Competition Law and the Challenges of Insular Economies

A Focus on French Polynesia and the Pacific Region

Concurrences
Paris – New York – London

106 West 32nd Street, Suite 144 New York, NY, 10001, USA
www.concurrences.com
book@concurrences.com

First Printing, March 2025
ISBN : 978-1-939007-58-2 (Paperback)
Library of Congress Control Number: 2025932424
Cover Design: Yves Buliard, www.yvesbuliard.fr
Book Design and Layout implementation: Nord Compo

Concurrences Books

Tributes

Harry First – A Global Vision for Competition Law, *S. Waller, A. Gavil, D. Bush (eds.), Forthcoming 2025*

James F. Rill – A Life in Antitrust, *2024*

Eleanor M. Fox – Antitrust Ambassador to the World, *2021*

Herbert Hovenkamp – The Dean of American Antitrust Law, *2021*

Frédéric Jenny – Standing Up for Convergence and Relevance in Antitrust, (Vol. I & II), *2019 & 2021*

Albert Foer – A Consumer Voice in the Antitrust Arena, *2020*

Richard Whish – Taking Competition Law Outside the Box, *2020*

Douglas H. Ginsburg – An Antitrust Professor on the Bench (Vol. I & II), *2018 & 2020*

Wang Xiaoye – The Pioneer of Competition Law in China, *A. Emch, W. Ng (eds.), 2019*

Ian S. Forrester – A Scot without Borders (Vol. I & II), *A. Komninos (eds.), 2015*

William E. Kovacic – An Antitrust Tribute (Vol. I & II), *2013 & 2014*

Practical Books

The DMA and more – Future application and margin of manoeuvre for national jurisdictions, *G. Muscolo & A. Massolo (eds.), 2025*

Artificial Intelligence and Competition Policy, *A. Abbott, T. Schrepel (eds.), 2024*

State Aid & National Enforcement, *J. Derenne, D. Jouve, C. Lemaire, F. Martucci (eds.), 2024*

The 2023 U.S. Merger Guidelines: *A Review, Sean Sullivan (ed.), 2024*

Competition Inspections in 25 Jurisdictions 2nd Edition – A Practitioner's Guide, *N. Jalabert-Doury (ed.), 2024*

EU Antitrust Enforcement – Law, Economics, History, *Policy & Practice, Wouter P. J. Wils, 2024*

The EU Foreign Subsidies Regulation, *Andreas Reindl, Isabelle Van Damme, 2024*

Compendium of Antitrust Damages Actions – ICC – 2nd edition, *J.W.H. Denton AO, F. Brunet, S. Williams, C. Inthavisay (eds.), 2023*

Pharmaceutical Antitrust: An Analysis of US and EU Law, *M. Thill-Tayara, G. Gordon (eds.), 2023*

Innovation Paradox in Merger Control, *G. Gurkaynak, 2023*

Antitrust and the Digital Economy, *Y. Katsoulacos (ed.), 2023 (in collaboration with CRESSE)*

Judicial Review of Competition Cases, *D. Ginsburg, T. Eicke (eds.), 2023*

Competition Law Treatment of Joint Ventures, *B. Bleicher, N. Campbell, A. Hamilton, N. Hukkinen, A. Khan, A. Mordaunt (eds.), 2022 (in collaboration with the IBA)*

Information Exchange & Related Risks, *Z. Marosi, M. Soares (eds.), 2022 (in collaboration with the IBA)*

Rulemaking Authority of the US Federal Trade Commission, *D. Crane (ed.), 2022*

The International Competition Network at Twenty, *D. Anderson & P. Lugard (eds.), 2022*

Competition Case Law Digest – 5th Edition, *F. Jenny, N. Charbit (eds.), 2022*

Competition Inspections in 21 Jurisdictions – A Practitioner's Guide, *N. Jalabert-Doury (ed.), 2022*

Perspectives on Antitrust Compliance, *A. Riley, A. Stephan, A. Tubbs (eds.), 2022 (in collaboration with the ICC)*

Turkish Competition Law, *G. Gürkaynak, 2021*

Competition Law – Climate Change & Environmental Sustainability, *S. Holmes, D. Middelschulte, M. Snoep (eds.), 2021*

Merger Control in Latin America – A Jurisdictional Guide, *P. Burnier da Silveira, P. Sittenfeld (eds.), 2020*

Competition Inspections under EU Law – A Practitioner's Guide, *N. Jalabert-Doury, 2020*

Gun Jumping in Merger Control – A Jurisdictional Guide, *C. Hatton, Y. Comtois, A. Hamilton (eds.), 2019 (in collaboration with the IBA)*

Choice – A New Standard for Competition Analysis? *P. Nihoul (ed.), 2016*

PhD Theses

The Economics of Digital Markets – Essays in Theoretical and Empirical Industrial Organization, *E. Arnaud-Joufray, 2024, Forthcoming 2024*

Abuse of Platform Power, *F. Bostoen, 2023*

Reform of Chinese State-Owned Enterprises, *X. Bai, 2023*

Competition & Regulation in Network Industries – Essays in Industrial Organization, *J-M. Zogheib, 2021*

The Role of Media Pluralism in the Enforcement of EU Competition Law, *K. Bania, 2019*

Buyer Power, *I. Herrera Anchustegui, 2017*

General Interest

Why Competition? Voices from the Antitrust Community and Beyond, *D. Crane, D. Gerard, R. Tritell (eds.), Forthcoming 2024*

Competition Law Dictionary, *D. Healey, R. Whish, W. E. Kovacic, P. Trevisán (eds.), 2024*

Great Antitrust Enforcers, *W. E. Kovacic, 2023*

Competition – How to Speak Like an Expert, *E. Combe, 2023*

Women and Antitrust – Voices from the Field (Vol I & II), *E. Kurgonaite & K. Nordlander, 2020*

The Wave and the Stone

Competition Law and the Challenges of Insular Economies

A Focus on French Polynesia and the Pacific Region

Forewords by Olivier Guersent and William E. Kovacic
Introduction by Benoît Cœuré
Postface by Gina Cass-Gottlieb

Editors
Johanne Peyre
Enzo Silvestro
Vivien Terrien
Teuraterai Emen
Yannick Lecornu

THE LEGEND OF THE WAVE AND THE STONE

Ta'aroa, the creator god, had created the sea smooth as a huge block of ice, without wrinkles or movement. But the sea was bored, because it's no fun being an inanimate, frozen thing. She decided to travel and to go beyond her borders. She knew full well that this was forbidden to her, that she was only entitled to half the world and that the other half belonged to stones, trees and men. So, she chose the darkest, blackest nights to disobey. Every night the sea set out to conquer the world.

At night, the sea began to swell slowly, gently, without making waves, to cover the whole world. The water rose silently, without waves, against the beach and the rocks, ripping away the sand and stones. It quietly swallowed the valleys and mountains, along with the houses of the people. Yet beneath the sand, there was still more sand. And behind the stone, there was still more stone. And the sea, defeated and weary, withdrew every morning. Then each evening it set out again to attack the world.

Ta'aroa the Great and the other gods were not to be awakened. She therefore carefully avoided the places of worship and sacrifice because they were tapu (forbidden and sacred). She would pass on either side of them and turn them into islands. No matter how worried the men were, the gods, who knew nothing, ignored their complaints. And little by little, the sea extended its domain.

But how do you stop the sea from advancing?

Arai, a young Polynesian boy, stood on the hill overlooking his village and watched the sea approach night after night. The gods seemed to be sleeping. Arai knew that soon there would be no more human life. So, he decided to stop the sea. But how could he do this?

He had observed that the sea seemed to carefully avoid the tapu (forbidden) places. One night, he went to the nearest marae (place of worship). He knew that by violating the tapu he was risking his life, but he wanted to stop the sea. He took a stone from the sacred altar and it seemed to burn his fingers. He hid it in a cave known only to him and waited.

He waited until the following night. When evening came, he fetched the stone and walked towards the sea. Then, hiding behind a tree trunk, he buried the stone in the sand.

The sea soon began to rise, advancing without a sound, to surprise the men in their sleep. It rose and rose and did not see the trap. All at once, it covered the sacred stone. It was already too late: there was a great wave and a loud noise, the stone was angry. Ta'aroa, warned, made his threat known with a thunderclap that stopped the sea.

The sea and man have been battling ever since. The sea would like to swallow him up, but every time it moves, it creates a multitude of noisy waves that are a warning signal for gods and men. Man then has time to build barriers, and the sea has always been able to be pushed back in time.

TE TU'A 'Ā'AI O TE ARU 'E TE 'ŌFAI MANA

Tē ha'umani noa ra te miti 'apāpāvai. Tupu iho ra tōna mana'o e 'a'e i te fenua. Terā rā, ti'a mai nei te taure'are'a tā'ī'ī ra o Arai nō tē tei fa'aū i te vāve'a a mau roa atu ai te he'era'a o te miti.

E ha'umani rahi tō te miti.

'Ua rahu o Ta'aroa, te Atua tinitini, i te miti 'apāpāvai e te mānino mai te tahi 'ata'a pape pa'ari huru rahi, te taratara 'ore e taimāmū. Tē ha'umani noa ra te miti, inaha i tōna mana'o e'ere roa i te mea au i te fa'aea noa. 'Ua 'ōpua a'e ra 'oia i te tere haere ē tāhiti roa atu i tōna 'ōti'a. Ua 'ite maita'i ho'i 'oia e tapu te reira, ua fa'aotihia te 'āfara'a o te fenua nōna 'āre'a rā te tahi atu 'āfara'a nō te 'ofa'i ïa, te aru e te ta'ata. Nō reira ïa 'oia i ha'a'eta'eta ai 'e a tāponi ai i te pō pōuri pa'opa'o.

I te mau pō ato'a e tere te miti nō te nīnīvaru i te fenua

I te tau pō, mara'a aunu'nu'u noa te miti, fa'a'ī marū noa ai ma te 'āueue 'ore ē 'ati a'e te fenua. 'Ua paremo o tahatai i te miti e 'ua nīnā roa te mau 'ofa'i, 'ua heru i te one e te 'iri'iri, horomi'i atu i te mau fa'a e te mou'a ē momi ato'a atu i te fare o te ta'ata. Teie nei rā i raro a'e i te one tē vai noa ra ā te one 'e i raro a'e i te mau 'ōfafa'i tē vai noa ra ā te 'ōfa'i. 'Aita te miti i manuia, 'e nō tōna rohirohi fa'aru'e iho ra 'oia i ta nā 'ōpuara'a ma te ti'afā i te mau po'ipo'i ato'a. 'Ia tape rā te mahana i muri mai, nā ni'a fa'ahou te miti i tāna peu 'e i tāna 'ōpuara'a i tē nīnīvarura'a i te ao.

'Ua māramarama maita'i 'oia ē 'eiaha roa o Ta'aroa e te mau Atua rau e 'ite i te 'ohipa o tāna e rave ra i te mau pō ato'a, nō reira 'oia a fa'ahahao noa ai i te mau vāhi tapu mai te mau Marae 'e te mau vāhi ha'amorira'a, a riro mai ai taua mau tuhara'a fenua 'ei motu 'āpī. E ahoaho tō te ta'ata, aita rā te mau Atua i hāro'aro'a noa a'e i te 'ohipa e tupu ra 'e te 'āehuehu o te ta'ata. Te 'ā'ano noa atu ra te pāhora fenua i po'i i te miti.

Nāhea rā i tē tāpe'a i te miti?

I te mau pō ato'a e ti'a mai o Arai i ni'a i te pu'u mou'a o tōna 'oire 'e tē 'ite noa ra 'oia i te miti i te fa'aenera'a i tahatai i te mau pō ato'a 'e tē piri noa mai ra e ru'i ē e ru'i atu. E au ra ho'i ē tē ta'oto noa ra te mau Atua. Ua 'ite maita'i o Arai i te mea ē tē vai ra te taime 'aita e ta'ata ora fa'ahou i ni'a i te fenua. Fa'aoti atu ra o Arai i te tāpe'a i te miti.

'Ua hi'o maita'i o Arai i te terera'a o te miti 'e ua 'ite 'oia ē tē 'ape'ape ra te miti i te mau vāhi tapu, fa'aoti a'e ra 'oia i te haere i te marae piri roa a'e iō na, noa atu tōna mata'u rahi i te pohe 'aita 'oia i 'ōtohe i tāna 'ōpuara'a e tāpe'a i te miti. 'Ua rave mai 'oia i te hō'ē 'ofa'i mai ni'a mai i te Marae, e au ra ïa e ahu rahi i tōna rima i te amora'a i taua 'ofa'i ra. 'Āfa'i tāpuni atu ra 'oia i tāua 'ofa'i ra i roto i te hō'ē ana matauhia e ana e ua tīa'i i reira.

'Ua tīa'i 'oia i te pō i muri mai 'e i te ahiahira'a ra haere atu ra 'oia e ti'i i taua 'ofa'i ra ma tē moemoe i te miti, huna atu ra i te reira i roto i te hō'ē 'āpo'o one i muri mai i te tahi tumu.

Te vāve'a māniania

Tē mara'a marū noa mai ra te miti i ni'a i te fenua ma tē 'ahehe 'ore, hitimahuta a'e nei te ta'ata i roto i tō rātou ta'otora'a. 'Aita te miti i fa'aea noa a'e i tē mara'a 'e ua horo haere ma te 'ore e ha'apa'o noa a'e i te 'ati e vai ra. 'Aita i maoro roa atu, 'ua 'a'e atu nā ni'a i te 'ōfa'i tapu, tāere roa : pahū vavā iho nei te miti i te hae o te 'ōfa'i mana. Ara iho nei o Ta'aroa e 'ua pi'i iho ra 'oia i te haruru pātiri, mau a'e ra te miti i tōna haere'a.

Mai reira mai te 'aro-noa-ra'a te miti i te ta'ata. Hina'aro ihoā te miti i te nīnā i te fenua, i te taime rā a hā'uti'uti ai 'oia, te tupututupu-ato'a-ra'a ïa te 'aru fāfati e āunauna ïa nō te mau Atua e te ta'ata. 'Aua'e maoti te reira a taimehia ai te ta'ata nō te patu i te pā fa'aruru miti rahi.

A WORD FROM THE PRESIDENT

Moetai Brotherson

President of French Polynesia

As President of French Polynesia, I am eager to share with you the vision that guides our actions to build an ambitious and balanced future for our territory. French Polynesia is a land of exceptional uniqueness: an archipelago spread across an area as vast as Europe, but populated like a mid-sized city. This geographical paradox, coupled with our distance from major markets, shapes the opportunities and challenges we face every day.

Our challenges are both historical and contemporary. The legacy of the Pacific Test Center has profoundly transformed our society, altering our economic structures and centralizing the population around Tahiti. Additionally, climate change is an immediate threat, particularly for low-lying islands such as those in the Tuamotu, where remediation efforts could become costly or even impossible. Yet, French Polynesia is rich in assets: some of the world's most beautiful landscapes, a vibrant and rich culture, and a resilient and innovative population.

Our ambition for the next decade is based on four main pillars. The first is sustainable tourism. We are not simply aiming to increase the number of visitors, but to rethink tourism so that it becomes an activity that respects the environment and our communities while generating income that directly benefits the local population. The second pillar is revitalizing our primary sector to regain food self-sufficiency and develop high-value-added productions like vanilla, sea cucumbers, and noni. The third pillar is the energy transition, leveraging local resources such as marine thermal energy, while reducing our reliance on fossil fuels. Finally, the fourth pillar is the digital revolution. Thanks to intercontinental cables that now connect Tahiti to the rest of the world, we have the capacity to develop a dynamic digital economy that creates jobs for our youth.

Competition regulation plays a key role in this strategy. In French Polynesia, the natural lack of competition, due to the size of our markets, can hinder innovation and economic efficiency. That's why the Polynesian Competition Authority is essential. It acts as a guarantor of economic fairness, allowing our markets to thrive while protecting consumers.

On the occasion of the tenth anniversary of our Polynesian competition regime, I want to share my belief that French Polynesia can meet these challenges and seize these opportunities through a balanced approach, combining respect for our cultural identity and openness to innovation. Our goal is to build a territory where every Polynesian can thrive, in a sustainable, supportive economy, looking towards the future. This project is not limited to addressing today's needs: it is about laying the foundations for a resilient Polynesia for future generations.

FOREWORD

"Defending competition for the benefit of innovation and consumers"

Oliver Guersent

Director-General of the Directorate-General for Competition, European Commission

In 2015, ten years ago, the competition law of French Polynesia was adopted, and the following year, the Polynesian Competition Authority (APC) began its operations. Since then, the APC and its staff have made a real difference in the competitive landscape of French Polynesia by fulfilling their assigned missions.

When we think of French Polynesia, the image of a lush archipelago in the middle of the blue Pacific immediately comes to mind. However, it is important to recognize that it consists of a multitude of islands and atolls, home to about 280,000 people, 69% of whom are concentrated in Tahiti.

In other words, what makes this territory naturally beautiful also influences the development of its economy and how competition operates. The small size of an island territory generally does not allow for the economies of scale and scope found in larger economies. Due to their limited domestic markets and production, small economies also tend to rely on imports. As a result, they face high transportation and input costs. Furthermore, French Polynesia is geographically remote from major maritime and air transport routes. All these factors contribute to high industrial concentration and significant barriers to entry. In such a context, the role of the Competition Authority is crucial in creating an environment where competition can thrive.

This is precisely what the APC has consistently done.

First, the APC has used its powers to support policies that promote competition. It can be consulted on any competition-related issue, including legislative proposals and other regulatory texts. In this regard, the APC has recently issued opinions in critical areas such as postal services, telecommunications, and energy, to name a few.

Beyond these advisory roles, the APC has actively enforced competition law in cases of violations. It has issued decisions against cartels, tackled abuses of dominant positions, and has not hesitated to impose interim measures when necessary.

With around thirty cases handled, the APC is also active in merger control, reviewing transactions that must be notified when jurisdictional thresholds are met.

Applying competition law through these conventional tools is essential to ensure that the competitive challenges faced by a small island economy like French Polynesia are not exacerbated by anti-competitive behavior from businesses.

In addition to these traditional tools, the APC monitors the creation and modification of commercial spaces to maintain a sufficiently competitive retail environment. In this context, it assesses whether a transaction creates or strengthens a dominant position.

The APC has courageously and effectively developed a rich portfolio of activities with a clear vision of how to strengthen competition in its territory.

The APC is also well aware of its broader regional context. It is a founding member of the Pacific Island Network of Competition, Consumer, and Economic Regulators (PINCCER), which was launched in November 2023. It co-leads the Competition branch alongside its New Zealand counterpart, the Commerce Commission (NZCC).

PINCCER will serve as a platform for regional cooperation and provide opportunities to address common challenges.

Exchanges between these jurisdictions can foster economic development and drive regional integration, as demonstrated by our experience in the EU. In the EU, we benefit from the European Competition Network (ECN), which includes the European Commission and the national competition authorities of all member states. I hope that the ECN can serve as an inspiration for cooperation in the Pacific region.

Both the APC and PINCCER can count on the support of the European Commission. For example, we have already helped fund several participants from the region to attend the PINCCER event held in Tahiti in February 2024, and we look forward to continuing our exchanges with the APC and PINCCER.

Looking ahead, the APC aims to further strengthen its expertise and enhance cooperation with other institutions and organizations in French Polynesia and internationally.

I congratulate the APC on this anniversary, which is marked by great success.

I wish it continued success in the years to come.

As authorities sharing the same values and principles – namely, defending competition to benefit innovation and consumers – it is with great pleasure that we stand alongside them.

FOREWORD

"This experience has a reach that goes beyond the Pacific"

William E. Kovacic

Professor and Director of the *Competition Law Center* at George Washington University

The extraordinary modern expansion of competition law as an element of global economic policy – including the adoption by roughly 120 jurisdictions of competition laws since the late 1980s – has provided many insights into what it takes to create and sustain an effective competition law regime. There is nothing quick or easy about it. Even nations that enjoy favorable enabling conditions and have substantial resources to devote to the task have found that the creation of an effective system is a slow growth and requires sustained effort. It can easily take twenty to twenty-five years to build and test the substantive commands and institutional framework that yield success.[1]

This volume provides promising signs that French Polynesia, at the tenth anniversary of the adoption of its competition law, is on a good implementation path. The development of an effective competition law system takes place through a virtuous cycle of experimentation, assessment, and refinement. The first decade of a new system is heavily experimental, as a nation creates institutional frameworks for policy implementation and applies law enforcement powers and other policy tools. French Polynesia is well within the mainstream of modern experience in terms of its accomplishments in this first formative decade.

Particularly impressive is the evident understanding of the leadership of the competition authority that the second phase of the virtuous cycle – assessment – is indispensable to future success. The volume not only reviews past work by the competition authority but also takes stock of economic conditions in French Polynesia. This stocktaking suggests priorities for the future application of the authority's powers and for enhancements to its mandate, institutional framework, and resources. The willingness of the Polynesian Competition Authority to carry out a review of its competition policy system and to diagnose obstacles to competition is most encouraging. No competition law system since the establishment in Canada in 1889 of the first national competition law has achieved success without an ongoing commitment to evaluate past performance and identify areas for improvement.

---

1 William E. Kovacic & Marianela Lopez-Galdos, Lifecycles of Competition Systems: Explaining Variation in the Implementation of New Regimes, 79 law & Contemporary Problems 85 (2016).

The assessment process would not be possible without an investment of resources in policy research. This investment provides the essential foundation for diagnosing commercial phenomena, deciding how to intervene to address apparent problems, and to select appropriate remedial solutions. Agency leadership must invest resources that may not yield immediately observable enforcement events but are vital to ensuring that future policy choices and interventions are wise. By establishing a norm that embraces research investments in building knowledge and capability, the Polynesian Competition Authority today has set a powerful example for future generations of leadership to follow.

This volume is important not only for French Polynesia, but also for the small islands of the Pacific. The volume documents efforts to build regional cooperative alliances that promise to enable each island nation to achieve results collectively that would be unattainable if each nation acted alone. The collaborative frameworks in the Pacific region are a valuable complement to larger international bodies that seek to promote the adoption of superior practices on a global level. By playing a central role in the formation of Pacific regional cooperative programs, French Polynesia is helping build a policy infrastructure that will benefit all nations in the region and supply a framework for emulation in other parts of the world.

Taken as a group, the developments sketched above constitute an impressive beginning for competition policy in French Polynesia and among the smaller island nations of the Pacific region. Capturing this experience has significance beyond the Pacific. By reporting on the early evolution of competition law in French Polynesia and joining the French Polynesian experience to broader developments in the Pacific region, this volume makes a valuable contribution to progress in the design and implementation of competition law globally.

INTRODUCTION

"We share a common vision with the Polynesian Competition Authority"

Benoît Cœuré

President of the French Competition Authority (national)

10 years ago, French Polynesia made the ambitious choice of competition.

Long-awaited, the reform initiated by country law no. 2015-2 of February 23, 2015 marked a real turning point: for the first time, a competition law saw the light of day in French Polynesia, entrusted to an independent administrative authority, the Polynesian Competition Authority (APC).

This modernization of the legal framework in French Polynesia met a pressing need on the part of consumers and businesses, who were aware of the benefits that more dynamic markets could offer them. This need was all the more pressing in French Polynesia, where the specific characteristics of the overseas territories – insularity, narrow markets and remoteness – reinforce the obstacles to competition, generating barriers to entry and a higher level of economic concentration than in mainland France.

The French Competition Authority (ADLC) is particularly sensitive these issues when acting in the French Overseas Departments and Regions, whose economic structures are similar to those of Polynesia. Protecting competition in the French overseas territories is one of our constant priorities, as set out in our roadmap for 2024-2025 .[1]

We share a common vision with the APC: that of free and fair competition, to the benefit of all. The challenges faced by overseas economies, as illustrated by the persistence of high living costs, call for constant vigilance on the part of competition authorities to preserve purchasing power and boost competition

The celebration of the tenth anniversary of the competition regime in Polynesia provides a valuable opportunity to salute the remarkable role played by the APC, which in just a decade has seized upon this reform to mobilize all its resources in favor of a more dynamic and open Polynesian economy.

This commitment was illustrated first and foremost in the area of enforcement, with landmark decisions sanctioning anti-competitive practices in the mobile telephony sector – where the APC was also able to take the measure of urgency when the situation required it, adopting the first precautionary measures in 2023 – as well as in beverage marketing and funeral services

---

1 Since its creation in 2008, the ADLC has handed down 46 contentious decisions (for a total of over 232 million euros in fines), 17 opinions and 81 merger control decisions.

Merger control is another essential facet of its action. To date, the APC has examined some thirty transactions, including several authorized subject to conditions, for preserving competition in key sectors for the Polynesian economy, such as maritime freight transport, health and tourism. At the same time, the APC exercised rigorous control over projects to create or modify retail space, going so far as to prohibit an operation in 2022 due to the high competitive risks in the retail sector.

In addition to these repressive and preventive missions, APC has established itself as a real force for proposal, placing its expertise at the service of public authorities. Through its many opinions, whether requested by third parties or on its own initiative, it has been able to enlighten public authorities and identify sources of purchasing power in areas as essential as hydrocarbons, car parts and basic necessities.

As the voice of French Polynesia throughout the world of competition, APC has also distinguished itself through its active role in international forums such as the International Competition Network (ICN) and the Organisation for Economic Co-operation and Development (OECD), and through the creation of the Pacific Network of Competition, Consumer and Regulatory Authorities (PINCCER), an initiative that testifies to its dynamism and regional influence.

Finally, it's impossible not to mention the close and fruitful collaboration that has linked the APC and ADLC since 2015. This cooperation, nurtured by exchanges of expertise and a shared vision, will continue to strengthen in the interests of both institutions.

Without claiming to be exhaustive, this brief retrospective provides an overview of the remarkable progress made since the introduction of competition law in French Polynesia. This success is also that of the men and women who, within the APC, have worked with conviction and professionalism in the service of consumers and the Polynesian economy. Their work is now recognized and celebrated in the pages of this book, which I invite you to discover.

Polynesian Competition Law: Protecting a Reef Barrier

Johanne Peyre

President of the Polynesian Competition Authority

If I draw from the fascinating world of marine biology to make an analogy with the competition code for the title of this editorial, it is primarily because a reef barrier, in my layman's eyes, acts like a dike that helps maintain a calm ecosystem, the lagoon, against the whims of Poseidon.

Just as a coral reef is a complex ecosystem where each species plays a crucial role, an island market is an economic ecosystem where each company interacts with others in a fragile harmony. A slight imbalance in a coral reef, whether caused by pollution, global warming or overfishing, can have disastrous consequences for the entire ecosystem.

Similarly, cartels, abuse of dominant positions, mergers or lack of control over commercial development can upset the economic balance and harm innovation, consumer welfare and, more generally, all the economic forces in the area.

And just as corals build the reef, businesses build the market. However, excessive growth or unfair practices can damage the economic ecosystem, just as excessive proliferation of one coral species can harm the reef's biodiversity

Finally, like our coral reefs, our economy is particularly vulnerable to environmental change and exogenous shocks.

Our economy, like our reefs, is a common good, requiring a subtle balance between protection and development, and therefore appropriate regulation of players and practices. This is the mission and raison d'être of the Polynesian Competition Code and its eponymous Authority.

This celebration of the tenth anniversary of our competition regime is an opportune moment to break with the dictatorship of immediacy, the modern despot before whom we too often kneel, to take stock of this first decade, to look back at the strategic orientations that presided over the creation of this regulatory framework, to measure the progress made, to note the failures and to define together the axes of progress to meet the challenges of the future.

The rules of the game: a lever for economic development

In an island economy marked by geographical and structural constraints, the adoption of a clear and adapted competitive framework is a visionary choice. The rules of the competitive game encourage innovation, reduce costs for consumers and boost the productivity of local businesses. In Polynesia, as in all market economies, competition is an effective lever in the fight against high living costs.

The competition regime was introduced in 2015 in reply to this ambition, and has partially met it. Emblematic decisions and opinions have been issued, helping to inform public policy and structure the economy.

A road travelled with limits

Since its creation, the Polynesian Competition Authority (APC) has established itself as a regulatory body capable of analysing complex situations and proposing concrete solutions. First of all, a large number of decisions have been handed down: most were favourable, while others sanctioned abuses. It's always tricky to objectivise the results of a long-term undertaking to clean up an economic system. Firstly, because the Authority does not decide how many cases it will have to deal with. Secondly, quantitative indicators do not reflect the complexity of a case, its potential impact, or even the number of economic agents who modify their behaviour out of fear of a potential sanction.

I believe that this cultural evolution of business leaders with regard to competition rules also owes a great deal to the awareness-raising initiatives undertaken by local players in recent years. Through events and workshops on competition issues, such as the Journées Concurrence and Ateliers Concurrence, the Authority has made available to an informed public the keys to understanding, as well as the tools and methods essential to bringing Polynesian companies into compliance. These meetings, dedicated to local players and practitioners, raise awareness and explain the principles of Competition law, share best practices and reinforce understanding of the economic stakes involved. I would like to take this opportunity to thank the many national and international experts who have volunteered to help us in this quest. Economic players and legal professionals are unanimous in welcoming this initiative, which will need to be sustained over the long term if it is to achieve its full impact.

At the same time, the APC initiated the creation of the Pacific Competition Authorities Network (PINCCER), which fosters cooperation and the exchange of expertise between the region's island economies. Here again, this dynamic must be maintained to ensure the continuous improvement of the teams making up each authority.

However, these ten years have also been marked by difficulties and setbacks. Firstly, in terms of governance. A historic first that the young Authority could easily have done without was the compulsory resignation of the first chairman of Polynesia's first independent administrative authority, which did not augur well for the future. We had to wait until 2021 for the Authority to find a stable working environment, after the end of the sequence of disruptions and interim appointments and its permanent installation in suitable premises.

Secondly, the Polynesian Competition Code has undergone a number of amendments, at a frequency which has been detrimental to the intelligibility of the law. Let's be clear: the evolution of a body of law is virtuous and highly necessary to enable it to keep pace with changing trends in society. However, the exercise must be carried out with a certain degree of rationality, failing which citizens and practitioners can quickly find themselves at a loss as to how to apprehend the matter in question in a positive light. For example, the abolition in 2018 of the ban on import exclusivities may have destabilised certain market dynamics, in addition to depriving the regulator of a useful tool in the fight against anti-competitive practices.

Similarly, failure to assess the impact of the adjustments made may lead to a different trajectory from that initially envisaged. In the case of the example cited above, French Polynesia being the only territory in the republican system to have opted for this position should enable a comparative analysis of the results recorded to be carried out.

Moreover, the Authority's response was not always as timely as third parties would have expected. Very recently, I have been forced to deplore abnormally long processing times, difficulties in maintaining fluid communication with claimants and, more generally, too great an asymmetry between the length of the procedure and the legitimate hopes of the partners.

In particular, this is the result of internal management that is still in need of improvement. In fact, the Authority does not yet have the latitude it needs to exercise its powers with serenity. While its activity and influence continue to grow, the Authority has very limited budgetary margins, particularly in terms of human resources. On this last point, the Authority's autonomy in terms of recruitment and payroll management was withdrawn in its early years, and it is now faced with increasing administrative complexity, with the corollary of a weakening of the resources devoted to its main missions.

Ambitious prospects for a sustainable economy

As we enter our second decade, we must learn from these successes and difficulties, and adjust our course to match our ambitions.

First of all, with regard to the Competition Code, it is essential to schedule periodic reviews – a three-yearly frequency would seem appropriate – in order to plan work, assess impacts, anticipate side effects, consult legal practitioners, and plan deployment.

It is equally important that the Authority be consulted on all economic texts. Following the example of the Economic, Social, Environmental and Cultural Council, the Authority's opinion could usefully be systematically brought to the attention of the representatives of the Assembly of French Polynesia, prior to examination in a committee. The introduction of this practice would enable the Authority's teams to respond, where appropriate, to requests for clarification from the deliberative assembly, thus helping to strengthen democracy while participating more effectively in the production of legislation and regulations. On this point, an ongoing dialogue must be established between the Authority and public authorities, so that the opinions issued by the Authority gain in readability and audience.

In addition, the Authority could be entrusted with the independent regulation of the key energy and telecommunications sectors, to ensure a more balanced and accessible market. In other latitudes, this responsibility has been entrusted to specific administrative authorities. By forging partnerships with them, the Authority could mobilise the expertise essential to understanding these high-stakes, highly technical fields.

Finally, the Authority's internal management procedures need to be rethought in the light of the above findings. The question of resources, both in terms of volume and allocation procedures, will determine our ambitions and our ability to meet the aspirations of all parties, public decision-makers and civil society alike.

In the words of the metaphor used in the introduction, our Competition law remains, like a coral reef, a living organism whose pulse needs to be checked at regular intervals to ensure that it is thriving, or, where necessary, under stress. This is the aim of this collection which, through the great variety of its contributors, will offer the reader keys to understand the past, apprehend the present and build the future.

Johanne Peyre is the President of the Polynesian Competition Authority. She is a lawyer specializing in competition law with experience at international law firms, and has also served as the Legal Director for competition and compliance at several publicly listed companies.

Enzo Silvestro has extensive experience working in ministerial offices and at the General Secretariat of the Government of French Polynesia. He has also been a member of the Board of Directors of the Port Autonome de Papeete and has taught at the University of French Polynesia.

Vivien Terrien is a member of the Board of the Polynesian Competition Authority and Vice-President of the French Competition Authority. He is a lawyer specializing in competition and European Union law, having also served as a référendaire at the European Court of Justice and taught at several universities in France and abroad.

Teuraterai Emen is responsible for the Bureau of Procedure, Communication, and Event Projects at the Polynesian Competition Authority. She has previously held the positions of Secretary General and Administrative and Financial Officer at the EPIC and the Tahitian Press Agency.

Yannick Lecornu has worked in international consulting, served as head of territorial policies for the State, as Chief of Staff for the Ministry of Economy and Finance of French Polynesia, and as General Director of the Chamber of Commerce and Industry. He has led several initiatives to modernize the regulation and oversight of the local economy.

INSTITUTE FOR SMALL MARKETS IN LAW AND ECONOMICS

Advancing Competition Law in Island Economies and Small Markets

ISLE is a non-profit organization driven by a team of volunteers eager to contribute to a better understanding of competition mechanisms and regulation in small market economies and island territories.

Indeed, the application of the general principles of competition law must take into account the structural characteristics and specific economic functioning of each territory, particularly when they are small and/or isolated. This observation calls for the mobilization of diverse analytical capacities in order to formulate tailored rules capable of meeting the objectives of harmonious development for each territory.

Through research work, sectoral studies, impact analyses on competition policies, the development of training, awareness tools, and communication programs, ISLE members aim to contribute to a better understanding by stakeholders of the externalities of competition rules, while addressing the challenges of the cost of living and the sustainability of economic practices.

With a view to dynamically leading these initiatives, the ISLE project is based on a bicameral governance structure, namely an administration through a steering committee chaired by Johanne PEYRE and thought leadership under the presidency of Professor William E. KOVACIC.

For more information, visit our website: www.isle-research.org

ACKNOWLEDGEMENTS

As we celebrate the tenth anniversary of the establishment of competition law in French Polynesia, I feel it is important to acknowledge the origins and human aspects behind any set of regulations and the tools dedicated to their implementation. Through the Code and the Polynesian Competition Authority, I would like to honor those whose dedication has helped build and develop this collective achievement.

My deep gratitude goes to the former presidents and members of the APC board, the general rapporteurs, the rapporteurs, the advisers, and the agents of the procedure office. Your work and dedication have anchored the culture of competition within our island economy, while shaping a credible and respected institution.

I also wish to acknowledge the work of legal and economic professionals, including lawyers and business advisors, who have helped support and structure the adoption of these rules by local economic players. My thanks also go to the businesses, the Polynesian Consumers' Association, and all those who, through their involvement and legal actions, have contributed to the life of competition law. By seeking the APC's intervention, challenging practices, and defending healthy competition among economic players, you have given meaning to this process.

My recognition also goes to the representatives of the Assembly of French Polynesia who, with the aim of equipping our territory with effective competition law tailored to its specificities, are responsible for the successes achieved and future accomplishments.

Finally, a special thank you to our critics, to those who, with admirable perseverance, attempted to weaken the foundations of this young Authority. Through their harsh criticisms and tireless efforts to destabilize, they provided, albeit unknowingly, the spur necessary to bring out the best in us. As an ancient saying from popular wisdom goes, they tried to bury us, not knowing that we were seeds.

May this book, beyond being a testimony to the journey we have undertaken, be a tribute to the women and men who turned this beautiful initial ambition into a tangible reality.

Johanne Peyre, President of the Polynesian Competition Authority

LIST OF CONTRIBUTORS

Joel Abraham

Léopold Biardeau

Jean Christophe Bouissou

Sophie Bresny

Moetai Brotherson

Arnaud Busseuil

Antoine Callot

Gina Cass-Gottlieb

Walid Chaiehloudj

Benoît Cœuré

Quitterie de La Poype

Pascal Devillers

Warren Dexter

Benoît Durand

Sean Ennis

Makalio Folituu

Edouard Fritch

Olivier Guersent

Arthur Helfer

Angélique Herbez-Fontaine

Patrick Hubert

Alejandro Ibarra

Nathalie Jalabert-Doury

Vincent Jaunet

Frédéric Jenny

Hironui Johnston

William E. Kovacic

Vinitesh Kumar

Hervé Raimana Lallemant-Moe

Yannick Lecornu

Jean-Luc Lemercier

Stanislas Martin

Marie Minetto

Emma Moisson

Elisabeth Moreau

Frederic Paillusson

Caroline Perdrix

Johanne Peyre

Jérôme Philippe

Henri Piffaut

Matthieu Pujuguet

Chloé Racine

Yvonnick Raffin

Stéphane Retterer

Teva Rohfritsch

Heiva Sage

Thibault Segalard

Igor Simic

Sarah Vidal

OVERVIEW

PART II
A DECADE OF DECISIONS AND OPINIONS FROM THE POLYNESIAN COMPETITION AUTHORITY – A REVIEW

PART III
CONTRIBUTION TO THE REGULATION OF KEY ECONOMIC SECTORS

PART I

The Genesis and First Steps of a Shared Ambition

In the Beginning There Was Determination

Jean-Christophe Boissou[*]

In February 2015, the promulgation of the law on competition in French Polynesia marked a crucial stage in the economic development of our territory. This text, debated at length and carefully drafted, responded to the need for a modern legal framework, adapted to the island's specific features while aligning with an international dynamic. Our government's motivations at the time centered on several strategic areas.

One of our first priorities was to promote the balanced operation of markets. We identified the need to regulate economic practices for healthy and transparent competition. The law established strict rules to prevent abuse of a dominant position, restrictive agreements and anti-competitive behaviour likely to distort markets. Our aim was twofold: innovation and the encouragement of private initiative protecting consumers from artificially high prices. This regulation was particularly crucial in an island economy like ours, where dominant players could easily emerge and disrupt competition.

At the same time, we aimed to modernise the local economy by drawing inspiration from international standards, adapting various tried and tested mechanisms to local realities. The legislative text drew its inspiration from European and American legislation and the Lurel law, taking account of the specific geographical and economic features of Polynesia. For example, the prohibition on exclusive rights for imports was designed to prevent the abusive capture of markets, while ensuring real benefits for consumers. This measure also made it possible to open up sectors previously blocked by monopolies, thereby stimulating the diversity of products available and boosting price competitiveness.

Another pillar of this reform was the establishment of an independent administrative authority. The creation of the Polynesian Competition Authority (APC), the first of its kind among the French territorial collectivities, reflected our stated political will to promote fair and rigorous market regulation. Conceived as an independent body, the Authority's mission was to ensure competition rules were applied, provide a framework for impartial arbitration and to raise awareness of these fundamental principles among economic players. Its independence was essential to guarantee objective decisions, free from external political or economic influences. However, certain provisions introduced subsequently, such as the power evocation conferred on the President of French Polynesia or the requirement of his agreement for certain mergers, have raised questions about balance between regulation and political power. It is crucial to ensure that these adjustments

---

* Jean-Christophe Bouissou was Vice-President of French Polynesia from November 2021 to May 2023. He also held ministerial positions, including Minister of Housing, Tourism, and Labor.

reinforce, rather than compromise, the initial objective of the Polynesian Competition Authority: to ensure fair, transparent and effective regulation at the service of all.

The law also aimed to reduce the social and economic inequalities exacerbated by island constraints, such as market concentration and high logistics costs. By making markets more accessible and competitive, we were protecting small businesses against abusive practices and guaranteed fair prices for essential products. This economic equity was essential to reduce disparities between the archipelagos and ensure better territorial integration.

Another major ambition of our government was to integrate Polynesia into a regional and international dynamic. By aligning local practices with international standards, our aim was to attract foreign investment, diversify the economy and strengthen the competitiveness of local businesses on external markets. This strategic openness promoted an image of reliability for investors, stimulating the exchange of know-how and technologies.

Finally, the law offered enhanced guarantees to consumers by improving transparency and introducing price control mechanisms. These measures were designed to improve purchasing power and access to quality goods and services. Unlike the previous period, when there was already a regulation of essential products, the provisions of the new code have strengthened these mechanisms. Tariff ceilings for essential products, drawn up in consultation with the Directorate General of Economic Affairs (DGAE), were consolidated by additional provisions in the Code, offering greater protection for Polynesians' purchasing power while affirming that markets should serve the general interest. The transitional provisions included allowed businesses to adapt gradually, minimising any short-term negative impact on consumers. This balanced approach demonstrated genuine consideration for the needs of citizens, while giving economic players time to comply with the new requirements.

Ten years later, being the former Minister for the Economy in the Polynesian government, I recall the debates and the defence of the bill before the Assembly. This text, the fruit of in-depth work and rigorous consultation, could not have seen the light of day without the essential mobilisation of the Directorate General of Economic Affairs (DGAE). Its expertise made it possible to adapt the principles of competition to local realities, while relying on recognised international standards.

At the time, Polynesian markets were faced with anti-competitive practices that were holding back innovation and weighing on consumers. The creation of the Polynesian Competition Authority was a strong and necessary response. With powers of investigation, sanction and injunction, this institution has become a key player in regulating markets and preventing abuses. Among the key measures, the price ceilings for essential products, drawn up in consultation with the DGAE, aimed to protect the purchasing power of Polynesians while affirming that the markets should serve the general interest. These ceilings also limited abusive commercial margins, thereby protecting the most vulnerable consumers.

The local economy was modernised pragmatically, adapting international models to the specific characteristics of Polynesia. With the support of renowned figures such as Bruno Lasserre, Chairman of the French Competition Authority at the time, we built a solid and appropriate regulatory framework. The ban on exclusive import is a notable example, opening markets while protecting the interests of small local businesses. In addition, efforts have been made to reduce disparities between the archipelagos, regulating essential products and offering tax and customs exemptions to ensure fair access to essential goods for all Polynesians.

Today, with the benefit of hindsight, certain aspects of the law need to be adjusted. Article LP. 111-9 imposes onerous administrative obligations on small businesses, which can hamper their dynamism. Similarly, the financial penalties, although clearly defined, are sometimes not enough to dissuade large groups. These shortcomings need to be remedied to improve fairness. Furthermore, the geographical and logistical constraints specific to the archipelagos have not always been fully taken into account. It is essential to adapt the regulations and means of control to meet the needs of the most isolated islands.

Polynesian competition law, rooted in a unique island reality, is inspired by international best practice. In comparison, the European Union imposes strict standards to prevent illicit cartels and abuses of dominant positions, while the United States adopts a more liberal approach, relying on ex post judicial remedies. China, meanwhile, combines modern anti-monopoly regulation with national strategic objectives, in particular to control its technology giants. These international examples show that French Polynesia has been able to develop a tailor-made framework, taking into account the logistical and geographical constraints that influence costs and access to products. However, there is still room for improvement, particularly in terms of harmonising sanctions with world standards in similar economies and making procedures more transparent.

To ensure that competition law continues to meet the evolving needs of our economy, several avenues for improvement are worth exploring. Investing in digitalization is essential to develop integrated digital tools for monitoring prices, simplifying administrative procedures and facilitating access to information for businesses and consumers. Strengthening the resources of the Polynesian Competition Authority by increasing its human and financial resources will enable it to carry out in-depth investigations and ensure proactive regulation. Training and awareness-raising for local businesses are also crucial to help them understand the rules and encourage them to adopt compliant practices, thereby preventing infringements. Harmonising notification thresholds and penalties with those of international models, while preserving local specificities, will contribute to better integration into global standards. Finally, reducing geographical disparities by adapting regulations to the realities of the archipelagos will ensure greater territorial equity.

Ten years after the law was passed, the progress made is undeniable. However, the work continues. By combining pragmatism, innovation and collaboration, it is possible to build a fairer and more inclusive economy for all Polynesians. As we celebrate this decade, it is also essential that we look to the future with ambition, strengthening this regulatory foundation to make it a model not just for Polynesia, but for island and developing economies around the world.

Teva Rohfritsch

Senator of French Polynesia

"My primary objective was to protect Polynesian consumers"[*]

On 25 June 2014, as a representative in the Assembly of French Polynesia, you voted in favour of the bill of the assembly of French Polynesia introducing a Competition law in French Polynesia. Can you remind us of the reasons behind this vote?

For me, competition has never been an end in itself, but a means of contributing to the emergence of a more dynamic and equitable economic environment. Our economic fabric, as you know, is the product of our history: it therefore has certain limitations, a high degree of bureaucratisation and concentration, and a lack of competition in certain key sectors.

In this sense, my vote was an initial response to this observation, and an important first step in the evolution of our economy. The introduction of a Polynesian Competition law could encourage the emergence of new businesses, stimulate innovation, and improve the quality of services offered to consumers. On this last point, my primary objective was to protect Polynesian consumers by offering them a wider choice of products and services at fairer prices, in particular by combating anti-competitive practices and abuse of dominant positions.

Politically and philosophically, I've always believed that enlightened regulation of passions is more effective than blind regulation of interests. To put it another way, my liberal vision of the economy encourages me to think in terms of healthy stimulation of interactions between companies, rather than administrative interventionism with deleterious externalities.

Finally, with a view to strengthening the economic attractiveness of our territory, I am aware of the importance of bringing Polynesian legislation into line with French and European Competition law. I am therefore proud to have played a positive role in this important vote in our territory's economic history.

---

* Interview collected by Yannick Lecornu.

Later, as Minister for the Economy, you brought about a more restrictive reform of the Competition Code, as well as of the internal workings of the Polynesian Competition Authority. What were the objectives of these reforms? Did they have the desired effect?

This reform was part of a drive to strengthen the effectiveness of our competition policy and better adapt our regulatory framework to the specific features of the Polynesian market. It was not restrictive, but aimed to draw the consequences of the first years of operation under the 2015 texts.

Competition law generally appears obscure to the general public. Is it the same for public decision-makers and legislators?

First of all, I'd like to make it clear that Competition law appears complex and technical even to specialised lawyers. This is due to the very nature of this field, which lies at the confluence of economics and law, and requires a detailed analysis of behaviour, market structures and interactions between companies.

For the general public, Competition law is often perceived as an abstract concept, too far removed from everyday concerns.

For public decision-makers, it all depends on their initial and continuing training, their specialisation and their appetite for the subject. As you know, an assembly elected by direct vote is the reflection of a society, so you'll find a wide variety of profiles and sensitivities, depending on the subject. That said, all public decision-makers and legislators must bear in mind that where there is honour, there is also responsibility.

Unlike the general public, participants in a legislative procedure have chosen to become involved in this type of project. They therefore have a duty to stay informed and to keep up to date, because while the technical terms, economic concepts and legal procedures involved may be difficult to grasp, the consequences of Competition law are very real, and have a direct impact on purchasing power and economic dynamism.

In your opinion, has Polynesian Competition law had a tangible impact on the lives of local consumers and businesses?

As I said at the start of our interview, the introduction of this right has undeniably raised considerable expectations in terms of economic dynamism and consumer protection. Fortunately, some of these expectations have been met. Indeed, the introduction of a competitive framework has encouraged the emergence of new players in certain markets, offering consumers a wider choice of products and services.

What's more, competition has exerted downward pressure on prices, improving consumers' purchasing power, particularly when it comes to telephone and digital services, as well as transport.

All this has been combined with a general improvement in service quality on the part of many companies to set themselves apart from their competitors and build customer loyalty. More generally, Competition law has helped to foster the emergence of a healthier, fairer business environment for all enterprises. Considering the starting point, this is an undeniable step forward.

At the same time, other expectations may not have been met, not least because of the slowness of procedures. As we know, the evolution of our economic system is a long-term undertaking, requiring patience, constancy, and determination. It also requires efforts to raise awareness. On this last point, while the introduction of "Competition workshops" for professionals is an excellent thing, as is the involvement of students in the organisation of the "competition days".

Although the company has been involved in "Competition days" for some time, there is still a long way to go when it comes to communicating with the general public.

Finally, I'd like to emphasise the great involvement of Polynesian companies in the deployment of competition rules. If few sanctions have been imposed on them, this is not due to any hypothetical laxity on the part of the Authority, but rather to the rapid adaptation of their behaviour to this new situation. To put it another way, it's a bit like the number of tickets issued for failing to wear a seatbelt in a car: if there aren't many, it's because people have understood the rule and are complying with it. The aim of the Polynesian Competition Authority (APC), like that of the police officer, is not to impose fines, but to enforce the rule. In this respect, the objective seems to have been achieved.

At a time when the high cost of living is a constant and almost universal concern, can Competition law help to meet citizens' aspirations?

Absolutely – in fact, it's one of the main levers in the hands of politicians. By encouraging new players to enter the market, Competition law limits the market power of existing companies and encourages them to lower their prices to remain competitive. By penalising anti-competitive practices, it helps prevent artificial price hikes. By encouraging a more efficient allocation of resources, it promotes innovation and investment, which in turn can lead to a more competitive market.

In time, this will translate into lower production costs and lower consumer prices. All for the benefit of the consumer.

So, if it works so well, why does the high cost of living remain such a recurrent theme in public debate? First, because a number of factors can limit the effectiveness of the competitive framework, such as market structure or exogenous shocks, which are particularly impactful in an import economy.

Secondly, because there's an asymmetry of temporality between the otherwise legitimate aspirations of the population, and the production of results from a public policy or an evolution of a legal framework. In my opinion, such impatience is the crux of the problem, and all democracies are currently facing it. In our modern societies, we can't stand waiting any longer, we want everything instantaneously, we react instead of planning.

Large-scale reforms can take several decades to take effect, which is why it's important to accompany their deployment with communication tailored to each individual.

The Polynesian Competition Authority had a rather chaotic start-up phase. What are the reasons for this? Should its status change?

And even then, chaotic is an understatement. With the compulsory resignation of its first president, it's fair to say that the story got off to a pretty bad start, and many thought it could never return to its original ambition. Others may even have nurtured the hope of seeing it buried forever. And yet, by dint of hard work and self-sacrifice, the Authority's renewed teams were able, step by step, to rebuild legitimacy, ethics, and effective working arrangements. In this case, for better or for worse, the human factor remains the source of our greatest weakness and our greatest strength.

As far as the Authority's status is concerned, I have to confess that my position has clearly evolved the last few years. While the botched start-up prevented any adjustment of the APC's scope and resources, the situation has calmed down, allowing us to consider the necessary evolution of this tool. As a first line of thought, I believe that the APC should be given a specific budget, under the supervision not of a ministry but of the Assembly of French Polynesia's economic commission. In this respect, dialogue between the APC and the APF must be constant. Second, the APC must regulate the key sectors of energy and telecommunications, in which the government is present as a shareholder or delegator. ARCEP and CRE, the national regulatory authorities, should support APC's development of these skills. Third, APC should be systematically consulted on economic issues, as the CESEC is. Fourth, cooperation with other administrative authorities needs to be strengthened, starting with the economic affairs and customs departments, and even APF's internal or specific commissions.

These first four ideas, which are simple and concrete, seem to me to be the right ones to support the development of the Polynesian Competition Authority.

Within the republican system, several territories are aspiring to greater autonomy and may, in the years to come, adopt specific rules governing competition. Based on the Polynesian experience, what advice would you give them?

The question of economic autonomy and local adaptation of Competition law is a major issue for all overseas territories. Believe me, it's a subject of constant discussion with my fellow senators. The French overseas territories have specific social contexts, unique economic characteristics, distinct regional environments and heterogeneous levels of development.

In this sense, the Polynesian experience can offer valuable lessons for all territories, as well as for national legislators. Following the example of our friends in New Caledonia, we have been able to find, through our own Competition Code, rules that are adapted, rather flexible, and relatively simple. With ten years' hindsight, we are now in a position to respond to any requests from our fellow citizens in the French overseas territories.

To return to your question, I'd like to offer two pieces of advice. The first is to be aware of the timeframe of the project: building and deploying a Competition Code is a process, means mobilising all players over the long term. The second is to rely on existing national and regional authorities. In our territories, we don't always have the constant availability of the expertise required in certain key sectors such as energy and telecommunications. We therefore need to find synergies to pool skills and benefit from an equal level of quality in all territories.

I've seen how a network specialising in competition issues, called the Institute for small markets in law and economics, has enabled experts to cooperate. This is an example of a concrete initiative that should be encouraged, and which could prove useful to the overseas territories if need be.

What do you see as the main challenges facing Polynesian Competition law over the next ten years?

Economics is a living matter. To keep pace with the times, our Competition law must continue to evolve. Building on the progress already made, it will have to adapt to the changing economic models of our society, which will undoubtedly see the emergence of new forms of competition.

To begin with, the rise of digital technology and online platforms is profoundly changing the rules of competition, and should logically impact us. Collaborative business models, such as Uber and Airbnb, raise new competition issues. In the coming years, we'll need to strike a balance between economic dynamism, innovation, and the protection of consumers and jobs.

Second, Competition law will have to take account of environmental and social issues. Tomorrow, it could be used to promote more sustainable and responsible economic practices. This is a growing concern for consumers, who are better informed and therefore more demanding.

Finally, the development of artificial intelligence and automation could lead to increased concentration in certain markets. Tools will therefore need to be put in place to detect and punish anti-competitive practices harmful to consumers.

Those, in a nutshell, are the main challenges I see. And I'm confident in our ability to meet them.

Édouard Fritch

Former President of French Polynesia (2014-2023)

*"It was an unprecedented experience for all those involved"**

Mr. President, the law establishing competition law came into effect just under a year after your election as President of French Polynesia. Could you explain the context in which this text was drafted and voted on at the time?

As part of the fundamental principles of democracy and good governance, French Polynesia chose to establish its own Competition Authority. This body was officially created by a law adopted by the Assembly of French Polynesia and holds extensive powers in the areas of investigation, decision-making, and sanctions. It complements the other local economic and legal institutions.

As a key player in economic regulation, the Competition Authority contributes to the structuring of a fair and competitive market while addressing the specific economic characteristics of French Polynesia. It also works to protect the interests of both consumers and businesses, thus fostering a harmonious and inclusive development of the local economic fabric.

Do you remember if the establishment of competition law in an administered economy like that of French Polynesia was met with unanimous support from the political class, or if, on the contrary, it was met with skepticism by some?

Any change or innovation can raise legitimate questions and concerns. However, the establishment of the Polynesian Competition Authority (APC) was part of a necessary and inevitable evolution. It is important to note that the Polynesian economy has historically been based on a counter trade model, largely relying on imports. In this context, it was natural for local economic players to question the relevance and implications of establishing such an institution in Polynesia.

Thanks to constructive dialogue and efforts to explain the initiative, it was gradually accepted by a large majority of stakeholders. The objective was to progress collectively while adjusting the approaches as the activities of the APC increased, in order to best meet local specificities and the expectations of economic players.

* Interview conducted by Maître Angélique Herbez-Fontaine, Lawyer at the Papeete Bar.

How did the Polynesian population receive and understand the establishment of an authority responsible for enforcing competition law?

It is essential to place these events in their historical context. French Polynesia was emerging from a period marked by a certain political instability, which inevitably had repercussions on the economic and social fronts. At that time, the concerns of the Polynesian population were more focused on tangible and immediate issues. Citizens were striving for the restoration of institutional stability and the revitalization of the economic dynamic.

Furthermore, it is important to remember that this context was part of a major global financial crisis, the impacts of which were felt both by local economic players and the population. These circumstances understandably heightened expectations toward public policies related to stability and economic resilience.

In light of the novelty represented by the establishment of such an authority, how did your government and you personally support the implementation of the Polynesian Competition Authority?

This was a unique experience for all the parties involved. It was necessary to understand and become familiar with the functioning mechanisms while scrupulously ensuring that the separation of roles and prerogatives was preserved. The independence of the Competition Authority is a fundamental principle that must be strictly respected. This process represented a phase of mutual learning for all the stakeholders involved.

The Polynesian Competition Authority was the first independent administrative authority established by French Polynesia. It has functional autonomy in legal matters as well as material autonomy.

Can you tell us what this independence meant in your relationship with the APC?

Under the separation of powers that applies to all stakeholders, once the rules of the game were clearly established for all, everyone could carry out their role with legitimacy and occupy their place within a structured framework. Although their roles were independent, they had the opportunity to be complementary while strictly respecting the defined limits and established principles. This respect for roles and boundaries was essential to ensure the success of the APC's mission and to strengthen the credibility of the community.

As President of French Polynesia, the competition code grants you the power of referral in matters of concentration, meaning the ability to authorize a transaction that the Competition Authority has not approved for reasons of public interest, or the ability to appeal decisions made by the APC. You did not use these powers during your mandate, but did you ever consider doing so?

I want to emphasize my deep respect for the principles and practices that guide our actions. The establishment of the Polynesian Competition Authority (APC) was part of a necessary framework, consistent with our commitments. As the primary person responsible for this initiative, it seemed imperative to me to strictly follow this course of action, fully in line with the powers granted to me by the competition code. To directly answer your question, it was never my intention to use my power of referral, and I have never done so, if my memory serves me correctly.

The Polynesian competition code also emphasizes the advisory role of the Authority, particularly the obligation for the President of French Polynesia and the President of the Assembly to submit any draft law or resolution instituting a new regime that would result in restrictions on the exercise of a profession or market access in terms of quantitative and geographical limitations, exclusive rights in certain areas or sectors, or the imposition of uniform practices regarding prices or sales conditions.
How have the opinions of the Polynesian Competition Authority been integrated into the legislative and regulatory process?

Thank you for your question. You raise a very pertinent point regarding the economic and structural specificities of French Polynesia, particularly of Tahiti. Due to the small size of the local market and the dominance of certain major groups, whether local or from mainland France, it is crucial to adopt a rigorous and balanced approach in decision-making and orientations, particularly in key sectors such as trade and other strategic activities.

In this context, the role of the Competition Authority, although consultative in some cases, is fundamental for ensuring regulatory mechanisms that serve as protective and preventive elements. This allows for the establishment of clear and fair principles while respecting local specificities.

Finally, it is important to remember that the separation of powers remains a key pillar of our democratic model. Each body performs a distinct role: some issue opinions, others legislate, while the executive implements the decisions. This framework ensures institutional balance, guaranteeing transparency and fairness in service to the public interest.

Competition law celebrates its 10th anniversary this year. Do you feel that, over the past decade, competition law has successfully integrated into the local economic landscape and contributed to developing the competitiveness of businesses in French Polynesia?

Regarding the first question, the answer is undoubtedly affirmative. Today, it has become common and essential for everyone to take the time to reflect on the right questions before engaging in any investment or major project. As for its impact on the competitiveness of businesses in French Polynesia, it has certainly made a significant contribution in this direction.

Have you noticed any changes in the practices of economic players in the territory, both in the public and private sectors?

As mentioned earlier, it has now become common and fundamental for everyone to take the time to carefully consider the relevant issues before committing to an investment or any major project. Our economic players have clearly understood this.

How would you assess the current level of collaboration between the country and the Authority regarding the implementation of competition law in the territory?

I will limit myself to addressing the period when I had responsibilities. During that time, the principles were clearly established: no interference in the APC's missions.

In your opinion, what have been the most significant positions taken by the Polynesian Competition Authority over the past decade?

I prefer to highlight the analyses and opinions issued, which have elicited varied reactions from the public and economic players, whether positive or critical. It is always challenging to strike a balance between seeking profitability in the business world, which can sometimes favor dominant positions, and maintaining a harmonious market in a restricted environment like that of French Polynesia. However, what I remember above all is that pragmatic reflection has always prevailed.

And what challenges will the Authority face in the coming years, given the country's economic prospects?

Many initiatives have been undertaken in the past, and it is now essential for them to flourish and endure. The main challenge for the Authority over the next decade will be to consolidate its organization, improve communication with institutions and citizens, optimize its internal functioning, and maintain its institutional independence, which is a fundamental element to ensure the full achievement of its mission.

Finally, with nearly 8 years of close collaboration with the Authority, what recommendations would you make to strengthen the effectiveness of competition law in French Polynesia for the future?

It is always delicate to make recommendations or suggestions for an independent Authority without risking misunderstandings. However, in a constructive spirit and with a general approach, several areas of focus could be considered for the Polynesian Competition Authority to address the specificities and evolving economic dynamics of the territory:

- Due to the limited size of the Polynesian market and economic concentration in certain key sectors (large retail, transportation, energy), it will be essential to maintain constant attention to ensure healthy and balanced competition.
- The strategic orientations of the territory in favor of energy transition and a sustainable economy will lead to significant transformations in sectors such as renewable

energy, maritime transport, or tourism. The Authority will need to adjust its tools and approaches to support these developments while ensuring fair conditions for all players.

- In a context where understanding and acceptance of competition principles are still developing, the Authority could intensify its educational actions, both with businesses and the general public, to better promote the benefits of fair competition and the applicable rules.
- Given that the economic dynamics of Polynesia are influenced by global and regional trends, the Authority would benefit from strengthening its cooperation with public authorities and other institutions to align with international best practices and anticipate market developments.

To tackle these challenges, the Competition Authority will need to combine vigilance, innovation, and education. Its role will be critical in guiding economic transformations while preserving a competitive, balanced market aligned with the objectives of sustainable development and the public interest.

Yvonnick Raffin

Former Minister of Finance and Economy of French Polynesia (2020-2023).

*"The dominant position of certain large groups, whether local or from the mainland, requires an economic governance based on rigor and balance"**

You were in charge of the Ministry of Economy under the leadership of President Edouard Fritch for three years, from 2020 to 2023. The Ministry of Economy and the Polynesian Competition Authority share the common goal of ensuring market efficiency, but they have very different means of action. How would you describe the institutional division of roles between this ministry, and more specifically between the General Directorate of Economic Affairs and the Authority?

As a preamble, it is essential to remember that the separation of powers between the various economic institutions ensures that public policies function optimally and coordinate effectively.

The relationship between the DGAE and the APC is based on a fundamental principle of complementarity. While the DGAE works on economic development and regulation within a political and strategic framework, the APC ensures compliance with competition rules in complete independence. This division makes it possible to ensure effective economic regulation, reconciling growth, consumer protection and market fairness.

Thus, the institutional framework in French Polynesia guarantees a balance between public intervention and respect for market principles, favouring structured, secure economic development in line with international standards.

The Polynesian Competition Authority is unique in that it is an independent administrative authority with functional autonomy over legal and material autonomy. Can you tell us what this independence meant for your relationship with the APC?

Within the framework of the fundamental principle of the separation of powers, which is binding on all stakeholders, the clarity of the rules of the game ensured that everyone had the legitimacy needed to carry out their duties. This structure made it possible not

* Interview conducted by Maître Angélique Herbez-Fontaine, Lawyer at the Papeete Bar.

only to preserve the independence of roles, but also to encourage synergies within a framework of strict respect for established prerogatives and principles. Maintaining this institutional balance was the sine qua non for ensuring the effectiveness of the APC's mission and consolidating the credibility of the community.

The Polynesian economy is characterized by being a managed economy, due to the significant geographical and logistical constraints of the territory. How can the liberal approach to competition law coexist within the same economy with the interventionism of the government, which is sometimes necessary given the local economic specificities?

The economy of French Polynesia is largely based on an import model, characteristic of a "comptoir" economy. Although its maritime territory covers almost 5 million km², most economic activity – around 90% – is concentrated in Tahiti, which has only 1,042 km² of land area. This concentration, combined with the limited size of the local market and the dominant position of certain major groups, both local and from mainland France, means that economic governance must be based on rigour and balance.

In this context, the definition of public policies, particularly in strategic sectors such as commerce, must be based on a pragmatic approach, where regulation and market structuring aim to guarantee healthy competition and a sustainable economic dynamic. The general interest must remain at the heart of decisions, while ensuring a fair distribution of resources and opportunities.

The institutional framework plays a decisive role in this balance. Each body has a specific remit: some are tasked with issuing opinions, others with legislating, while the executive is responsible for implementing decisions. This distribution of roles helps to guarantee transparency and fairness, while consolidating the legitimacy of political choices in the service of the economic and social development of French Polynesia.

You were in office during the Covid-19 health crisis, which hit French Polynesia hard. During this crisis, when strong economic measures had to be taken, what was the relationship between your ministry and the Authority?

The need to restructure the APC became clear with the new governmentHowever, the priority was not to focus on the APC, but to put in place the conditions essential to the survival of our economy, the preservation of jobs and the establishment of mechanisms for a rapid and effective economic recovery.

Over the past ten years, the Polynesian Competition Authority has issued numerous opinions on the functioning of the local economy, as well as on reform projects. What insights have the Authority's opinions provided you regarding the economic perspectives at stake?

During my ministerial term, the Polynesian Competition Authority played a key role in helping economic players adapt to the new regulatory framework.

Its opinions have fostered a better understanding of the local market, supported economic reforms and strengthened market regulation in the general interest. They have also contributed to the development of more effective public policies, guaranteeing sustainable and balanced growth for the economy of French Polynesia.

The metropolitan competition law today involves the Ministry of Economy to a large extent in carrying out its missions, notably by extensively involving the DGCCRF (the equivalent of the DGAE) in identifying anti-competitive practices and exercising its investigative powers. Do you think that Polynesian law would also benefit from evolving in the same direction?

Simply copying and pasting external models is not enough when it comes to adapting regulations to local realities. During my term of office, I have ensured that collaboration between the Ministry and the Polynesian Competition Authority is both close and effective, while respecting the autonomy of the institution. As the executive, we ensured active coordination, particularly through the appointment of the Government Commissioner, appointed by the Government on the recommendation of the Minister of Finance. This approach has helped to anchor the APC's actions in a pragmatic vision that is consistent with the economic challenges facing French Polynesia.

This year marks the tenth anniversary of competition law in French Polynesia. Do you feel that, over the past decade, competition law has successfully integrated into the local economic landscape and contributed to developing the competitiveness of the local economy?

The answer is undoubtedly yes, because in an economic context such as that of Polynesia, its action has clearly strengthened the ability of economic players to adapt to market demands, by promoting a more structured environment conducive to sustainable growth.

Have you observed any changes in the practices of economic players in the territory, both in the public and private sectors?

Today's private sector players adopt a rigorous strategic approach before allocating resources to a major investment or project. This pragmatic approach allows to optimise the economic and social benefits controlling the risks. For public-sector players, on the other hand, the logic is fundamentally different: their actions are not part of a competitive dynamic, but of a public service mission. This means that resources must be managed in the public interest, requiring an approach tailored to the specific challenges of the public sector.

In your opinion, what have been the most significant positions taken by the Polynesian Competition Authority over the past decade?

The analyses and opinions formulated, which naturally elicited contrasting reactions from the public and economic players are significant contributions. The most important thing is that the decisions have always been guided by a pragmatic approach, giving priority to the general interest and economic efficiency.

Are there still sectors today where the development of competition is a priority, considering the economic prospects of French Polynesia?

As highlighted above, the economy of French Polynesia is based on a limited territory of 1,042 km², which has a direct influence on the structure of its markets. On the one hand, the concentration of economic power among a few local players shapes the dynamics of competition; on the other, the limited size of the market makes it difficult for truly open competition to emerge. This reality calls for appropriate regulation and proactive public policies to ensure a balance between competitiveness, economic development and consumer protection.

Finally, in your opinion, what are the upcoming challenges that the country will need to overcome to ensure healthy and effective competition in Polynesian markets?

The Competition Authority of French Polynesia must adapt its action to the territory's economic specificities, reconciling effective regulation and sustainable development. Faced with a small market marked by high economic concentration, its vigilance will be essential to guarantee balanced competition, particularly in strategic sectors such as mass retailing, energy and transport.

The changes brought about by the energy transition and sustainable development mean that its tools need to be adapted to manage these developments without holding back innovation. At the same time, we need to step up our educational initiatives aimed at businesses and the general public in order to instil a genuine competition culture.

Finally, in an environment influenced by regional and global dynamics, the AMF will have to step up its cooperation with the public authorities and competent institutions to anticipate market developments and align itself with best practice. Its action will be decisive in structuring a more transparent, competitive and resilient market, serving the objectives of economic development and general interest.

Pascal Devillers

President of the Administrative Court of Polynesia

"Competition has paid off: telecommunications and air transport are prime examples"[*]

As President of the Administrative Court, you are on the front line of competition law enforcement in Polynesia, a jurisdiction that has long evolved without a specific local legislative framework. What do you see as the main challenges faced by the Administrative Court in establishing and enforcing competition law in Polynesia?

To say that the Administrative Court of French Polynesia is on the "front line" in the application of competition law in French Polynesia is very kind, but this should not obscure the fact that the judge is most often regarded as the "natural judge of competition". In 1987, the legislator decided to modify the normal order of jurisdictional competence by assigning the litigation of the Conseil de la concurrence (which became the Autorité de la concurrence in 2008), which has the nature of an independent administrative authority, to the Paris Court of Appeal, and ultimately to the Cour de cassation. The French Constitutional Council partially accepted this derogation from the principle that the annulment or reversal of decisions taken by administrative authorities (including independent administrative authorities), in the exercise of prerogatives of public power, fall within the jurisdiction of the administrative courts, thereby enshrining this "fundamental principle recognised by the laws of the Republic", in its important decision no. 86-224 DC of 23 January 1987.

However, rather than conferring jurisdiction by means of a summary reference to the Authority's acts in this field, the legislator has opted for a precise enumeration of certain decisions mentioned in certain legislative articles, excluding all merger-related disputes, which are heard by the Conseil d'Etat. Judicial case law is thus essential in matters of unfair competition, restrictive practices and market transparency.

In Polynesia, the Administrative Court, which judges the legality of public action, whether through regulatory or individual acts adopted or contracts signed, is called upon to deal with competition law issues and potentially to apply the rules contained in the French Polynesia Competition Code, a jurisdiction reserved for French Polynesia by the statutory organic law. More marginally, national and European rules will be applied to locally applicable acts of state authorities. This is notably the case for the

---

[*] Interview conducted by Thibault Segalard, journalist at Tahiti Infos.

Tahiti airport concession, on which we will most likely have to rule in 2025, or for contested government or military contracts. It should also be noted that the decisions of the Polynesian Competition Authority can be contested in the first and last instance before the Paris Administrative Court of Appeal, which has jurisdiction to hear them under article R. 311-2 of the Code of Administrative Justice, and therefore before the administrative jurisdiction, unlike the Competition Authority on mainland France.

As far as the Administrative Court of French Polynesia is concerned, Polynesian competition law is indeed made up of a body of very recent rules since they were instituted by the country's competition law no. 2014-15 LP/APF of June 25, 2014, just ten years ago. Of the 18 decisions handed down under the Polynesian Competition Code, only 7 concern the application of the code's substantive rules, while the other 11 relate to disputes between Polynesian Competition Authority (APC) staff and French Polynesia, including, all the same, a president and a general rapporteur of this institution.

But beyond the application of the new code, which has not presented us with insurmountable difficulties, the difficulty lies more in understanding the often very dense and complex regulations governing certain professional activities, when it comes to checking the legality of a regulation or administrative sanction. There are also societal obstacles to the application of competition law, insofar as monopolies and oligopolies exist.

When you think of the introduction of competition law, the conflicts between Onati and Pacifique Mobile Télécom immediately spring to mind. Aside from this case, what other major competition law cases has the Administrative Court ruled on?

Disputes between Onati and the other two telecoms operators account for no fewer than 15 court rulings, and the disputes are highly complex and varied: challenges to orders approving reference interconnection tariffs, to articles of the French Post and Telecommunications Code relating to the determination of these reference interconnection tariffs, to an order approving the allocation of an investment subsidy to SAS Onati for the deployment of 4G in remote archipelagos, to the refusal to disclose documents relating to the public service delegation concluded between OPT and SAS Onati, to the refusal to repeal article LP. 28 of the Country law of 7 December 2009, insofar as it excludes from the regulatory framework applicable to public service delegations those entrusted by public establishments (clearly OPT) to their subsidiaries, the refusal to modify the deployment schedule set out in the specifications for the authorisation to operate as a mobile telephony operator.

And in addition to these disputes, in which each party endeavours to limit the competitive advantage deemed unduly granted to others by the regulations, we are also involved in liability litigation, to obtain compensation for damage caused by rules that the court has declared illegal.

Other important cases involving high prices for consumers, the main focus of competition law, included challenges to the list of basic necessities (PPN) and fast-moving consumer goods (PGC), which classify certain products in these categories, reducing margins and favouring certain types of business, administrative fines for improperly collecting trade discounts on certain essential products, or disputes between shipowners over decrees setting maximum selling prices for diesel fuel used to power the engines of commercial vessels engaged in inter-island shipping, on the grounds that they would give an advantage to a competitor.

What recurring competition law complaints have you observed? Are there any sectors or practices that are particularly prone to litigation?

At this point, we should mention the particular role played by the court as guarantor of transparency and equality between candidates in the field of public procurement, public contracts and concessions/public service delegations, which contribute to a large part of French Polynesia's GDP and employment. Two types of litigation in particular fall within the scope of competition rules: pre-contractual injunctions (référés précontractuels) and contract annulment proceedings (recours en annulation d'un contrat) when – as is most often the case – an unsuccessful competitor is involved.

Under article L.551-24 of the Code of Administrative Justice for French Polynesia, the pre-contractual summary procedure is used to reshuffle the deck if a candidate for a public contract considers that a rule of the tendering procedure, or the way in which it was carried out, favours, de facto or deliberately, a category or certain candidates, in disregard of the applicable advertising and competitive bidding rules. The judge then has the power to annul the procedure for awarding the contract and to order the procedure to be repeated, purging it of the defect that affected it. On average, summary proceedings are heard within 15 days. Since this provision was introduced in 2009, 237 cases have been referred to the court on this basis, 22 of them since the beginning of 2024.

How would you assess the effectiveness of the legal measures put in place to promote competition in French Polynesia? In your opinion, in which sectors could competition be developed to enhance its effectiveness?

It's very difficult for me to answer this question, for which I have very little data or information. Indeed, as President of the Administrative Court, I cannot assess whether these measures are effective in combating monopolies or quasi-monopolies, cartels or abuses of dominant positions. On the other hand – and this is the citizen speaking – perhaps we can question the maintenance of rules that hinder competition and serve to protect abusive margins to the detriment of consumers' interests – local development taxes, exclusive import agreements, etc. – which, in my opinion, are not in the interests of consumers.

In your opinion, what is the importance of an administrative jurisdiction for the application of competition law in a small island economy like Polynesia?

In the exercise of its regulatory function, the administrative judge occupies a position that is far from negligible. As I mentioned at the start of this interview, all decisions organising the exercise of an economic activity are subject to their control. The judge also controls the use by public authorities of their powers of sanction, but also, upstream, of approval or authorisation.

Our intervention in the field of competition can also be incidental when, for example, we are asked by a competitor to cancel a building permit granted for the construction of a hotel or supermarket. On a more ad hoc basis, French Polynesian or State authorities may request an opinion from the tribunal on competition issues, such as, for example, this year's request for an opinion on the possibility of creating a quasi-regulated system adapted to the specific sectoral and geographical characteristics of the telecommunications sector in French Polynesia.

How does the Administrative Court integrate and take into account the opinions and recommendations of the Polynesian Competition Authority when handling competition cases?

We do, of course, take into account the authorised opinions issued by the APC, to which, incidentally, the parties that benefit from them do not fail to refer. They weigh heavily in our assessment of the legality of the issues submitted to us, and this has of course been the case in the many disputes involving the telecommunications sector, with some decisions even quoting extracts from them when they best reflect the singular context of an issue to be decided. We quote them extensively in our decisions, not as an argument of law, but as the argument of an organisation specialised in the field of competition.

Finally, how do you see competition regulations evolving in French Polynesia over the next ten years? What do you see as the priorities for development?

With the APC, French Polynesia has equipped itself with a fine tool, made up of competent and motivated people, in a working atmosphere that we hope will no longer feed into the hearings of the Administrative Court. This tool must be put to good use, and its reports and proposals taken into account, without pusillanimity.

The high cost of living is the number 1 problem of a fractured population, with considerable disparities in wealth leaving more and more poor people by the wayside. Yet competition has borne fruit: telecommunications and air transport are striking examples. It is in the common interest that regulation should be stepped up in the fields of mass retailing and luxury hotels, for example, where dominant positions, nurtured and constantly reinforced by the margins charged, are the most visible. And competition law should undoubtedly be complemented by a proactive fiscal policy.

Jean-Luc Lemercier

Chairman of the Territorial Audit Office of French Polynesia

*"The APC's actions are also favourable for public authorities, since greater transparency encourages the management of public funds"**

What role does the CTC play in monitoring and promoting competition in French Polynesia? To what extent does this contribute to the territory's economic development?

The Chambre territoriale des comptes does not intervene directly in the field of competition. However, through occasional analyses, we touch on these issues or come very close to them. Competition law, as it has developed in Polynesia, has its origins in the economic crisis of 2008. The aid allocated to Polynesia at that time was subject to a number of conditions, including the emergence of competition law. In a more recent context, competition issues are increasingly present among the population, which is sensitive to inflation and believes that competition lowers prices.

The role of the CTC is not to deal with competition, this is why the APC was created. Our role is to be the guardian of public financial order, guaranteeing sound management of public funds while informing citizens about how they are used. However, there are two aspects that link us to the competition. Firstly, we exercise financial control over the Polynesian Competition Authority (APC). A few years ago, we published a report on its management, recommendations. Competition is also reflected in our analyses, in particular through subjects chosen by citizens through a participative platform. For example, in 2023, the subject of the local development tax TDL was chosen, a subject linked to the protection and emergence of Polynesian "champions".

Another example is our recent report on Air Tahiti Nui (ATN) and the country's tourism policy, which highlights the challenges associated with opening up to international competition, which affects the national operator and its public subsidies. Finally, our audits of public entities - municipalities, inter-municipal bodies or companies receiving public funds - include the examination of public procurement contracts, a key area for competition. In this way, our work contributes indirectly to the development of this right in Polynesia.

---

* Interview conducted by Thibault Segalard, journalist at Tahiti Infos.

As for the impact of these missions on economic development, competition is a "crest line" that needs to be handled with care. The example of ATN is a good illustration of this equation: balancing opening up to competition and protecting local interests to protect both the economy and taxpayers.

What specific difficulties do you encounter in the financial control of public entities in the context of a progressively liberalised economy?

Paradoxically, and this is a note of hope, we are encountering few difficulties. We have a solid legal framework - the *Financial Jurisdiction Code* - which gives us the prerogatives we need to effectively audit public entities. Although the Polynesian economy has begun to liberalise, I agree that there is still progress to be made. The APC plays an essential role in this, by encouraging greater competition.

It is in the interests of public bodies, whether they are lawmakers or economic agents, to encourage this dynamic and foster the emergence of competition in the region. For our part, we have the tools we need to carry out our control missions.

Has the introduction a *competition code* in Polynesia enabled you to strengthen the financial control of public bodies and companies under public management?

Absolutely, to a certain extent it has strengthened financial control, since this code gives us a valuable additional tool. Its adoption was a necessity, marking real progress. In French Polynesia, we lack many codes, such as the public health code, which sometimes complicates our controls. Without a code, there is no legal basis and therefore lack of tools for our inspections. The *Competition Code, on* the other hand, provides a legal basis that strengthens our ability to act.

Have you seen any concrete changes in the Polynesian economy since the introduction of competition law? Which public sectors are most affected?

The introduction of competition rules facilitated the establishment of the APC, which today has developed a solid body of case law governing competition. This jurisprudence provides a framework for actions of economic players in this area, and that is very positive. This regulatory framework is essential for the strategic sectors most affected, such as energy, telecommunications and basic necessities.

The APC plays a decisive role, as demonstrated by the decisions taken on energy regulation. Without its presence and recommendations, such a decision would not have been taken. In short, the APC has reached a certain maturity. It is already shaping competition issues in French Polynesia through its opinions and decisions, and will continue to do so. I am convinced of this.

In your opinion, has the Competition Authority contributed to better management of public funds, particularly in terms of transparency and accountability of public players?

Undeniably. Since it entered its mature phase, the APC has had a positive impact on all local players. Concrete examples, such as the lowering of costs in the telecoms or funeral services sectors, show that its action translates into direct savings for the consumer. What's more, the APC's actions are also beneficial to the public authorities, since greater transparency encourages better management of public funds. Today, the Authority's role is accepted, understood and necessary. This is no mean feat.

How has competition law influenced the behaviour of local public companies and public services in Polynesia?

Competition law is an essential legal foundation. Public players and companies must respect and comply with these constraints or face sanctions, whether from the APC or under criminal law. As far as public companies and services are concerned, it is important to understand that competition law applies to all companies. All have had to adapt to the constraints. Before the code existed, there were no rules, so it was complicated to enforce anything.

What additional measures would you consider to strengthen compliance with and enforcement of competition law?

In my view, there are two key areas. The first is to take inspiration from best practices elsewhere. I'm a great believer in benchmarking. For example, by reassessing the relevance of certain provisions such as the exclusive importer clause, which is still in place here but has been withdrawn elsewhere. We could ask ourselves why it has been withdrawn elsewhere. We need to think about what is happening beyond French Polynesia. Which brings me to my second point, which is the regular evaluation of existing systems. Taking stock 5 or 10 years after the adoption of a regulation would make it possible to adjust public policies and measure their impact. We need to know what has worked and what hasn't, and whether the objective has been achieved. In my opinion, this would be essential for improving competition law and the CPA's action.

PART II

A Decade of Decisions and Opinions from the Polynesian Competition Authority – A Review

Sophie Bresny

General Rapporteur of the Polynesian Competition Authority

*"Informal contacts are numerous and help to clarify texts and case law"**

Island economies, especially when they far from continents, usually suffer from high prices, but there is not always agreement on the explanation for this phenomenon. Sometimes structural reasons are cited, such as transport costs, and sometimes anti-competitive ones, such as more frequent collusion between market players. In your experience, what should we make of this debate?

Before looking at the difference between structural and anti-competitive reasons for high prices in island economies, it's worth taking a closer look at what each encompasses.

Firstly, the *structural reasons* are mainly linked to the specific geographical and economic characteristics of island territories. They include:

– *Additional supply costs*:

Due to their insularity (double insularity for some, such as French Polynesia), island economies are subject to additional supply costs, notably linked to sea and air transport. In French Polynesia, for example, sea transport represents an additional cost factor of around 8% of a product's selling price, which is not substantial but not negligible. However, the remoteness and isolation of French Polynesia are not enough to explain all the additional costs, which are also due to the size of the market.

– *Small markets*:

Island markets are often small, which limits the economies of scale that local companies can achieve. This is a natural obstacle to the establishment of a competitive market. French Polynesia is dependent on imports, particularly for consumer goods. Of these, 28% come from mainland France, 14% from other European Union countries, and the remainder from the United States, China, Australia and New Zealand. Regional circuits are therefore not favoured. This is particularly the case for food industry products, electrical equipment and pharmaceuticals.

* Interview conducted by Patrick Hubert, partner based in Paris in the Antitrust & Competition department at the law firm Orrick.

– *The concentrated, integrated structure of island markets* (particularly in Polynesia) is the result of 2 cumulative factors.

Firstly, upstream, the importation of goods is highly regulated. Local producers benefit from customs protection. What's more, demand is often undervalued, while local supply is often overvalued, leading to shortages of a number of products. It then becomes necessary to resort to import quotas, forcing importers to buy under unfavourable conditions, which are passed on to consumers in the form of higher prices. Secondly, importers often benefit from exclusive import rights for one or more brands that are legal in French Polynesia. In addition, in many sectors there is vertical integration of import, production and distribution activities. Producers have no incentive to improve production quality or diversity. The retail sector is also highly concentrated

– *A specific regulatory framework*:

This also contributes to higher prices by increasing the cost of entering island markets. This represents around 8%, or as much as the additional supply costs mentioned above. French Polynesia, for example, has introduced a wide range of market protection measures designed to protect domestic industrial and agricultural production. Imports are highly restricted by both tariff barriers (around twenty import duties and taxes, representing almost 30% of the CIF value of imports, but much more on certain products, notably those subject to the local development tax (TDL) or specific taxes) and non-tariff barriers (import bans or quotas, notably on agricultural products). Other regulatory provisions are also likely to have an impact on prices: price regulation, which the Authority's opinion of 2 April 2019 on basic necessities showed to have price-increasing effects in particular; local tax exemption, which already favours powerful players to the detriment of new entrants; restrictions on foreign direct investment, which limit the market entry of new operators or producers; old and unreviewed health rules with sometimes anti-competitive effects.[1]

Secondly, *anti-competitive reasons* are mainly linked in island economies to *corporate practices* that restrict competition in these markets. These practices include:

– *Cartels and concerted practices*[2]:

Companies can collude to fix prices artificially. For example, in the funeral services sector in French Polynesia, 12 companies took part in concerted meetings to fix the prices of their funeral services for deaths linked to COVID-19, causing them to rise.[3] Cartels also exist, of course, in large non-insular economies, but it may be that the smaller size, more limited number of players and the existence of barriers to entry, which make it difficult for "dissident" players to enter, encourage the emergence and maintenance of cartels on the scale of a small, isolated economy.

---

1 APC, Opinion no. 2019-A-01 of 2 April 2019 on the effects of regulation on the competitive operation of goods markets.
APC, Opinion no. 2019-A-02 of 19 September 2019 on import and distribution mechanisms in French Polynesia.
ISPF, Points Etudes et Bilans de la Polynésie française, n°1391, October 2023.

2 Article LP. 200-1 of the French Competition Code.

3 APC, Decision no. 2022-PAC-01 of 5 September 2022 concerning practices in the funeral services sector.

– *Abuse of a dominant position*[4]:

Companies in a dominant position can exploit this position to impose high prices. For example, in the mobile telephony sector for residential customers in French Polynesia, VINI offered loyalty programs and differentiated rates when its subscribers contacted its competitor's subscribers by SMS or phone.[5]

The difference between anti-competitive and structural reasons for high prices in island economies lies in their origin. The former stem from the behaviour of companies through the pricing structure of their products, in particular margins and anti-competitive practices, on which the Polynesian Competition Authority is competent to act, unlike the latter, which depend more on the will of the local government in terms of competition policy, but which the Authority can clarify through opinions.

Solutions to these high prices must therefore take into account both the structural characteristics of island economies and the anti-competitive practices of companies. By way of illustration, in 2022, the difference in consumer prices between French Polynesia and mainland France will remain 31% higher, based on a comparable average consumer basket that is intermediate between the consumption structures of the two territories. This gap far exceeds those observed in the French overseas departments (16% in Guadeloupe, 14% in Martinique and French Guiana, 10% in Mayotte and 9% in Réunion).

Has the Authority succeeded in setting up an efficient investigation department despite the impact of distance and isolation, and the small size of an economy where everyone knows everyone else and where developing specialist careers is not easy?

In my opinion, the *efficiency of an investigating department* is measured against a multiplicity of criteria, some applicable to all competition authorities, others specific to island territories, and in particular to French Polynesia.

Generally speaking, the efficiency of an investigation department is measured by the extent to which it achieves the objectives set by law and defined by the AMF's Board of Directors[6], in relation to its resources. As far as the general tasks assigned to the Investigation Department are concerned, the team's day-to-day work is no different from that of other departments: the aim is to combat cartels and abuses of dominant position by searching for clues, collecting evidence and drafting grievance notifications; to monitor mergers and acquisitions; and finally, to investigate requests for opinions, mainly at the request of the President of Polynesia. A special feature of Polynesia, and also of New Caledonia, is that we also investigate commercial development operations.

4 Article LP. 200-1 of the French Competition Code.

5 APC, Decision no. 2018-PAC-01 of 6 June 2018 concerning practices implemented in the mobile telephony sector aimed at residential customers.

6 APC, Annual Report 2023. Available on the APC website: https://autorite-concurrence.pf/rapport-annuel-2023/

The difficulty of working in Polynesia stems from the number of compulsory files to be processed within tight deadlines, with no visibility on the actual workload on a daily basis. On average, we have 25 working days to process a merger[7], 15 working days for a commercial development[8] and one calendar month for an opinion, except in emergencies, when the time limit is reduced to 15 days.[9] This means we have to be particularly reactive, while maintaining our litigation activity. In 2024, my team of 5 rapporteurs handled 25 cases.

In such a context, it is essential to be able to recruit specialists in competition law and, if possible, people who have already had experience as rapporteurs, so that the team is immediately operational. However, it is also important to encourage the transmission of knowledge by integrating into the department people who are perfectly familiar with the territory and its challenges. It's a delicate balancing act. Last but not least, we need to succeed in retaining resources, which is a considerable challenge given that it is difficult to make a career within the same authority. By signing a partnership agreement with the University of Polynesia on 8 October 2024, setting out the terms and conditions of enhanced cooperation in competition law training for students of Masters degrees in public law and business law, the Authority has committed itself to a policy of greater openness towards the region's dynamic forces.

As for insularity, it is both an asset and a challenge for the investigating department, particularly when it comes to carrying out investigations. The confidentiality of investigations can sometimes be difficult to maintain in a territory where everyone knows everyone else. While we all know how difficult it is for suppliers to report potentially anti-competitive behaviour by their customers (supermarkets, restaurants, hotels, etc.) for fear of reprisals, in an insular context the effects can quickly be devastating in the absence of alternative solutions. The investigating department must be able to ensure the anonymity of reports and create a climate of trust to reassure complainants. This trust can only be built up over the long term in the context of successful litigation cases, and the role of the general rapporteur is central in this respect.

Companies in a dominant position need to be clear about their increased responsibility as a dominant player. Informal contacts are numerous and help to clarify texts and jurisprudence. The fact that we are an island encourages these exchanges, which I welcome, as they benefit all economic players by promoting the dissemination of best practices in competition law. But informal contacts sometimes turn into formal ones, with the opening of litigation files. The current major challenge for the Investigation Department is to be able to bring its litigation cases to a successful conclusion, so as to put the Board in a position to sanction deviant behaviour. On this point, there is still some way to go to clear up referrals. The time it takes to investigate and draw up a notification takes time, and this time is not always adapted to the small size of the territory and the economy, which require rapid solutions.

---

7 Article LP. 310-5 of the French Competition Code.

8 Article LP. 320-3 of the French Competition Code.

9 Article LP. 620-2 of the French Competition Code.

Does cooperation with other competition authorities help you overcome the disadvantages of small size and isolation?

Cooperation between the investigating departments of competition authorities has traditionally been organised in two different ways: formal cooperation as set out in legislation, and informal cooperation created within the forums of international or regional bodies, or as a result of privileged bilateral relations. The main aim of both types of cooperation is to adopt common, best practices in order to improve legal certainty for businesses through the effective application of competition law. Formal cooperation also facilitates cross-border litigation. The investigation department of the Polynesian Competition Authority is no exception, and relies on both types of cooperation.

For the investigation department of the Polynesian Competition Authority, *informal cooperation with its counterparts* is fundamental in more ways than one. The size of my department and the demands resulting from the missions entrusted to us, oblige us to constantly train ourselves and to understand the practices of other authorities, so as to be able to efficiently handle our own cases and improve our performance and responsiveness.

The Authority's investigation department is not large enough to specialise its rapporteurs by mission. There are 6 of us, including the general rapporteur, and each must be able to deal with a merger, an authorisation to set up a commercial development, an anti-competitive practice including in a network industry, or to draft an opinion on a draft text from the Pays the sector concerned. This lack of specialisation has several immediate practical consequences:

- We are often faced with tight deadlines to resolve procedural difficulties which are new to us, but which other authorities, notably the French Competition Authority (ADLC) or the New Caledonia Competition Authority (ACNC) (for the control of commercial developments) have already encountered. Being able to benefit from the rapid support of our counterparts enables us to respond effectively to our needs. When you only deal with two or three mergers a year, you may legitimately ask yourself questions about the assessment of a controlling company's decisive influence on the business of a controlled company, or about the effective way to negotiate commitments.
- We have no specialised support services (economics or investigations departments). We therefore need to be sufficiently trained to be able to handle economic analyses in-house, or to efficiently gather evidence of anti-competitive practices. On average, we receive one training session per month on subjects as diverse as IT investigations, financial analysis, quantitative techniques in merger control and the handling of business secrets. On 4 May 2022, the Authority signed a technical assistance framework agreement with the ADLC, which provides for the implementation of these training courses.

Informal exchanges are also supported by the existence of three specialised forums where the Polynesian Competition Authority's investigation department can maintain regular contact with its counterparts and deal with practical competition issues: the PINCCER network (Pacific Island Network of Competition Consumer and Economic Regulators), the OECD and the ICN cartel working group. While the last two forums need no introduction, the first, the PINCCER network, a regional initiative created in 2023, enables discussions between departments in the Pacific zone facing the same constraints resulting from insularity, narrow markets and high cost of living.

We also regularly organise bilateral meetings on subjects of common interest, notably with the ACNC, whose size, missions and insular territory in which it operates are common factors that bring us closer together in the day-to-day exercise of our appraisal missions.

But while informal cooperation between competition authorities is essential to the APC's investigation service, the legislator has also provided for *formal cooperation*, which is just as important.

Article 2 of Act no. 2018-643 of 23 July 2018, amending Order no. 2017-157 of 9 February 2017, extending and adapting to French Polynesia certain provisions of Book IV of the French Commercial Code relating to competition inspections and sanctions, introduced a system for exchanging information between the Authority and the ADLC.[10] This text enables the Authority to ask the ADLC or the Minister in charge of the economy to carry out investigations on its behalf, and vice versa, since the information gathered in this way can be legally used in notifications of grievances in particular

This text has been applied to date, on the initiative of the ADLC, which asked the Authority to carry out investigations on its behalf in a case of air freight transport of pets in Polynesia, which was the subject of a penalty decision.[11] To assist the ADLC in its investigation, the Authority interviewed members of the animal health unit of the Polynesian Biosafety Directorate.

In this case, Goldenway International Pets (GIP) was fined 65,000 euros for abuse of a dominant position. By linking the quarantine service, on which it had a de facto monopoly, with two other services linked to road transport and the organisation of air freight transport, GIP created a leverage effect and prevented any competition.

Finally, some cases require *coordination between competition authorities, including those not expressly provided for in Polynesian law*, but for which the ICN[12] recommendations serve as a basis for discussion, and the practice established by the European Commission in particular, through "weavers", documents by which companies authorise the authorities to communicate confidential information relevant to the case to each other. These waivers of confidentiality in merger investigations enable the competition authorities, on a bilateral basis, to discuss the merger and conduct joint analyses to promote more informed decisions and enable the case to be examined more rapidly.

Indeed, in the context of merger control, certain operations can have a global dimension. In 2023, the worldwide transaction to sell 100% of the Bolloré Logistics subsidiary of the Bolloré Group to the CMA CGM Group, valued at 4.65 billion euros, is a perfect

---

10 Article 9 bis of Ordinance n°2017-157 of 9 February 2017 extending and adapting to French Polynesia certain provisions of Book IV of the Commercial Code relating to competition controls and sanctions.

11 ADLC, Decision no. 22-D-05 of 15 February 2022 concerning practices in the air freight transport of live animals.

12 ICN Recommended practices for merger notification and review procedures, working group comments, Original Comments (April 2004), Amended (April 2018), page 35.

illustration. In this case, the Authority cooperated closely with the European Commission and the ACNC. After examining the transaction, the Authority authorised it subject to structural and behavioural commitments, in particular the resale, to a purchaser subject to the Authority's approval, of Bolloré Logistics' maritime freight transport organisation activities relating to French Polynesia.[13] The Commission's cooperation with the Polynesian Competition Authority extended to the approval of the purchaser of the business to be divested, with CMA CGM choosing Balguerie as the buyer for both divestment packages.

However, this cooperation in no way denies the specific characteristics of the region, and leaves the Authority fully autonomous. It simply makes it more efficient. Cooperation with other investigating departments is necessary, effective and must continue.

Competition law is practiced not only by competition authorities, but also by in-house counsel and lawyers. Ten years after the introduction of modern competition law, what do you think of the bar's degree of maturity on competition issues?

Between the time I took up my post on 1 May 2023 and the present day, I have seen a marked change in the interest shown by local law firms in competition matters. The Authority's advocacy role is encouraging the emergence of specialists. For the past 2 years, the Authority has been organising competition days (in January 2023 for the 1st edition, and in February 2024 for the 2nd) and competition workshops (in November 2023 and 2024) to which the economic, administrative, legal and academic communities are invited. These events, in the form of conferences or case studies, help to disseminate the competition culture. They show companies that they need to call on the services of lawyers in certain complex legal situations (drafting a referral to the Authority, responding to a notification of grievances, M&A projects, etc.), and show lawyers that they may benefit from specialising.

The Papeete bar has many lawyers specialising in business law and restrictive competition practices. For the most part, their practice focuses on defending cases of breach of commercial relations and unfair competition. But the Authority's growing activity will inevitably interest a growing number of legal professionals. When it comes to mergers and authorisations for the creation of retail outlets, companies are increasingly choosing to outsource the preparation of their notification files to local law firms who are familiar with Polynesia's territorial network. Only the major groups manage their files internally through their legal departments, or call on the services of metropolitan law firms specialising in competition law for contentious cases.

In practice, however, only a limited number of local lawyers are currently involved in cases handled by the investigating department. There are 3 or 4 firms that are beginning to specialise, the risk being that these firms will eventually find themselves in a position to refuse clients who are both plaintiffs and defendants in the same cases. Indeed, the size of the Polynesian market and the concentration of economic activity

---

13 APC, Decision 2024-CC-01 of 27 February 2024 Acquisition of sole control of Bolloré Logistics SE by CMA CGM SA

in the hands of a small number of families could in future create situations of conflict of interest for these law firms specialising in competition law. It should also be pointed out that lawyers also specialise in specific sectors of the economy (mass retailing, network industries, etc.).

What I've also noticed is that SMEs that are beginning to learn about competition law no longer hesitate to call on certain local lawyers, who in turn no longer hesitate to contact the investigating department either to pass on information or to ask about the procedures for an official referral to the Authority. Until recently, the majority of referrals of facts or practices likely to constitute an anti-competitive practice[14] were drafted by metropolitan law firms. This situation is likely to change in the future, and is excellent news both for companies, who will benefit from advice tailored to the territory, and for the Authority, which will have regular contacts.

Long-term relationships with the same law firms are desirable, as they help establish a climate of trust. We will often be adversaries in litigation before the AMF Board, but we can also be partners in leniency applications, for example, and trust in this context during initial informal exchanges is vital. Last but not least, we must not forget that the Investigation Department carries out investigations on its own initiative or with the judicial authorisation of the liberty and custody judge[15], where the presence of counsel is required by law, even if it is not mandatory. By definition, law firms in mainland France will not be able to travel to assist their clients, whereas local lawyers will be able to attend.

However, here again, the specialisation of a lawyer in a field such as competition law will probably oblige law firms to recruit young people with specialised studies, and it is to be hoped that the University will be able to meet this demand so that students from Fenua will be able to pursue careers in this field.

---

14 Art LP. 620-5 and A. 631-1 of the French Competition Code.

15 Articles 3 and 5, Ordinance no. 2017-157 of 9 February 2017 extending and adapting to French Polynesia certain provisions of Book IV of the Commercial Code relating to competition controls and sanctions.

Competition and Import and Distribution Mechanisms

Antoine Callot*
Administrative Court of Grenoble

1. On September 19, 2019, the APC adopted an initiative opinion regarding the importation and distribution mechanisms in French Polynesia.[1] This was a general study aimed at identifying the main factors contributing to the high cost of goods in French Polynesia.
2. The investigation led to hearings, questionnaires, a public consultation, as well as the use of a large database from the Polynesian Directorate General of Economic Affairs (DGAE) on price breakdowns.
3. It helped identify the factors driving up the costs of various goods and led to the formulation of about fifty proposals to reduce them.

I. Small Island Economies and Competition

4. Economic literature describes the economy of French Polynesia as a "small island economy." These economies suffer from a double disadvantage. Their small size prevents them from reaching a critical mass that would allow for efficient local production due to low economies of scale, while their remoteness from main markets penalizes their exports. Consequently, imports are more important. Moreover, even where local production exists, it is necessarily

---

* Antoine Callot is an administrative judge and public rapporteur at the Administrative Court of Grenoble. He previously held the position of Deputy General Rapporteur at the Polynesian Competition Authority. The views expressed are personal and do not engage these institutions

1 Opinion No. 2019-A-02 of September 19, 2019, regarding the importation and distribution mechanisms in French Polynesia.

concentrated, which can be done at the expense of competitive intensity and facilitates the maintenance of dominant positions, cartels and collusive arrangements.

5. In addition, particularly on volcanic islands such as Polynesia, there is a concentration of activity on the coast and a low availability of available land, while production and distribution activities are large land consumers.

6. While such economies have specific characteristics that justify focusing on import and distribution circuits, it must be noted from the economic analysis that a high degree of competition remains relevant. On the other hand, public authorities' actions and competition authorities' control need to be adapted, particularly by adopting lower thresholds for merger control, regulating natural monopolies[2] as a priority, and adapting tools to combat collusive behaviors or abuses of dominant positions. Specifically, on this last point, the goal is to reduce the standard of proof required by competition authorities to demonstrate effects on consumers, which will be more easily presumed, and to prioritize tackling exclusive import and distribution agreements.[3]

7. In view of these problems common to small island economies, but also the frequent protests against the high cost of living, especially in the West Indies and Reunion, many reports have been written on these issues, before and after the APC, by the French competition authority[4], the Caledonian authority[5] or the national parliament.[6]

---

2 See article on telecommunications.

3 See on these adaptations *Competition for Small Market Economies*, Michal S. Gal, Harvard University Press, 2003. See also, *Small economies and competition policy: a background paper*, OECD Global Forum on Competition and *Word Development Reports*, 2002, World Bank, p. 142

4 ADLC, Report on the import and distribution mechanisms for consumer products in New Caledonia, 21 September 2012. ADLC, Opinion no 18-A-09 of 3 October 2018 on the competitive situation in the construction materials markets in Mayotte and La Réunion. ADLC, Notice no. 19-A-12 of 4 July 2019 concerning the operation of competition in overseas, see also *French Competition Authority, The French Competition Authority publishes its recommendations to the New Caledonian government authorities regarding the food retail sector and the competition control bodies (Gouvernement de la Nouvelle-Calédonie), 21 September 2012, e-Courses September 2012, Art. No. 58526, voir aussi French Competition Authority, The French Competition Authority issues an opinion regarding competition in the building materials markets in Mayotte and La Réunion, 3 October 2018, e-Concertions October 2018, Art. No. 88067, voir aussi Jean-Philippe Kovar, Overseas territories: The French Competition Authority delivers a general diagnosis of competition in the French overseas territories and recommends strengthening its powers, 4 July 2019, Concurrences N° 4-2019, Art. No 92383, pp. 191-19.*

5 New Caledonia Competition Authority (ACNC), Opinion no. 2020-A-07 of 28 December 2020 on the price formation mechanism for mass consumer products in New Caledonia. Notice n° 2023-A-03 of 31 October 2023 on the request for an opinion concerning the draft resolution amending the regulatory part of the commercial code applicable in New Caledonia relating to spare parts and replacement cars, *see also Nils Vitalis, New Caledonia: The New Caledonian Competition Authority issues an important opinion on the price formation mechanism of consumer products in New Caledonia, which is an opportunity to make a comparative approach between the opinions of the metropolitan, Polynesian and New Caledonian competition authorities on this issue, 28 December 2020, Concurrences N° 2-2021, Art. No 100610, pp. 219-222.*

6 National Assembly, 'The Octroi de Mer, a Strategic Issue for the Overseas Economies,' Information Report No. 659 presented on behalf of the Delegation for Overseas by Mr. Mathieu Hanotin and Jean-Jacques Vlody, January 29, 2013, XIVth Legislature. Senate, April 15, 2015, report presented on behalf of the Finance

8. The APC also promoted its geographical location and the creation of the regional network of Pacific competition authorities (Pacific Island Network of Competition Consumer and Economic Regulators) to address this issue with several of its counterparts in the region;

II. The Polynesian Specializations and the APC opinion

A. *The observation: higher prices than in other ultra-marine territories*

9. The studies conducted by the French Polynesia Statistical Institute (ISPF) comparing the cost of local, ultra-marine and metropolitan goods baskets, show higher prices in Polynesia than in the mainland and that in the overseas departments and regions (DROM), regardless of the basket chosen, with very significant differences for food and non-alcoholic beverages (Fisher's index 48% higher).

10. Food is also the main source of expenditure for Polynesian households and is even more important because the population is small (over 30% of the budget of the poorest compared to 12% for the wealthiest).

11. This observation is at first sight paradoxical. The index is rising even though food products are subject to a full range of market protections (regulated prices, import quotas and bans, health rules) and are the core business of large retailers, which at the same time experienced strong growth and buy cheaper than small shops. It is even less intuitive that price reductions have been observed following market openings for competition in other sectors, such as mobile telephony and air transport. This paradox is probably due in part or in whole to the uncompetitive structure of the market, rather than to the isolation of the territory, and it is a very illuminating sign of the lack of effectiveness of the existing consumer support mechanisms.

B. *Price level determinants*

12. From a large database, covering various products with free and regulated tariffs, the APC was able to determine the price structure and distinguish the costs related to the approach phase towards Tahiti, the cost of moving away from the territory, duties and taxes falling under import regulations and margins earned by importers and then local retailers, partly linked to market structure.

Committee on the draft law amending Law No. 2004-639 of July 2, 2004, relating to the Octroi de Mer, by Mr. Éric Doligé, Senator. Hearing of April 11, 2019, by the Delegation for Overseas of the National Assembly of the Interministerial Delegate for Competition in the Overseas Territories.

Breakdown of the consumer price of current consumer products

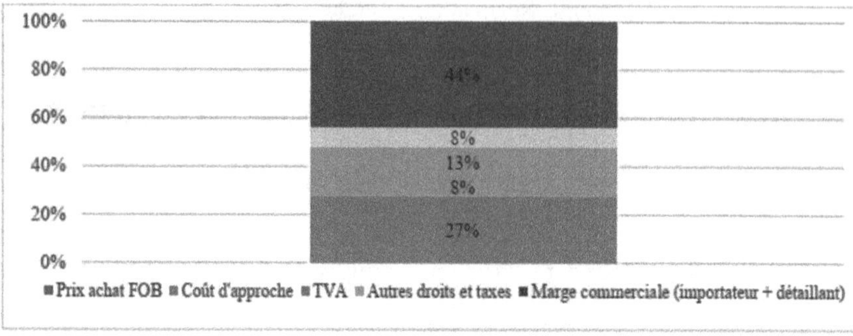

Source : APC

13. On the sample collected, for the various categories of products, apart from the initial purchase price representing about a quarter of the price, the average delivery represented only 8% of the cost of a product, taxes around 20% and the balance was the commercial margin of the various importers and distributors for (which – it is worth to recall – does not limit itself to their profit but also covers their expenses).

14. Thus, contrary to what is sometimes claimed by public authorities and some companies, the reason for high prices is not only and not even predominantly in the remoteness of the territory, but also in the lack ofthe regulatory and competitive structure of the import and distribution sector.

C. *Possible actions on structural determinants related to the geographical position of French Polynesia*

15. The geographical characteristics of the Polynesian territory necessarily affect prices. French Polynesia is a small market of 275,000 inhabitants, narrower than those of Réunion or the Antilles, located 18,000 km from the metropolis and more than 4,000 km from the first metropolises of the pacific zone, and very fragmented (118 islands over 2.5 million km). It is referred to as "double insularity".

16. As a result, it has a very large trade deficit, with only 7% being covered by local production. Apart from hydrocarbons, there is also a very strong predominance of the metropolitan area and the European Union in imports, 46% of which are from the EU, 28% of which are from France, even if a significant share of agricultural goods come from the StatesUnited States and New Zealand and manufactured goods from China. In addition to the privileged customs regime of which the European Union is blessed, explanations are also cultural, linked to the presence of hexagonal and regulatory signs, with issues such as compliance with CE or NF standards and the requirement for French-language labelling of food products.

17. However, the share of the price of products related to transport and, therefore, to distance remains relatively limited and is not, as such, a fatality. In particular, the analysis of the sea freight market, with a quasi-monopoly on the link with

the French Republic and that of the Acconage (handling by dockers and storage), shows that excessive regulation limits any competition, meaning that significant cost savings could be achieved at this stage.

18. The APC has thus carried out a detailed analysis of the *cost of* transport from the metropolitan area on the main line, excluding handling and taxes. If it is not known that airlines can save money by serving French Polynesia, due to its low economic weight, the imbalance of the waters (boats are forced to leave almost empty) and the impossibility for its main port to accommodate the largest ships (even the largest container ships from Europe are not operating at full capacity), the high concentration on the line from Europe (38% of the tra c) also has an effect on tariffs, which are higher than for comparable routes on competing routes, including Noumea. To expand the maritime offer, only a deepening of the Papeete harbor would allow for supporting the global maritime transport industry's drive for economies of scale, which notably involves increasing the size of ships and at least accommodating medium-sized container ships.[7] This is a frequent topic in French Polynesia, but no concrete action has been taken to date, with the risk of marginalization of the link, which could lead to a systematic transshipment of goods in a New Zealand port, further lengthening the time and costs.

19. Regarding docking, the prices are very high, both compared to major global ports and to the DROMs and other ports in the region. Only the Nouméa stopover has similar prices, and the Caledonian press has already denounced a cartel situation there. However, this activity is highly regulated, and inefficiencies can be observed. Indeed, the rates are not competitive but are set by decree and regularly increased. While three service providers operate there, they have been chosen by the government without any competitive bidding since 1987, and they share the clientele in what could resemble a collusion. Furthermore, they each have their own lifting equipment, which hinders economies of scale, as the cranes located on the same quay are not all active at the same time. This situation is not optimal. In fact, there is neither competition 'on the market' due to the regulated prices, nor competition 'for the market,' due to the lack of regular re-tendering for service providers based on prices and service quality. This leads to a rent-seeking situation for the three operators, who take advantage of their financial capacity to develop parallel activities (land transport, raw material imports, shipping agencies, etc.).

20. Other actions could be taken to reduce the level of customs duties, particularly for neighbouring countries, and to take account of the international trade gravity equation, which means that the most natural and effective trading structure for a given country is to trade with neighbouring countries with high GDP (in this case, the United States, New Zealand, Australia or even China.

21. French Polynesia has a very wide range of tariff and non-tariff protections, which account for a much larger share of the price than the approach fees.

22. Some 20 tariff barriers were identified, with an average tax rate of 29.5%, which increases the price of imported products and weighs on consumers'

7 Polynesian Territorial Chamber of Accounts, Final Observation Report, 'Autonomous Port of Papeete,' September 3, 2018.

purchasing power. There is also a complex tangle of non-tariff barriers with different regimes, such as import bans (deli or pineapple), goods under the tendering regime (rice or flour), import quotas (fruit and vegetables) and health or technical rules whose legitimacy is contested, and which have anti-competitive effects (yoghurts, honey, meat).

23. Such import restrictions, rational when they are temporary and allow local businesses to establish themselves in their market (educational protectionism), are no longer justifiable if they artificially and sustainably support a non-competitive activity. In this case, these protections lead to a net loss of welfare for the economy, effectively making consumers finance a few local industrial jobs, even though there is no certainty that these jobs would disappear if these barriers were reduced or removed. On the contrary, the gains in purchasing power on imported products could shift towards a demand for local goods and services, made more attractive (due to the lower price of intermediate goods). The price reduction would also have a positive impact on the country's attractiveness, particularly in the tourism sector.[8] This is the choice that has been made by other small island economies such as the Republic of Mauritius or the Seychelles.

24. The APC's opinion particularly emphasized two measures that are especially questionable in this regard: the local development tax and agricultural product import quotas.

25. *The local development tax (TDL),* introduced in 1998, applies to 147 tariff items taxed between 2% and 82%, including a wide range of everyday consumer goods such as jams, soaps, fruit juices, mineral waters, pareos, beer, tablecloths and napkins, or toilet paper. The objective is to give a competitive edge to local production and protect employment in French Polynesia. However, this tool does not seem to be the most relevant. Criticisms focus both on the particularly high rates applied to everyday products, which account for a significant portion of household budgets, and the overly broad base, which also targets goods not produced locally,[9]

26. as well as the use of a customs classification that is too unspecific. Ultimately, only 1,200 industrial jobs are affected by the sectors protected by the TDL, and these are sectors where the local added value is often very low, often just simple assembly or packaging of imported products such as beverages or hygiene products. Furthermore, there is no indication that these industries would not be viable without this support, and on the contrary, they lose, due to these protections, all incentives for innovation and lowering prices for consumers. Thus, this tool, which evolves mainly according to the actions of different interest groups on the government, does not achieve its objectives, notably due to the lack of a proper evaluation of its effects, industry by industry.

---

8 Bernard Poirine and Jean-François Gay, 'The Cost of Protectionism in a Small Island Economy: The Extreme Case of French Polynesia,' *Région et Développement*, 2015, 42, pp. 133-156. B. Poirine, *Tahiti, A Protected Economy*, L'Harmattan, 2012.

9 This criticism was, however, partly addressed with the removal of 20 price positions in 2019, including on iconic products such as chocolate and smoked salmon.

27. An effective reform would thus consist in limiting such taxes over time to allow for the emergence of an industry while limiting the associated rent effects, and in implementing countermeasures to protection, with controllable and transparent criteria related to performance, innovation, the preservation or creation of jobs, or the incorporation of local inputs into the production process. As for *the quotas on imported fruits and vegetables*, decided monthly during agricultural conferences, they actually benefit only the agricultural producers, but to the detriment of all other actors: processors, importers, distributors, and of course consumers. In particular, the chronic underestimation of demand (despite the public health importance of these products, whose consumption should be encouraged) and the overestimation of supply by the producers leads to excessively high prices and frequent shortages. Producers have no incentive to improve the quality, diversity, or cost of their production, as they are guaranteed to sell it. Moreover, the distribution of quotas between importers is opaque, and the lack of predictability of future quotas prevents them from negotiating prices with their suppliers. In this sector, as in all sectors relying on imports, since it is known that the welfare losses generated by non-tariff barriers are higher than those of tariff barriers, local production would be better protected by simple customs duties, in order to maintain local incentives for quality improvement and productivity. Tariff barriers are also revenue-generating and are better able to limit shortages than quotas or simple imports. To achieve the goal of stimulating local production, a targeted approach in the agricultural sector, through actions of structuring and pooling, would be more effective than the quota policy.

28. *Other regulations that protect local producers have also been examined.* This is notably the case with tax exemption schemes and the regulation of foreign direct investments, which limit the entry of potential foreign competitors into several sectors and often favor projects that merely replace existing infrastructure, without adding new capacity (especially in the hotel industry). Such measures can be seen as a subsidy to already existing businesses, particularly the larger ones, thus reinforcing an already structural concentration. At a minimum, independent competitive scrutiny of projects seeking to benefit from tax exemptions, potentially by the APC, would allow for an analysis of these projects within the broader context of the economic sector to which they belong.

D. *The issue of market structure*

29. For a consumer price of 100, the purchase cost of the goods, approach costs, and duties and taxes each represent just over half of the price. The remaining balance, estimated on average at 44%, consists of the margin for distributors, importers-wholesalers, and retailers. This commercial margin is primarily used to cover the costs related to marketing (structural costs, storage, distribution, communication), and the remainder constitutes the net margin or profit for businesses.

1. Local production: the risk of hyper-concentration and conglomerates

30. The protections enjoyed by local producers are very strong, which limits competition from imports, and this segment is highly concentrated, particularly

in the food industry. The APC's Concentration Observatory, for example, examined the degree of concentration in several food industries (industrial charcuterie, fishmongers, beverage manufacturers, dairy products, and bakeries-pastry shops). With the exception of bakeries-pastry shops, a relatively fragmented sector, the other four sectors experience very high levels of concentration. This is also why the APC issued a specific opinion concerning the pork sector[10] and why some of its competition or concentration cases have focused on the beverage sector.[11]

31. There are therefore rent-seeking situations, which lead to very high prices and a lack of incentives to improve the quality or diversity of production. Additionally, there is strong vertical integration, with the presence of groups involved in both importation, production, and distribution activities, as well as conglomerate diversification across various business sectors, beyond just the food industry, often in hospitality. This is notably the case with the leading producer in the food sector, which is also active in hospitality, distribution, transportation, real estate, textiles, printing, advertising, and container production. These activities offer strong complementarities with beverage production and give the group the ability to provide a comprehensive service to clients such as cafés, hotels, and restaurants.

32. Such consolidations require great vigilance to avoid their market power leading to discriminatory practices against competitors, such as the implementation of a "price police," by imposing recommended or minimum resale prices on retailers, which directly contravenes the competition code (Article LP 420-1). Other practices include land acquisition and retention to prevent the emergence of competing

33. production or exerting pressure on downstream sectors (such as shops, hotels, or restaurants) either to impose exclusive or preferential supply agreements, or symmetrically, to refuse sales or provide services under deteriorated conditions to competitors.

2. The import sector: an irrational multiplication of intermediaries

34. The long supply chain, which involves passing through an intermediary called "wholesale importer" or "brand agent," responsible for transportation, storage, delivery, and advertising of products, remains the majority model in French Polynesia, although a short circuit is developing where a distributor is supplied by their purchasing centers and on their own storage platforms, particularly for private label brands. Both circuits are often – and importantly – accompanied by exclusivity in the importation of a brand, either by law (contractually) or in practice.

---

10 Opinion No. 2020-A-01 of May 11, 2020, regarding the competitive situation in the pig farming sector.

11 Decision No. 2019-PAC-01 of August 22, 2019, regarding practices implemented in the beverage marketing sector, annulled by the Paris Court of Appeal by a ruling on January 21, 2021, on procedural grounds, and referred back to the APC for a new examination on the merits. Merger decisions of June 27, 2019, No. 2019-CC-052, and December 8, 2023, No. 2023-CC-02 and 03, which led to commitments from the Brasserie de Tahiti group, see also Jean-Louis Fourgoux, French Polynesia: *The Polynesian Competition Authority fines a distributor nearly 2 million euros (235 million FCP) for abuse of dominant position, imposing discriminatory and excessive pricing on its beverage suppliers for the provision of refrigerated display units (Wane), August 22, 2019, Concurrences No. 4-2019, Art. No. 92404, pp. 198-20.*

35. However, the financial situation of wholesalers is quite favorable and dynamic, with increasing profit margins that are higher than those in mainland France. While using importers remains useful due to their negotiating capabilities, economies of scale, and commercial services, even if it involves an intermediary and therefore an additional margin, the difficulty lies in the fact that due to import exclusivities, these economies of scale do not benefit consumers. Indeed, reducing the margin would require effective competition between importers. However, these exclusivities exclude intra-brand competition, while the very small size of the market significantly reduces inter-brand competition and the number of substitute products, which is already limited for well-known brands.

36. As a result, there is considerable freedom in price setting by importers, and productivity gains are actually captured by the importer, especially since many importers are also distributors and can then use their market power over imports to favor their own distribution channels at the expense of those of their competitors. This may explain the maintenance of strong profitability in a sector that, at first glance, appears competitive due to the high number of importing companies.

37. However, these practices cannot be quickly and easily addressed by competition law, and the prohibition of cartels and abuses of dominant position, whose procedures are long and complex, while the situation is particularly unfavorable to the consumer. That is why all the French overseas territories allow for a general prohibition of exclusive import agreements, unless companies can demonstrate that they bring a benefit to the consumer. The competition authorities in mainland France (competent for the DROM) and New Caledonia frequently sanction such agreements and seek to strengthen the effectiveness of these measures. French Polynesia, which removed this prohibition from its law in 2018, is therefore clearly going against the trend.

3. Distribution: a dual and highly concentrated retail sector

38. One group occupies more than half of the retail space in supermarkets and hypermarkets "under a brand," while a dense sector of small local shops and convenience stores, particularly in the islands but also in Tahiti, remains in parallel. This survival is likely related to their proximity and certain commercial practices, such as merchant credit, but it is also an indication of a small price differential between these stores and large retailers, due to the existence of regulated prices (basic necessities or PPN and fast-moving consumer goods or PGC), but also the fact that the volume effect enjoyed by large retailers does not always lead them to reduce their prices but often results in increased margins.

39. Thus, in its 2019 opinion, the Polynesian Competition Authority described the retail sector as follows: one player is the *price maker* and sets prices for the entire market at a high level, benefiting from very high profitability, while other groups align with these high prices, unable to engage in a price war. Moreover, there is a phenomenon of conglomerate vertical integration, as this group is also active in the agri-food production, importation, and hotel sectors. This concentration is likely to have effects on both upstream and downstream markets by giving it considerable leverage in negotiations with manufacturers and importers, who cannot do without

this distribution channel, which often represents more than a third of their sales, and with its competitors in retail who need the products it has exclusive access to.

40. Again, closer market surveillance is necessary to prevent price pressures, threats of delisting, and discriminatory commercial practices, particularly in terms of supply conditions.

41. Such behaviors are made possible by the small size and isolation of the Polynesian market, which foster an implicit collusion phenomenon among actors. However, consultations conducted reveal that these actors also take advantage of the significant income inequality in French Polynesia (with a Gini index higher than in mainland France) by setting their prices based on the willingness to pay of the wealthier consumers, thus prioritizing high unit margins over volume effects. There is, therefore, an alignment among actors and a form of high-price equilibrium, due to the differentiation of demand between, on the one hand, modest consumers who are likely to buy only low-priced products (basic necessities and consumer goods), and on the other hand, wealthier consumers whose demand is relatively inelastic to price, and on whom businesses often prefer to focus. A comprehensive reflection on price regulation and its effectiveness – sometimes counterproductive – is therefore necessary.

42. To combat excessive concentrations in the distribution sector, the Polynesian Competition Authority (APC) has also been equipped with an effective tool for controlling the creation of commercial spaces, through prior consultations on opening projects, which has allowed it to reject certain projects.[12] However, this tool is insufficient given such structural imbalance. Another mechanism exists to put an end to potential price distortion, namely structural injunctions, which allow the imposition of asset disposals on dominant groups, if necessary. However, this mechanism was removed in 2018, again going against what is done in other overseas territories. Although this mechanism has never been applied, one can imagine that it has a deterrent effect, since its implementation requires demonstrating the existence of high prices in a sector where one actor is dominant, thus making it in the best interest of the dominant actor to avoid charging exorbitant prices.

III. Follow-up to the Opinion

43. The intensity of competition in French Polynesia is generally low. Upstream, transportation is hindered by the dominant position of one operator on the main maritime route – from Europe – and the high cost of handling.

44. Regarding local production, industries take advantage of this isolation to negotiate more protection from the authorities in the name of employment, although the effects are highly debatable. Once protected, they have little incentive to reduce their prices or better satisfy consumers. At the intermediate stage of importers-wholesalers, a certain degree of competition still appears to exist, but brand exclusivities limit its effectiveness. Downstream, the dualism and high concentration in the large distribution sector are not favorable to competitive dynamism. Finally, the presence

---

12 Decision of September 12, 2022, No. 2022-SC-09 regarding the opening of a retail store under the 'Carrefour' brand with a sales area of 1830m2 located in the municipality of Paopao, Moorea.

of large integrated groups, as well as the captive nature of the island's clientele, further dampens competition and makes it difficult to challenge their market power.

45. However, the question of market structure is crucial. It alone can reduce costs and redistribute part of the margins to consumers. But more importantly, it guarantees the effectiveness of other measures, particularly regulatory ones, that could be decided but will be in vain if they are not accompanied by action on competition. For example, if price regulation were lifted or relaxed to promote competition on prices rather than alignment with ceiling prices, it is still necessary for the different brands to engage in real price competition for these products. However, such a measure would be futile if the actors continue to follow the behavior of the dominant player and maintain high prices.

46. There is therefore a need to remove barriers to entry into the market, facilitate the creation and development of businesses, establish fair competition conditions, and strengthen a competition culture. For this reason, the September 2019 opinion from the APC presented – in addition to the main structural measures mentioned above – a set of measures concerning land issues, the pooling of small actors, and particularly consumers, who suffer from a lack of representation in French Polynesia, as well as price transparency to combat the "high price bubble."

47. Several subsequent thematic opinions have enabled these proposals to be implemented and adapted to other sectors, such as the pork industry,[13] spare automotive parts,[14] or hydrocarbons.[15]

48. For its part, the Polynesian government has implemented several reforms, although they have remained of limited scope: reform of the TDL in 2019[16], reform of the regulated pricing system,[17] implementation of detailed price monitoring systems (the DGAE's price weather forecast).

49. However, the main structural reforms do not appear to have been accomplished to date. In the absence of successive governments making a true choice between an open market economy and a managed economy, private actors continue to take advantage of this intermediate situation to develop a rent-seeking economy and capture margins, to the detriment of the most modest consumers. The APC's actions, even in the area of anti-competitive practices, will be doomed to have only marginal effects if they are not accompanied by bold political choices.

---

13 Opinion No. 2020-A-01 of May 11, 2020, regarding the state of competition in the pork industry.

14 Opinion of December 23, 2021, No. 2021-A-04 on the competitive functioning of the repair and spare parts trade sector for motor vehicles (automobiles).

15 Opinion of April 21, 2022, No. 2022-A-01 regarding the state of competition in the supply of hydrocarbons in French Polynesia.

16 See Opinion of April 2, 2019, No. 2019-A-01 regarding the effects of regulation on the competitive functioning of essential goods markets.

17 See the opinions of the APC of March 30, 2022, No. 2022-AO-01 on a draft law of the Country regarding the conditions for regulating prices of certain products and services and amending the legislative part of Book I of the Competition Code, and December 5, 2022, No. 2022-A-05 on a draft decree approving a voluntary price-blocking agreement for certain products by retail businesses with a focus on food (or "basket of products with blocked prices"). *See Alain Ronzano, Competition Policy: The Polynesian Competition Authority issues several recommendations regarding the government's project to strengthen the regulation of essential goods and mass-market products prices, March 30, 2022, Concurrences No. 2-2022, Art. No. 106154.*

Price Control Mechanisms in Polynesia

Frédéric Paillusson*
Polynesian Competition Authority**

1. In a recent study[1], the Institut de la statistique de la Polynésie française (hereafter "ISPF") noted that consumer price levels in French Polynesia will be 31% higher on average than in mainland France in 2022, according to the Fisher synthetic index. This price differential is comparable to that observed in New Caledonia, but far exceeds those observed in the overseas departments. The ISPF notes in particular that these price differences are partly explained by the high cost of food products.[2] In French Polynesia, the additional cost of food reaches 80% for a household consuming a metropolitan basket, whereas this additional cost is "*only*" 17% for a household consuming a Polynesian basket.[3]

2. These price differences are compounded by a lower standard of living in French Polynesia than in mainland France, with a median monthly income estimated at 1,630 euros.[4] As a result, the high price level weighs more heavily on household purchasing power, and spending on essential needs (food, housing, transport)

---

* Frédéric Paillusson is deputy general rapporteur at the investigation department of the Polynesian Competition Authority.

** The views expressed are those of the author and do not necessarily reflect the position of the Polynesian Competition Authority.

1 ISPF, Points Études et Bilans de la Polynésie française no. 1391 – *Prices 31% higher in French Polynesia than in mainland France in 2022*, October 2023.

2 *Ibid.*

3 *Ibid.*

4 ISPF, Points Études et Bilans de la Polynésie française no. 1268 – *Des fortes inégalités salariales en Polynésie française*, November 2021.

"*represents 62% of the budget of Polynesian households, whereas it accounts for only 44% of the budget of households in mainland France*".[5] In Polynesia, food also accounts for 10 percentage points more of spending.[6]

3. All these data illustrate why the issue of high living costs has become a central political topic in French Polynesia, and a source of dissatisfaction for the population.

4. As already emphasised in the past[7], the causes of high living costs are manifold. French Polynesia is a small island economy, heavily dependent on imports[8] but protected by tariff and non-tariff barriers (quotas, import bans) which raise the price of imported products and protect local production. The Polynesian economy is also characterised by weak competitive dynamics in many sectors.

5. Faced with this situation, one of the solutions favoured by the public authorities was price regulation, with the central aim of curbing inflationary drift and making basic products accessible to the entire population.

6. For nearly a decade, the Polynesian Competition Authority (hereinafter the "Authority") has had the opportunity to examine a number of local laws aimed at addressing the issue of high living costs, and to make a number of recommendations through its consultative mission.

7. This *advocacy* effort on the part of the Authority has been evident from the very first years of its activity. On the occasion of two structuring opinions[9], the Authority attempted to shed light on the determinants of the high cost of living, by carrying out two successive sectoral surveys on strategic sectors for the Polynesian economy: imports, distribution and basic necessities. Subsequently, the Authority will be invited to take another look the various price-control mechanisms in place in the territory, in opinions to be issued in 2022[10] and 2024.[11]

8. On the occasion of these notices, the Authority has carried out an analysis of the various price control mechanisms provided for in the Polynesian Competition Code (I.), and of the impact of these mechanisms on the markets concerned (II.)

---

5 ISPF, Points Études et Bilans de la Polynésie française no. 1391, cited above.

6 *Ibid.*

7 See, for example, the hearings of Mr Philippe Liou, Acting Director of the ISPF, Ms Florence Bouliou, Head of the ISPF Prices Department, and Ms Johanne Peyre, Chairman of the Authority, Minutes no. 7 of the Commission of Inquiry into the Cost of Living in Territorial Authorities Governed by Articles 73 and 74 of the Constitution, 6 April 2023.

8 In French Polynesia, 94% of consumer goods are imported

9 Opinion no. 2019-A-02 of 19 September 2019 relating to import and distribution mechanisms in French Polynesia and opinion no. 2019-A-01 of 2 April 2019 relating to the effects of regulation on the competitive operation of staple goods markets.

10 Opinion no. 2022-AO-01 of 30 March 2022 on the conditions governing the prices of certain products and services, amending the legislative part of Book 1 of the French Competition Code, and opinion no. 2022-A-05 of 5 December 2022 on a draft order approving an agreement for the voluntary freezing of prices of certain products by predominantly food retailers (or "basket of price-blocked products").

11 Opinion no. 2024-AO-05 of 29 July 2024 on a draft law amending Book 1 of the French Competition Code and relating to the price control of certain products and services benefiting from a special tax or customs regime.

I. An arsenal of regulations to control prices

9. Similar to the situation in mainland France, the French Competition Code enshrines the principle of price freedom (article LP. 110-1), a principle protected by the constitution. However, the Competition Code provides for a number of derogations, enabling the Council of Ministers to control prices in order to pursue a number of general interest objectives (A.), which the Authority has had occasion to comment on (B.).

A. *On exceptions to freedom*

10. The Competition Code establishes a relatively simple classification of exceptions to price freedom, enabling the Council of Ministers to regulate prices, and distinguishes between temporary measures (1.) and permanent measures (2.). It also lays down the methodology for setting prices and margins (3.).

1. Temporary measures

11. Article LP. 110-1 of the French Competition Code provides that the Council of Ministers may take price control measures against risks of "*excessive price rises or falls*", for a period not exceeding six non-renewable months, "*motivated by a crisis situation, exceptional circumstances, a public calamity or a manifestly abnormal market situation in a given sector*". By way of example, the Council of Ministers has adopted a measure to freeze the revision of rental contracts for a period of six months, between February 2024 and August 2024.

2. Permanent measures

12. Article 110-1 provides for a further derogation from price freedom, allowing for permanent price controls, after consultation with the Authority, in sectors or areas where price competition is limited "*due to monopoly or oligopoly situations, lasting supply difficulties or commercial under-equipment*".

13. Article LP. 110-2 provides for a new possibility of derogations to price freedom based on the pursuit of three objectives, namely: "*the impact on household budgets*", "*the economic development of French Polynesia*" or "*the correction of disparities linked to the remoteness of the archipelagos*". Within this framework, the Council of Ministers is authorised to regulate the maximum selling prices of products or services contained in three lists:

- A non-limitative list of essential products and services (hereinafter referred to as "PPN"), covering products and services required for daily living, personal health and natural disaster relief. PPN are also exempt from duties and taxes, including VAT, and are covered by the country's inter-island sea freight. The list of PPN products has recently been extended, bringing the total to 63 PPN products;
- A non-exhaustive list of fast-moving consumer goods and services (hereinafter "PGC") normally used by households in everyday life. Unlike PPNs, PCGs are subject to duties and taxes. Only some of them are subject to inter-island freight charges and VAT exemptions. The list of PGC products has also recently been extended, bringing the total to 36 PGCs; and finally

- A non-limitative list of products or services necessary for the economic and social development of French Polynesia, such as inter-island freight, hydrocarbons, port handling, etc.

14. Article LP. 110-3 allows the Council of Ministers to introduce a system of controlled price freedom, by "*subjecting the evolution of the prices of these goods or services to compliance with a defined calculation formula or to administrative approval*", when this measure is necessary to protect the purchasing power of users, the economic development of French Polynesia or the correction of disparities linked to the remoteness of the archipelagos. This measure has been used in the real estate sector, for example, to control the revision of residential rents after August 2024, beyond the six-month period allowed by article LP. 110-1.

15. Article LP. 110-4 provides for the possibility of signing a price moderation agreement between French Polynesia and a professional organisation or group of companies representing a branch or sector of activity. This arrangement has a number of similarities with the "*Bouclier Qualité-Prix*" *(Quality-Price Shield)* in French overseas departments and territories, introduced by the Lurel law.[12]

16. The final price-control mechanism enables the Ministerial Council to regulate all "*products or services benefiting from a special tax or customs regime*". To date, this mechanism has not yet been incorporated into the Competition Code, but it could come into force in 2025. This price control mechanism also consists of a non-limitative list in which all products and services benefiting from a tax or customs exemption granted by the country would be likely to have their prices administered. It would appear that the triggering event for such a framework would be a selling price deemed excessive by the authorities.

17. In addition to these general provisions of the Competition Code, there are various sector-specific price regulations, such as regulated prices in the healthcare sector, regulated professions, etc., which will not be discussed in here.

3. Regarding the calculation methodology

18. Article LP. 111-1 also lays down the procedures for setting sales limit prices, in three different ways:
    - the imposition of a maximum margin, either in absolute or relative terms (i.e. as a percentage), applied to the cost price of products[13];
    - setting a ceiling price[14]; and
    - the introduction of a specific system setting a maximum selling price at different stages or taking into account the specific characteristics of the good or service.[15]

19. These margins and prices constitute a maximum, "*whatever the number of intermediaries in the* distribution *circuit*", in order to put pressure on the various

---

12 Article L. 410-5 of the French Commercial Code, created by Law no. 2012-1270 of 20 November 2012.

13 This is the delivered warehouse price for imports and the invoice price for local products.

14 This is the only method available for services.

15 A number of specific regimes already exist for various agricultural and food products, such as copra, flour and bread.

intermediaries to share a contained margin and prevent the multiplication of intermediaries.

20. Until now, the Polynesian administration has favoured margin control over price ceilings. Within this framework, the administration has frequently resorted to controlling margins in relative terms (i.e. as a percentage) as the preferred methodology for price control.

B. *On the objectives pursued by price-control mechanisms*

21. When the first PPN regulations were introduced, decree no. 171 CM of 7 February *1992* did not any general interest objective likely to justify price controls. When the various price-control measures were codified in the French Competition Code, the Polynesian legislator endeavoured to take the Authority's recommendations into account when identifying the precise general interest objectives pursued by each of the different price-control mechanisms.

22. In its first opinion of 2019 on regulated prices, one of the main reservations expressed by the Authority on PPNs was the lack of a precise definition of the general interest pursued by this price control mechanism. In particular, it seemed vital that the laws of the land should be able to clearly identify the general interest objective pursued, so as to be able to ensure that the restrictions on competition induced were justified and proportionate.

23. In its codification efforts, the legislator has taken into account, at least in part, the Authority's recommendations, by highlighting the objectives pursued and defining in greater detail the products and services likely to fall under each of the price-control mechanisms. With regard to PPN and PGC, article LP. 110-2 provides for three types of objectives, namely (i) household budgets, (ii) the economic development of French Polynesia and (iii) the correction of disparities linked to the remoteness of the archipelagos. The Conseil d'Etat has confirmed that these three objectives are in the public interest, and may justify a derogation from the principle of price freedom.[16]

24. The observer will not fail to note that the various objectives pursued under article 110-2 go well beyond the fight against high living costs. The same price-control mechanism can also be used to support Polynesia's economic development, or to correct disparities between the archipelagos.

25. This is the first difficulty raised by the Authority with regard to price-control mechanisms. The effectiveness of price-containment mechanisms in combating the high cost of living must be weighed against other public policies, in particular to support local production. In this respect, it may be recalled that customs regulations provide for a certain number of tariff barriers (import duties and taxes) and non-tariff barriers (quotas, import bans, etc.) limiting the pressure of imports on local industry and employment, but at the cost of higher prices for imported foodstuffs, on which Polynesian households largely depend in their daily lives.[17]

---

16 Conseil d'Etat decision no. 4666687 of 9 December 2022, *Fédération générale du commerce et autres*.

17 As a reminder, 94% of consumer goods are imported into French Polynesia.

26. Protecting local production can therefore have a significant impact on food prices, and limit the impact of price-control mechanisms. However, as the Authority emphasised, resolving the trade-off between combating high living costs and protecting local production is "*complex and falls outside the scope of competitive regulation alone*".[18]

27. In this respect, one of the contributions of the Authority's position papers is to emphasise that the issue of high living costs, to a large extent, is not only linked to Polynesia's geographical remoteness, but also to the public policies in place, including tax and customs policies, as well as price regulations.

28. With the proliferation of price-control regimes, a second difficulty lies in the overall coherence of these price-control mechanisms. This problem is illustrated by the latest price-control mechanism, "*for products and services benefiting from a special tax or customs regime*", due to come into force in 2025.

29. In its opinion of 2024[19], the Authority noted the difficulties encountered by the initiator of the text in identifying an unprecedented objective of general interest likely to justify the creation of a new price control mechanism. In this case, the sponsor of the text indicated that the new mechanism was intended to ensure that the tax and customs exemptions granted by the country would have a moderating effect on prices. Such an objective of price moderation appears very close to the fight against high living costs, already covered by the other price control mechanisms provided for in articles 110-2 and 110-3 of the French Competition Code.

30. As a result, this new instrument is bound to create a certain amount of overlap with other existing price control mechanisms, given the proximity in terms of objectives pursued. Under these conditions, the need to create a new mechanism, with a broad scope of application, is obvious. Moreover, price controls, as a derogation from the principle of price freedom, should be seen as an exceptional measure, limited by strict conditions of application.

31. A third difficulty identified by the Authority concerns the match between the resources deployed and the objective pursued. With regard to the fight against the high cost of living, the Authority has had occasion to note that the PPN and PGC schemes, as well as other price regulation schemes, such as the one on fuel prices, benefit all consumers equally, whatever their income. In all its opinions on price regulation, the Authority has emphasised the windfall effects of these price regulations for the benefit of well-off households. Thus, a regulated price affects all Polynesian consumers, but "[without] *fulfilling its function of providing access to these products for the most disadvantaged*".[20]

32. Although the aim of price control mechanisms was to make essential products accessible to the most disadvantaged, it has to be said that regulations are not targeted at this category of consumers. In this respect, the Authority has recommended refocusing the various mechanisms on priority target groups.[21]

---

18 Opinion no. 2019-AO-01 of 2 April 2019, paragraph 182.

19 Opinion no. 2024-AO-05 of 29 July 2024, cited above.

20 Opinion no. 2019-A-01 of 2 April 2019, paragraph 181.

21 See, for example, opinion no. 2024-AO-05 of 29 July 2024, cited above, paragraph 81.

33. The Authority has identified a number of difficulties in defining the general interest objectives of the various price control mechanisms. The diversity of public policies pursued, the multiplication of price-control mechanisms, implying overlaps in their scope, and the difficulty of focusing price-control instruments on the populations most exposed to the high cost of living are all challenges to the effectiveness of price-control mechanisms in French Polynesia.

II. A pile of legislation of questionable effectiveness

34. In the wake of the positions taken by the Autorité métropolitaine de concurrence (hereinafter "ADLC ")[22], the Authority has warned public authorities against excessive recourse to price regulation, given the limited capacity of price regulation mechanisms to resolve observed market malfunctions. The Authority has described the many obstacles to the implementation of effective price regulation: firstly, the negative effects induced (A.), and secondly, the lack of evaluation of these policies (B.). All these factors suggest that price controls should be used with caution, pointing to a possible change of approach to the issue in Polynesia (**C.**).

A. *On the effects of mechanisms*

35. Price regulation presents several risks of distortion of competition, whatever the markets concerned. Indeed, when public authorities take the place of market mechanisms, they come up against difficulties in determining regulated prices, given the complexity of the price-setting process (determination of costs, multiplicity of products concerned, inflation trends, etc.) and the asymmetry of information between the administration and the economic players concerned.

36. In its opinions[23], the Authority has tried to alert the political authorities to the distortions that may be created by price control mechanisms, and has drawn up a typology of the risks incurred by price or margin controls, distinguishing between risks relating to a regulated price that is too high (**1.**) and risks relating to a regulated price that is too low (**2.**).

1. Risk of too high a maximum price

37. The Authority has identified a "*cleat effect*", i.e. the alignment of retail prices with the maximum price or margin reference (in value terms) made public by the authorities. This risk is particularly significant in markets where companies are able to maximise their margins by sticking to the maximum authorised margin, due to the weakness of the competitive dynamic.

38. The reality of this phenomenon was observed by the Authority in its 2019 opinion, in which it noted that "*in 80% of cases, the price charged* [for a PPN product] *is a price with almost the maximum margin. In less than 5% of cases, prices are*

---

22 See, for example, opinion no. 09-A-45 of 8 September 2009 on import and distribution mechanisms for mass-market products in overseas departments, and no. 08-A-07 of 7 May 2008 on the organisation of the fruit and vegetable sector.

23 For a recent example, see the aforementioned opinion no. 2024-AO-05 of 29 July 2024.

more than 15% below the maximum price".[24] The Authority had also noted a homogenisation of PPN prices, in contrast to free-price products.

2. Risks associated with a maximum price that is too low

39. The Authority has identified four types of risk involved in setting prices or margins too low:

- *Deterrent effect*: a margin that is too low can dissuade wholesaler-importers from sourcing all, some or most of their products at regulated prices.
- *Bypass effect*: too low a margin can encourage wholesaler-importers to adapt by switching to similar or analogous products, or products with similar characteristics but not on the list of regulated products. This behaviour is encouraged by overly precise definitions and restrictive names.
- *Degradation effect*: too low a value margin on a regulated product may encourage wholesaler-importers and retailers to favour the supply of less expensive products. In this case, importers may prefer to source lower-priced, lower-quality products that generate higher margins.
- *Compensatory effect*: excessively low margins on regulated products encourage wholesaler-importers and retailers to pass on this "loss of earnings" to the price of free products. The offsetting effect can therefore also contribute to inflation on unregulated products.

40. The Authority has also identified an inflationary effect of the percentage margin method, which is commonly used in French Polynesia to set regulated prices, in particular for PPN and PGC. Indeed, with a percentage margin, the margin increases correlatively with the increase in the price of goods, which serves as the basis for calculating the regulated margin.

41. Under such a price control mechanism, there is no incentive for operators to lower their production costs or their delivered warehouse price. Conversely, economic operators have an incentive to pay a high purchase price, enabling them to increase their margin by the same amount on the basis of this purchase. There are also a number of ways in which traders can artificially inflate the purchase price: use of intermediary structures, over-invoicing, back margins, and so on.

42. From a quantitative standpoint, the Authority looked at price trends for several PPN products between 2006 and 2016, despite the relative lack of data on the subject. The results are mixed. When vegetables were added to the PPN list in 2013, the Council of Ministers anticipated a 5% drop in store prices. However, the Authority noted a disparate trend for this product category: some saw their prices fall, while at the same time, the prices of lettuce (+100%), tomato (+30%) and cucumber (+12%), also classified as PPN, rose.[25] A similar phenomenon of rising retail prices for fresh fish (composed mainly of tuna) has been observed, starting with classification of tuna as PPN in 2007.[26] In February 2019, tuna was removed from the list because "*the administrative framework has had little*

---

24 Opinion no. 2019-A-01 of 2 April 2019, paragraph 121.

25 Opinion no. 2019-A-01 of 2 April 2019, paragraph 80.

26 Opinion no. 2019-A-01 of 2 April 2019, paragraph 84.

effect on selling prices" according to the Council of Ministers, but was again classified as PPN in 2020.[27]

43. This calculation method also appears to be a source of tension during periods of high inflation. Where the aim of regulated prices would be to maintain or even lower prices, the calculation method actually accompanies high inflation by passing it on to the final price. In this respect, it may be noted that the Council of Ministers recently decided to change the methodology for calculating the margin of certain PPN products to a margin in absolute value, in order to limit the upward trend of PPN products.

44. This stance follows the post COVID-19 inflationary episode, which hit food products in particular, including products classified as PPN. The local press reported an increase of +14.3% on a reference basket of 25 PPN food products between November 2021 and June 2022.[28] Significant increases have been reported for poultry (+20.9%) and bluefin tuna (+33%), both of which are highly consumed in French Polynesia.

45. On the basis of the few data available, the results are therefore mixed. Although price rises are not systematically observed, PPN products have not escaped the inflationary trend of the past decade. In particular, it appears that the price control mechanisms for PPN products were unable to curb the upward trend in food prices.

B. *On the failure to measure the effectiveness of these mechanisms*

46. With the exception of the temporary price control measures provided for in article LP. 110-1, most of the regulated price regimes provided for under the French Competition Code are permanent. Moreover, as mentioned above, recent years have seen a proliferation of price-control mechanisms.

47. In its opinions, the Authority has had occasion to question the effectiveness and evaluation of these various legal price-control regimes. The Authority's analysis, in opinion after opinion, shows that the regulations in force are piling up, without being "*systematically and regularly evaluated*".[29] This is all the more worrying given that these are measures infringing the principle of freedom of prices and trade, which should be subject to regular assessment, for example the form of economic studies, in order to know whether they should be retained, amended or even abolished.

48. Since 2019, the Authority has been making recommendations to encourage public authorities to collect data on the effectiveness of these framework mechanisms and, more generally, to assess their impact on the markets concerned.

49. This is a fundamental point raised by the Authority in its opinions. Indeed, it is possible that price control systems do not always fulfil the functions assigned to them, insofar as their objectives are not sufficiently defined upstream (see above), but also are not sufficiently evaluated after implementation.

---

27 Tahiti Infos, *Le thon en PPN, peine perdue*, 21 April 2020

28 Tahiti Infos, *PPN, la flambée continue*, 8 June 2022.

29 Opinion no. 2024-AO-05 of 29 July 2024, paragraph 92.

50. This recommendation by the Authority appears particularly important in the current context of frequent recourse by the public authorities to price control mechanisms when it comes to responding to public concerns about the high cost of living. Price-control measures, such as PPNs and PGCs, have become important policy instruments, attracting a great deal of interest from the local media and, more generally, from the general public, not only as regards changes to the list of products concerned, but also as regards any increase (or decrease) in prices or authorised margins.

51. The creation of new price-control regimes could thus be explained by a desire to display vigorous public action aimed at resolving the problems of high living costs by means of administered prices. This trend was recently illustrated by the creation of a new price control measure for products and services benefiting from tax or customs exemptions, even though its objective and scope of application appear to be largely redundant with previous measures.

52. In its opinions[30], the Authority questioned the appropriateness of creating a new category of regulated prices in addition to the many other legal price-control regimes. This argument was strengthened by the fact that, under constant law, the Council of Ministers would be able to implement this price framework using the various price-control instruments already provided for by the regulations, whether the list of PPNs, PGCs or other instruments.

53. This leads to a second set of remarks concerning the need to collect data on the effect of these price control measures in French Polynesia. The Authority has had the opportunity to collect data on the evolution of PPN prices, with mixed results in terms of the ability of these mechanisms to ensure price moderation. To date, no objective assessment of the effectiveness of price regulation, or of its real impact on the markets concerned, has been carried out by public authorities. In particular, it would be interesting to study whether regulated prices have actually protected everyday consumer products from the post-COVID inflationary episode, as reported in the local press.

54. In any case, data on the impact of these various price-control measures will be a decisive contribution to the public debate on the ability of these measures to achieve their intended objectives, and in particular, the legitimacy of these instruments as the preferred response of public authorities to the issue of high living costs, a pressing political and social challenge in French Polynesia. Such data would also enable us to assess the relevance of price control regimes, in a context where price regulation measures have continued to expand, affecting an ever-increasing number of products and services.

C. *Towards a new model for fighting the high cost of living?*

55. As part of its consultative role, the Authority took a radical stance, recommending the abolition of permanent regulation of essential products, or at the very least, the refocusing of the list of regulated prices on products that meet the basic needs of

30 See, in this respect, opinion no. 2024-AO-05 of 29 July 2024 or opinion no. 2022-AO-01 of 30 March 2022.

the population. This recommendation has not been followed by the public authorities, since the opposite phenomenon has been observed over the past decade, with increased recourse to administrative price controls.

56. Several years after taking this stance, the French Minister of the Economy announced his intention to reform the price control mechanism for PPN and PGC products. According to the Minister's statements, the aim of this reform project would be to reduce the list of PPN and PGN products subject to price controls, by retaining just one restrictive list of products. At this stage, a reform project is underway within the Ministry of the Economy, and a possible entry into force is envisaged in the course of 2025.[31]

57. To compensate for the reduction in the scope of regulated prices, the project is also likely to make use of the moderation agreements provided for in article LP. 110-3 of the French Competition Code. These moderation agreements do not consist directly in setting administered prices or margins, but in providing a framework through agreements signed between the Pays and the representative bodies of local distributors.

58. This provision differs from the others in that it is a contractual measure negotiated by the signatory companies. It is also non-binding for non-signatory companies. This measure bears a number of similarities to the "*Bouclier Qualité-Prix" (Quality-Price Shield*) in French overseas departments and territories, introduced by the Lurel law.[32] The implementation of such a scheme would be likely to mitigate certain distorting effects identified by the Authority, such as the offsetting effect on unregulated products, but also to maintain a certain degree of price competition on regulated products.

59. It should also be noted that, during debates in the Polynesian Assembly, certain effects of price controls identified by the Authority were discussed by representatives of the Assembly. In particular, the representatives were interested in the offsetting effect between regulated prices and free-price products, but also in the inflationary effect of the methodology used to calculate regulated margins. In particular, the local press reported that the Minister of the Economy had confirmed the existence of "*surcharges" on unregulated products to offset the regulated prices of PPN products.*[33]

60. These positions take up the substance of the Authority's analysis, as well as some of the recommendations it has made the past decade, calling for caution with regard to regulated price mechanisms and, in particular, for the reduction of regulated price lists to a series of specific products.

61. It is still too early to say whether these positions mark a turning point in the Polynesian approach to price control mechanisms. However, it can already be said that this subject provides an interesting perspective on the usefulness of the Authority's consultative function in French Polynesia. Since its first years of activity, the Authority has taken up this subject, in order to shed new light on

---

31 Tahiti Infos, *Des PPN à consommer avec modération*, 28 November 2024.

32 Article L. 410-5 of the French Commercial Code, created by Law no. 2012-1270 of 20 November 2012.

33 Radio 1, *L'exécutif allonge encore la liste des PPN... avant de la détricoter*, 28 November 2024.

the ability of administrative price controls to bring about a lasting reduction in prices and provide a credible response to the problem of high living costs.

62. By highlighting the contrasting effects of price controls on the economy, the positions taken by the Authority have had the merit of calling into question certain public policies marked by a certain dirigisme, even if its recommendations have not systematically been incorporated into regulations. In their most technical aspects, the Authority's recommendations are frequently incorporated into the successive reforms carried out by the country. On the other hand, more radical positions taken by the Authority, such as the abolition of permanent price regulation for PPN products, have not often been followed by the public authorities.

63. This aspect is perhaps also what characterises the role of a competition authority, which is namely to bring a singular voice to public debate, by analysing the impact of certain regulations on competitive dynamics and, where appropriate, proposing bold solutions. Over the past decade, the Authority's consultative role has enabled a dialogue to be established between the Authority, political decision-makers and civil society on issues that have a substantial impact on the Polynesian economy and, more generally, on the local population, which continues to be severely affected by the high cost of living.

64. In the decade to come, it will be necessary to take stock of regulatory developments and, in particular, to observe whether price control mechanisms have retained their importance in the regulatory framework or whether, on the contrary, a shift towards a less dirigiste approach has been adopted to combat the high cost of living in French Polynesia.

Transportation of Hydrocarbons: The Action of the Polynesian Competition Authority

Arnaud Busseuil[*] and Heiva Sage[**]
Polynesian Competition Authority

I. A major economic challenge

1. French Polynesia is an overseas collectivity spanning an area of over 4 million km² (the size of the European Union), and only 4,167 km² of land divided into 118 islands, 76 of which are inhabited. As such, it has many of the characteristics of a Small Island Economy[1] and is heavily dependent on imports, particularly of hydrocarbons.

2. In 2021, according to the Polynesian Energy Observatory, the level of energy dependency was 93.9%. That same year, more than 70% of local electricity production was based on thermal sources, while the transport sector alone required the import of more than 368,000,000 litres of hydrocarbons. This structural dependence means high costs and increased economic vulnerability. In addition, the supply of hydrocarbons relies on specific port infrastructures whose limitations (depth of passes, storage capacity) have a direct influence on logistical and pricing costs.

---

* Arnaud Busseuil holds a doctorate in public law, special- ising in constitutional law, and is head of the Department of the Presidency and the Board of the Polynesian Competition Authority.

** Heiva Sage holds a doctorate in public law, specialising in public finance, and is an advisor to the President and Board of the Polynesian Competition Authority.

1 Valérie Angeon, Jean-François Hoarau. *Small island economies: a world of their own?* Région et Développement, 2015, Small island economies: new conceptual and methodological perspectives, 42, pp. 5-13

3. This situation gives rise to two major concerns for the region, which are linked but distinct. On the one hand, there are risks of supply disruptions, particularly for the archipelagos at the end of the logistics chain, and it is up to the competent authorities to alleviate this problem, in particular through direct intervention in a competitive market. On the other hand, these authorities are in a relatively weak position in terms of negotiations and the costs borne by the community may rapidly no longer correspond to the actual costs borne by the carriers.

4. Supply is governed by an agreement between the Polynesian government, importing companies, and sea carriers. This agreement, which was signed in 2006 and expired in 2016, provided a framework for sea freight. Since then, the tariff framework has been modified, with notable effects on the competitiveness of the prices applied.

II. Intervention by the Polynesian Competition Authority

5. As soon as it was set up[2], the President of French Polynesia asked the Polynesian Competition Authority (hereafter "the Authority") to examine the competitive situation in the transport of hydrocarbons. This initial request was made in the context of a project to renew a tripartite agreement between the French Polynesian government, companies importing petroleum products and companies transporting these products. Agreement No. 6.0294 of 7 July 2006 relating to the transport of hydrocarbons to French Polynesia having expired in 2016, this new draft agreement was an opportunity to organise the pooling of transport and to revise the factors used to determine the cost of freight in the price structure for hydrocarbons.

6. In 2021, during the negotiations for a new renewal of this agreement, the Authority again examined[3] the operation of the sector to determine whether its 2016 recommendations had been followed, in whole or in part, and to note any changes in the competitive conditions for the supply of hydrocarbons. This could, if necessary, justify reductions in the price of freight with the aim of "*stimulating business activity, reducing the cost of producing thermal electricity and increasing the purchasing power of Polynesian consumers, and motorists in particular*".[4]

7. In practical terms, this shipping agreement had two objectives[5]:
   - set the cost of freight used in the pricing structure for hydrocarbons;
   - encourage pooling between carriers.

---

[2] The Authority took up its duties on 1 January 2016 following its creation by Country Law No. 2015-2 of 23 February 2015.

[3] Decision No. 2021-DAA-01 of 28 June 2021; Pursuant to Article LP. 620-4 of the French Polynesian Competition Code, "[t]*he Authority may take the initiative of issuing an opinion on any matter concerning competition. It may also recommend that the government of French Polynesia implement the measures necessary to improve the competitive operation of the markets*".

[4] Opinion No. 2016-A-02 of 7 November 2016 on the state of competition in the hydrocarbons sector.

[5] Opinion No. 2022-A-01 of 21 April 2022 on the state of competition in the hydrocarbon supply sector in French Polynesia, § 122.

8. In the Authority's view, the choice of contractual arrangements is a wise one insofar as it strikes a balance between *"freedom and constraint and between protecting the interests of Polynesian professionals and consumers"*.[6]

9. The Authority's Opinion No. 2022-A-01 of 21 April 2022 on the competitive situation in the hydrocarbon supply sector in French Polynesia therefore seeks to strike a balance between flexibility for operators, security of supply and reasonable prices for the country and consumers.

10. On the subject of pooling between carriers, which will not be developed further here, although the Authority *ultimately* considered its 2016 opinion[7] that the pooling of purchases of petroleum products from Asian refineries by the three companies importing petroleum products did not appear to be economically justified, since it derogated from the principle of price competition and was likely to have anti-competitive effects, the Authority did nevertheless acknowledge that pooling the transport of these products was justified by the specific configuration of the territory's petroleum product supply. Its 2022 opinion reiterates this analysis and proposes possible solutions to the Polynesian government, in particular through incentive mechanisms.

11. The Authority's analysis of the cost of freight also attracted considerable media and institutional attention. According to its conclusions, for the year 2021, "*the difference in freight costs is therefore estimated to have been almost one billion francs*"[8] (approximately 8.4 million euros). It was therefore deemed necessary to come back to this major point of the 2022 opinion in greater detail.

III. Determining the cost of freight according to convention

12. In its opinion, the Authority points out that the wholesale and retail prices of a number of finished petroleum products imported into French Polynesia are administered and governed by a "price structure" based in particular on a "CIF scale value" set for each of the petroleum products concerned.

13. This CIF value (Cost of Freight Insurance) is made up of the purchase price, or FOB (*Free On Board)*, calculated according to the market price of hydrocarbons[9], the cost of insurance (at the rate actually applied) and the cost of freight. This last point is the subject of the opinion under review.

14. In this case, the "CIF scale value" is therefore the basis for determining wholesale fuel prices, but also the basis for determining retail fuel prices. The Authority is right to point out that this value has an impact on most economic activities and consumers (pump prices, electricity prices, etc.). It also points out that this value can represent between 30% and 100% of the regulated wholesale and retail prices of imported hydrocarbons.

---

6 Opinion No. 2022-A-01 of 21 April 2022 on the state of competition in the hydrocarbon supply sector in French Polynesia.

7 Opinion No. 2016-A-02 of 7 November 2016 on the state of competition in the hydrocarbons sector.

8 Opinion No. 2022-A-01 of 21 April 2022 on the state of competition in the hydrocarbon supply sector in French Polynesia, § 261.

9 According to a formula set out in Article 3 of Order No. 898 CM of 27 August 1990, as amended, fixing the general framework for the sale prices of certain hydrocarbons imported into the territory of French Polynesia.

15. Based on the fact that, according to data provided to the Authority by the Directorate General for Economic Affairs, the cost of freight represented an average of 11% of the "CIF Value Scale" between 2015 and 2021, applied to very large volumes for the region, the Authority has rightly perceived the potential savings that a reduction in freight costs could generate for the region and/or consumers.

16. Thus, while the methodology set out in the agreement for determining prices should overcome the risks associated with the vertical integration of players, the Authority nevertheless had to ensure that the level of fares resulting from the agreement was not excessive for French Polynesia in relation to the costs actually borne by the carriers. To do this, the Authority had to check the basic formula for freight rates.

17. This time, it realised, as it did in its 2016 opinion, that while this formula was indeed based on indices representative of market values, it was also accompanied by a number of additional elements likely to be the subject of debate. The formula to be analysed by the Authority was therefore as follows:

Freight rates in USD per metric tonne = *Flat rate x (Worldscale index + 15) x (vessel deadweight / average number of tonnes unloaded in Papeete)*

- The *flat rate* is a rate published by the *Worldscale Association Limited* and the *Worldscale Association Inc.* for the delivery year.
- The *Worldscale* index is the monthly average, calculated over the last full calendar month prior to the vessel's loading date, of the *Worldscale* index for a given route, as published by *S&P Global Platts* (in this case the Singapore-Sydney route) by vessel type (in this case 30 KT "*medium range*" (MR) vessels).
- The deadweight represents the maximum load that a ship can safely carry.
- The average number of tonnes unloaded in Papeete is the average tonnage of all types of oil unloaded in Papeete over the calendar year preceding the date of arrival of the vessel. It is equal to the total tonnage unloaded in the year in question divided by the number of voyages made during that year.

IV. Recommendations and key reforms

18. As the French Financial Markets Authority (AMF) points out: "*the choice of an agreement seems judicious, insofar as it represents a good balance between freedom and constraint and between protecting the interests of Polynesian professionals and consumers*"[10]. There are many issues behind this choice. It guarantees greater transparency and enables non-integrated importing companies (those that do not transport via a subsidiary or a company in the same group) to have their products transported fairly, without discrimination.

---

10 Opinion No. 2022-A-01 of 21 April 2022 on the state of competition in the hydrocarbon supply sector in French Polynesia, § 121.

19. The Authority furthermore carried out a critical analysis of the draft agreements submitted during the investigation in order to submit proposals for improvement to the government, with the following guidelines: (i) to ensure a balance between flexibility for the players and security of supply at a reasonable rate; (ii) while correctly calibrating the determination of the freight rate in favour of a formula that is less costly for the Polynesian economy.

20. Determining the cost of oil transport to French Polynesia under the agreement is based on various technical parameters specific to this area of activity.

21. The Authority made 15 recommendations[11] aimed at improving the regulation of maritime oil and gas freight, including:

    - elimination of unjustified margins: revision of the freight calculation methodology to ensure a better correlation between rates and actual costs;
    - the use of reliable market indices (*Worldscale*, *Platts*): alignment with transparent market values to avoid arbitrary adjustments by carriers;
    - encouraging the pooling of transport: optimising journeys, limiting the number of empty runs and introducing incentives for importers to pool their loads;
    - greater tariff transparency: carriers and importers are required to provide supporting documents (contracts, invoices, freight indices) to the public authorities.

22. The Authority's study also revealed differences in the application of freight costs between different operators, with an impact on the pricing structure for hydrocarbons in Polynesia. Better supervision of the reference indices was recommended to ensure greater transparency.

23. These recommendations are based on objective values (such as the *Worldscale* and *Platts* indices), which limits the risk of arbitrary tariff adjustments by the integrated players, while taking into account the real additional costs associated with supplying the Polynesian territory, which include in particular the shallow depth of the channel (11 metres) and the limited storage capacity.

24. On the basis of various comparisons, the Authority highlighted elements of the agreement that need to be adapted to current practices. Among these are the reference indices such as the *flat rate* and *Worldscale* index relating to the routes followed. The opinion stresses the importance of applying a *more realistic flat rate, covering journeys as far as Papeete*, on the one hand, and *opting for the flat rate for the route actually used, on the other.* This change better reflects carriers' real costs, but also *eliminates mark-up coefficients that are no longer justified, particularly in the case of the Worldscale index.* A similar questioning was developed with regard to the mark-up coefficient linked to ship capacity, because of the leeway available to optimise routes. The opinion proposes, as an alternative, that the latter coefficient be maintained if its determination is based on encouraging the pooling and optimisation of voyages to Papeete in order to limit their number.

---

11 Six of them are based on incentives to transfer. These will not be dealt with in this report

25. The range governing the freight rate was also analysed and revealed an asymmetry in its application. The initial aim of this formula was precisely to abstract from endogenous data in favour of exogenous market values. However, the rates observed were often higher than the conventional ceiling and almost never lower than its floor. This benefited the carriers alone, to the detriment of Polynesian consumers and non-vertically integrated importers, who were able to make super-profits during periods of low prices, while being protected from price rises. The opinion rightly points out that the recommendation to *remove this range* is consistent with the recommendation to limit the formula for calculating the unit price of freight to a combination of the *flat rate* and *Worldscale* index, which are appropriate for the situation of freight of petroleum products to French Polynesia and, more generally, to the islands of the South Pacific.

26. This argument is also valid to compensate for *the exclusion of the fuel surcharge clause in the price structure.* It comes into play as a variable, plus or minus, once the actual consumption of a completed trip is known. From a competitive point of view, it favours importers who are able to make intra-group compensations. In fact, the combination of the *flat rate* and the *Worldscale* index makes it possible to assess the real rate almost instantaneously, and the formula already incorporates fluctuations in bunker prices.

27. The opinion also calls into question a final component of the cost of freight, demurrage, which is a charge for delays in loading or unloading charged to importers by the carrier. The recommendation is based on charging these costs only for unforeseeable events not covered by insurance, not involving the liability of a third party, and occurring in French Polynesia. At present, these costs are billed in an unjustified manner.

V. A concrete impact

28. The Authority's opinion revealed that the prices charged were out of line with the actual costs borne by carriers, and examined the causes. With this newly-gained knowledge of the sector, the result of a meticulous 10-month investigation, the Authority has made concrete proposals for changes to the method used to calculate the cost of freight, to the benefit of the government and consumers, while maintaining a subtle balance of incentives for carriers.

29. The "*ex officio* referral for an opinion", for which no time limit is imposed[12], has enabled the Authority to gather important information on the operation of the market studied and its developments since 2016. In this case, the Authority's highly technical analysis of the breakdown of the method of calculating the cost of freight showed that the additional costs invoiced to the Country were based on elements defined in an agreement to which the Country was a co-signatory. The fact remains, however, that the uniform rates ($57.37 per tonne) charged

---

[12] On the other hand, mandatory or optional notices under articles LP. 620-1 and LP. 620-2 of the Competition Code provide for publication deadlines of one month, or 15 days in the event of an emergency declared by the President of French Polynesia, the latter case being regular.

by the three transport companies and accepted by the Country corresponded to the floor of the 2006 agreement, which was no longer in force. Time will tell whether an investigation has been or will be carried out into this matter. In 2023, the Country confirmed to the Territorial Audit Chambre (hereinafter referred to as the "CTC") that it had only been able to discover this practice on the advice of the APC.[13]

30. Over the years in question (2017-2021), the amount of freight invoiced to the Country was higher than the market cost, which led to significant profits for the carriers, financed by consumers and taxpayers through the Hydrocarbon Price Regulation Fund, known as the "FRPH".[14] According to the CTC, which followed in the footsteps of the Authority to investigate the matter further, the cumulative undue profit for transporters over this period is 5 billion Pacific francs (around €42 million), and damage to motorists of 80 CFP francs (€0.67) per full tank of petrol.[15]

31. The results also highlighted structural weaknesses in the governance of the sector. The Authority insisted on the need for stronger regulation to avoid excessive rent and to increase competition between carriers.

32. As a result of the Authority's recommendations, the Polynesian government adopted Decree No. 2638 CM of 8 December 2022, abolishing the range for freight rates and aligning them more closely with market indices. The formula is now based on market indices, which constitute an objective foundation. French Polynesia now relies on the services of a specialised company to compile the indices, which improves transparency and reduces the asymmetry of information in relation to the oil companies.

33. However, the question of pooling transport remains to be resolved, because despite the incentives offered, it has not yet been implemented by the players in the sector.

34. In addition, an *ex officio* referral for an opinion is an interesting tool for the Authority. It enables it to gather, in a calm atmosphere free from the concerns of procedural deadlines, important information to support the data it possesses for understanding the operation of certain specific markets that are outside its usual scope. In addition, these opinions may not only lead to recommendations in the context of the opinion itself, as in the present case, but may also help detect practices that could subsequently be the subject of investigations into anti-competitive practices. It should be remembered that as long as the information obtained during the investigation of the notice has been collected legally, it can be used in an investigation file that is opened subsequently.

---

13 CTC, Final observations report – Collectivity of French Polynesia: energy policy, financial years 2017 et seq., 19 April 2023, p. 59.

14 This fund was set up by deliberation No. 97-98 APF of 29 May 1997 creating a special account called the Hydrocarbon Price Regulation Fund (FRPH). Its purpose is to prevent sudden fluctuations in the price of hydrocarbons intended for domestic consumption, and also to set specific selling prices for certain professional categories (EDT, fishermen, power stations, pearling companies, etc.).

15 CTC, Final observations report – Collectivity of French Polynesia: energy policy, financial years 2017 et seq., 19 April 2023, pp. 61-62.

VI. Is the role of the Authority changing?

35. The Authority played a key role in correcting pricing practices in the hydrocarbon freight sector. Its intervention has revealed unjustified discrepancies and proposed structural reforms that benefit consumers and public finances. The challenge for the future now lies in establishing a sustainable framework that ensures ongoing transparency and a better balance between market players, thereby guaranteeing an effective reduction in freight costs and better protection for the Polynesian economy.

36. The Authority's effectiveness in this area has led the government to consider strengthening its powers in energy regulation. On 6 May 2024, the Authority was consulted on a draft law giving it responsibility for regulating gas and electricity.[16] However, the hydrocarbons sector remains excluded from this regulation, which raises questions about the political will to maintain direct control over such a strategic sector.

37. The supply of hydrocarbons is a crucial issue for the Polynesian economy, and effective regulation could optimise costs for consumers while guaranteeing the long-term future of the market.

---

16 Opinion No. 2024-A-04 of 30 May 2024 on a draft country law relating to sectoral regulation in the field of energy, § 107, see also *French Competition Authority, The French Competition Authority issues its opinion on the competitive functioning of electric vehicle charging infrastructure, 30 May 2024, e-Competitions May 2024, Art. No. 119123.*

Funeral Services: The First Agreement Decision by the Polynesian Competition Authority Sets the Tone

Nathalie Jalabert-Doury* and Emma Moisson**
Mayer Brown

1. In early November 2022, the Polynesian Competition Authority (APC) published its first ever cartel decision. This decision imposes cumulative penalties of just over XPF 6 million (around €50,000) on 11 small funeral companies for colluding to fix prices during the Covid-19 pandemic period.
2. The case was triggered by reports from the Te Tia Ara consumer association and the Directorate General of Economic Affairs (DGAE). The Polynesian Authority, which referred the matter to itself in March 2021, conducted the procedure smoothly, resulting in a penalty decision less than 18 months later.
3. While the companies and the case are modest, this decision is a strong act on the part of the Polynesian Authority to illustrate how a competition authority can watch out for abuses in times of health crisis, when Polynesia has been particularly hard hit by the Covid-19 crisis, with 636 deaths at the end of the "Delta" wave on 27 October 2021[1] and a GDP loss of 10% in 2020 alone.[2]

---

* Nathalie Jalabert-Doury is the head of the Antitrust and Competition department at Mayer Brown in France and co-leads the firm's European Antitrust department.

** Emma Moisson is a trainee lawyer at Mayer Brown.

1 Decision No. 2022-PAC-01 of 5 September 2022 relating to practices implemented in the funeral industry, point 111, see also Alain Ronzano, French Polynesia: The Polynesian Competition Authority cleans up the funeral industry by severely sanctioning a horizontal price agreement (HPP Funéraire...), 5 September 2022, Concurrences No. 4-2022, Art. No. 110026.

2 Institut de la statistique de la Polynésie française, "Estimation du PIB 2020", *Collection Points Référence de la Polynésie française*, February 2021, no. 1234.

4. This first cartel case dealt with by the Autorité Polynésienne is reassuring in that it applies classic, tried and tested principles at French and European level to the various levels of analysis (I). On the substance, it is emblematic of the competition difficulties that can arise in conditions of health crisis when companies are legitimate in taking joint action but must have the strength to resist going beyond that, even though they do not feel they are breaking the rules (II). Finally, in terms of fines, it appears that much remains to be done in Polynesia because the Authority does not have all the tools at its disposal, but it has nevertheless done its utmost here to aim for effectiveness (III).

I. The application of classic, tried and tested principles

5. The decision recalls that under the terms of Article LP 200-1 of the French *Competition Code*, concerted actions, express or tacit agreements or coalitions between undertakings are prohibited when their purpose or effect is to prevent, restrict or distort competition on a market in Polynesia, in this case the market for funeral services in the company's home islands.

6. The decision quotes extensively from French decision-making practice and EU case law. While the latter is not directly applicable in Polynesia, it provides a useful guide, as does French practice, given that the terms and concepts on which the Polynesian rules are based are very similar. In so doing, the Polynesian Authority is incorporating a base of decision-making practice and precedents that it does not yet have directly at its disposal. On all the points of convergence between the regimes, this approach is to be welcomed in that it reinforces legal certainty and predictability.

A. *An adversarial procedure with clear guidelines, but in the event little use is made of it by the companies concerned*

7. While the Polynesian Authority can carry out inspections and seizures[3] – as it has done in other recent cases[4] – this was not the case here, as the practices were reported, made public and the information provided by the companies during their hearings was sufficient to feed the investigation file.

8. A reading of the decision shows that the adversarial procedure was organised quickly but surely, with hearings of the companies (the statements in the procedure of at least 10 of the 12 respondents are cited in the decision), a notification of grievances (end of October/beginning of November 2021), a report (March 2022) and a hearing (29 August 2022).

9. However, it seems that the adversarial debate was not very fruitful, as only 2 of the 12 companies submitted written observations in response to the statement

---

3 *French Competition Code*, art. LP 500-1 et seq., resulting from Order no. 2017-157, 9 February 2017, art. 5.

4 As it was able to do in the asphalt roadworks sector (CA Papeete, First President, 6 April 2022, no. 21/00003).

of objections. Some of them are very small individual companies with an annual turnover of less than 5 million XPF (i.e. less than 50,000 euros).[5]

10. It is a fact of life for the APC that the companies involved in its proceedings can be very small and that they simply do not have the means to ensure their representation, or even probably to benefit from legal advice in proceedings that are cumbersome for the parties involved, in a context where competition law is itself still in its infancy. All these circumstances call on the Polynesian Authority to use both education and repression to develop a competition culture.

B. *A case illustrating the broad scope of the competition rules*

11. As article LP 100-1 of the French *Competition Code* very clearly states, "the rules set out in this Code [on competition] apply to all production, distribution and service activities, whether carried out by public entities, or on their behalf, or by private entities".

12. While the sale of products obviously falls within this scope, some people sometimes have a little more difficulty conceptually considering that services as specific and regulated as funeral services are subject to the same competition rules. However, this is in fact the case, and over the last decade in mainland France, competition cases have concerned new sectors for which operational staff had clearly been unprepared for this possibility (banking services, *trading*, etc.).

13. Following the example of the National Authority, the Polynesian Authority even considers that compliance with competition rules is even more important in the health and social protection sector, where competition is already reduced due to the regulations applicable to preserve the budgetary equilibrium of the health insurance service.[6]

14. Moreover, all forms of economic activity are subject to these competition rules, including when services are provided by very small enterprises (VSEs) or even by sole proprietors – which was the case for several of the businesses involved in this case.[7]

15. This is classic: "even a natural person may constitute an undertaking within the meaning [of the antitrust prohibition] if it carries on an economic activity. An economic activity is any activity consisting in offering goods or services on a given market".[8]

---

5 Decision, art. 2the penalty imposed on Min Chiu Junior Moorea amounts to XPF 48,825 and represents between 0 and 1% of its turnover. Assuming that this penalty corresponds to the maximum range of 1% of its turnover, its turnover would be a maximum of XPF 5 million

6 Decision, point 118.

7 Decision, points 25 et s.

8 European Commission, decision in case COMP/C.38.279/F3 of 2 April 2003 relating to a proceeding pursuant to Article 81 of the EC Treaty, *Viandes bovines françaises*, paragraph 104; CJEU, 23 April 1991, Case C-41/90, *Höfner and Elser*, paragraph 21; CJEU, 17 February 1993, Case C-159/91 and Case C-160/91, Poucet and Pistre, paragraph 17. C-160/91, *Poucet et Pistre*, point 17, see also, European Court of Justice, The EU Court of Justice holds that the concept of an undertaking encompasses every entity engaged in an economic activity regardless of the legal status of the entity and the way it is financed (Höfner / Macrotron), 23 April 1991, e-Competitions April 1991, Art. N° 107351.

16. Finally, the context of crisis does not make it possible to escape the application of competition rules, which is the result of consistent case law in French law[9] as well as in European Union law.[10] The only effective exclusions are set out in article LP 200-5 of the French *Competition Code*, namely practices resulting from the application of a regulatory provision, and those exempted on the grounds of their contribution to economic progress.

17. The decision therefore finds that the context of crisis is neither an excuse nor a mitigating factor[11] , but the decision recognises the special nature of the context in assessing the reduction for failure to contest the grievances[12] (see III, C below).

C. *A standard of proof for the classic agreement of will*

18. As regards the standard of proof, the Polynesian Authority endorses the principles adopted by the French Competition Authority and the courts of the European Union.

19. Thus, the Polynesian Authority points out that an agreement of wills is established "when the companies have expressed their common will to behave on the market in a given manner, without the need for a written document, any particular formalism, contractual sanctions or other coercive measures".[13] In this case, a number of pieces of evidence were collected, including the initial tariff document stamped and signed by nine of the companies concerned and communicated to the various companies that took part in the discussions and to the public authorities (the Covid-19 crisis centre, the CHSP, etc.), as well as two subsequent versions, this time signed by the 12 companies. The authority has also gathered several statements from the companies to establish the conditions under which these documents were drawn up and then implemented.

20. Some companies have only jointly approved tariffs, others have taken the initiative by issuing reminders and contacting the authorities; others have only half applied the agreed tariffs, or have not applied them at all, because Covid has not taken responsibility for their deaths.

21. Without using the terms "single, complex and continuous infringement", the Polynesian Authority states that "by agreeing on the terms of an action plan, the undertakings know that they are in agreement and are aware of the expected

---

9 French Competition Authority Décision 18-D-15 du 26 juillet 2018 relative à des pratiques mises en œuvre dans le secteur de la distribution de médicaments vétérinaires, point 206, see also, French Competition Authority, The French Competition Authority fines wholesale distributors of veterinary medicinal products and their professional association for anticompetitive practices (Alcyon / Coveto / Centravet), 26 July 2018, e-Competitions July 2018, Art. N° 8747.

10 ECJ, 20 November 2008, aff. C-209/07, see also Competition Authority v/ Beef Industry Development Society Ltd, Barry Brothers (Carrigmore) Meats Ltd, ; ECJ, 18 December 2008, aff. joined cases C-101/07 P and C-110/07 P, Viande bovine française, point 87, see also Richard Burton, The EU Court of Justice rules on the capacity of reduction agreements in an Irish beef case (Beef Industry Development Society / Barry Brothers), 20 November 2008, e-Competitions November 2008, Art. N° 44500.

11 Decision, point 125.

12 Decision, point 137.

13 Decision, point 82.

consequences".[14] The 12 companies concerned are therefore considered to have participated in a prohibited concertation for the entire period (from 24 March 2020 to 26 October 2021).

22. The Polynesian Authority has therefore clearly taken advantage the procedural facility provided by the single, complex and continuous infringement, which makes it possible to assess the anti-competitive nature of certain practices globally and to hold the companies liable for the various manifestations of the concerted action relating to the joint plan that they approved, even if they did not participate in each of them.[15]

23. Consequently, all the undertakings are considered to have participated in the concerted action established based on these various events. It is not clear from reading the decision what overall plan each company adhered to, but the monolithic nature of the practices does not seem to have required further elaboration.

D. *Classification as an anti-competitive object*

24. Article LP 200-1 of the French *Competition Code* requires, as does the French text,[16] the demonstration of an anti-competitive object or effect. Where a practice involves a "sufficient degree of harmfulness with regard to competition",[17] it is not necessary to establish that the practice has had restrictive effects on competition. In addition to the content of the agreement and the economic and legal context in which it takes place, the objectives pursued by the parties must also be considered in order to determine the degree of harmfulness necessary to classify the practice as a restriction by object.[18]

25. Based on European and national decision-making practice,[19] the Polynesian Authority considers that it is dealing with a practice with an anti-competitive object "insofar as the fixing of common prices to be applied by competing undertakings constitutes a concerted practice which necessarily has an anti-competitive object".[20]

26. In this respect, it is irrelevant to the Polynesian Authority that the undertakings were unaware of such an anti-competitive object, or even of infringing the competition rules, since they did not conceal themselves in any way. In this respect, the decision is in line with French and European case law, for which the intention

---

14 Decision, point 83.

15 CJCE, 8 July 1999, aff. C-49/92 P, *Commission/Anic Partecipazioni*, see also European Court of Justice, The EU Court of Justice holds that the Commission does not have to prove the existence of an agreement as well as a concerted practice regarding a cartel in the chemical industry (Anic), 8 July 1999, e-Competitions July 1999, Art. N° 108006.

16 *French Commercial Code*, art. L420-1.

17 CJEU, 11 September 2014, Case C-67/13, *Groupement des cartes bancaires (CB) c/ Commission*, paragraph 49, see also Martine Behar-Touchais, Restriction "by object": The Court of Justice of the European Union returns to a strict conception of the anti-competitive object (Groupement des Cartes Bancaires), 11 September 2014, Concurrences N° 4-2014, Art. *N° 69844, pp. 110-118.*

18 *Ibid*, point 53.

19 CJEU, 25 October 1983, aff. C-107/82, *AEG/Commission*, point 43; Cour d'appel de Paris, 16 May 2013, n° 12/01227, Kontik, see also Michel Debroux, Retail prices: The Paris Court of Appeal rejects a distributor's action of toy and fancy goods for anticompetitive practices, who challenged the existence of resale price maintenance (Kontiki), 16 May 2013, Concurrences N° 3-2013, Art. N° 53676, p. 72.

20 Decision, point 90.

of the parties does not constitute a necessary element for the characterisation of an infringement by object, just like error as to the lawfulness of the conduct.[21]

27. It should be noted that during the hearings held by the Polynesian Authority, the companies themselves agreed with the objections and the decision, confirming the existence of a concerted practice, themselves emphasising the existence of checks and reminders, where necessary, or even the higher (or even too high) nature of the tariffs thus established. This enabled the Polynesian Authority to characterise a particularly stable cartel that was very serious in nature, even though the companies were not aware that they were participating in an infringement.

II. A health crisis creates particularly dangerous conditions for businesses

28. This first Polynesian case is reminiscent of a number of cases in mainland France where, in the context of a health crisis, companies have somewhat lost sight of the applicable rules in an attempt to respond to the crisis more effectively.

29. Unsurprisingly, the Polynesian Authority's response was the same as that of the other competition authorities: the existence of a crisis cannot justify the implementation of prohibited practices.

A. *When raising awareness among health authorities during a crisis leads to an agreement*

30. When the pandemic arrived in Polynesia, measures were quickly taken to adapt the conditions of care for deceased people infected or suspected of being infected with the SARS-CoV-2 virus. According to Order no. 1322 CM of 27 August 2020, people who died because of the Covid-19 virus were to be buried immediately and the coffin closed, with a number of precautionary measures recommended (cost of equipment and individual protection, disinfection of equipment, etc.).

31. The Polynesian Social Protection Fund (CPS) has also set limits on the amounts covered, with a list of associated benefits (i.e. up to XPF 150,000 for an adult).

32. Against this backdrop, funeral undertakers have obviously approached the public authorities to obtain coverage for the specific services associated with Covid-19 and an increase in the flat-rate amount of coverage – an action that is not contested by the Authority.

33. What is clear, however, is the fact that the companies have discussed together the tariffs applied by each of them to support these requests for revaluation. If companies put themselves in such situations, it is more often than not because the authorities with which they exchange information ask them to do so or suggest

---

21 CJEU, 18 June 2013, Case C-681/11, *Schenker*, paragraph 43, see also Norman Neyrinck, Milia Chamas, The EU Court of Justice decides that a firm that has infringed Article 101 TFEU is unable to escape the imposition of a fine merely because the illegality of its conduct was erroneously assessed by its legal counsel (Schenker), 18 June 2013, e-Competitions June 2013, Art. N° 63670.

that they do so in order to facilitate the investigation of their requests. So, there is only one step from authorised collective action to prohibited practice.

34. After several meetings, the companies drew up a document formalising their agreement on common rates. The document, stamped and signed by nine companies, provides for a price breakdown of XPF 234,540, significantly higher than the fixed price set by CPS.

35. The document was then sent by the companies to the authorities (CHSP, Covid-19 crisis centre) to obtain financial support for Covid services. The table will be completed at a later date to reach 260,940 XPF.

36. This was in no way a secret consultation between companies, and the decision recalls that the companies mentioned during the proceedings how the proposed fee schedule was also intended to facilitate the care of the deceased and prevent families from travelling too far: The aim of the practices was to "make it easier to take care of Covid's deceased"; "to be able to obtain financial responsibility from the CPS for all the services billed to families"; "to prevent families from travelling too far to meet their funeral director and to allow the local funeral director to intervene quickly"; "to encourage families to go to the operator closest to the deceased's home, thanks to identical prices".[22]

37. This is not surprising. It should be remembered that competition law has only been in force in Polynesia since 2017, and this type of practice is still often encountered in France, where competition rules have been in force for many years.

38. The decision is a reminder of the rigor of the law:

> *Incentives or encouragements, tolerances or approvals given by administrative authorities do not constitute a basis for exemption from anti-competitive behaviour. The exemption process must be preceded by a legislative act. A fortiori, mere information brought to the administration's attention and its passive attitude, as in this case, cannot exonerate or constitute a mitigating circumstance for an anti-competitive agreement.*[23]

B. *A novelty in Polynesia, an established practice in many jurisdictions*

39. Decisions by competition authorities concerning practices during periods of crisis are not uncommon. In fact, periods of crisis give rise to additional costs and leave less time for competitive tendering, so that some may be satisfied with harmonised tariffs. Sometimes, the setting of rates is even organised by regulation – in which case it does not constitute an infringement since it is the applicable texts that set the rates applicable by all.[24] On the other hand, if it is organised between companies, it may be prohibited, as it has been in this case.

---

22 Decision, point 95.

23 Decision, point 125.

24 Art. LP 200-5 and Decision, point 125.

40. We all remember the case of beef, dealt with by the European Commission in 2003.[25] In this case, linked to the mad cow epidemic, beef consumption plummeted in France and the market stabilisation measures adopted by the authorities were deemed unsatisfactory. As the situation hardened, with farmers setting fire to meat of non-French origin, the Minister of Agriculture brought together the professional organisations of farmers and slaughterers, inviting them to agree on a fair purchase price scale and to put a stop to imports.

41. The Commission's decision sanctions the federations concerned: while the State may have strongly encouraged the conclusion of the cartel, it is only if anti-competitive behaviour is "imposed on undertakings by national legislation or if that legislation creates a legal framework which, in itself, eliminates any possibility of competitive behaviour on their part" that the prohibition on cartels is inapplicable.[26]

42. Another particularly telling example is the distribution of veterinary medicines during the bluetongue (FCO) epidemic, which was dealt with by the French Competition Authority in 2018.[27] France experienced several outbreaks of bluetongue, a viral disease transmitted from one infected animal to another by midge bite. This disease, which can cause significant economic losses for livestock farmers, has led to the introduction of large-scale vaccination campaigns.

43. During the first vaccination campaign in 2008, the authorities were unprepared and sought to make vaccines available as quickly as possible by instructing wholesale distributors to deliver the vaccines without providing any compensation. The distributors took care of storage, handling and delivery for some time, before finally contacting the authorities to ask for compensation. The authorities asked the distributors, both directly and via their federation, for proof of the expenses incurred, and on this basis agreed to pay 4 cents (excluding tax) per dose delivered.

44. Clearly, the health authorities here themselves contributed to the practices by failing to take appropriate measures upstream (for example by issuing invitations to tender) and by seeking to establish a single compensation downstream based on individual or collective contacts with players who had previously worked without remuneration. However, this was not taken into account by the Autorité, which focused on the fact that the distributors "took advantage of the health emergency caused by the rapid spread of bluetongue and the absence of a call for tenders to knowingly mislead the public purchaser as to the true logistical costs of delivering the vaccines borne by each of them, thereby compromising the proper use of public funds".[28]

---

25 European Commission, Decision in Case COMP/C.38.279/F3 of 2 April 2003 relating to a proceeding pursuant to Article 81 of the EC Treaty, *Viandes bovines françaises*, cited above.

26 Decision, points 151 and 152.

27 French competition authority, décision n° 18-D-15 du 26 juillet 2018 relative à des pratiques mises en œuvre dans le secteur de la distribution de médicaments vétérinaires, point 206, see also Michel Debroux, Transaction: The French Competition Authority fines various anticompetitive practices (non-aggression pact, distribution costs agreement) carried out by several companies and their professional federation (Alcyon / Coveto / Centravet), 26 July 2018, Concurrences N° 4-2018, Art. N° 88165, pp. 111-112.

28 Decision, point 206.

C. *The competition authorities have a role to play in alerting companies and/or adopting derogations in the event of a crisis*

45. When the Covid-19 epidemic broke out, several authorities took the lead in alerting companies to the risks, the need for vigilance and the exemption mechanisms they felt were justified.

46. This was particularly the case for the European Competition Network[29] , which brings together the European Commission and the EU's national authorities, which issued a joint statement in March 2020 informing businesses that the extraordinary nature of the situation might require cooperation from businesses to ensure the fair supply and distribution of essential products to consumers and that they would not open investigations into such cooperation.

47. At the same time, however, the authorities warned that they would not hesitate to act against companies that took advantage of the situation to commit infringements: "the ECN will not hesitate to take action against companies that take advantage of the situation to organise cartels or abuse their dominant position".

48. The message was clearly relayed in the Commission's communication of 9 April 2020 setting out the temporary framework for cooperation in response to emergency situations (Covid-19):[30] "practices by undertakings which opportunistically seek to exploit the crisis as a screen to conceal an anti-competitive agreement" will not be tolerated.[31] The Autorité de la concurrence (French competition authority) issued the same warning in its opinion on a request for an opinion from the Médiateur du cinéma (film industry ombudsman), in which it stressed the established case law according to which "a crisis situation cannot in itself rule out the anti-competitive nature of an agreement".[32]

III. A sanctioning power that becomes clearer based on this decision

49. The procedures for setting fines in Polynesia are similar to those used by the National Authority, with the same recent trend of removing the reference to damage to the economy. Unlike the National Authority, the Polynesian Authority has not adopted guidelines to explain the method for setting its penalties, but for the time being seems to be adopting the national guidelines, which is a good thing pending the development of its own practice. Lastly, the approach taken to the issue of not contesting a complaint is also entirely consistent.

---

29 *Antitrust: Joint Statement by the European Competition Network (ECN) on Application of Competition Law during the Corona Crisis.*

30 Temporary framework for assessing anti-competitive practices in cooperative ventures set up between companies to respond to emergency situations arising from the current Covid-19 pandemic.

31 Decision, point 20.

32 Autorité de la concurrence, avis n° 21-A-03 du 16 avril 2021 relatif à une demande d'avis du Médiateur du cinéma sur les modalités de sortie des films en salle, point 62, see also Jean-Philippe Kovar, COVID-19: The French Competition Authority specifies the conditions for exemption of an agreement between distributors on a common calendar for the release of films when movie theaters reopen, 16 April 2021, Concurrences N° 4-2021, Art. N° 103325, pp. 181-183.

A. *Penalties essentially determined by the seriousness of the offence, even though the text applicable at the time also referred to damage to the economy*

50. The decision was handed down under the terms of article LP 641-2 applicable at the time, which provided that

> *the financial penalties shall be proportionate to the duration and seriousness of the acts complained of, and shall take account in particular of the extent of the damage caused to the economy, the distortion caused on the market or markets concerned, the actual and potential effects on consumers, in time and in space, the situation of the organisation or undertaking penalised or of the group to which the undertaking belongs and the possible repetition of the prohibited practices referred to in Articles LP 200-1 and LP 200-2. [...].*

51. Since the French Polynesian law 2021-40 of 7 September 2021, the text no longer refers to damage to the economy, the distortion caused on the markets concerned or the actual and potential effects on consumers, in time and space, which is reminiscent of the national equivalent, which also required the amount to be determined based on the damage to the economy.[33]

52. The reference to damage to the economy was a French specificity that had to be eliminated at national level in 2021 to harmonise the procedures for determining penalties within the EU. Moreover, economic damage was always particularly complex to quantify, giving rise to lengthy and ultimately unsatisfactory debates between evaluation (possible) and precise quantification (generally impossible). The vagueness of the criterion was therefore a good reason for abolishing it in Polynesia too.

53. Although the Authority's decision refers to the text applicable to the facts, at no point does it expressly refer to damage to the economy. It only refers to the seriousness of the practices, assessed in accordance with national decision-making practice on the basis of :

- the nature of the infringement and of the costs, as well as the nature of the competition parameter(s) concerned ;
- the nature of the activities, sectors or markets in question ;
- the nature of the people likely to be affected;
- the objective characteristics of the offence.[34]

54. The decision therefore provides a useful guide to what its practice will be under the new text: calculating penalties that are proportionate solely to the duration and seriousness of the offences and to the situation of the company penalised.

---

33 *French Commercial Code*, art. L 464-2, in the version prior to Order no. 2021-649 of 26 May 2021.

34 Decision, point 113.

B. *Methodology clarified, even though the Authority does not (yet) have guidelines for setting fines*

55. The decision cites the case law of the Paris Court of Appeal and the French Supreme Court (Cour de Cassation)[35] to emphasise that the text does not impose any method for determining penalties, and only sets the maximum amount.

56. Although Article LP 630-1 of the French *Competition Code* states that "the Polynesian Competition Authority shall draw up guidelines specifying in particular [...] the methods for determining the penalties that it may impose", it has not yet done so, which is quite understandable given its early years of experience in this area.

57. In the meantime, the decision indicates that the Polynesian Authority is more or less in line with the National Authority's methodology[36] – all other things being equal, since the coefficients of the National Authority's methodology are linked to a penalty ceiling of 10%, whereas it is only 5% in Polynesia.

58. Firstly, the decision defines the annual value of sales on the affected market for each undertaking in order to calculate the basic amount of the fines, so as to ensure that they are proportionate to the infringement in question. In this case, the Authority used the amounts invoiced for Covid-19 deaths during the first wave of Covid-19 until 30 June 2021, given that there were more deaths during the second wave. The annual value of sales for all the companies involved is XPF 25 million (around €200,000).

59. In order to take account of duration, again in line with the national guidelines, the Authority applies a coefficient of 1.3 for an infringement period of 19 months between 24 March 2020 and 26 October 2021. This seems to correspond to the method used to determine the duration of the infringement under the old guidelines, i.e. a coefficient of 1 for the first year and half for subsequent years.[37]

60. Gravity is taken into account in the form of an additional coefficient of 25%, which is still broadly in line with the arrangements proposed in the national guidelines, i.e. the application of a coefficient of between 15% and 30% for horizontal price-fixing cartels.

61. The AMF then adjusted the penalty to take account of the greater involvement of two of the companies concerned (origin of the contacts, role in coordinating the exchanges, monitoring of the application of the agreement) with an increase for aggravating circumstances of 15% for one and 5% for the other.

62. Lastly, the Authority had to check that the financial penalties thus defined did not exceed 5% of the amount of turnover excluding tax achieved in French Polynesia

---

35 Paris Court of Appeal, 21 January 2016, No 2014-22811, *Inéo Réseaux Sud-Ouest SNC and Others*; Cass. com, 27 September 2017, n° 16-12907, *Spie Sud-Ouest e.a*, see also Alain Ronzano, Sanctions: The Paris Court of appeal follows the French Supreme Court in refusing to take into account the fact that a company belongs to a group of companies for deterrence purposes when no infringement is attributable to the parent company (Info Réseaux Sud Ouest / SPIE Sud Ouest), 21 January 2016, Concurrences N° 2-2016, Art. N° 79606.

36 Autorité de la concurrence, Communiqué relatif à la détermination des sanctions pécuniaires of 30 July 2021.

37 The new communiqué on penalties provides for each year to be taken into account in full: Communiqué on the determination of financial penalties of 30 July 2021, point 34.

by the companies concerned during one of the last three financial years. In this respect, the Authority is obliged to point out that it has not obtained the turnover of certain companies despite several reminders. However, it considers that it is in a position to estimate this turnover on the basis of the companies' declarations and the threshold does not appear to have been reached.

C. *Application of additional reductions for failure to contest grievances*

63. Polynesian law still allows the AMF to take into account the fact that no statement of objections has been lodged[38] and has not moved towards a settlement procedure like national law.[39]

64. If a company does not contest the statement of objections, it may benefit from a halving of the maximum fine (and in practice from a limited reduction in the fine itself), which does not always allow the fine to be adjusted sufficiently. Hence the adoption at national level of a settlement procedure that makes it possible to arrive at an acceptable range of fines within which the AMF will have to rule.

65. It does not appear from the decision that the companies signed statements of non-contestation of grievances like those used in France, but they were indeed granted non-contestation of grievances. As a result, the companies obtained a halving of the maximum fine (2.5%) and a 10% reduction in the fine, which is not expressly provided for in the text, but which was customary before the national Authority in proceedings prior to the transition to the settlement procedure.[40]

66. It would certainly be useful in the future to allow the Polynesian Authority to conclude real transactions rather than these 10% reductions, which are hardly satisfactory.

*

* *

67. In total, the fines handed down in this case range from 48,825 to 3 million XPF (i.e. approximately 400 to 25,000 euros), apparently representing for some companies around 2% of their total turnover, which is actually quite substantial for a first decision in a context of crisis and concerning very small companies.

---

[38] *Competition Code*, art. LP. 614-2, III.

[39] *French Commercial Code*, art. L464-2, III.

[40] See, for example, Autorité de la concurrence, decision no. 07-D-26 of 26 July 2007, see also Alain Ronzano, Bid rigging: The French Competition Council sanctions an anticompetitive practice on the market of suppliance of high-voltage cables (Nexans), 26 July 2007, Concurrences N° 4-2007, Art. N° 56151.

Company	Sales value (XPF)	Severity coefficient	Duration	Individualisation	Reduction No statement of objections	Fine (XPF)	Share of sales
Min Chiu	9 185 548	25 %	1,3	+ 15 %	– 10 %	3 069 982	0-3 %
Tehei Services	6 273 848	25 %	1,3	–	– 10 %	1 823 337	0-2 %
HPP Funeral	4 022 873	25 %	1,3	+ 5 %	– 10 %	589 842	0-3 %
Vaxelaire	1 537 243	25 %	1,3	–	– 10 %	446 761	0-2 %
Maraetefau	1 254 500	25 %	1,3	–	– 10 %	364 589	0-1 %
Teave Julienne	1 145 660	25 %	1,3	–	– 10 %	85 928	0-3 %
Maruhi Services	451 980	25 %	1,3	–	– 10 %	101 250	0-3 %
Loïc Funéraire	361 700	25 %	1,3	–	– 10 %	101 728	0-2 %
Raromatai	218 880	25 %	1,3	–	– 10 %	61 560	0-1 %
Min Chiu Junior	168 000	25 %	1,3	–	– 10 %	48 825	0-1 %

68. This decision therefore sets the tone: the Autorité will be particularly vigilant about prohibited practices that harm consumers. This is the price to pay for maintaining and, if possible, developing competition in an area that is not only insular but also isolated.

69. This decision sets the tone: the Authority will be particularly vigilant about prohibited practices that harm consumers. Maintaining and, if possible, developing competition in a territory that is not only insular but also isolated comes at this cost.

The Effectiveness of the Polynesian Competition Authority: The Example of the Telecommunications Sector

Patrick Hubert* and Quitterie de La Poype**
Orrick

1. The French island territories are marked by a scissor effect between the high general level of prices and the low incomes of a large proportion of the population, a situation that is particularly pronounced in Polynesia, where there are many small islands far from Tahiti, implying high logistical costs.
2. Price differences between the DROM-COM and mainland France have been the subject of numerous studies. One of the most recent, Report No. 1549, submitted by the French National Assembly on 20 July 2023, found that the telecoms sector was especially affected. The report cites only the French overseas departments and territories, where mobile services were 35% more expensive than at national level, and packages 65% more expensive[1], but similar conclusions could be drawn for French Polynesia.
3. Two kinds of explanations can be put forward: structural explanations relating to the small size of the territories and their difficulty access, and explanations

---

* Patrick Hubert is a partner at the Paris office of Orrick, in the Antitrust & Competition department.

** Quitterie de La Poype has been a lawyer at the Paris office of Orrick since September 2022.

1 Autorité de régulation des communications électroniques, des postes et de la distribution de la presse (ARCEP), *Les services de communications électroniques dans les départements et collectivités d'Outre-mer, année 2021. Observatoire des marches des communications électroniques* [online], 7 July 2022, p. 27. Available at: https://www.arcep.fr/fileadmin/cru-1677573101/reprise/observatoire/march-an2021/obs-marches2021-OUTRE- MER_juil2022.pdf.

based on concentration and the functioning of the markets. Because of the lack of competitors or their behaviour, competition is said to be sub-optimal.

4. All over the world, telecoms markets are highly regulated, and public authorities have implemented reforms to open them up to new entrants. However, the behaviour of the players involved, essentially that of the historically dominant players, has hampered this opening-up by hindering the deployment of competitors, thereby making price competition difficult or ineffective. One of the most classic problems is the need for a new entrant to have access to the dominant operator's network under economically acceptable conditions. In the fixed telephony market, the dominant operator is often the owner of the cables: the new entrant must be able to access this network, which does not belong to it. In mobile telephony, the problem is posed in slightly different terms: each operator must be able to circulate communications on the network of all the others, so that its customers can access all subscribers, regardless of their operators. On the surface, there is less asymmetry because each operator is dominant on its own network; however, the operator with the most developed network can easily make access too difficult or too expensive. It is up to competition law and the authorities responsible for enforcing it to solve these problems posed by the behaviour of dominant operators.

5. In island markets, this dual approach – regulatory and then competitive – has long been illustrated in the DROMs. The aforementioned report by the French National Assembly notes that the number of operators in the DROMs is more or less equal to the number in mainland France, but that it has been necessary for the Autorité de la concurrence to intervene on numerous occasions against the locally dominant operator (France Télécom, Orange or Société Réunionnaise du Radiotéléphone (SRR), depending on the place and the time).

6. With a time lag, the same sequence can be seen in French Polynesia, where opening up the market by regulation has run into difficulties that the Polynesian Competition Authority (APC) has sought to resolve.

I. The opening up of telecommunications markets by the Polynesian authorities

7. The Assembly of French Polynesia initiated opening up of these markets by Deliberation No. 2003-85 APF of 12 June 2003, which provided for the opening up to competition of mobile telephony services and the provision of Internet access, and the allocation of a public telecommunications service to the incumbent operator, Office des Postes et Télécommunications (OPT) (through its subsidiary SAS Onati), which would retain a de jure monopoly on external links (voice and data and on fixed networks) and, finally, a system of authorisation for telecommunications operators competing with the incumbent operator, both for mobile telephony and for the provision of Internet access.

8. The main innovation was the opening up of the mobile telephony and Internet markets to allow Polynesian consumers to benefit from competition between operators. However, long after the reform came into force, its full impact had yet to be felt. Indeed, it was only in 2010 for fixed telephony and 2013 for mobile

telephony was the second operator authorised to enter the market. For a long time, the mobile telecoms sector was characterised by a duopoly, made up of the incumbent operator's subsidiary OPT and Pacific Mobile Telecom (PMT), which markets mobile services under the Vodafone brand. It was not until 2020, 17 years after the reform, that a third player, Viti, began to market mobile communications services, although this rollout has encountered difficulties.

9. Twelve years after the telecommunications sector was opened up to competition, French Law No. 2015-2, adopted on 23 February 2015, introduced a modern competition law and an independent authority responsible for enforcing it, the APC, endowed not only with sanctioning powers but also with the ability to adopt precautionary measures to resolve urgent situations without waiting for a decision on the merits of the case.

II. The APC's first intervention in the sector of telecommunications: The handling of PMT's complaint

10. Intervention by a competition authority to resolve market failures is by nature very different from regulatory intervention, as it generally requires a complaint to be lodged. It was not until 2021 that the APC received its first complaint on the merits, accompanied by a request for interim measures, from PMT[2], which claimed that it had been unable to deploy a 'local loop' in the remote islands of Tahiti because it did not have access to the Natitua cable, owned by the incumbent operator Onati, which links the islands together.

11. PMT put forward two complaints: the impossibility of access to an essential infrastructure in the case of fixed telephony, and access, which was certainly physically possible, but on excessively onerous terms, in the case of mobile telephony.

12. If the complaint concerned an issue specific to French Polynesia, not transferable to other geographical markets, the problem itself – access to an essential, irreplaceable infrastructure vital for market access – is a classic one. Relying on counter-arguments, also classic, Onati argued that the Natitua cable was not irreplaceable, as it was possible to transmit communications from one island to another via microwave transmission, to which PMT responded that it had not deployed this technology, which, moreover, would not have allowed communication between islands that are very far apart from each other.

13. Such access was also necessary for mobile telephone communications. this time Onati had made an offer access to PMT, PMT complained that it was being offered access to the Natitua cable on terms that were too onerous to enable it to offer consumers prices on the downstream market that were as low as those charged by Onati. It was therefore a margin squeeze, or margin squeeze, that was invoked, a practice that is also common in this sector and often condemned by other competition authorities[3].

---

2 Decision no. 2021-PAC-01 of 8 December 2021 relating to a request for interim measures submitted by Pacific Mobile Telecom in the telecommunications sector, concerning the provision of iti- nérance for mobile data access.

3 See in particular, Court of Justice, 10 April 2008, T-271/03, *Deutsche Telekom AG*; and the annual report of French Competition Authority, *Etude thématique. Les pratiques de ciseau tarifaires*, 2008, p. 147 to 177.

14. To date, the APC has not yet given its decision on the merits of this case, but it has nonetheless addressed the merits by ruling on the request for precautionary measures.

15. On this occasion, it noted that the dominant's practices "are likely to cause serious harm to the functioning of competition" but nevertheless rejected the request for interim measures, in the absence of irreversible damage.

16. Nonetheless, this lengthy and precise decision is enlightening for market players. The APC has used concepts and methods that are well known in the telecommunications sector, notably those applied by the European Commission and the French Competition Authority, but has applied them to specific situations, particularly with regard to island-to-island links.

III. Second speech: Dealing with Viti's complaint

17. A second case confirms this dual approach; it is more spectacular as, this time, the APC has issued interim protective measures, at the request of the third telecoms operator, Viti,[4] relating to the mobile telephony market.

18. As mentioned in the introduction, this market is characterised by the fact that each operator has a monopoly on its own network, which means that, in order for its competitors' customers to be able to call its own customers, it must offer roaming services to its competitors. The practice of other authorities has shown that even an operator that is not dominant on the downstream market can be condemned for abuse of a dominant position if it does not provide access to its network under acceptable conditions[5].

19. From a certain point of view, the APC was therefore faced by Viti with a classic problem: the conditions of access (or roaming) to Onati's mobile network were abusive. The contribution of this decision lies in the application of a classic problem to a situation that was not: in the remote islands of French Polynesia, Onati was not only dominant on its own network, but in fact the only one to have deployed a mobile network.

20. In general, a mobile phone operator can, even in the face of abuse by another operator, at least allow each of its customers to call other customers using its own network; but this was not possible in the remote islands because Viti did not have a network there. Typically, different operators can negotiate mutual roaming agreements in a kind of balance of power, which is not always easy to achieve, especially for the smaller operators. However, in this case, Viti had no choice but to negotiate a completely asymmetric roaming agreement, as the prospect of installing its own network in remote, sparsely populated islands was distant, placing it in a difficult negotiation position against Onati.

---

4 Decision No. 2023-PAC-01 of 31 March 2023 relating to a request for interim measures submitted by Viti for practices implemented in the telecommunications sector, concerning roaming services in remote archipelagos.

5 See in particular Decision No. 12-D-24 of 13 December 2012 concerning practices implemented in the mobile telephony sector aimed at residential customers in mainland France, partially confirmed by a ruling of the Paris Court of Appeal No. 2013/01006 of 19 May 2016.

21. In a detailed analysis of the potential anti-competitive nature of the practices observed, the APC indicated (without, however, giving a definitive ruling on the merits) that they were likely to create a price squeeze, to be discriminatory[6] (PMT benefiting from better conditions) and, lastly, to be unfair in relation to the costs incurred by Onati.[7]

22. With regard to the existence of a margin squeeze, based on the decision-making practice of the French and European competition authorities, APC made an interesting application of the correction made to the equally efficient competitor test, which now admits that competition can also come from competitors who are not as efficient, or at least not yet as efficient, as the dominant operator.[8] This correction was particularly appropriate to the situation in view of the considerable imbalance in the forces present.

23. On this basis, APC questioned Viti's request for interim measures. Article LP 641-1 of the *Polynesian Competition Code* states that precautionary measures may be ordered if a practice "causes serious and immediate harm to the general economy, to the economy of the sector concerned, to the interests of consumers or to the complainant company".

24. The APC first observed that the development of Viti was particularly beneficial for competition in French Polynesia. This new entrant allowed for breaking the Onati/PMT duopoly. However, getting down to the nitty-gritty, the APC studied Viti's commercial behaviour and concluded that Viti was developing commercial offers, such as unlimited packages, that had not previously been available in French Polynesia.

25. However, on the basis of the roaming proposed by Onati, Viti had decided not to develop in the remote archipelagos, thereby depriving 12% of the territory's population of the competitive opportunities it could have offered. The APC considered that this constituted serious and immediate harm to the sector and to consumers.

26. The APC also found that there was serious and immediate harm to the interests of Viti, once again looking at a very specific situation. By not serving the remote archipelagos, Viti avoided the very high cost of asymmetric roaming and was thus able to operate financially satisfactorily on the other islands. It could be deduced from this that there was no serious and immediate threat to Viti.

27. However, the APC considered that the company's interests had to be assessed for each geographic market: the financial survival of the company conditional on the abandonment of certain geographic markets was not sufficient to conclude that the company's interests were not being met.

---

6 See in particular Court of Justice, 17 July 1963, C-13/63, *Italian Republic v. Commission*, specifying that discrimination consists not only in treating similar situations differently, but also in treating objectively dissimilar situations identically; or Court of , 19 April 2018, C-525/16, *Meo – Serviços de Comunicaçoes e Multimedia*.

7 See in particular Paris Court of Appeal, 7 April 2022, No. RG 20/03811, *Google*, on excessive pricing.

8 See in particular Decision No 2023-PAC-01, cited above, § 90; European Commission Communication of 27 March 2023, "*Amendments to the Communication from the Commission Guidance on the Commission's Enforcement Priorities in Applying Article 82 of the EC Treaty to Abusive Exclusionary Conduct by Dominant Undertaking*" – see Annex, pts 2(b) and 3.

28. The decision was upheld by the Paris Court of Appeal on 6 July 2023[9] (with the exception of one point relating to the benchmark to be used to calculate the new offer).

*

* *

29. For French Polynesia, these decisions confirm that structural reforms of regulated markets need competition law, applied by competition authorities, to produce their full economic effects. They also show the value of entrusting this role to a locally competent authority that seeks to apply the general concepts of competition law, which are more or less identical in every country in the world, to the specific features of local markets, both in terms of market history and geographical constraints.

---

9 Paris Court of Appeal, 6 July 2023, no. 23/06177.

The Acquisition of Bolloré Logistics by CMA CGM: Impact of the Decision

Jérôme Philippe*
Freshfields

1. On 31 January 2024, the Polynesian Competition Authority (APC) conditionally authorised the acquisition of Bolloré Logistics and its subsidiaries by CMA CGM. This decision merits comment because not only does it mark a change in merger control in French Polynesia, but it also lends itself particularly well to comparison, since three authorities – the European Commission, the APC and the New Caledonian Competition Authority (ACNC) – intervened in parallel on this merger to assess situations that are legally and economically quite similar, although not identical.[1]

2. In April 2023, CMA CGM announced that it was entering into exclusive negotiations with the Bolloré group to acquire the latter's transport and logistics business. According to press reports, the deal would be worth around €4.6 billion.

3. Schematically, the transaction led to a slight horizontal concentration on the *freight-forwarding* markets, as CMA CGM had acquired CEVA Logistics, active on these same markets, in 2018-2019. But above all, and this was the crux of the competition issues that were to be examined, the transaction resulted in a more significant vertical integration between the world's third-largest container liner shipping operator and a major freight forwarder and logistics provider operating in around 150 countries.

---

* Jérôme Philippe is a partner in the Paris office of Freshfields Bruckhaus Deringer, where he heads the antitrust, competition and trade team.

1 The merger has also been the subject of other decisions by other competition authorities, but in more distant economic and legal contexts.

4. As a reminder, a freight forwarder is a major intermediary responsible for organising the transport of goods, whose activities generally include customs clearance, warehousing and a number of ground services. Freight forwarders can organise ground transport to and from the airport or port, even if they do not usually carry it out themselves as they do not have their own means of transport.

5. The APC's decision of 31 January 2024 is obviously not the first to authorise a merger subject to remedies, but *it is the first to do so for a merger with an international rather than a local dimension.*

6. It comes against a backdrop of an increase in the number of merger decisions from 2022 onwards, after a series of 4 years of low merger activity (only 6 mergers reviewed in 4 years from 2018 to 2021, of which only 1 resulted in remedies).

Year	Merger decisions	Of which with remedies
2024	4	1
2023	3	2
2022	5	3
2021	1	0
2020	2	0
2019	2	1
2018	1	0
2017	4	1
2016	5	1

7. After this lean period, the number of merger decisions has been around four per year since 2022, returning to the levels of the first two years.

8. Above all, it is immediately apparent from the figures that *the APC's intervention rate is high*: the proportion of mergers for which the APC requests modifications as remedies was already high in the first few years (3 decisions with remedies out of a total of 15 decisions, or 20%, between 2016 and 2021), but *it has increased further since 2022*, with 5 decisions with remedies out of a total of 12 merger decisions, i.e. an *intervention rate of over 40%.*

9. Such a high rate of intervention does not necessarily reflect a stricter approach on the part of the APC compared with other competition authorities, as a reading of the decisions shows very similar reasoning on the part of the various authorities, as confirmed by the *CMA CGM/Bolloré Logistics* decision. Rather, it should be seen as a reflection of the *greater concentration of Polynesia's island economy, which leads the APC to intervene more frequently in mergers*, even though it conducts the same type of analysis as the national authority or the European Commission. This can be seen as one of the public authorities' responses to the specific characteristics of an overseas island economy.

10. In terms of the types of remedies requested by the APC, the *CMA CGM/Bolloré Logistics* decision stands out. It is the second merger decision by the APC to impose structural remedies (i.e. divestitures). But it is the first to impose a remedy

that completely cancels out the effect of the merger on the territory, i.e. imposing the divestiture of the entire target in the territory.

11. In the previous decision involving a structural remedy, which also concerned maritime transport but this time the inter-island transport of goods and passengers, in 2017 the APC imposed the sale of two vessels (one on the Tahiti-Îles Sous-le-Vent route, the other on the Tahiti-Tuamotu de l'Est-Gambier route).[2] These were injunctions issued by the APC and not commitments proposed by the purchaser. This structural remedy was intended to recreate a competitor while strengthening the buyer's position in Polynesia. *The* CMA CGM/Bolloré Logistics *decision, on the other hand, seeks to nullify the effect of the transaction in Polynesia.*

12. *With this exception, all the other remedies requested by the APC prior to* CMA CGM/Bolloré Logistics *were behavioural in nature*: they concerned two transactions in the distribution sector.[3] two transactions in the tourism and hotel sector,[4] one transaction in the food production sector[5] and one transaction in the medical sector.[6]

13. Last but not least, *this is the very first time that the APC has been involved in a global transaction.* Almost all previous mergers, with or without remedies, local transactions. The only non-local transaction previously controlled was, in 2020, the acquisition of joint control by CMA CGM of the Dubreuil Aéro group, which in particular operates French Bee, one of the airlines serving Polynesia from France and the United States. Even if it went beyond the strict scope of Polynesia, this operation was much more modest in size than the acquisition of Bolloré Logistics.

14. Because of its size, the *CMA CGM/Bolloré Logistics* merger gave rise to *multiple filings* with a number of authorities, including three that were responsible for monitoring similar situations:
    - *the European Commission*, which was responsible for merger control in Guadeloupe, Martinique, French Guiana, Réunion and Mayotte;
    - *the APC*, which was in charge of control for French Polynesia; and
    - *the ACNC*, which was responsible for inspections in New Caledonia.

15. Although the legal status of these territories differs, resulting in differences in administrative powers, *there are important points in common, particularly in the economic sphere*:
    - Guadeloupe, Martinique, French Guiana and Réunion are overseas departments, Mayotte is an overseas department and region, French Polynesia and Saint-Martin are overseas collectivities governed by Article 74 of the Constitution, and New Caledonia is a collectivity governed by Title XIII of the Constitution, they all have very strong economic ties with mainland France, and all are in a situation where their foreign trade is largely, and often predominantly, with mainland France;

---

2 APC, decision no. 2016-CC-01 of 10 March 2017.

3 APC, decisions n° 2023-CC-02 and 2023-CC-03 of 24 October 2023.

4 APC, decisions n° 2022-CC-02 of 8 June 2022 and 2016-CC-04 of 5 December 2016.

5 APC, decision no. 2019-CC-02 of 6 June 2019.

6 APC, decision no. 2022-CC-03 of 14 June 2022.

- All of them come under the French administration for the regalian aspects and come under or originate from a French administrative organisation model for the non-regalian aspects;
- to varying degrees, all have local consumption patterns based largely on imports, very often from mainland France;
- all tend to be less integrated into their regional economies than they are with the European economy, despite the distance;
- all have a high degree of economic concentration, given their island location[7] and the small size of their local economies;
- All of them face a recurring problem of the cost of living, recognised by numerous official reports but which is struggling to be resolved;
- All are highly dependent on maritime trade, and this dependence was exacerbated during the Covid-19 pandemic.

16. Given these economic and local organisational similarities, it is obviously tempting to engage in a little comparative exercise on the way in which the various competition authorities in charge of the *CMA CGM/Bolloré Logistics* merger have dealt with situations which, although not identical, are at least similar.

17. With regard to the definition of the relevant markets, the three authorities consider that there is a market for the maritime transport of containers, and within this there are two main segments, *deep-sea* and *short-sea*. Given the location of the territories concerned and CMA CGM's business, they all focus on the deep-sea shipping segment.

18. Traditionally, this market is defined geographically by lines, each end of which is a large geographical area (for example, a Europe-North America line).

19. On the European side of the line, there may be a Northern Europe/Southern Europe segmentation, which only the Commission will examine, without formally adopting it.

20. With regard to the regions at the other end of the lines concerned, a traditional segmentation would have been to consider Central America and the Caribbean, the east coast of Africa and the islands of the Indian Ocean, and finally Australia and Oceania.

21. However, the authorities will all be looking at substitutability between ports in the French overseas departments and collectivities and other ports in the region, and within the French overseas collectivities at substitutability between ports:
    - Are the ports of Guadeloupe, Martinique, Saint-Martin and French Guiana substitutable with other Central American and Caribbean ports for *deep-sea* activity from Europe, and are they substitutable with each other?
    - Are the ports of Réunion and Mayotte substitutable with other ports in East Africa and the Indian Ocean for *deep-sea* shipping from Europe, and are they substitutable with each other?

---

7 With the exception of French Guiana, which is obviously not an island from a geographical point of view, but whose economy is nonetheless very similar to an island economy.

- Are the ports of Papeete and Nouméa substitutable with other ports in Australia, New Zealand and Oceania for *deep-sea* activity from Europe, and are they substitutable with each other?

22. The authorities will all conclude that it is appropriate to examine the market situation on routes departing from or arriving in Europe and connecting *each of* the territories concerned.[8] They will rule out both the substitutability of ports in the territories concerned with other ports in the region, and the substitutability of ports in the territories concerned with each other. This market delimitation is based on various types of criteria:
    - geographical isolation and distance from other ports, particularly in Polynesia and New Caledonia;
    - the absence or limited nature of *feeder* services (short-distance services) between the territories concerned and other ports in the region, and between the ports concerned themselves (excluding Mayotte);
    - taxation, specific to each territory, and the absence of fiscal integration with the other countries in the region; this is one of the reasons why, despite the existence of a line between Auckland and Papeete, the two ports are still considered to be non-substitutable;
    - specific customs obligations for the territories concerned;
    - the minority nature of trade with the region compared with trade with mainland France, whether for reasons of standards, tax or customs, or consumer preferences;
    - the absence of many international forwarding agents from the ports in the territories concerned.
23. Ultimately, CMA CGM's position will be analysed in all cases on the Europe-French Polynesia, Europe-New Caledonia or Europe-Caribbean or Indian Ocean routes.
24. Similarly, the APC will also examine the operation on the North America-French Polynesia, Asia-French Polynesia and Oceania-French Polynesia routes.
25. For each line, the authorities will have to make a distinction according to the direction of travel, as the economics of the two directions are not at all the same given the much higher volume of imports than exports for the territories concerned.
26. As regards freight forwarding, the three authorities will again consider a market by territory to assess the position of Bolloré Logistics and CEVA Logistics.
27. In all cases, *the competition authorities will easily rule out the existence of competition problems arising from the horizontal combination between Bolloré Logistics and CEVA Logistics*. The combined market share of the two entities remains moderate, and the new entity will each face a significant number of competitors.
28. *The authorities' attention will be focused on the vertical integration between carrier CMA CGM and freight forwarder Bolloré Logistics.*

---

8 Some will formally define the market in this way, others will choose to formally leave the market open but nevertheless conduct the analysis on this segmentation.

29. By way of comparison, the various authorities have noted the following CMA CGM market shares in excess of :

Authority	Line	Market share of CMA CGM
APC	Europe → French Polynesia	90-100] % with VSA
APC	French Polynesia → Europe	[90-100] % with VSA
APC	French Polynesia → Asia	[90-100] %
ACNC	Europe → New Caledonia	[60-70] %
CE	Northern Europe → Martinique	[90-100] % with VSA
CE	Martinique → Northern Europe	with VSA
CE	Mediterranean → Martinique	[70-90] %
CE	Martinique → Mediterranean	[70-90] %
CE	Northern Europe → Guadeloupe	[90-100] % with VSA
CE	Guadeloupe → Northern Europe	with VSA
CE	Mediterranean → Guadeloupe	[70-90] %
CE	Guadeloupe → Mediterranean	[70-90] %
CE	Northern Europe → French Guiana	with VSA
CE	French Guiana → Northern Europe	with VSA
CE	Mediterranean → French Guiana	with VSA
CE	French Guiana → Mediterranean	with VSA
CE	Europe → Réunion	[70-80] % with VSA
CE	Europe → Mayotte	[70-80] %

30. It should be noted that, in calculating CMA CGM's market share, both the APC and the European Commission have taken into account all the participants in the *Vessel Sharing Agreements* (VSAs) of which CMA CGM is a member, considering that the other VSA members can only exert a lesser competitive pressure.

31. Given the existence of such very strong positions on some of the upstream markets, APC examined whether this situation was likely to lead to the exclusion of some of Bolloré Logistics' freight forwarding competitors on the downstream market.[9] It therefore sought to assess the risk of an "input foreclosure", the input here being the transport of goods by *deep-sea* containers.

32. In other words, the risk envisaged by the APC is that the new group, through its control of container transport in certain markets, could deprive competing freight forwarders of access to its volumes (total foreclosure) or at the very least force them to work on less favourable terms than those enjoyed by its now integrated freight forwarder.

33. Firstly, the APC eliminates this risk on routes out of Polynesia, regardless of CMA CGM's market share, because volumes there are too low for a possible

---

9 The APC first examined the risk of "customer foreclosure", i.e. the risk that the newly integrated freight forwarder would address its volumes only to CMA CGM and exclude other carriers. However, it quickly dismissed this risk, noting that the limited downstream market share of Bolloré Logistics and CEVA Logistics would not allow them to implement such a policy successfully.

squeeze out of this very narrow segment to have any impact on the structure of the freight forwarding market.

34. *The APC therefore focuses on routes to Polynesia*, and more specifically on the only route to Polynesia on which CMA CGM has a significant share, namely the Europe-Polynesia route, on which CMA CGM, together with the other VSA participant Marfret, has a market share of over 90%.

35. The APC rules out the risk of total foreclosure on the grounds that the new group would not have the capacity to absorb the additional volume that this would represent for freight forwarders. It therefore focuses on the risk of partial foreclosure.

36. According to the APC,

> *A situation of partial foreclosure could take the form of discriminatory treatment organised by the new entity against freight forwarders competing on the market for the organisation of freight transport. Such a strategy could take the form of CMA CGM granting less advantageous commercial conditions e.g. prices, volumes, quality of service, etc.) to the new entity's competitors, thereby reducing their competitiveness on the market for the organisation of transport vis-à-vis the new integrated entity. This type of partial foreclosure of the market may dissuade rivals from entering or expanding on the market, or even encourage them to leave it.*[10]

37. The APC notes that CMA CGM owns 12 of the 13 vessels of the VSA "Panama Direct Line" (PAD), which account for more than 90% of the Europe-Polynesia route, with the remainder divided between 4 competitors. In addition, the PAD alone accounts for 42% of all the volumes handled by forwarding agents in Polynesia and, with its weekly frequency and transport time of just 30 days, is the preferred method of supply from Europe. The APC points out that the PAD is the only maritime option for perishable products imported from Europe.

38. APC concludes that the PAD is a critical input for freight forwarders. It adds that with only one vessel out of the 13 in the PAD, the other PAD member, Marfret, would not be able to absorb the volumes needed to provide an alternative for freight forwarders in the event of a dispute between them and CMA CGM.

39. APC also examined dynamic competition, looking in particular at the possibility of an existing competitor such as MSC, or a potential competitor such as Maersk or SeaTrade, launching a direct service without transhipment to compete with the PAD. It notes, however, that the market's history shows outflows rather than inflows, and that the depth limit of the port of Papeete constitutes a barrier to entry for operators wishing to use large vessels (over 2,400 TEU).

40. Finally, the APC points out that the forwarding agents present in Polynesia are too weak to be able to exert counter-power on the new group.

41. It concluded that the new group would have the capacity for partial foreclosure.

42. It then examines the incentives for implementing such a policy and concludes that the new group could increase its downstream volume and the

---

10 APC, decision no. 2024-CC-01 of 31 January 2024, § 107.

corresponding margin without necessarily incurring significant upstream costs. It concludes that the new group could have economic incentives to implement such a policy.

43. In addition, the APC also notes a risk that the integrated freight forwarder could have access to the conditions that its competitors offer to CMA CGM.

44. Faced with these risks identified by the APC, CMA CGM proposed a structural commitment consisting of the disposal of the Bolloré Logistics Polynesia business and the Bolloré Logistics France business relating to French Polynesia.

45. However, the commitment provides for two exceptions concerning certain current multidestination customers of Bolloré Logistics, either appearing on a limited list or carrying out less than of their business with CMA CGM to or from French Polynesia, in order not to artificially "break" the new group's relationship with global customers.

46. This commitment to sell is coupled with a commitment to strict separation and to maintain the business, under the supervision of a trustee, between the *closing of* the merger and the sale.

47. Furthermore, CMA CGM undertakes not to develop any freight forwarding activity to or from French Polynesia for a period of 5 years, with the exception of the global customers already mentioned.

48. The reasoning followed by the APC appears to be very similar to that of the European Commission. The Commission also looked at the risk of total or partial input foreclosure in the island markets (and Guyana) in which CMA CGM, alone or in VSA, has a significant share of the line. It also successively examined the capacity and incentives to implement such a policy. Like the APC, it also examined dynamic and potential competition, as well as the possible countervailing power of buyers, and came to the same conclusion. Finally, it also eliminated the risk of customer foreclosure.

49. However, in the case of Réunion, the Commission has agreed not to take into account the whole of the VSA in which CMA CGM participates, because the partner in the VSA is the MSC group, which has 10 of the 16 vessels in the VSA and is particularly powerful in the region. CMA CGM's individual market share of less than therefore eliminates the risk of input foreclosure.

50. Despite CMA CGM's significant individual market share to Mayotte, the Commission also ruled out the risk in this territory given the strong pressure from MSC and potentially stronger competition from Maersk.

51. In response to the Commission's concerns, CMA CGM proposed structural divestiture commitments for Bolloré Logistics' activities in Martinique, Guadeloupe, Saint-Martin and French Guiana.

52. Lastly, the ACNC also carried out an analysis of partial foreclosure of inputs, centred on the PAD service, considered more efficient by freight forwarders and customers than the MSC competitive service, which takes longer and involves transhipment in Sydney.

53. Unlike the Commission and the APC, however, the ACNC authorised the transaction on the basis of behavioural commitments, considering that they would

be sufficient to remedy the risk of foreclosure while preserving the efficiencies linked to vertical integration.

54. The purchaser has undertaken to reserve at least of its volumes from Europe for third-party freight forwarders, not to discriminate on price against competing freight forwarders by proposing general terms and conditions and accessible and transparent pricing scales, and to set up a programme to raise awareness among the management and sales teams of the entities concerned. These commitments are for a period of 5 years, which may be extended twice by the ACNC for all or part of the commitments, giving a maximum duration of 15 years. An independent trustee will be responsible for monitoring the commitments.

55. It is quite rare to be able to carry out a comparative examination of the same merger by several authorities with sufficiently similar market situations. The exercise shows a high degree of parallelism in the analyses and conclusions, even if a divergence ultimately emerged as to how to resolve the competition risks identified.

56. In addition to its interest, the *CMA CGM/Bolloré Logistics* decision is particularly important for the APC in that it marks the first time that the APC has reviewed a global transaction in parallel with other authorities as part of a *multi-filing of* the acquirer.

57. The fact that the APC, which is still a very young authority, not even 10 years old, has been fully aligned with the European Commission since its first "parallel decision", not only on the analysis and conclusions but also on the remedies, is indicative of the authority's growing power, in terms of positioning, expertise, management of the entire review process and ability to convince the parties of the need to fully address its competition concerns.

Regulating Merger Transactions in French Polynesia: Lessons from the *Brasserie de Tahiti Case*

Arthur Helfer[*], Igor Simic[**] and Marie Minetto[***]
Bredin Prat

I. Introduction

1. Since 2015, the Polynesian Competition Authority (hereinafter the "APC") has issued around thirty merger control decisions.
2. Decisions no. 2023-CC-02 and no. 2023-CC-03,[1] adopted in the *Brasserie de Tahiti* case after an in-depth examination, is an important milestone in the first ten years of the APC's existence.
3. These decisions provide guidance on how parallel transactions should be examined, particularly when they are carried out by the same acquirer (II.).
4. They also illustrate the competition issues specific to overseas territories, particularly related to the high prices of mass consumer products (III.). Finally, they

---

* Arthur Helfer, Partner, Bredin Prat.
** Igor Simic, Partner, Bredin Prat.
*** Marie Minetto, Associate, Bredin Prat.

1 Decision no. 2023-CC-02 relating to the acquisition of sole control of SARL Toa Distribution, which operates a predominantly food supermarket under the name "Happy Market Faa'a", SARL Société de gestion d'approvisionnement et de marketing, which recently obtained authorisation to open a predominantly food Happy Market supermarket, and SCI Ofai by Brasserie de Tahiti; Decision no. 2023-CC-03 on the acquisition of exclusive control Société de distribution et d'exploitation commerciale, which operates a hypermarket-type business with a predominantly food product offering under the Hyper U banner in Pirae, by Brasserie de Tahiti.

confirm the importance, for competition authorities operating in these territories, of having tools complementary to the control of concentrations (IV.).

II. The Polynesian Competition Authority's handling of parallel transactions

5. The analysis of so-called 'parallel' concentration operations can be carried out using different methods (A.). In its decisions of October 24, 2023, the APC applied the so-called 'combined' approach, which involves examining each operation while considering the changes induced by the other (B.).

A. *Rules applicable to the analysis of "parallel" mergers*

6. The competition authorities are regularly called upon to rule on mergers notified at the same time and likely to affect the same markets.

7. When they can be described as "interdependent" – i.e. single transactions[2] – such transactions are the subject of a single decision analysing the overall change in market structure brought about by "all of these transactions taken together"[3]

8. Conversely, when the conditions are not met to classify them interdependent, such transactions must – in principle – be analysed separately.[4]

9. While the consequences of this principle are clear from a procedural point of view (transactions must be notified separately and notification thresholds assessed individually), its implications from the point of view of competitive analysis on the other hand, are less obvious – the question then being how to take account, in substance, of any competition problems *specifically linked to the combination of these transaction.*[5]

10. Historically, the competition authorities have provided different answers to this question.

---

2 Aut. conc. *merger control guidelines*, § 77 et seq. See also: Consolidated Jurisdictional Notice of the European Commission on the control of concentrations between undertakings (hereinafter "*the Consolidated Jurisdictional Notice*"), § 38 et seq. As the European Commission points out in its Consolidated Jurisdictional Notice, this approach "reflects the philosophy that [...] transactions that constitute a whole in terms of the economic objectives pursued by the parties should also be assessed the context of a single procedure". For the record, under French law, transactions are qualified "interdependent" if (*i*) they are carried out by the same acquirer, (*ii*) there is a conditional link between them, and (*iii*) they each constitute, in themselves, a concentration (see in particular : Aut. conc. *merger control guidelines*, § 79). It should be noted that for the European Commission, transactions are said to be "interdependent" when they are linked by a reciprocal conditionality, but can only then be qualified as a "single transaction" if they also result in "an acquisition of control of one or more undertakings by the same person(s) or undertaking(s)" (criterion of the 'result' of transaction, which is the first of the three conditions set out in the Autorité de concurrence's guidelines).

3 Consolidated Jurisdictional Notice, § 40.

4 At the European level, paragraph 40 of the consolidated Judicial Communication states that 'as long as the different operations are not interdependent and the parties would complete one of the operations even if all the others failed, it seems appropriate to assess these operations individually under the merger regulation.

5 The risk then is that each decision is limited to analysing the effects specific to one of the operations (without taking the other into account) and that none of the decisions ultimately analyses the scenario in which the parallel operations are *all* carried out.

11. In several cases, the authorities have applied a *rule known as "combined treatment"*.[6]This approach, which consists of considering each of the transactions in the analysis of the other, is based on a single post-merger scenario, common to all the decisions and in which all notified transactions are carried out.

12. It therefore essentially involves examining the notified operations as if they were interdependent, without considering any potential intermediate scenarios in which only certain operations would be carried out.

13. In other cases, the competition authorities have opted for *a so-called "priority rule*", which consists of dealing with transactions sequentially, following an order of priority derived (generally) from the date of notification of each transaction.[7] This approach, which is now favoured by the Commission[8], is based on the following principles involves analysing the first notified transaction *without taking account* of the second and then examining the second *on the assumption that the first will be implemented.*[9]

---

6 This approach was notably adopted by the European Commission in the PriceWaterhouse/Coopers & Lybrand decisions (decision IV/M.1016 of May 20, 1998) and KPMG/Ernst & Young (decision COMP/M.1044 of February 4, 1998). See also: decisions COMP/M.2389 of December 20, 2001 (Shell/DEA) and COMP/M.2533 of December 20, 2001 (BP/E.ON); decisions COMP/M.1630 of January 18, 2000 (Air Liquide/BOC) and COMP/M.1641 of February 9, 2000 (Linde/AGA); also see Geraldine Emberger, John Kemp, The EU Commission clears a merger between two leading audit and accounting companies addressing the issue of possible collective dominance (Price Waterhouse / Coopers & Lybrand), May 20, 1998, e-Competitions May 1998, www.concurrences.com/39374; also see Michael Rauber, The German Competition Authority clears a merger in the energy market with remedies, including the divestiture of gas stations, pipeline supply contracts, and the granting of infrastructure access for aviation fuel delivery at Frankfurt airport (Shell/DEA), December 19, 2001, e-Competitions December 2001, www.concurrences.com/25731; also see Wilmer Hale, The EU Commission approves an acquisition by an industrial gas producer of part of a rival subject to complex remedies (Air Liquide / BOC), January 18, 2000, e-Competitions January 2000, www.concurrences.com/121756.

7 This approach was notably implemented by the Commission in the decisions KarstadtQuelle/MyTravel (decision COMP/M.4601 of May 4, 2007) and TUI/First Choice (decision COMP/M.4600 of June 4, 2007), as well as in the decisions TomTom/TeleAtlas (decision COMP/M.4854 of April 14, 2008) and Nokia/NAVTEQ (decision COMP/M.4942 of July 2, 2008), in the decisions Western Digital Ireland/Viviti Technologies (decision COMP/M.6203 of November 23, 2011) and Seagate/HDD Business of Samsung (decision COMP/M.6213 of November 19, 2011), and more recently in the decisions Dow/DuPont (decision COMP/M.7932 of March 27, 2017); Chemchina/Syngenta (decision COMP/M.7962 of April 5, 2017) and Bayer/Monsanto (decision COMP/M.8084 of March 21, 2018); also see Stanislas Martin, Collective Dominance: The European Commission revisits the analysis of collective dominance in the travel sector and reaffirms the principle that an initial notified concentration is examined without considering the consequences of a second operation immediately following in the same sector (TUI/First Choice-KarstadtQuelle/MyTravel), June 4, 2007, Concurrences No. 3-2007, www.concurrences/13822; also see John Gatti, Mary Loughran, The European Commission clears an acquisition in the navigable digital map databases sector (Nokia/NAVTEQ), July 2, 2008, e-Competitions July 2008, www.concurrences.com/37707; also see www.concurrences.com/59294, also see www.concurrences.com/59294, also see www.concurrences.com/86504.

8 See notably: Bertuzzi Alexandre, Blanco Thomas Soledad, Forestier Laurent, Goppelsroeder Marie, Hariton Cyril, Impellizzeri Alessandra, Kovo David, Tew Julia, Vande Walle Simon, Deisenhofer Thomas, Ramondino Marco, Bove Roberto, and Notaro Giovanni, The EU Commission Conditionally Approves a Merger in the Seeds, Traits and Pesticides Markets to Protect Innovation and Product Competition (Bayer/Monsanto), March 21, 2018, e-Competitions March 2018, Art. N° 114428. Also see the press release issued by the European Commission in connection with the aforementioned Bayer/Monsanto decision (Mergers: Commission Clears Bayer's Acquisition of Monsanto, Subject to Conditions, March 21, 2018).

9 Even today, the two approaches coexist and are alternately used by competition authorities, as illustrated by the Western Digital/Hitachi and Seagate/Samsung cases, which were analyzed using the combined approach by the Federal Trade Commission and the priority rule by the European Commission (see notably: Agathoklis Murino Andrea and Tennis Bradley T., Mergers in the Information Technology Industry in the US: An Overview of Leading Cases, January 22, 2015, e-Competitions US Mergers in IT, Art. N° 70930).

14. The advantages and limitations of each of these approaches are now well known.

15. On the one hand, the combined approach is generally advocated for reasons equal treatment and fairness, as a sequential analysis may prove unfair to the party notifying its operation second, which must then bear alone the risk of prohibition, or the burden of commitments linked to the combination of operations[10]

16. As merger control is prospective in nature, some authors also point out that there is nothing to prevent the examination of a transaction from taking into account changes in the market structure that are likely to occur in the near future and with sufficient certainty, in particular as a result of the existence of another transaction – provided that the latter is notified (and therefore known) before the first transaction is authorised.[11]

17. On the other hand, several arguments are traditionally put forward in favour of the "priority" rule:

- a literal reading of the texts applicable to merger control, which (more often than not) only mention the possibility of examining several transactions together in the specific case of interdependent transactions (or in the equally specific case of successive transactions);
- a concern for consistency between procedure and substance, which would mean reserving the global approach for cases where the transactions concerned are to be analysed in a single decision; or
- the desire to avoid prohibiting several operations on the sole grounds that their accumulation poses a problem, even though some of them, taken in isolation, could (or even should) be authorised.

18. Finally, the analysis of decision-making practice shows that the combined approach presents a risk of instrumentalisation of merger control perspective of a combined analysis of the two transactions may encourage third parties active in the same sector to notify another transaction at the same time solely to impede the first.[12]

B. *Special case of parallel transactions notified by the same purchaser*

19. These decisions provide an interesting illustration of the problem so-called "parallel transactions", where the transactions concerned are carried out by the *same acquirer*.

---

10 See for example: Levy Nicholas, *European Merger Control Law: A Guide to the Merger Regulation*, edition n° 21, Matthew Bender Elite Products, LexisNexis, November 2024, § 10.06 et seq.

11 This argument was also recently taken up by the General Court of the European Union in the case of *EVH et al. v. European Commission*, in which the applicants criticised the Commission for having analysed *together* parallel transactions for which the classification as a "single transaction" had nevertheless been rejected and which were consequently the subject of two separate decisions (Trib. EU, 17 May 2023, 11 judgments, *EVH*, aff. T-312/20, et al; then Trib. EU, 20 December 2023, 11 judgments, *EVH v Commission*, Case T-53/21, et al.)

12 Such a scenario is far from being purely theoretical, illustrated by the *PriceWaterhouse/Coopers & Lybrand* (decision IV/M.1016 of 20 May 1998) and *KPMG/Ernst & Young* (decision COMP/M.1044 of 4 February 1998) cases, in which the European Commission was only able to authorise one of the transactions because the second was abandoned during the investigation of the first.

20. In this case, Brasserie de Tahiti planned to carry out four transactions,[13] each formalised by a sale agreement dated the same day. Three of these transactions were interdependent. The fourth, on the other hand, could not be linked to the first three because there was no conditional link between them.

21. Noting the lack interdependence between the first three operations (on the one hand) and the fourth (on the other), the APC logically adopted two decisions.

22. Then, noting the simultaneity of the four transactions, the APC decided to use the combined approach.[14]In accordance with this approach, the APC therefore analysed the two sets of transactions together, using in each decision a single post-transaction scenario in which all the notified transactions were carried out.[15]

23. Methodologically, this choice was not straightforward. The combined approach, already debated in the case parallel transactions envisaged by different acquirers (see *above*), seems in our view even more debatable in the case of parallel transactions notified by the same acquirer.

24. In such a case, it could be imagined that the competition authorities would *require* the acquirer, before or at the time of the formal notification of the transactions concerned, to state explicitly:
   - whether it intends to carry out all the transactions together or only some of them (in particular if the competitive analysis would not allow the competition authority to approve all the transactions notified to it); and
   - in the latter case, which operation it intends to prioritise.[16]

25. This choice, made at the pre-notification stage, would allow the competition authority either to consider the transactions as mutually conditional and therefore interdependent, or to treat them separately, both procedurally and substantively,

---

13 Acquisition a first seller of (i) all the shares in SARL Toa Distribution, (iiSARL Société de gestion d'approvisionnement et de marketing, and (iii) société civile immobilière Ofai, and acquisition from a second seller (iv) all the shares in SA Société de distribution et d'exploitation commerciale (a company operating a hypermarket in Pirae under the Hyper U name).

14 See § 14 and 15 of decision no. 2023-CC-02 ("Simultaneously with this transaction, the BDT group notified the Autorité of a second merger consisting of the acquisition of all the shares in SA Société de distribution et d'exploitation commerciale, which operates a hypermarket in Pirae under the Hyper U banner. The competitive analysis carried out in this case therefore takes account of this second notified transaction"). See also sections 14 and 15 of Decision 2023-CC-03.

15 See § 35 of decision no. 2023-CC-02, in which the APC notes that *the notifying party, after completion of the notified transactions, will be a new player on the food market through the target company, a second target which is to be active in the same sector in the near future* **and a third target (which is the subject of a second notified transaction***)* *active on the food retailing market. The transaction is therefore likely to produce horizontal effect.*

16 From a strictly legal point of view, it is also possible to wonder whether the use of the combined approach, in a case where the transactions (*i*) are notified by the same acquirer and (*ii*) are each subject to a condition precedent linked to obtaining the authorisation required under merger control, is not such as to characterise, *in itself*, a de facto conditionality, and therefore to render the transactions interde- pendent – in particular if the agreements materialising each transaction are concluded on the same day (as the case here) or if the transactions were all part of the same overall economic project (see in this sense Aut. conc, *Guidelines on merger control*, § 81-82: "In order to determine whether several transactions are effectively interdependent, the Authority may take into account several factors, such as the formalisation of the transactions in a single instrument, the simultaneous conclusion of their agreements or the declarations made by the parties themselves, in any form of communication (internal documents, public statements, etc.)").

by applying a priority rule dictated by the acquirer's own choice – and which the dates of formal notification could, where appropriate, reflect.[17]

26. In *Brasserie de Tahiti*, there were certainly two legitimate reasons for using a combined approach.

27. The first reason is that, in the case in point, a sequential analysis of the two transactions *would probably not have led to a different result* from the one arrived at by the APC by applying a combined approach.

28. As the acquirer was a new entrant on the downstream market for food retailing, and as the two targets were present exclusively on this market but in different geographical areas, the transaction did not raise any horizontal competition concerns, regardless of the approach adopted.

29. Similarly, at the vertical level, an analysis of the decisions shows that evaluating each transaction separately would likely have led to the same outcome – that is, requiring behavioral commitments of the same nature as those ultimately proposed by the acquirer. The risks of foreclosure identified by the APC were not primarily related to the size of the market shares acquired by the acquirer in the downstream markets, but to the very principle of vertical integration, in a sector where many players are already vertically integrated.

30. The second reason for using a combined approach in the *Brasserie de Tahiti* case is the *clear economic unity* of the two notified transactions, which was reflected in the purchaser's decision to sign the various sales agreements and then notify the transactions on the same day each time, as the decisions expressly point out.

31. While the APC's choice in this case appears fully consistent and justified, it would be interesting to know whether it would follow the same approach if the choice of method had a greater impact on the outcome of its analysis.

III. Analysis of mergers in overseas territories

32. The specific characteristics of the overseas territories, which have been pointed out on numerous occasions by the competition authorities (A.), largely explain the analysis carried out by the APC in its decisions of 24 October 2023 (B.).

A. *The specific features of competition in the overseas territories*

33. The competition authorities have long been aware of the unique characteristics of the economies of the French overseas territories, whether in the context of merger operations[18] or in the context of their consultative activities.

---

17 In choosing to carry out a combined analysis of the two transactions, the APC also departed from the practice other competition authorities and, in particular, the European Commission. By way of illustration, mention may be made of the decisions relating to the concomitant acquisitions of Fels (decision M.2495 of 21 February 2002) and Ytong (decision M.2568 of 9 April 2002) by Haniel, notified respectively on 4 September 2001 and 16 October 2001 – a case in which the Commission applied the priority rule by analysing the first transaction without taking account of the second, then the second by including in the analysis the increase in market share linked to the first.

18 See for example Aut. conc. métropolitaine, décision n° 20-DCC-72 du 26 mai 2020 relative à la prise de contrôle exclusif de la société Vindémia Group par la société Groupe Bernard Hayot, *see also* French Competition Authority, The French Competition Authority clears merger in food retail sector in La Réunion after in-depth

34. In its first opinion on the mechanisms for importing and distributing FMCG products in the overseas departments in 2009, and then again in its opinion on the operation of competition in overseas France in 2019,[19] the Autorité de la concurrence métropolitaine (hereinafter "ADLC") has drawn up a detailed report on the functioning of competition in overseas France.

35. In these opinions, the ADLC noted that prices were still significantly higher in the overseas territories than in mainland France (between 7% and 12.5% according to 2015 INSEE figures)[20]

36. According to the ADLC, these price differences, which are particularly high for FMCG products (between +28% and +38% on average in 2015), can be explained by by various characteristics specific to overseas economies, including:
   - the isolated and narrow nature of most of these economies, resulting in very high approach and supply costs;
   - the existence of a large number of tax measures designed to protect local production[21] which have the effect of increasing prices for consumers;
   - the high concentration of players in the food retail market; and
   - the presence of vertically integrated players in the supply chain, many of whom also have exclusive import agreements.

B. *Taking these characteristics into account in the case of Brasserie de Tahiti*

37. The two decisions handed down by the APC on 24 October 2023 are part of the context described above. They illustrate the particular attention paid by the competition authorities to the problems of combating the "high cost of living" and, as such, to the competition problems linked to vertical integration of the main players in food retailing.

38. In these decisions, the APC carries out a classic vertical analysis a methodological point of view. After recalling the triptych of capacity-incentives effects analysis, it examines the risks of input foreclosure (on the one hand) and customer foreclosure (on the other).

39. The specific analysis of each of these risks shows, however, that the APC has been extremely vigilant in the context described above.

40. *As regards the risk of input foreclosure*, the APC notes that Brasserie de Tahiti holds a very strong position on the upstream markets, in particular the drinks supply market. It also notes that this position is protected by a number of specific

---

investigation, subject to conditions (Vindémia / Groupe Bernard Hayot), 26 mai 2020, e-Competitions May 2020, Art. www.concurrences.com/95118

19 Aut. conc. métropolitaine, avis n° 19-A-12 du 4 juillet 2019 concernant le fonctionnement de la concurrence en outre-mer.

20 *Ibid*, p. 16 et seq.

21 French Polynesia has introduced various types of measures to protect local industrial and agricultural production. These measures are both tariff-based (collection of import duties and taxes, such as the local development tax or the consumption tax for prevention) and non-tariff-based (import bans or quotas, particularly in the agricultural sector).

features of the island territory, such as regulatory advantages, local development taxes and various import bans.[22]

41. Given the small number of outlets that the purchaser will have after the completion of the two transactions, a conventional analysis in another context would, however, probably have led the APC to exclude (or strongly relativise) the risk of input foreclosure by Brasserie de Tahiti – such a strategy could not be profitable given the extremely limited market share that the latter will hold downstream.

42. On the contrary, in this case, the APC identifies a risk of foreclosure linked to the interest that the new entity could have in increasing the price of its products and/or in reducing the conditions of sale of its products vis-à-vis its downstream competitors,[23] which would ultimately lead to higher prices for consumers in competing shops.

43. *Regarding the risk of customer foreclosure*, the APC again seems to be increasing its vigilance. Despite the acquirer's limited position on the downstream market after the transaction,[24] the APC confirms the existence of a risk customer foreclosure on the grounds that one of the target shops (Hyper U in Pirae) is among the 10 largest customers of Brasserie de Tahiti's competing importing wholesalers.

44. Notwithstanding the extremely high asymmetry between the market shares held by the new entity on the upstream market and on the downstream market,[25]the APC therefore concludes there is a risk anti-competitive vertical effects justifying commitments – drawing inspiration on this point from the decision-making practice of the ADLC in the food distribution sector on Reunion Island.[26]

IV. Limits to behavioural commitments and the importance of instruments complementary to merger control

45. Drawing the consequences of its analysis summarised above, the APC made the authorisation of the two transactions conditional on the implementation of behavioural commitments (A.). The specific limitations of this type of commitment illustrate the need for the APC to have additional tools that go beyond the strict framework of merger control (B.).

---

22 Decisions no. 2023-CC-02, § 58 and 59 and no. 2023-CC-03, § 62 and 63.

23 Decisions no. 2023-CC-02, § 66 and 67 and no. 2023-CC-03, § 69 and 70.

24 In addition, the analysis of horizontal effects shows that the downstream market share of the Brasserie de Tahiti group will remain moderate, at less than . Traditionally, a risk of customer foreclosure is analysed when the new entity a market share of more than 30% on the downstream market.

25 Brasserie de Tahiti is a new operator on the downstream market and will only own three shops following the transactions, one of which is not yet in operation.

26 See Aut. conc. métropolitaine, decisions no. 20-DCC-72, cited above; no. 18-DCC-142 of 23 August 2018 relating to the acquisition of exclusive control of the companies SDRO and Robert II by the company Groupe Bernard Hayot; no. 11-DCC-134 of 2 September 2011 relating to the acquisition of exclusive control of assets of the Louis Delhaize group by the company Groupe Bernard Hayot. [27] Decisions no. 2023-CC-02, § 89 and no. 2023-CC-03, § 92.

A. *Commitments accepted by the APC as part of the decisions commented on*

46. In this case, the commitments proposed by Brasserie de Tahiti and accepted by the APC[27] cover in particular:

- a commitment to separate the Brasserie de Tahiti group's predominantly food retailing activities from its other activities (*commitment no. 1*);
- an undertaking by Brasserie de Tahiti to maintain the same conditions in the upstream market (where its position is particularly strong) regarding competing downstream retailers as it does with regard to the target shops, together a (more general) guarantee of non-discriminatory access to the drinks produced by the acquiring group (*undertaking no. 2*); and
- a commitment by Brasserie de Tahiti to ensure that the target shops acquired and operating downstream reserve a minimum proportion of their bottom of the beverages concerned for the group's upstream competitor suppliers, accompanied (again) by a general guarantee of non-discriminatory access to the target shops for the group's upstream competitors (*commitment no. 3*).
- These commitments are for a period of 5 years, renewable once, and are accompanied by the appointment of an agent to monitor them.
- Given the importance of vertical integration issues in overseas France, particularly in the FMCG distribution sector, and given the small market shares acquired by Brasserie de Tahiti downstream (making any structural divestment commitment unthinkable), the use of such behavioral commitments is easy to understand.
- In practice, however, the ability of these commitments to address (in the long) the risks identified by the APC in its decision seems limited.

B. *The inherent limits to such commitments*

47. Generally speaking, behavioral commitments give rise to much debate as to their effectiveness, particularly from the point of view of their implementation and monitoring by the competition authorities.[28]The latter are generally not in favour of them and consider that their use should be exceptional.[29]

48. Classically, behavioral commitments are intended to preserve the competitive structure of markets *for the time being*, particularly in dynamic and evolving markets, in order (*i*) to give the various operators concerned (competitors, customers, suppliers) time to commit to strategies that will eventually enable them to compete effectively with the new entity, or (*ii*) to facilitate the entry of new operators into the market. This temporary function, which distinguishes behavioral commitments from structural commitments, is linked in particular

27 Decisions No. 2023-CC-02, § 89 and No. 2023-CC-03, § 92.

28 See the Autorité de la concurrence's 2019 study on behavioural commitments.

29 Commission Notice on remedies acceptable under Council Regulation (EC) No 139/2004 and under Commission Regulation (EC) No 802/2004, § 17.

to the fact that behavioral commitments are by definition always adopted for a fixed period.[30]

49. Given the structural characteristics of the overseas economies, the behavioral commitments made mandatory by the decisions in question will probably not be sufficient on their own to resolve the competition issues identified *above*.

50. Other instruments will therefore have to be mobilised, including by the APC, to deal with these issues. In addition to the traditional powers that the APC has in the same way as most competition authorities (control of anti-competitive practices and consultative powers in particular), the APC will probably be required, in this respect, to mobilise the powers that it has under the control of commercial developments, powers that enable it, in particular, to give an *ex ante* opinion on all new commercial establishments or shop extensions with a surface area exceeding 300 m².[31]

51. The APC's activity in this area is already exponential, with 13 decisions handed down in 2024 (compared with just three in 2023).

52. There is no doubt that this dynamic will continue in the coming years, complementing the active role played by the APC in merger control.

---

30 *Ibid.*

31 *French Competition Code*, art. LP 320-1-1.

The Oversight of Commercial Arrangements in French Polynesia: A Case Study of Carrefour Moorea

Matthieu Pujuguet*
Belgian Competition Authority

I. Presentation of the commercial development control mission

A. *Legal framework and objectives*

1. Introduced in 2015 by the *Polynesian Competition Code*, which came fully into force in February 2016, the control of commercial developments is governed by articles LP 320 to LP 320-5 of the Code. These provisions introduce the principle of prior authorisation for the opening or extension of any retail business with a sales area in excess of 300 m². The aim is to ensure that projects do not create or significantly strengthen a dominant position. As we shall see, this *a priori* control of structures, although original in the case of internal growth operations such as the opening or extension of retail premises, is useful the context of an island territory with a number of specific characteristics. However, certain conditions must be met in order to give this *a priori* control all the scope it deserves – and no more. We will also expand on this last point below.

---

* Matthieu Pujuguet is Senior Advisor to the Presidency, in charge of international affairs and coordination of sector enquiries for the Belgian Competition Authority. Previously, he was Acting General Rapporteur at the Polynesian Competition Authority.

2. There are three main objectives behind the introduction of the control of commercial developments and its incorporation into the remit of the Autorité, alongside the more usual tools (a priori control of mergers, sanctioning anticompetitive practices and advisory role):

   - *Preserving local competitive dynamism*

     One of the major challenges is to prevent the formation of overly powerful monopolies or oligopolies, which could harm commercial diversity and impose restrictive practices on local consumers and suppliers. Ultimately, the question arises as to whether this mission is also aimed at directly protecting small operators, who are often fragile in the face of powerful economic groups, even when they are not very efficient. If so, this would be a significant departure from the fundamental missions of competition law – even if the adaptation of the latter to the specific characteristics of the islands should lead us to take seriously the legitimacy such departures *from the doxa.*[1]

   - *Maintaining a territorial balance economic activity*

     In French Polynesia, and specifically in Tahiti where commercial land is scarce, there is a high risk of retail concentration in the most accessible or profitable areas. This phenomenon can lead commercial depopulation in other areas, exacerbating territorial inequalities. A priori control can make it possible to distribute retail infrastructures fairly, insofar as the Authority is required by law to take account commercial development considerations in its decisions[2] – something that the Government Commissioner is quick to point out if it is forgotten.

   - *Protecting consumers*

     By guaranteeing a multiplicity operators on the market, this *ex-ante* control of commercial developments is supposed to lead to competitive prices, better quality of service and a commercial offering tailored to the needs of local populations.

3. This system is original in that it controls internal growth operations, which are not usually covered by competition law.[3] It is shared only with New Caledonia and may be justified by certain characteristics specific to these island territories.

---

1 At the very least, it is important not to refrain from asking questions a priori, even when the answers seem obvious to a competition law practitioner accustomed to the context of the major continental economies.

2 Without, however, having the technical competence or expertise to do so – which is a major weakness of the system. If the Authority is to take Polynesian regional planning into account in its decisions to control commercial developments, there is no indication of how this should be done or what criteria should be used. In this respect, the Authority could consider drawing up guidelines on the subject, which would introduce predictability for the parties or third parties, while facilitating the work of the Authority's investigating staff, who would then know how to carry out the task assigned to them *ex officio* by the *Competition Code*. should be noted, however, that this consideration of planning is presented as a possibility for the Authority. The Authority may well decide to ignore this invitation, albeit at the risk of being criticised for doing so by the Government Commissioner precisely for reasons of technical incompetence. In fact, this is the line it has followed until now.

3 Or at least not at *first*, as administrative authorisations are in most cases (as in mainland France, for example – although the market configuration there is very different from that in French Polynesia) based on considerations relating to commercial town planning.

B. *Specific features of the Polynesian economy*

4. The Polynesian economy has a number of characteristics that set it apart from markets in mainland France. These include

- *Exacerbated insularity*

  French Polynesia is made up of 118 islands spread over an oceanic area equivalent to that of Europe. Each island constitutes an isolated local market, where inter-island trade is often complex and costly. These geographical barriers can exacerbate trade imbalances, favouring the dominance of already well-established operators. In particular, the double insularity experienced by islands other than Tahiti is a distinctive and rather unique factor. This term refers to the fact that the constraint is twofold for these islands, as they face double insularity in that all (or almost all) goods are unloaded (or produced) on the island of Tahiti before being subsequently shipped to the other archipelagos

- *Significant economic concentration*

  Like other sectors in French Polynesia, given the narrowness of the downstream market, the food and non-food retail sector is dominated by a few large groups, including the "Wane group" (Carrefour, Champion, Carrefour Market, Easy Market, etc.). These players control not only distribution, but also major segments of logistics and supply, limiting the ability of new entrants to compete effectively.

- *A scarcity of land*

  The availability of land for commercial use is limited. This constraint increases installation costs for new operators and can discourage local initiatives. On the other hand, the dominant groups, already having access to strategic locations, enjoy a decisive competitive advantage.

  These specific features impose a sort of vigilance on the part of the Authority to ensure that the market operates competitively. In addition, beyond this purely competitive objective, the *ex ante* control provided for also makes it possible to take account of the socio-economic effects of projects, such as job creation or the effects on local infrastructures – even if the Authority's analysis does not focus primarily on these elements.[4]

C. *The authorisation procedure*

5. The control of commercial developments follows a rigorous procedure, organised in several stages, each designed to ensure a full and impartial assessment of the projects submitted. the Authority itself states on its website:

> *In order to maintain a sufficiently competitive climate in the retail sector, the Polynesian Competition Authority controls the creation and modification of commercial premises. To this end, any person wishing to create, extend*

---

4 When the Authority examines the projects, these can at least taken into account as efficiency gains, offsetting (at least in part) any anti-competitive structural effects.

or transform a retail area larger than 300 square metres is subject to the provisions of Competition Code and the Authority's internal regulations. The operations concerned by the control of retail premises are defined in article LP 320-1 of the [Competition Code].[5]

1. Project notification

6. Any project developer wishing to open, extend or convert[6] a sales area exceeding 300 m² must therefore notify the Polynesian Competition Authority of their project. This notification includes a detailed file that must include:

- A precise description of the project, including its location, sales area and the products or services proposed;
- an economic impact , describing the potential effects local competition, employment and regional planning;
- the commitments or remedies that the project sponsor is prepared to implement to limit any competitive risks identified.

7. As with merger control, which is also an *ex ante* control of structures, and with which the task of controlling commercial developments has many similarities, this notification stage is essential to enable the Authority to prepare itself to examine the specific issues at stake in the project. As a result, it is often accompanied by a pre-notification phase, the scope of which is less defined in the regulations, and which enables the notifying party to calibrate and detail its application until it can be considered formally notifiable to the Authority. This phase consists of a period of informal exchanges between the project promoter and the general rapporteur (and more generally, the Authority's investigation department). This pre-notification phase is not without its challenges, since once the application has been formally notified and declared complete by the procedure department after verification by the appraisal department, the deadlines (for appraisal and decision) officially begin to run, leaving little room for manoeuvre. However, it would be possible to declare the file incomplete as long as it does not comply with the requirements of the *Competition,* and in particular the relevant appendix. On the other hand, the *Competition Code* does not explicitly provide for the possibility of suspending the investigation deadlines if a request for information sent to the notifying party results in the latter taking too long to reply, as is the case, for example, in in-depth merger inspections.[7]

---

5 Actually LP 320-1-1.

6 It should be noted that the law has been slightly rewritten to give greater clarity to the types of transactions concerned. There was some debate about the case of shop extensions where the sales area, as defined by the *Competition Code*, was less than 300 m² prior to the transaction and became than this threshold as a result of the transaction. The current wording is now sufficiently explicit for it to be understood that these projects do fall within the scope of a priori control.

7 However, the use of this mechanism is limited and cannot serve as a viable solution for a poorly prepared file. It is therefore in the best interests of both the notifying party and the Autorité to make the most of all the possibilities offered by the pre-notification phase, especially as the considerable freedom allowed for discussion can make it particularly effective and a real heuristic.

2. Competitive analysis

8. Once the draft has been notified, the Authority publishes a press release within 5 working days (on its website and/or in the *Official Journal*). Interested third parties then have 7 days to submit any comments they may have. This is followed by the competitive analysis phase or, to put it another way, the examination of the file as notified. This examination may be simplified or in-depth.

9. In the first case, which is supposed to concern the simplest applications, the Authority's decision is taken very quickly, no later than 15 working days after the date of notification of the complete application. The investigation period is short, often limited to a maximum of 7-10 working days. Once the investigation has been completed, a meeting of the college must be convened and held to rule on the case. The decision taken by the panel is then notified to the party submitting the project, which has 15 calendar days in which to assert its right to protection of business secrets. The Authority must also publish the meaning of the panel's decision within 5 working days of the decision. Finally, once the business secrecy protection procedure has been completed, the Authority publishes the decision (on its website and/or in the *Official Journal*), and forwards it to the President of French Polynesia.

10. In the second case, the decision period is extended to 35 working days the date on which the Authority is notified of the complete file. The procedure is different in that it is partially adversarial: once the first phase of the investigation has been completed, the investigating department produces a report which it sends to the notifying party and the Government Commissioner. The notifying party and the Government Commissioner then have 5 working days to submit their observations in response. The rest of the procedure is identical to that of the simplified review (apart from the time limits), with a meeting convened and held, publication of the meaning of the decision, notification of the decision and procedure for protecting business secrets, and finally publication of the decision. There is one major difference, however: the panel meeting is not open to the notifying party or to any witnesses under the notified review procedure, whereas it is under the in-depth review procedure.

11. The appendix to the notification form for a commercial development operation provides more information on the criteria for simplified review. These may include:

> *where the notifying party can demonstrate that it is in a situation in which there is only a very slight likelihood of an effect on competition in the market or markets concerned [...] The notifying party may then dispense with completing section 4 of the notification form and limit itself to a presentation of the reasons why the transaction is not likely have an effect [,] on competition in the market or markets concerned. Such a situation may correspond to:*
>
> *1° A change of sign by the same operator with no change of activity and no other change of structure [...] ;*
>
> *2° A takeover by a new operator with no capital ties to an existing company in French Polynesia;*
>
> *3° An extension to the sales area of less than of the existing area, in any case limited to 150 m².*

12. The purpose of the Authority's appraisal is to assess impact of the project on the market concerned. This assessment may include:

- *Quantitative studies*

  Econometric models can be used to simulate the effects of the project on market shares, prices and supply.

- *Consultations with stakeholders*

  The AMF's investigating department may seek comments from the parties concerned, whether local economic operators, local authorities or consumer associations.

13. This phase may also include requests for additional information or modifications to the project. For example, the AMF's appraisal department may ask the project sponsor to reduce the sales area or propose commitments to mitigate the competitive risks identified, for example at the report stage of the in-depth review.

3. Authority's decision

14. At the end of the investigation phase, a meeting of the AMF Board is held to decide on the notified project. At this meeting, the Authority may take one of the following decisions:

- *Unconditional authorisation*

  If the project does not present any significant competitive or territorial risk, it is authorised as notified.

- *Authorisation subject to conditions*

  If moderate risks are identified, the Autorité may accept commitments or modifications to the project (reduction in sales area, restrictions on certain products, etc.) proposed by the notifying party during the procedure. It may also order the notifying party to take any measures necessary to ensure that sufficient competition is maintained after transaction.

- *Refusal of authorisation*

  If the competitive risks are deemed too high and the remedies proposed are insufficient, the project is prohibited.

15. In reaching its decision, the Autorité Article LP 320 of the French *Competition Code*, which states that: "Operations relating to commercial development likely to have a substantial effect on competition are prohibited".

II. Case study: The *Carrefour Moorea* case

A. *Context and issues*

16. In 2022, Société commerciale de Moorea, a subsidiary of the Wane group, submitted request for authorisation to set up an 1,830 sq.m Carrefour supermarket in Maharepa, in the commune of Paopao, on the island of Moorea. The aim of the project was to consolidate the presence of the Wane group in Moorea, which is already the leading retailer in French Polynesia. Present in Moorea through its Champion brand, the group already held a significant share of the local market, giving it a potentially dominant position in several areas of the island.

17. The Carrefour Moorea project had clear strategic objectives for the Wane Group:

- *Strengthening the Wane Group's retail offering on the island*

  With a slightly more upmarket positioning and a broader, more diversified offering than Champion, Carrefour aimed to capture a varied customer base, including residents and tourists.

- *Increasing the presence of the Carrefour brand in the Pacific Islands through franchising*

  The Maharepa site was intended to serve as a model for other possible developments in French Polynesia and elsewhere in the Pacific.

18. However, several issues emerged during the appraisal, calling into question the viability of the project in terms of its economic and competitive impact.

19. *The main difficulties concerned:*

1. *Greater concentration*

   The Wane group already controlled a significant share of the food retail market in Moorea through its Champion brand and its other commercial activities. The arrival of Carrefour would have reinforced this dominance, further reducing the room for manoeuvre of smaller local operators.

2. *Impact on competitors*

   At the time, two competing projects were being developed on the island (Painapo Market and Happy Market). These projects, led by independent operators, aimed to diversify the retail offering on Moorea. The arrival of a new player as powerful as Carrefour would probably have led to the abandonment of these initiatives, reducing competitive diversity and limiting choice for consumers.

3. *The risk of discrimination in procurement*

   The Wane group, which also operates in the supply chain, was likely to favour its own brands to the detriment of competing shops. This risk of discrimination would have further weakened the position of independent players.

4. *Potential impact on local economy*

   Although the project put forward arguments such as the creation of jobs and a broader offer for consumers, these advantages were deemed insufficient to offset the risks identified. In particular, the Authority feared that small and medium-sized local businesses, which are often essential to the island's economy, would be crowded out.

B. *The Authority's arguments as developed in the decision*

20. In its decision of 23 June 2022, the Polynesian Competition Authority concluded that the Carrefour Moorea project presented significant risks competition and the local economy. This analysis was based on the following factors:

- *Strengthening of the dominant position*

  The Wane group already had a very large market share in the food distribution sector in Moorea. The establishment of Carre- four would have increased this share by a further 10 to 20 points, consolidating a dominant position that would have been difficult for other operators to challenge.

- *Substitution for competing projects*

  The Authority identified the risk that the arrival of Carrefour would result in the abandonment of the competing projects mentioned *above*. Painapo Market and Happy Market, which were in the development phase, would have had little chance of survival in the face of such a powerful player. This substitution would have been detrimental to the diversity of the retail offering, an essential element in maintaining healthy competition on the island.
- *Risk for the competition*

  The project would have reduced the intensity of competition in Moorea by eliminating potential players, while consolidating the dominance of the Wane group. This reduction in competition could have led to an increase in prices and a reduction in the quality of services offered to consumers.
- *Risk of discriminatory treatment of downstream competitors by Wane group companies active in the upstream markets for the supply and import of food products*

  As a result of the strengthening of the Wane group in Moorea and throughout French Polynesia through this project, there was an increased risk that the Wane group's import and supply would treat Carrefour's competitors on the downstream market – of which they are the essential suppliers – with less favourable treatment and service. It would have been rational to act in this way, the companies in the group had the means to do so, and lastly, the consequences of such a strategy would have been substantial.
- *Inadequacy of proposed remedies*

  Following the inspection department's report, the Société commerciale de Moorea proposed commitments to mitigate the risks identified. These included a reduction in the food sales area and undertakings concerning the fair treatment of downstream competitors. However, the Authority considered that these remedies were insufficient to remedy the structural problems identified. They would have ensured sufficient competition or prevented foreclosure effects on independent operators.
- *Cumulative effects*

  Finally, the Authority considered the cumulative effects of the project on the local economy. If Carrefour had been authorised, the market would have been permanently unbalanced, limiting opportunities for new entrants for a long time to come and increasing consumer dependence on a small number of players.

C. *Scope of the decision*

21. Similar to the decision to authorise, with injunctions, the proposed takeover of the *Taporo* ships by SNP, a subsidiary of the Martin group (Brasserie de Tahiti) in 2017, the prohibition of the Carrefour Moorea project for lack of satisfactory commitments marked a turning point in the application of controls on commercial developments in French Polynesia. This decision demonstrated the Authority's ability intervene proactively to protect a fragile island market.

22. *There are many lessons to be learned from this decision:*

1. *Protecting competitive momentum*

   By preventing excessive market concentration, the Authority has preserved the opportunity for independent operators to develop their activities, thereby ensuring greater commercial diversity. In the final analysis, it is competition, which was threatened by the Carrefour Moorea project, that has been preserved, in accordance with the Authority's explicit mission.

2. *Strengthening competition regulation and asserting the independence of the AMF*

   This decision has sent a clear signal to operators: commercial development projects are examined with the utmost rigour, paying particular attention to local circumstances and potential effects on competition. Above all, by opposing a major economic player such as the Wane group, the Autorité has confirmed its determination to exercise its role impartially, regardless of the economic or political pressures that sometimes arise during investigation or at board meetings.

3. *Creation a robust and coherent local decision-making practice*

   This decision constitutes an important reference for future competitive analyses in French Polynesia. It provides a methodological framework and evaluation criteria that can be reused to examine other similar projects, in particular with regard to the evaluation of

23. commitments in the event of a major competitive risk being identified, or for developments relating to the behaviour of subsidiaries of an integrated group active upstream and the consequences of this behaviour on players competing other subsidiaries of the integrated group active on the downstream market. In this respect, the reasoning was very similar to that used in the *Taporo* case in 2017 (merger, phase 2), in which similar issues had arisen.

III. Review and outlook: What does the future hold due diligence on commercial development projects in French Polynesia?

A. *Putting things into perspective: Controlling commercial developments in the French overseas territories (excluding French Polynesia and New Caledonia)*

24. In the other French overseas territories, the control of commercial development operations is quite different. It is not a matter for the Autorité de la concurrence (which is also responsible for sanctioning anti-competitive practices and controlling mergers in overseas France). Furthermore, the objective is not primarily to prohibit transactions "likely to have a substantial effect on competition". Rather, it is a regulation relating to commercial planning, which involves players such as the Commission départementale d'aménagement commercial (CDAC) or the Commission nationale d'aménagement commercial (CNAC). Any project creates or extend a retail development must first be submitted to the CDAC, which is

made up of representatives of the State, local authorities and qualified individuals. CDAC decisions may be appealed to the CNAC.

25. It is true that the Lurel Act of 20 November 2012 reaffirms the importance of competition in combating the high cost of living – a very specific issue in overseas France. It also imposes regulation of trade margins in strategic sectors (notably food and fuel) and encourages the emergence of new players to break up rent-based situations. However, the Autorité de la concurrence does not have the power to take *ex ante* decisions on commercial development, so competition concerns, if they exist, are not the sole guide to the authorisation or prohibition decisions taken by the Commissions. Environmental considerations (standards, impact on car traffic, etc.), land-use planning and employment are at least as important – with a great deal of attention paid to food distribution networks, which are seen as a key variable in reducing the high cost of living in the French overseas territories.

26. Regarding commercial development projects, the Autorité de la concurrence can only issue advisory opinions, possibly accompanied by recommendations, or deal *ex post* with the anti-competitive effects of authorised projects, which it does not fail to do where necessary.

B. *Strengths and limitations of the Polynesian system*

27. The control of commercial developments is an essential tool for preserving the economic and competitive balance in a (doubly) insular economy such as French Polynesia. However, although this system has proved its usefulness in emblematic cases such as the Carrefour Moorea case described *above*, it has structural and operational limitations that sometimes reduce its effectiveness.

1. Strengths of the system

a) Protecting fragile local markets

28. Regulation makes it possible to preserve effective competition in an environment where geographical and economic barriers encourage concentration. By preventing the big groups from being outrageously dominant, it guarantees opportunities for local operators and, ultimately, it is the competitive dynamic that is preserved, to the benefit of the end consumer, who is offered better prices and a diversified, higher-quality offering.

b) Reducing territorial imbalances

29. The control of commercial development limits the excessive concentration commercial infrastructures in certain areas, thus contributing to a more harmonious development of the territory, again to the benefit of the final consumer and his consumption behaviour.

c) Adapting to the specific characteristics of islands

30. Unlike continental regulations, this scheme takes account of the specific economic and geographical features of the islands, making it a tool for French Polynesia.

2. Identified limits

a) Control thresholds may be too low

31. Currently set at 300 m², this threshold creates an administrative overload, forcing the Authority to examine many insignificant cases, despite the introduction of a simplified examination when the *Competition Code* was amended. This situation diverts precious resources that could be better spent on projects with a strong economic impact. After years of practice, it is no doubt now possible to reach a consensus on this issue, which was not possible during previous reforms of the *Competition Code*, when the 300 m² threshold was ultimately left unchanged.

b) A risk of procedural complexity

32. Although the procedure is clear, project promoters, particularly small operators, may perceive this control as an excessive administrative constraint, thus slowing innovation and economic initiative. In this respect, while the introduction of a simplified review is a step in the right direction, it would undoubtedly be possible to reduce the complexity of the procedure for the notifying party, as well as for the staff of the Polynesian Competition Authority. In particular, at the risk of having to amend the law again, one may question the necessity of a session of the board for this type of decision (at the very least concerning the simplified procedure).

c) What justification is there for ex ante control of internal growth operations?

33. It's a debate that has agitated many economists. Some take offence at the fact that an institution can stick its nose into internal growth operations (without buying a competitor, and therefore without the immediate disappearance of a player), which are supposed to be neutral for competition (from their point of view). While the debate can be taken seriously and may lead to an increase of flexibility in the procedures relating to this transaction, the fact remains that the major cases handled by the Autorité have demonstrated with utmost clarity that these transactions do indeed have undeniable effects on current and potential competition. It would be a bad decision to simply abolish the dis- positive on the grounds that it would distance the Authority from the heart and essence of competition law. The specific nature of Polynesia's territory and its competitive dynamic (with certain players already holding very strong positions in the predominantly food retailing sector) gives this tool its full legitimacy.

d) How to consider the possibility offered to the Authority to analyse the effects of transactions on regional planning?

34. As it stands, it must be said that the AMF's investigation department did not consider itself competent to deal with this issue. This is understandable, as these considerations are so far removed from competition law. Important though they are, they would need to be addressed by specialists.

3. Reform proposals

35. To maximise the efficiency and usefulness of the system, several reforms can be envisaged. These proposals aim to lighten the administrative burden, strengthen the methodology and optimise the impact of regulation on local economic development.

a) Increasing the control threshold

36. Raising the threshold to *500 m²* would enable the Authority to refocus its efforts on projects with a real economic and competitive impact. This increase would contribute to:

- reduce the volume of notifications for minor cases, thereby freeing up resources ;
- encourage small operators to develop their projects without fear of disproportionate administrative obstacles;
- strengthen the legitimacy of the Authority's actions, by focusing on the most strategic projects.

b) Increasing regional cooperation

37. Strengthening the partnership with New Caledonia (which has the same jurisdiction) could benefit both jurisdictions by sharing feedback, pooling certain resources (in particular, for training rapporteurs and developing econometric or mapping tools),[8] aligning procedures and investigation – thus creating a harmonized framework that would give stakeholders visibility and predictability on a regional scale.

c) Greater transparency and consultation

38. After many years of practice, it is undoubtedly time for the Authority to consider drawing up and publishing guidelines, which will provide greater visibility on the procedure and criteria for assessing projects.

d) Suggest that the effects on spatial planning be analysed by systematically requesting the opinion of the DCA (Direction de la construction et de l'aménagement) or another competent authority

39. In this case, it is recommended that the law be enshrined, and recourse to it should be limited to cases undergoing in-depth scrutiny.

e) Evaluate the advisability of introducing simplified decisions, without going before the college

40. For cases where there is no competition at stake, it would be possible to streamline and shorten procedures by allowing the general rapporteur to take the authorisation

---

8 The technical assistance of the French Competition Authority could be sought here, as it has developed considerable expertise in commercial mapping and analysis of catchment areas (for proposed mergers).

decision directly, without convening a meeting of the college. This is done in many authorities for simplified merger control cases and relieves the workload of the college. In this case, the decision is ultra-simplified (less than one page) and contains few (if any) reasons. This approach seems to be consistent with the principle of good use of resources, in that it allows more resources to be allocated to cases that require them. In this respect, the case of the Polynesian Authority is striking, with many *ex-ante* control decisions and opinions (all of external origin), but few decisions on anti-competitive practices (mainly due to lack of time).

f) Regularly evaluate the effectiveness of the scheme

41. The idea is to set up a periodic assessment (every 3 or 5 years, for example). This would enable the system to be adapted, if necessary, to economic and social developments in French Polynesia. In addition to monitoring the effects of decisions (e.g. 2 years later) on competition and the local economy, such a periodic assessment could include wider consultation with stakeholders in the sector to identify any necessary adjustments.

IV. Conclusion

42. The *Carrefour Moorea* case is a perfect illustration of the importance of controlling retail developments in French Polynesia to preserve the competitive dynamic, which is sometimes threatened by large-scale projects likely to have a lasting effect on the operation of the market and the incentives to enter it. This system is unique. It is the result of a clear political will, and the Polynesian Competition Authority strives to apply it as effectively as possible. This tool is effective most of the time, and cannot be called into question outright, given the specific territorial and competitive characteristics of French Polynesia, and particularly the well-established positions of certain major players in the predominantly food retail sector. However, it needs to be adjusted to meet current and future challenges.

43. **Why reform?**

- To reduce the administrative burden and concentrate efforts on projects with a significant impact, as the Authority is overwhelmed by projects with little competitive impact.
- To improve the quality of competitive analyses, guaranteeing increasingly robust and transparent decisions.
- To strengthen regional cooperation and consolidate best practice in the Pacific.

Makalio Folituu

President of the Polynesian Consumer Protection Association Te Tia Ara

*"We've come so far, and expectations are high"**

French Polynesia has had a Competition Code for ten years now. As a representative of the interests of Polynesian consumers, what is your assessment of this first decade?

The introduction of competition rules can only be welcomed by an association such as ours, as it can help improve consumer protection by regulating corporate behaviour. As far as the initial objective is concerned, I therefore welcome this innovation.

In actual fact, since we've come to the point of taking stock, it has to be said that things haven't quite gone to plan. To date, the Polynesian Competition Authority (APC) has struggled to investigate cases of interest to consumers. One case in point is our referral of a suspected tied sale in the telecoms sector. We submitted it in 2021, but to date it has gone unanswered! While I can understand the argument that it takes time to conduct a thorough procedure, I cannot accept that nothing has happened after 40 months. When I asked the Chairman of the Authority about this delay, she replied that she had no power over the investigating departments. I understand the need to maintain a separation between the appraisal department and the board to guarantee the independence of the appraisers, but it is absolutely essential that this department be managed and that the objectives be met.

Seen from the outside, this gives the impression of an administration working with the tools and methods of the past, whereas we are soon entering the second quarter of the twenty-first century. Perhaps it's time to strengthen the Authority's human and organisational resources to bring it up to date with the times. With this in mind, I have already proposed the introduction in the regulations of an enforceable time limit for investigating a referral. Without this, it will be impossible to meet consumers' expectations, of which there are many.

However, the APC has made a number of decisions in favour of consumers...

Fortunately. Rulings on practices in the funeral services sector, a case opened on our initiative, and in the mobile telephony sector for residential customers represent real progress for all Polynesians.

---

* Interview conducted by Yannick Lecornu.

Similarly, the work of the APC in controlling mergers in the health, tourism, and import sectors has helped to avoid the excesses of the past. More recently, when CMA CGM wanted to take over Bolloré Logistics, the APC made the transaction conditional on the resale of Bolloré Logistics' maritime activities in French Polynesia. It was a courageous decision – we all know how powerful these major international groups can be – and a strategic one for the future of supplies to the territory. Thanks to this decision, the competitive structure of the market has been preserved, to the benefit of the consumer. For an island economy like ours, and considering the weight of our imports, this is essential.

As you can see, I do recognise the progress made in recent years. I know that Competition law and the APC have helped to clean up economic life. But we had such a long way to go, and expectations are high. By way of example, if I go back for a moment to the undertakers' case, the APC sanctioned the companies. They were found guilty of colluding at the expense of Polynesian consumers. Now, to obtain compensation, the aggrieved consumers must take their case to another court. Put yourself in the shoes of the victim of this anti-competitive agreement – it's Kafkaesque! I hope that the Assembly of French Polynesia will take the necessary measures to facilitate compensation for victims, and that the APC will quickly step up to meet the challenges ahead.

The role of the APC remains unclear to the general public. Do you know the reasons for this? Is it because consumers' interests are not sufficiently taken into account by the APC?

It's understandable that the public is still not very familiar with the role of the APC. You know, if you ask the general public about the role of the Overseas Issuing Institute (IEOM) or the Territorial Audit Chambre (CTC), you're likely to get similar answers. And yet, like the APC, these organisations respond to very concrete needs and, to a certain extent, impact people's lives through their actions.

Not everyone is fortunate enough to have studied, to have access to information and to understand the workings of all these bodies. It's for these people that we are committed to Te Tia Ara on a daily basis.

If the APC suffers from a lack of notoriety, it's primarily due to the nature of the issues it deals with. When the APC expresses an opinion on the concentration of five-star hotels, it doesn't excite the crowds because very few Polynesians frequent this type of establishment. As far as imports are concerned, it's a very technical issue and part of the economy that's invisible to the general public. On the other hand, if you start talking about post office boxes, telephone subscriptions, the price of medications, TDL or shopping in supermarkets, you'll immediately attract the attention of consumers because they'll feel directly concerned.

Then there's the problem of communication. The language of the APC is not accessible to the average person. When you use terms like "structural injunctions" or "exclusive import rights", you've already lost the majority of people. APC needs to learn to express its positions simply, without sacrificing legal rigor. This can be done. As a member of the Economic, Social, Environmental, and Cultural Council (CESEC), I can tell you that there are technicians who are well-versed in this exercise of outreach. As Boileau said, "*What is well conceived is clearly stated, and the words to say it come easily.*"

Isn't it also the role of the Te Tia Ara association to facilitate this transmission to the general public?

You're right. It's also our responsibility to Polynesian consumers. To do this, it is essential that the APC includes us more in its communication strategy, that it gives us the keys to understanding the meaning of its decisions so that we can relay them to the population.

Over the past few years, we've taken a few steps towards a lasting partnership. In 2021, for example, I took part in the recruitment panel for the APC president. This jury was essentially made up of people from outside the government, which enabled us to make an independent decision. It was also an opportunity to learn more about Competition law and the role of the APC. In short, to share our knowledge.

Since then, we've had other opportunities to talk, but the timing has been too unpredictable. For the APC, it's essential to maintain dialogue with Te Tia Ara, but also with civil society as a whole. As I said earlier, I'm also heavily involved in the CESEC. Here too, we need to talk about competition more often. The APC must fulfil this mission.

Te Tia Ara's recent successes, notably before the administrative court, attest to the growing recognition of consumer rights in case law. Does your approach to the APC pursue the same objective?

With very limited resources, our association is concerned with all consumer issues. From the introduction and extension of a bank balance that cannot be seized, to the fight against undue commission charges on bank accounts, we have achieved a number of successes for the benefit of all Polynesians. Our association has also been a member of the Personal Over-Indebtedness Commission since it was set up in 2012. The follow-up of all these cases requires constant involvement from our team of volunteers.

This is also one of the reasons why I would like to develop closer ties with the APC's teams. We could even consider having an office on their premises, so that we can work cross-functionally and benefit from the rapporteurs' expertise.

By submitting a first request to the APC in 2021, I also wished to take a first step towards this cooperation, and I am now patiently awaiting the fruits of this initiative. I am convinced that it is by working together that we will be able to improve the economic efficiency of our territory and the protection of our consumers in the future.

Quiet on Set! Competition in Progress…

In this book, which traces the first ten years of the Polynesian Competition Code, we wanted to give a voice to all the players involved, particularly the representatives of the economic actors. However, through a remarkable collective discipline worthy of a perfect competitive equilibrium, the latter preferred to avoid speaking out in any way that might alter the harmony of the market or a dominant position... on the debate. Rather than seeing this as a risk of collusion, the reader is invited to interpret this unanimous silence as a resounding sign of great satisfaction and deep contentment. After all, the absence of comment is not only a highly obliging gesture, but also a form of eloquence in itself.

PART III

Contribution to the Regulation of Key Economic Sectors

The Opening of the Polynesian Telecommunications Sector to Competition

Antoine Callot*
Grenoble Administrative Court

1. The Polynesian Competition Authority (APC) did not initiate the opening up of the telecommunications sector to competition, which was a political decision prior to its creation by the Bill of the Assembly of French Polynesia no. 2015-2 of 23 February 2015. On the other hand, its deployment coincided with the arrival on the market of the incumbent operator's first competitors in the early 2010s, which quickly made this one of its preferred areas of intervention. At a crucial time for their survival, the aim was to prevent the incumbent operator from using its commercial behaviour or influence strategies to hinder the reform and development of its competitors. The APC therefore played its dual role of competition watchdog and advisor to the government. Telecommunications have already given rise to three contentious decisions and nine opinions.[1]
2. This article takes a look back at this trend, recalling how the opening to competition was successful, but under supervision (I), the role played by the APC, in a virtuous dynamic with the administrative judge who also took up the issue of competition (II), and finally the challenges ahead to ensure the sustainability of this reform (III).

---

* Antoine Callot is an administrative judge and public rapporteur at the Administrative Court of Grenoble. He previously served as deputy general rapporteur at the Polynesian Competition Authority. The views expressed are personal and do not represent these institutions.

1 See appendices 1 and 2 for details.

I. Successful opening to competition, but under scrutiny

A. *A network industry long governed by a public monopoly*

3. Like energy and transport, the telecommunications sector is a network industry, requiring heavy investment in infrastructure (submarine cables, masts and antennas, copper or fibre optic networks), and therefore high fixed costs. For this reason, most countries have opted to create monopolies to roll out this network, the incumbent operators, which have often taken the form of public companies such as the Office des Postes et Télécommunications (OPT) of French Polynesia. As they are highly vertically integrated, these companies have been active in all segments, from infrastructure to the provision of services to end consumers (individuals and businesses).

4. Investment was all the more important in French Polynesia because, like many of its Pacific counterparts, it is both a very isolated and very large territory (76 inhabited islands over 2.5 million km²). This "double insularity" required, and still requires, very substantial public support from the country and its financial partners, particularly to deploy submarine cables to remote archipelagos, but for a long time this has led to very high tariffs for consumers.

5. Gradually, however, certain segments of these markets have been opened up to competition. Indeed, while it is economically rational for certain "essential infrastructures"[2] such as wireline or submarine cable links, when they have the character of a natural monopoly, to remain a monopoly and not be duplicated, other segments, such as the provision of services to consumers, have every interest in being open.

6. From the 1990s onwards, market economies gradually put an end to the monopoly situation of incumbent operators, by distinguishing between monopoly activities, subject to regulation, and market activities.

B. *Late opening to competition, but a remarkable success for consumers*

7. The telecommunications sector in French Polynesia was opened up to competition more recently and only partially, or more so in any case than in the European Union, the United States and most Pacific island states (Australia, New Zealand, Samoa, Tonga, Fiji, Papua New Guinea, Solomon Islands, Vanuatu, for example). This situation is regularly denounced, notably by three reports on OPT and its subsidiaries published in 2008 by the Chambre territoriale des comptes, and has led to censure by the Conseil d'Etat[3] The first texts date back to 2003, but the actual opening up, i.e. the arrival of competitors to OPT, dates back to 2011 for the Internet and 2013 for telephony services.

---

2 An infrastructure to which access is essential in order to carry out a competitive activity in an upstream, downstream or complementary market, but which cannot be reproduced under reasonable economic conditions by competitors.

3 In its decision no. 343991 of 2 February 2011, Haut-commissaire de la République et société Digicel, the Conseil d'Etat censured a provision of a local law limiting foreign investment in cell phone operators.

8. But this opening up quickly became synonymous with a spectacular drop in prices, both for mobile telephony and Internet access, encouraging a veritable explosion in usage at a strategic time when access to new technologies, such as broadband, is essential, both for private use and for a competitive economy. According to data from the Institut de la Statistique de la Polynésie Française (ISPF), while the general price index rose by 11.5% between 2014 and 2024, the index for telephony and internet access services fell spectacularly, by 62.7%.[4]

9. Today, three players coexist:
   - Onati, a subsidiary of OPT, which operates the Vini brand and has a legal monopoly on external telecommunications (submarine cables) and wireline networks (copper and optical fibre), and a de facto monopoly on domestic networks on most islands other than Tahiti, Moorea and Bora Bora.
   - Pacific Mobile Telecom (PMT), which started trading in 2013 under the Vodafone brand and has its own network on the main islands, but roams on the Onati network on the other islands.
   - Viti, which started out as a fixed-line Internet service provider in July 2011 and has been offering mobile voice, SMS and data services since early 2020.

10. The challenge for the competition authority has been to keep pace with this trend, without forgetting the public service objectives of guaranteeing a service at a reasonable price to all users, regardless of their location.

C. *A monitored process*

11. The telecommunications sector is a *club* business, in which each operator has its own subscriber network. It's also a mature market, with a customer equipment rate approaching 100%. Whereas the incumbent public operator has built up its network with public funds, and has built up its customer base in the absence of any competition, new entrants have to finance their network with private funds, and win their customers from among those of the incumbent operator. The result is a very strong competitive disadvantage at the time of market entry, which explains why, after enjoying a legal monopoly until 2003, the incumbent continued to enjoy a de facto monopoly, despite the opening of the market to competition, for almost another ten years. While by its very nature, the incumbent operator has no incentive to encourage competitors to enter the market, it is essential to ensure that it does not abuse its dominant position to limit mobility between operators, and to enable competitors to build up their own customer base on their own merits.

12. When the incumbent operator remains active in both network management and the retail market, it also has a special responsibility to offer its wholesale services to its competitors in the downstream market at a non-discriminatory rate, which falls within the scope of tariff regulation.

13. For this reason, over and above intentions, the success of regulatory opening to competition and the monitoring of anti-competitive practices are crucial.

---

[4] Source: ISPF website. See also the article in the daily Tahiti Infos of 27 December 2021, "Le coût de la vie sauvé par la téléphonie".

Competition law is precisely designed to ensure that the rules of the game are respected. In this context, competition authorities act *ex post*, to condemn and correct infringements of the rules through injunctions, financial penalties or the negotiation of structural and behavioural commitments. In fact, the decision-making practice of competition authorities shows that most incumbent operators were sanctioned for a wide range of anti-competitive practices when the sector was opened up to competition[5] and has led to record fines in France, of over €350 million (40 billion CFP Francs) for France Télécom in 2015, for example, in relation to its offers to businesses. The authority also has an *ex ante* advisory role for the regulator, which is all the more crucial when technical and technological choices, however seemingly insignificant, have a competitive impact. This applies not only to pricing, but also, for example, to the need or otherwise to duplicate infrastructures, or the choice of whether or not to use satellite constellations for Internet access in remote areas.

14. These various issues have all, on various occasions, been addressed by the litigation decisions and opinions handed down by the APC.

II. A privileged area of intervention for the fledgling APC

A. *Several litigation decisions concerning suspected anti-competitive practices*

1. The incumbent operator's defence of its customers and Commitment Decision No. 2018-PAC-01

15. On the occasion of its first contentious decision of 6 June 2018, the APC looked into practices implemented in the mobile telephony sector aimed at residential customers.

16. Despite the market entry of a new operator, in 2017 the incumbent operator Vini – then a subsidiary of OPT – still held around 85% by volume of the retail market for mobile telephony services. PMT then called upon the APC to assess practices it deemed to be anti-competitive, in particular price differentiation on the retail market for mobile services between "on-net" (internal to the Vini network) and "off-net" (between operators) calls, without justification by the underlying costs of these services, and foreclosure of retail customers through excessive commitment periods and certain clauses in Vini's loyalty program. The combined competitive risk of these practices was to dissuade consumers from opting for the new entrant's offers, reinforcing the *club* effect on the incumbent operator's network.

17. Given the urgency of this situation, which could result in the new entrant's outright exit from the market, the Authority obtained commitments from Vini to behave in a non-discriminatory way towards its competitors, and not to take advantage of its

---

5 For example: abusive use of customer files, price discrimination between calls on its network and calls outside its network, price scissors, refusal of access to infrastructures, obstruction of the installation of equipment by an alternative operator on unbundled lines, lack of transparency between the activities of network manager and operator, etc.

dominant position on the market, for example by limiting commitment periods to an excessive length, or differentiating its tariffs between calls to its own network and to those of competitors.[6]

2. The issue of roaming services and access to the incumbent operator's network by new entrants

18. In French Polynesia, local roaming is known as "asymmetrical". Onati is the only operator to have deployed a network across the entire territory. It is therefore also the only operator able to offer its competitors (PMT and Viti) access to its network on islands that they have not yet covered. This position presupposes open access, under fair and non-discriminatory pricing conditions.

19. Given the strategic importance of the first years of business for new entrants, they asked the APC to take urgent measures to obtain such access.

20. In the case of precautionary measures, which in French Polynesia as in mainland France are similar to the summary proceedings procedure before the administrative judge, the conditions laid down in article LP. 641-1 of the French Competition Code require a causal link to be established between the practices complained of and a serious and immediate harm to the company's interests, to the general economy, to the sector concerned or to consumer interests.

a) Decision 2021-PAC-01 on precautionary measures

21. In 2021, PMT lodged a complaint with the APC concerning mobile data roaming services on seven islands in the Tuamotu and Marquesas archipelagos, recently linked to Tahiti by the Natitua submarine cable. The incumbent operator has a monopoly on access to external data from the cable, and has deployed 4G sites on these islands. PMT accused the incumbent operator of implementing a strategy aimed at driving it out of the mobile data market on these islands, first by simply refusing to offer roaming, and then by offering it on abusive access conditions.

22. The APC took the view that, on the basis of the evidence presented, the initial refusal and then the pricing conditions proposed by Onati for this service appeared likely to constitute a practice contrary to article LP. 200-2 of the French Competition Code, which punishes the abusive exploitation of a dominant position by a company, and were likely to cause serious harm to consumers and to the functioning of competition in this sector. To date, Onati has been the only company able to market packages including mobile data access in the islands concerned.

23. However, it rejected the request on the grounds that the harm to PMT, the industry and consumers was not immediate or irreversible. Examination of the case is therefore continuing on the merits.

---

6 For a detailed analysis of the decision, see Concurrences no. 4-2022, November 2022, article no. 109478, *L'application du droit de la concurrence par les trois autorités françaises de concurrence en outre-mer (Nouméa, 27 July 2022), Les contributions de l'Autorité polynésienne de la concurrence.*

b) Decision 2023-PAC-01 on precautionary measures

24. At the end of 2022, the APC received a complaint from Viti, which considered that Onati's tariffs for roaming services in the remote archipelagos were excessive, leading it to withdraw its mobile telephony services on these islands as of 1 November 2022.

25. The APC considered that the proposed tariffs, which required Viti to cover one third of the cost of covering these islands with a telephone network, despite its very small market share of around 1%, tended to protect the customer base of the dominant operator and its main competitor (PMT) from the competitive pressure of the latest entrant, and limited competition in the retail market for mobile telephony services, irrespective of the efficiency of the operators, at a critical time for Viti's development. They were therefore likely to constitute an abuse of a dominant position.

26. In this case, the conditions necessary for the pronouncement of precautionary measures were deemed to have been met, since by depriving not only the inhabitants of the remote archipelagos, but also all those wishing to travel there, of the benefit of a Viti package enabling access to mobile telephony services, they were likely to lead to the company being driven out of the market in the short term, and did not enable consumers to benefit fully from the opening up of the sector to competition.

27. The APC enjoined Onati to propose to Viti, within a maximum period of ten weeks, a tariff offer for roaming access in the islands of the "remote archipelagos" enabling it to exercise effective competition.

28. This decision, contested on appeal, was confirmed by the Paris Court of Appeal in decision no. 23/06177 dated 6 July 2023, with the exception of a marginal modification to the injunction provided for in article 1 of the decision, as the Court considered that it should concern only the fixed part of the roaming tariff and not its variable part.

*

* *

29. In addition to its role as market "policeman", which has seen some fruitful developments, the APC has also been very active in its advisory role.

B. *Effective implementation of the new regulations has been facilitated by the combined actions of the APC and the administrative judge.*

30. As part of its consultative role, it is not the APC's responsibility to check the legality of draft legislation submitted to it, but rather its impact on competition. On the occasion of its nine opinions, and drawing inspiration in particular from countries that liberalised the sector earlier (mainland France, the United States, Pacific Rim countries), the APC has consistently reminded the Polynesian government of the main principles for successfully opening up the sector to competition, on the basis of recommendations adapted to the Polynesian context.

31. For its part, the administrative judge[7] exercises a control of legality and has the capacity to censure certain texts or decisions adopted by the government, including on the basis of a competitive analysis (Conseil d'Etat, 3 November 1997, decision no. 169907, Société Million et Marais), as long as the promotion of competition is provided for by a text, which is explicitly the case of the Polynesian Post and Telecommunications Code.[8] On nearly twenty occasions, the administrative courts have been called upon to examine the conditions for implementing this process, particularly by new market entrants.[9]

32. So, while the competition authority and the administrative judge are two independent and autonomous entities, on the one hand the administrative judge has on several occasions drawn inspiration from the APC's competition analyses and recommendations, sometimes to censure government decisions or shortcomings, and on the other hand, in order not to incur the judge's censure again, the government has referred to the APC the texts implemented following these annulments. In this way, we can speak of a virtuous dynamic engaged between the two institutions in their respective functions, to the benefit of the consumer.

33. Without going into the detailed content of each of these decisions and opinions, it may be useful to give an overview of the diversity of fields in which this approach has taken shape.

1. The question of additional licenses

34. In 2017, the President of French Polynesia referred to the APC for its opinion on applications for prior administrative authorisations, from Viti to become a cell phone operator and from PMT to become an internet service provider.

35. Opinion no. 2017-A-02[10] recommended that the government grant the requested authorisations without delay, in view of the expected benefits for businesses and consumers (low prices, quality and diversity of services offered). At the same time, it pointed out that the effectiveness of these benefits was nevertheless conditional on the exercise of effective and fair competition, with operators in a position to compete on equal terms, and proposed a series of far-reaching improvements to current regulations.

36. Having initially refrained from issuing these authorisations, in June 2018 the TAPF sanctioned it.[11] After recalling the favourable opinion of the administrative services

---

7 Tribunal administratif de la Polynésie française (TAPF) in first instance, Cour administrative d'appel de Paris in appeal, Conseil d'Etat in cassation and for the examination of draft Country laws.

8 CPT, article D. 212-2: "*The competent authorities of French Polynesia shall ensure: (...) 2° the exercise of effective and fair competition between mobile telecommunication service operators, Internet access providers and call-back procedure providers, for the benefit of users; 3° the definition of conditions of access to networks open to the public and of interconnection of networks, in particular mobile telecommunication service networks, which guarantee the possibility for all users to communicate freely with each other, as well as equal conditions of competition in the field of mobile telecommunication service (...)*".

9 See appendix 3: decisions by the administrative courts concerning the opening up of the Polynesian telecommunications sector to competition.

10 APC, opinion no. 2017-A-02 of 22 September 2017 on the granting by the government of authorisations to provide telecommunications services to Viti and Pacific Mobile Telecom.

11 TAPF, decisions no. 1700414 of 12 June 2018 and no. 180002 of 26 June 2018.

(DGEN) and the APC, it took full advantage of its prerogatives and on the basis of an analysis of the competitive situation in the sector and the business plans of the candidates for installation, it considered that "*French Polynesia has a duty to ensure the development of effective and fair competition*" and that "*French Polynesia cannot reasonably maintain that the market for mobile telephony operators is already sufficiently lively and that the entry of a third operator would undermine the existing situation of effective and fair competition.*"

2. The issue of fair pricing for the incumbent's interconnection tariffs and upstream services

a) The challenges of fair, cost-oriented pricing

37. The APC has issued a number of opinions on tariffs for access to infrastructures over which OPT still has a monopoly, and on interconnection tariffs, i.e. the prices for services that the various operators charge each other. Unlike roaming tariffs, which are the result of commercial negotiation, the Post and Telecommunications Code stipulates that they are regulated and determined by the government.

38. This is a fundamental issue, as the successful entry of new operators into the market presupposes the removal of the barriers to entry that protect the incumbent operator. To achieve this, access to the incumbent's network and monopoly infrastructure must be guaranteed under transparent, fair and non-discriminatory conditions. However, a vertically integrated operator who is also active on the retail market has an interest in bidding up the price of these services in order to maximise its profits. This is neutral for the operator, but discriminatory for its competitors, sometimes to the point of a "price squeeze", when the price charged does not allow competitors to compete on the downstream market. Conversely, it is also important to prevent new entrants from concentrating solely on the most profitable activities, leaving the incumbent operator with sole responsibility for the network.

39. This is why, at least during the market opening phase, the tariffs charged by each operator to the other must be geared to each operator's costs, and are therefore often asymmetrical during the first years of market opening, allowing new entrants to benefit from the incumbent's economies of scale, even though they have not yet reached critical size.

b) The APC's initial proposals on how to set rates

40. As early as its opinion no. 2017-A-02, the Authority pointed out the strong dependence of alternative operators on the OPT. It therefore recommended broadening the scope of wholesale services covered by the interconnection regime, and legally and accountably separating OPT's monopoly activities from those carried out in a competitive environment, in order to place all operators on an equal footing.

41. Subsequently consulted on the adoption of a new regulatory framework for setting interconnection rates for mobile call termination, the Commission made recommendations on pricing principles in its opinion no. 2020-A-02. Recalling the balance to be struck between the need to orient tariffs towards costs, to have tariffs low enough to develop usage, and the possibility of using asymmetrical tariffs, she considered that the Long-Term Incremental Average Cost (LTIAC)

model proposed in the text had the advantage of homogenising the conditions for calculating tariffs, was consistent with the maturity of the Polynesian market, but carried the risk of not pushing tariffs downwards, and advocated determining a medium-term trajectory for tariff evolution.

42. However, some of these proposals have not been followed, and the tariffs have given rise to a large number of administrative disputes.

c) Resolute action by the administrative judge to ensure fair rates

Inclusion of roaming charges in the tariff

43. The two new market entrants, PMT and Viti, pay roaming fees to Onati on all islands not covered by their own mobile network. However, in the draft decree detailing the methodology for determining the costs of mobile termination tariffs, this expense was excluded from the cost base, while Onati was able to include the cost of rolling out its network. In its opinion no. 2020-A-02, the APC recommended that the government reinstate these costs in the cost base, but this recommendation was not followed in the decree adopted.

44. An action for annulment was lodged with the TAPF[12], which based its decision on this recommendation to annul the order and remove this service from the exclusions to the regulatory cost base, in order to ensure *"effective and fair competition between, on the one hand, the operator who has control over the essential infrastructure that is the network, and on the other hand, the service operator who does not"*.

Cancellation of interconnection tariffs

45. In several rulings handed down in 2021 and 2022, the TAPF annulled the tariff decrees issued by the Polynesian Council of Ministers on the grounds that they had merely renewed the interconnection tariffs previously in force and were not strictly cost-oriented. It thus first cancelled the 2021[13] tariffs, then the 2022-2023 SMS tariffs.[14]

d) The APC, guarantor of legal certainty for new tariff decrees

46. Drawing the consequences of the various administrative court rulings, the government was forced to repeal several tariff decrees and propose new tariffs. These were then submitted to the APC for its opinion, and received favourable opinions on 17 October 2022[15] and 17 May 2023[16], since they were deemed to meet the objections of the administrative tribunal and enable the re-establishment of free and undistorted competition between operators.

---

12 TAPF, decision no. 2100234 of 29 March 2022

13 TAPF, decisions no. 2100101 and no. 2100108 of 14 December 2021

14 TAPF, decision no. 2200067 of 22 November 2022

15 APC, opinion no. 2022-A-03 on the integration of roaming services

16 APC, notice no. 2023-A-01 for SMS tariffs

3. The question of separating the incumbent's monopoly and competitive activities

47. In its opinion no. 2017-A-02, the APC addressed the question of the OPT's role. Under current regulations, OPT has a very extensive monopoly, particularly on networks for which it continues to receive public funding. However, to ensure that new entrants have free access to monopoly infrastructures under fair conditions, without sacrificing network development and maintenance, requires a very detailed understanding of costs. In this respect, the company managing the infrastructure is much better informed than the regulator or potential entrants about the cost of its own network. These information asymmetries can lead to incorrect cost estimates, generate significant barriers to the development of new offers, and distort the effectiveness of regulation.

48. The usual solution is to ensure strict separation between the incumbent operator's entities carrying out monopoly activities and those operating in the competitive arena, at best by creating legally distinct structures, if not, functionally, for example by creating subsidiaries within the group, which have their own budget, staff and resources, and *at a minimum*, in accounting terms, with internal procedures for distinguishing activities.

49. In French Polynesia, however, the opposite is true. Whereas in another network industry, electricity, TEP, the transmission provider, is clearly separate from EDT, the producer and distributor, in telecommunications, Onati, created in 2019, has become the sole operator for OPT, reinforcing the opacity of costs, including for the regulator.

50. At the same time, French law no. 2018-42 of 27 December 2018 amended the regulatory regime for public service delegations, removing from it those awarded by public establishments to their subsidiaries. The stated aim was to enable OPT to continue entrusting its subsidiary Onati with the management of mobile telephony and internet access networks without competitive bidding. Following a dispute initiated by PMT, the Conseil d'Etat, acting on a referral from the TAPF, ruled on 29 December 2023 (no. 488288) that these provisions, by virtue of their generality, infringed the constitutional principles of freedom of access to public contracts and equal treatment of candidates. Drawing conclusions from this decision, the TAPF issued a ruling on 25 June 2024, enjoining the President of French Polynesia to convene the Council of Ministers to repeal these provisions within two months of notification of the ruling.

51. In response to a proposal to modify this procedure and create an adapted quasi-public service regime, again exempting the OPT from carrying out a competitive bidding process to delegate the public services for which it is responsible to one of its subsidiaries, the APC issued an opinion on 1 October 2024.[17] In its opinion, the APC considers that – except in situations where private initiative is lacking – there is nothing to justify a derogation from the competitive bidding procedure,

---

17 APC, opinion no. 2024-a-07 of 1 October 2024 on three draft local laws amending local law No. 2009-21 of 7 December 2009 on the regulatory framework for public service delegations in French Polynesia and its public establishments and the Post and Telecommunications Code.

which must remain the preferred solution for the delegation of public services, and reiterates the need to separate, at least functionally and not just in accounting terms, the entities entrusted with a public service mission and those operating in Onati's competitive markets.

52. On 29 April 2024, the APC also issued an opinion on external telecommunications via submarine cables and satellite links[18], following Google's plan to deploy a cable network passing through Tahiti and the development of satellite constellations for Internet access. While this opening up of the upstream market appears to be a positive step, enabling better coverage of the Polynesian territory at a lower cost, this opinion was an opportunity to reiterate once again the need to regulate OPT's wholesale services, in order to offer non-discriminatory access to infrastructures to its competitors.

4. The question of universal deployment of the new operators' network

53. As early as its 2017 opinion, and then in an opinion specifically issued on this subject on 24 July 2023[19], the APC indicated that, while the Polynesian regulatory framework imposes the deployment of all operators on all archipelagos, such a requirement generates inefficiencies and distorts the normal play of competition. By failing to ensure the economic equilibrium of players, except at the cost of very high tariffs for consumers, it is detrimental to the objective of reducing the digital divide and providing access to different services for all Polynesians.

54. The APC recommended distinguishing between densely populated areas, where infrastructure-based competition between operators would be possible, and sparsely populated areas, where competition would be limited to services, but where infrastructure would be shared. However, while several types of pooling were theoretically possible, Onati unilaterally deployed its own 4G network on all the islands served by the new Natitua submarine cable, benefiting from a substantial subsidy from the French government of almost 250 million francs. The challenge now is to reconsider how other operators roll out their own networks, excluding islands where it makes no economic sense to duplicate networks, and to regulate the rates offered by Onati for access to its 4G network.

55. This distinction, which the government failed to implement quickly enough, has also been the subject of recent litigation. On 2 November 2024, the TAPF[20] censured the stipulations in PMT's specifications setting out a universal roll-out timetable for the period 2027-2036, as being vitiated by a manifest error of assessment. The TAPF took up the competitive analysis carried out by the APC, pointing out that the principle of developing "infrastructure-based competition" was not based on any regulatory provision.

---

18 APC, opinion no. 2024-AO-03 of 29 April 2024 on a draft law amending the Post and Telecommunications Code.

19 APC, opinion no. 2023-A-02 of 24 July 2023 on the conditions for deploying and financing telecommunications networks in the sparsely populated islands of French Polynesia.

20 TAPF, decision no. 2400179, Pacific Mobile Télécom, 12 November 2024

5. Number portability

56. The APC has regularly argued that smooth mobility between operators is essential, as it helps to limit *club* effects to the benefit of the incumbent operator. While certain practices relating to re-engagement periods or the homogeneity of tariffs between *off-net* and *on-net* calls have already been addressed by decision 2018-PAC-01, examined *below*, another issue by its very nature falls not within the remit of the operators themselves, but within that of regulatory power alone: that of number portability, which enables people to change operator without changing their telephone number.

57. This option is essential because it strengthens the power of the consumer, who can opt for the most competitive offers without having to change his or her telephone number, and thus facilitates the acquisition of market share by the most innovative operators. However, while the French Post and Telecommunications Code has provided for such an implementation since 2013[21], it was still not effective in 2023, necessitating the intervention of the administrative judge referred to by the operator Viti.

58. In a ruling handed down on 12 September 2023, the TAPF[22] ordered French Polynesia to enact regulatory measures enabling number portability between operators.

59. French Polynesia then introduced these provisions into the French Post and Telecommunications Code with a decree[23] of 13 December 2023[24]. However, this text left it to a new decree to specify the terms and conditions of application, in particular "*subscriber information, quality of service obligations for porting and maximum service interruption times, transmission times between operators for the information required to process the subscriber's request, and other specifications required to implement portability*", for an entry date of 1 December 2024 only. In the absence of effective implementation, the TAPF issued an enforcement decision on 30 April 2024[25] imposing a fine of 11.8 million CFP francs on the country.

*

* *

60. The combined intervention of the courts – to enforce the competition aspect of the telecoms reform – and the competition authority – whose competitive analysis helps to clarify the judge's reasoning and reinforce the legal certainty of the new texts – has thus proved its worth. It is also noteworthy that the more open market conditions brought about by these various decisions have resulted in a

---

21 CPT, article LP. 212-20 introduced by local law no. 2013-4 of 14 January 2013

22 TAPF, decision no. 2200830 of 12 September 2023

23 Order no. 2376 CM of 13 December 2023 on the implementation of mobile number portability in French Polynesia

24 CPT, article A. 212-20-17 on the retention of mobile numbers by subscribers wishing to change operator, and article A. 212-20-18 setting out the obligations of operators when a subscriber indicates that he or she wishes to retain the mobile number assigned to him or her by the outgoing operator.

25 TAPF, decision no. 2400039 of 30 April 2024

significant increase in the new entrant's market share, the arrival of a third player, and the emergence of more advantageous offers. As a result, volumes of voice calls, SMS and mobile data have continued to rise, and 2022 saw the arrival of the first unlimited offers.

61. However, the need for, and frequency of, such intervention by the supervisory authorities is also indicative of a more structural problem, linked to the lack of independent regulation of the sector, which will be discussed below.

III. A fragile, unfinished process

A. *The need for an independent sector regulator*

62. Despite the isolation and complexity of the Polynesian territory, the opening up of the telecommunications sector to competition has been a success. Alongside increasing broadband coverage, prices have fallen sharply, making these services more accessible to consumers.

63. However, this success has been achieved at the cost of close, ongoing monitoring of market opening by both the APC and the administrative courts. Despite the existence of certain tools, such as summary proceedings before the courts or precautionary measures before the APC, the risk of such a *modus operandi* is to intervene *a posteriori*, in a repressive rather than preventive manner. And yet, when it comes to opening up to competition, the first few years are crucial for new operators, and regulatory or behavioural barriers can quickly prove disastrous, even over a very short period.

64. In reality, the abundance of – often redundant – opinions issued by the APC and the repeated censures by the administrative courts are the symptom of a structurally unfinished reform, due to the maintenance of functional and organic links between the government and the incumbent operator – OPT and its subsidiary Onati – whose strategic role has been maintained and even strengthened since the opening up of the telecommunications sector to competition. At present, regulation of the sector is the sole responsibility of the Council of Ministers, who represent half of the Board of Directors of OPT, the industrial and commercial public establishment of French Polynesia.

65. If the reform is to be sustainable, we need to go further and depoliticise the management of the sector, by providing French Polynesia with a regulator independent of the government, as is the case in all developed countries that have opened up their network industries to competition (this is the role of ARCEP in France). A regulator of this kind guarantees the effectiveness and efficiency of regulation, providing both political authorities and industry players with impartial means of reconciling diverse and often conflicting interests, as well as stability and predictability in the rule of law, which is conducive to private investment.

66. The regulator could be responsible for granting individual operating authorisations, setting regulated tariffs, drafting operators' specifications, determining areas of shortage and infrastructure pooling arrangements. It would also have a role in arbitrating disputes between operators over tariffs or commercial conditions, which are not covered by the present article but are sometimes virulent. The government,

for its part, would retain its regal role in allocating frequencies (after receiving the regulator's assent) and setting major public service objectives. Such a reform would in no way deprive the country of the possibility of demanding that political objectives such as accessibility and universal service be taken into account, but it would have less leeway in determining the best means of achieving them.

67. The advantages of such an evolution are well known and documented: limiting conflicts of interest and the capture of the regulator; limiting political opportunism and political alternations in regulatory choices; limiting information asymmetries if accompanied by a broad obligation of transparency, data communication and functional and accounting separation between monopoly activities and competition. There is also a political advantage in delegating to an independent authority the responsibility for taking certain measures which are in the country's long-term interest, but which run counter to short-term vested interests. Such reforms restore confidence and visibility among operators, and create an environment conducive to investment in the sector – and hence employment – and to the development of offerings, in the interests of consumers and the economy as a whole.

68. The same reasoning also applies to other sectors where infrastructures are predominant and can create bottlenecks, such as energy or port activity, which are also strategic because they have an effect on the economy as a whole.

B. *A new role for the competition authority?*

69. With this in mind, the solution usually advocated is to create independent sector-specific regulatory agencies, endowed with resources, guarantees of independence and expertise, and decision-making powers, particularly in terms of tariffs and authorisations.

70. The APC has taken advantage of its geographical location and the creation of the Pacific Island Network of Competition Consumer and Economic Regulators to discuss this issue with several of its counterparts in the region, including Australia, New Zealand and Fiji. Unlike the larger countries (France, the UK and Germany), and following the example of Spain and the Netherlands, all three have chosen to entrust the bulk of their network industry regulatory tasks to the same independent authority as that responsible for competition matters. For example, the Australian Competition and Consumer Commission (ACCC) and the Commerce Commission of New Zealand (ComCom) have a triple mission: i) the fight against anti-competitive practices (role devolved to the APC in French Polynesia), ii) consumer protection (role devolved to the government through the DGAE in French Polynesia) and iii) the regulation of network industries (role devolved to the government through the DGEN and the SDE). They justify this plurality of missions by their common objective, which is to protect the long-term interests of consumers.

71. In a note for the OECD, Mr Ergas and Mr Fels underlined the potential for synergy between regulation and competition within the same independent administrative authority: "[t]he *advantage of* [this] *approach, at least in theory, is that it broadens the range of instruments that the authority can use. For example, it may be that the most effective solution to a particular regulatory problem is to restructure the market in such a way as to promote competition, and then vigorously enforce*

the competition rules. By "internalising" competition law and regulatory instruments in the same authority, the authority may be more inclined to mix and match problems and instruments effectively, thus avoiding the "silo mentality" that can compromise good decision-making. At the same time, there may be cases where identifying an effective regulatory solution requires a competition impact analysis, which such an integrated authority may find easier to carry out."[26]

72. Polynesia's only independent administrative authority, the APC, could thus be entrusted with the task of regulating networks in sectors characterised by natural monopolies (energy, telecommunications and, where applicable, transport). While such a reform would need to be carefully thought through, particularly with regard to the composition and conditions of appointment of the college and the versatility of the investigating departments, it would limit the risk of the regulator being captured by special interests, while offering substantial economies of scale in a small economy in a field requiring rare skills, and providing greater visibility for institutional and economic players.

73. In 2024, this process took a significant step forward, not in the field of telecommunications, but in energy. Indeed, the President of French Polynesia asked the APC for an opinion on a draft Country law by which he wished to transfer the mission of sectoral regulation of energy to the APC, which gave rise to an opinion of 30 May 2024.[27]

IV. Conclusion

74. In its early years, the telecommunications sector was a privileged playground for the APC. Its creation coincided with the effective opening up of the sector, and more than in any other field, it was able to make use of its various prerogatives. Through its contentious powers, as arbiter of competition, it has been able to prevent the incumbent operator from hindering the emergence of new competitors, notably through emergency procedures. Through its consultative powers, it has advised the government on the principles of effective competition and the concrete measures to be implemented to limit barriers to entry, particularly in the face of the risk of censure of its texts by the administrative judge.

75. Despite its initial successes, which have enabled and accompanied an explosion in usage, this reform is nevertheless incomplete and fragile, lacking independent regulation of the sector, a severing of ties between the incumbent operator and the Polynesian government, and a genuine functional separation between OPT-Onati's various activities. The time has come to set up an independent regulatory authority, whose functions could be combined with those of a competition authority. The Polynesian government, for its part, would remain the sole decision-maker on social and political objectives, such as regional planning, equal access for users and the promotion of the development of uses.

---

26 Free translation of an extract from the note by Allan Fels and Henry Ergas, *Changes in Institutional Design of Competition Authorities (OECD Roundtables on Competition Policy)*, 17-18 December 2014. Quoted by APC opinion no. 2024-A-04.

27 APC, opinion no. 2024-A-04 of 30 May 2024 on a draft law on energy sector regulation.

APPENDIX 1: APC telecommunications litigation decisions

APC telecommunications litigation decisions
2023-PAC-01: Request for interim measures submitted by the company Viti for practices implemented in the telecommunications sector
2021-PAC-01: Request for interim measures submitted by the company Pacific Mobile Télécom in the telecommunications sector concerning roaming services for mobile data access
2018-PAC-01: Practices implemented in the mobile telephony sector for residential customers

APPENDIX 2: APC telecommunications advisory opinions

APC telecommunications advisory opinions
2024-AO-03: Opinion on a draft law amending the Post and Telecommunications Code in French Polynesia
2024-A-07: Opinion on three draft Country laws amending Country law no. 2009-21 of 7 December 2009 relating to the regulatory framework of the public service delegations of French Polynesia and its public establishments and the Post and Telecommunications Code
2023-A-06: Notice concerning the setting of reference interconnection tariffs (TRI) for mobile call termination (TAM) for the mobile operators Onati, PMT and Viti for 2024 and 2025
2023-A-03: Opinion on a draft order temporarily regulating the rates and conditions of fixed Internet access offers in sparsely populated areas
2023-A-02: Opinion on determining the conditions for deploying and financing telecommunications networks in the sparsely populated islands of French Polynesia
2023-A-01: Opinion on setting reference SMS mobile termination interconnection tariffs for the mobile telephone operators ONATI, PMT and VITI for 2022 and 2023
2022-A-03: Opinion on setting reference mobile termination interconnection tariffs for the mobile telephone operators PMT/VODAFONE and ORA/VITI for 2022 and 2023
2020-A-02: Opinion on a draft Country law amending the Post and Telecommunications Code (reference interconnection tariff)
2017-A-02: Notice relating to the granting by the government of authorisations to provide telecommunications services to Viti and Pacific Mobile Télécom

APPENDIX 3: Administrative court rulings on the opening up of the Polynesian telecommunications sector to competition

Judicial body	Decision number	Applicant	Decision date	Sense of decision
TAPF	1300592	PMT	7 October 2014	Cancellation of wholesale services from OPT to PMT (failure to negotiate)
TAPF	1700414	Viti	12 June 2018	Rejection of Viti's application to become a telephone operator overturned
TAPF	1800002	PMT	26 June 2018	Rejection of PMT's application for approval as an Internet service provider overturned
TAPF	2100101-2100108	PMT-Viti	14 December 2021	Reference interconnection tariffs for 2021 cancelled
TAPF	2100234	PMT	29 March 2022	Cancellation of the exclusion of roaming purchases from the regulatory cost base of reference interconnection tariffs.
TAPF	2200067	PMT	22 November 2022	Cancellation of reference SMS interconnection tariffs for 2022-2023
TAPF	2200350	Viti	25 April 2023	Dismissal of the challenge to the subsidy paid to Onati for the roll-out of 4G in remote archipelagos
TAPF	2200387	PMT	25 April 2023	Dismissal of the challenge to the subsidy paid to Onati for the roll-out of 4G in remote archipelagos
TAPF	2200359	PMT	6 June 2023	OPT ordered to disclose public service delegation agreement with Onati
TAPF	2200830	Viti	12 September 2023	French Polynesia ordered to issue the regulatory measures provided for in article LP 212-20 of the CPT (number portability between operators).
TAPF	2200941	PMT	12 September 2023	Dismissal of the appeal against the public service delegation agreement between OPT and Onati (lateness of the application)
TAPF	2300126	PMT	12 September 2023	Transmission to the Conseil d'Etat of the challenge to article LP 28 of Country law no. 2009-21 (delegation of public services without competitive bidding)
TAPF	2300053	PMT	26 September 2023	Motion to cancel the reference interconnection tariffs for 2022-2023 rejected

Judicial body	Decision number	Applicant	Decision date	Sense of decision
Council of State	488288	PMT	29 December 2023	Paragraphs 2 to 5 of article LP 28 of Country law no. 2018-42 infringe the constitutional requirements of freedom of access to public contracts and equal treatment of candidates.
TAPF	2300182	Viti	30 January 2024	Motion to cancel deployment schedule for 2018-2030 rejected
CAA de Paris	22PA00799-22PA01197	French Polynesia-Onati	5 February 2024	Confirmation of decisions no. 2100101 and 2100108 (annulment of interconnection reference tariffs for 2021)
TAPF	2400039	Viti	30 April 2024	Settlement of the penalty payment provided for in decision no. 2200830 (failure to implement number portability between operators) in the amount of 11,800,000 F CFP
TAPF	2300126	PMT	25 June 2024	Injunction to the President of the FP to repeal paragraphs 2 to 5 of article LP 28 of Country law no. 2009-21 (delegation of public service without competitive bidding in telecommunications)
TAPF	2400179	PMT	12 November 2024	Cancellation of the PMT deployment schedule for the period 2027-2036

Transport: Analysis of Infrastructures, Barriers and Regulations in Island Markets

Henri Piffaut*
European Commission
Polynesian Competition Authority
Competition Authority of New Caledonia

1. The transport sector is key to any economy, enabling the exchange of both people and goods. In the Pacific island economies, its importance becomes even more central, as the well-being of the inhabitants in many islands depends largely on their interconnection with other islands, and even with the continents. This chapter focuses on transport competition policy in the Pacific Island economies, drawing mainly on the respective practices of the competition authorities in New Caledonia (ACNC) and French Polynesia (APC), as well as relevant examples from French and European practice. Competition policy is not only about litigation and merger control, but also about advising public authorities, particularly in the form of opinions. This role is all the more important and legitimate given that this type of sector, because of the externalities it entails, is most often subject to economic regulations that influence the profitability of activities, the incentives to invest in infrastructures, and even the number of players operating there.

---

* Henri Piffaut is an advisor to the European Commission – DG COMP in Brussels, specializing in foreign subsidies. He is also a member of the Board of the Polynesian Competition Authority and a member of the forward-looking committee of the New Caledonia Competition Authority (ACNC). Previously, he served as Vice-President of the French Competition Authority and advisor to the Deputy Director-General in charge of mergers at DG COMP. The views expressed are personal and do not engage these institutions.

2. Due to the geographical remoteness of these economies and their dependence on supplies from Europe, the transport sector plays an important role in price formation: APC has estimated that, on average, the cost of approach, which includes freight but also the handling of goods and on-site transport, represents around 8% of the price (including VAT) of a good[2]

I. Introduction

A. *Transport definition and characteristics*

1. Definitions

3. An island's transportation infrastructure is essential for its connectivity, economic development and tourist appeal. Given geographical and environmental constraints, they generally include a combination of roads, ports, airports and, in the case of archipelagos, local shipping systems. Some islands have a public transport network to facilitate travel. It should be noted, however, that island geography can severely restrict the scope for increasing road network capacity. Almost all inhabited islands include one or more harbor infrastructures to handle local or tourist traffic, inter-island transport of people and goods, or the import of containers transported over long distances by cargo ships. It should be noted that like road networks, ports are most often the result of investments by public authorities and are constrained by physical geography and road connections. Even if many of these infrastructures charge for their use, for the most part they could not remain viable or be the subject of investment without help from the public authorities.

4. Within the airport infrastructure, a distinction is made between international and local airports, depending on the origin, number and scale of flights handled. The intensity of use of local airports varies. In all cases, an airport is strongly constrained by its physical geography and the scale of the investment and expenditure it requires. Airports are often managed by private companies on the basis of concessions, or in the form of régies. For the same reasons as for port infrastructures, airports may be financially dependent on public intervention.

5. Port and airport infrastructures form the basis of a value chain that spans many levels. It includes activities ranging from the organization of transport, the reception and maintenance of ships or aircraft, and the unloading of goods to final distribution, via handling, storage, transport and transformation processes. As many of these activities involve significant fixed costs, the volume of traffic demanded by an island, or even an archipelago, may not be sufficient to ensure the minimum critical mass for sufficient profitability, taking into account the demand's ability to pay. Here again, public intervention may be necessary to satisfy demand.

---

[2] Opinion no. 2019-A-02 of September 19, 2019 on import and distribution mechanisms in French Polynesia.

2. Market failures

6. Transport infrastructure markets often fail to allocate resources efficiently or meet needs optimally. This can lead to negative externalities and high social costs, requiring public intervention through subsidies or regulation to correct distortions.

7. First of all, these markets present negative externalities, such as environmental impact, accidents (mainly road accidents), the consequences of which are often borne by society (in the form of public spending on health and reduced productivity), and infrastructure maintenance, which is not fully reflected in any user fees paid.

8. The second shortcoming affecting transport markets is the existence of situations of substantial market power in the form of natural monopolies, high market concentration due to market size, geographical constraints or regulations limiting the number of players. On islands or archipelagos, for example, it may be economically inefficient to duplicate transport infrastructures such as airports or ports. If the behavior of the operator of such infrastructure is not regulated, this can lead to excessive prices, lower quality of service and inefficiencies. The problem is exacerbated when the owner of this infrastructure is also vertically integrated into other related activities, where several players may be in competition.

9. The third failure often encountered relates to access issues. Certain types of transport infrastructure, such as roads, bridges and public transport services, are public goods, meaning that their use by one individual does not prevent their use by others (non-rivalry), and that it is difficult to exclude users, even in the event of congestion. This may require public intervention in the form of subsidies or regulation.

10. Similarly, the profitability constraint can lead to routes not being served, resulting in situations of economic and social exclusion. Public intervention is then necessary to guarantee accessibility and territorial equity.

11. The fourth category of market failure is information asymmetries, particularly between service providers and customers. Customers of transport services may lack information on the quality, safety or environmental impact of the services they use (e.g., their choice of airline or freight forwarder). This can lead to demand for lower-quality services, or to decisions based on incomplete information. Similarly, in some markets, such as air transport, pricing structures are complex and sometimes not very transparent. This makes it difficult for customers to compare offers and choose the best option, and can cause inefficiencies in users' decision-making.

12. Fifthly, time constraints can lead to poor resource allocation decisions. Transport infrastructure projects often require large initial investments and long payback periods. In such cases, there may be an incompatibility between the profitability prospects of private investors (and their financing) and the characteristics of the project in question. This time myopia can lead to under-investment.

13. Finally, transport services and infrastructure form part of complex value chains, and often need to be coordinated with other modes of transport. Lack of coordination can lead to reduced or less efficient use of transport resources, to the detriment of users or certain categories of customer.

3. Entry and exit barriers in transport markets

14. Transport markets also often have high barriers to entry and exit. This plays an important role in competitive dynamics.

15. The construction of infrastructures such as airports, roads, ports, or even the building of vehicle fleets (boats, buses, planes) requires very high initial investments, thus limiting the entry of new players. What's more, access to essential resources (such as land or rights of use) is often regulated or monopolized, creating a significant barrier to new entrants. Furthermore, the transport sector is heavily regulated to guarantee safety, sustainability and reliability. These regulatory requirements (licenses, safety certifications, environmental standards, etc.) are certainly justified, but they are also complex and costly to comply with. There are also often significant economies of scale and scope. Air transport, for example, is subject to significant economies of scale and scope. Fixed costs are material with the acquisition of aircraft, and each aircraft has a capacity to fill.

16. What's more, managing aircraft fleets and their routes enables their use to be optimized, leading to substantial savings. Airlines face high barriers to entry, due to the cost of purchasing or leasing aircraft, airport access rights and competition from major groups. There are also barriers to exit, as the resale of aircraft fleets or the closure of infrastructures can be costly. Airlines reduce their costs by operating a fleet on several routes. This makes it difficult for new entrants to compete on cost with established players.

17. Exit barriers in the transport sector are also often high. Companies often own expensive and specific assets (aircraft, port infrastructure, etc.) which cannot be easily reused or resold for other activities. What's more, selling or dismantling infrastructure can be costly in terms of labor, environmental regulations and land restoration constraints. Furthermore, transport companies, particularly in the utilities sector, are often bound by long-term contracts. These contracts include costly or restrictive exit clauses. Initial investments in infrastructure and transport vehicles generate high levels of debt. In the event of exit, it is often difficult to cover these debts without a constant cash flow.

4. Positive externalities

18. Transport and transport infrastructure generate beneficial effects for society that are not directly included in the price of services. These positive externalities benefit the economy, the environment and social cohesion far beyond the usefulness of user demand.

19. In this way, transport and transport infrastructure benefit economic and social development by facilitating access to markets for local and foreign companies, thus stimulating economic growth and investment. What's more, well-designed transport infrastructures can reduce workers' commuting times, improving overall productivity by enabling them to reach their place of work more quickly. Companies also benefit from faster, more reliable logistics.

20. The development of this sector can also benefit social cohesion and the reduction of inequalities by improving access to public services (education, health) for remote

populations and offering more equitable access to resources and opportunities for all. Last but not least, connectivity enables greater social inclusion, notably with the availability of public transport that makes it easier for people without vehicles to get around.

21. It is clear from the above that the transport sector is based on high fixed costs and barriers to entry and exit (with the exception of small-volume means of transport such as trucks). The scale of these fixed costs and barriers often results in highly concentrated markets, or even natural monopolies. This can necessitate economic regulation of access. As a result, the value chain may comprise several highly concentrated links, and situations of market power may exist. Another characteristic is that their availability is often of vital importance to the economic zones they serve, especially islands. This means that when their provision is not economically viable, or could come up against natural monopolies, public intervention is often necessary.

B. *Gradual application of competition law to transport*

22. As an illustration of the special features and central role of the transport sector for economies, this sector has long benefited from specific measures for the application of competition law in the EU.

23. For example, while regulation 17[3] had empowered the Commission to implement articles 85 and 86 (now 101 and 102) of the Treaty, regulation 141[4] excluded from the scope of regulation 17 "*agreements, decisions and concerted practices in the transport sector which have as their object or effect the fixing of transport rates and conditions, the limitation or control of transport supply or the sharing of transport markets*" and "*the abuse of a dominant position, within the meaning of Article 86 of the Treaty, on the transport market*". Gradually, the rules specific to the transport sector were replaced by the application of ordinary competition law. This process was completed with the adoption of regulation 1/2003.

24. Specific rules on possible exemptions for agreements under Article 101(3) remained in place until 2024, while the last vestige, the block exemption regulation for maritime consortia, was not extended beyond April 25, 2024. Nevertheless, a specific framework remains in place for the control of state aid.

25. This slow movement is the product not only of the difficulties of integrating the different national markets and the policies that accompanied them, but is also explained by the specific features of transport markets. The gradual abandonment of a dedicated regulatory framework shows, however, that these specificities can be taken into account within the framework of ordinary competition law for anti-competitive practices. It should nevertheless be noted that the transport sector is a major source of competition cases in Europe, whether in terms of anti-competitive practices, merger control or state aid control.[5]

---

3 Regulation 17/62: OJ 1962 013/204.

4 Council Regulation 141/62, OJ 1962 124/2751.

5 See Broca, Hubert de, Marta Mielecka Riga, and Anatoly Suboès, ' Transport', in Jonathan Faull, Ali Nikpay, and Deirdre Taylor (eds), Faull & Nikpay: The EU Law of Competition, 3rd Edition (2014; online edn, Oxford Academic).

II. Competition policy and government action

26. Because of its specific nature and importance to the economy in general, the transport sector is subject to dedicated policies. This raises the question of how to link transport and competition policies. At European Union level, the answer lies both in the control of State aid (which monitors the intervention of public authorities in the competitive game) and in the collegiality of the European Commission's action, which ensures that all transport policy projects take into account their impact on competition, and vice versa. In the French hexagon, the same control of State aid applies, while the hexagonal Competition Authority (ADLC) can (and sometimes must) issue opinions on the competitive impact of economic regulations. In New Caledonia and French Polynesia, the competition authorities may issue opinions on their own initiative or in response to a referral from the public authorities, but there is no State aid control, even though European practice informs the opinions of the APC and ACNC.

A. *Transport notices in New Caledonia and French Polynesia*

27. There is no State aid control system in the Pacific Islands. The concept exists by capillary action in French Polynesia and New Caledonia, where the competition authorities can draw on the European legal framework when issuing opinions on government reform projects in sectors with high externalities, such as transport. The issues addressed in these opinions include the relationship between competitive markets and public service obligations. A public service obligation entails costs that can be borne by demand, by public funds or by other activities. The first option can be socially regressive, since it leads to higher costs and therefore higher prices, which can drive out the most vulnerable part of demand. The second option is subject to budgetary constraints, as public authorities do not have unlimited funds at their disposal. In this case, the public authorities can either take charge of the activity themselves, or let a third party do so, while compensating for the extra costs. It is important not to over-compensate for the laoer, to avoid public rents distorting competition in other markets. Finally, the third is to allow companies to earn extra profits on other markets to compensate for the additional costs generated by public service obligations, which raises questions in terms of distortions of competition.

28. This problem has arisen in particular for inter-island connections, whether by sea or by air. Because of the high proportion of fixed costs, such links are not always profitable with a sufficiently high frequency.

B. *Impact of state aid*

29. In its opinion (2016-A-01) on competition on maritime services between Tahiti and Moorea, the APC examined whether existing tax exemption measures could distort competition. It found that the tax reduction applied only to taxpayers contributing capital to productive investments in French Polynesia, and thus included, within the meaning of European state aid law, a selective advantage as it applied to specifically defined investments. Even if European law did not

apply, the French tax exemption scheme in French Polynesia was identical to a scheme that the European Commission had considered compatible aid for other French territories. The APC nevertheless recommended introducing a criterion of effect on the competitive operation of a market as part of the analysis of a tax exemption project. This would enable it to analyze the impact of a project on competition and the creation of any distortions, particularly with regard to the approvals previously granted to operators in the market concerned.

C. *Public service obligations*

30. A 2016 country law in French Polynesia had provided that the transport activity would be carried out in a competitive framework, through the award of an operating license that would individually set out the public service obligations and how they were to be provided, for a fixed period. The APC, in a notice dated February 7, 2017 examined the determination of the conditions for granting and withdrawing the operating license.[6]

31. The deliberation in question was aimed at facilitating market access conditions by distinguishing between areas where competition can be freely applied and those where additional obligations should apply. For sea transport, islands with no particular service problems included Moorea, Bora Bora, Raiatea, Huahine and Tahaa. Isolated or poorly served islands that could be subject to special operating arrangements or licensing restrictions included islands such as Rapa, Maupiti, Fatu Hiva, the North-East Tuamotu Islands, the East Tuamotu Islands, the Gambier Islands and others. In the air transport sector, the draft deliberation provided for a threshold of 1,000 commercial movements per year, above which free competition would be allowed, while special obligations could be imposed below. In addition, the draft favored the establishment of foreign operators in the air sector, and created the possibility of granting exceptional authorizations in the maritime sector. APC noted that the competition zones covered the vast majority of flows (for the maritime sector, over 99% of passenger flows and over 2/3 of freight tonnages transported; in the air sector, around of air passenger flows and almost of freight transported by air). Operators of scheduled inter-island public transport companies were to be remunerated out of revenues collected from users, according to approved fares that were to "*correspond to normal operating conditions, taking into account French Polynesia's aids and contributions to the financing of public service obligations*".

32. In its opinion, the APC noted that the constraints imposed on carriers' activities appeared to be justified by an objective of general interest, relating to the effectiveness and efficiency of the transport system thus organized. The APC validated the demand-based criteria for determining the competitive nature of a route, and noted that the introduction of a system of operating licenses ensured clarity for users, enabled data-driven management and monitoring of the constraints imposed on operators.

---

6 Opinion No. 2017-AO-01 of February 7, 2017 on the draft deliberation on the operating license and public service obligations in maritime and air inter-island transport.

33. Firstly, APC pointed out that the new regime would help lower barriers to market entry by facilitating access to licenses in areas of free competition, enabling foreign operators to enter the inter-island air transport market, and clarifying and relaxing the derogation regime in the maritime transport markets.

34. Secondly, the draft increased transparency and objectivity on the markets by clearly defining public service obligations and organizing the collection of information for statistical and sector monitoring purposes, and by separating the consultative body (the inter-island transport observatory) from the body responsible for awarding licenses and monitoring compliance with them.

35. Lastly, APC considered that the project laid the foundations for sector regulation by introducing clear procedures for granting operating licenses and sanctions, as well as general monitoring of the sector and individual operators.

36. It should be stressed that, with regard to the risk of cross-subsidies, the APC rejected a prohibition in principle and stated that their effect must be assessed on a case-by-case basis, depending on the markets concerned, the fares, services and products they support, and the position of the competitors involved. It added that they could lead to efficiency gains, since a public compensation mechanism would be more cumbersome and time-consuming than compensation between ships and companies, which is directly linked to market trends and the company's costs and revenues.

D. *Aid to the airline industry*

37. In its opinion of December 13, 2022[7], the ACNC noted that the domestic and international airline sector was heavily subsidized on both the demand and supply sides. Local airlines were almost exclusively state-owned, and held a dominant position in the markets concerned. In particular, the public authorities supported the investment of local public carriers through the overseas tax exemption scheme, while the New Caledonian public authorities also provided support such as loan guarantees, subsidies (without competitive tendering) for loss-making routes or international routes, and compensation for carriers' financial losses. On the demand side, public authorities also granted aid linked to territorial continuity with France or within New Caledonia. The ACNC noted that these schemes were insufficiently controlled and that, as they stood, they would be prohibited in principle or subject to authorization within a national framework. In addition, the ACNC emphasized the de facto identity of the organizer, regulator and shareholder of New Caledonian airlines.

38. Alongside structural measures concerning operators, their links, airports and sector regulation, the ACNC advocated ensuring the efficiency of public aid to the sector, drawing inspiration from European policy on the control of State aid, through adapted subsidy and pricing regimes. This would involve identifying routes benefiting from public support and those to be operated under a regime inspired by the

7 ACNC opinion no. 2022-A-04 of December 13, 2022 on the competitive operation of the air transport sector in New Caledonia.

Public Service Obligation (PSO) in force in the European Union, and abolishing the obligation to validate fare grids for routes outside the PSO. Finally, it suggested introducing a passenger aid scheme independent of carriers. More generally, it proposed drawing up a regulatory framework for the allocation of public aid to companies, which it could oversee, in order to ensure healthy competition on New Caledonian markets for goods and services, including air transport.

E. *Opinions on economic regulations*

39. In its opinion of June 19, 2017, the APC examined a draft law of the country that reformed the regulation of access to and exercise of the professions of cab entrepreneur and delivery vehicle.[8]

40. The APC welcomed the fact that the project removed a certain number of barriers to entry by facilitating access to the cab and delivery vehicle sectors for new entrants. However, it also suggested going further by eliminating other barriers, such as the maintenance of a *numerus clausus* and the possibility of refusing a license to operate on the basis of a mismatch between supply and demand.

41. In addition, APC noted that the project – with multi-transport licenses, marauding and pre-booking-allowed for the diversification of the land transport offer, enabling the satisfaction of new consumer demands, the development of the sector and the stimulation of competition. The APC nevertheless recommended that these reforms be accompanied by beoer market monitoring and consumer information tools.

42. Lastly, APC noted that the project would contribute to beoer consumer protection and, ultimately, greater demand by making it compulsory to install time meters in cabs and to display regulated fares in vehicles.

43. In notice dated May 14, 2018 examined the competitive operation of international air transport serving French Polynesia[9]. The APC first noted that the weighted average price rose steadily between 2013 and 2016 on the Papeete – Los Angeles route in a context of scarce supply, while over the same period prices had fallen on the London – Australia route. In examining the possible causes of this divergence, APC first noted that regulation, even if it could be made more open, has not been a major brake on the development of competition or had, in itself, a negative influence on the evolution of ticket prices.

44. Secondly, the costs borne by airlines (notably fuel and ground handling charges, taxes and fees) did not explain the change in ticket price. On the other hand, the optimization of airline revenues (yield management) in a context of exploiting the scarcity of seat supply seemed a more relevant explanatory factor. Finally, APC noted that code-share agreements could, in certain cases, lead to restrictions of competition. In the absence of any prior control mechanism for this type of agreement in French Polynesia, APC invited airlines to carry out a self-assessment of the competitive risks of their agreements or conventions, in order to correct any anti-competitive aspects.

---

8 APC Opinion No. 2017-A0-02 of June 19, 2017 on the draft law of the country regulating the activity of private road transport with driver, using vehicles with fewer than ten seats.

9 APC Opinion No. 2018-A-01 of May 14, 2018 on international air transport.

It also recommended that French Polynesia modify the system of indirect approval of agreements by referring the maoer to the Polynesian Competition Authority on the basis of article LP 620-1 I of the French Competition Code.

F. *Conclusion*

45. The notices have the following characteristics:

46. Firstly, as far as public services are concerned, they are agnostic as to how they should be delivered.

47. Secondly, whatever the model chosen by the public authorities, there may be competition (and public spending control) issues. Firstly, borrowing from the practice of State aid control, the authorities have sought to alert us to the need to put in place a mechanism that limits the subsidies granted to their minimum. This limitation has two dimensions: to reduce the burden on the community and also to avoid distorting competition beyond what is necessary. Secondly, competition authorities are particularly aoentive to the risk of cross-subsidization. On the one hand, excessive subsidies could be used to finance distortions of competition in other markets. On the other hand, public authorities could encourage the creation of rents on other markets to finance PSOs privately.

48. Thirdly, to prevent these problems from arising, these opinions emphasize the need for relevant information and accounting separation between activities subject to PSOs and those that are free on the market. In addition, the public authority should ensure that it benefits from a continuous flow of information to avoid the realization of competitive risks. A consequence of this position is the suggestion to have a regulator with the powers and means necessary to ensure that the PSO is respected and that competitive risks are minimized.

49. The opinions cited in this section mainly concern means of transport. Although none of the cases or opinions concerned port or airport infrastructure, it should be emphasized that the issues raised by potential PSOs would be similar, and that investment aid measures would be assessed against the criteria established by European state aid control: identification of a market failure, proportionality of the aid and incentive effect for investment.

50. With regard to public control of access to economic sectors, opinions advocate objective criteria and the abandonment of limitations on the number of players when demand is sufficient.

III. Anti-competitive practices and merger control

A. *Relevant markets*

1. Passenger transport

51. As a general rule, competition authorities follow a point-to-point approach when defining passenger transport markets. Substitutability between air and sea transport modes is assessed on a case-by-case basis, and depends in particular on the type of passengers, the distance and duration of journeys, the frequencies available and the

fares[10]. In its opinion on the maritime service between Tahiti and Moorea, using a point-to-point approach, the APC considered that on the maritime service between Tahiti and Moorea, several types of customer could be distinguished: daily traffic and tourist traffic, which tends to operate at weekends. The substitutability of sea transport with air transport appeared limited, given that the price of an air ticket was around 4 to 5 times that of a sea crossing on this route, and that the timetables and geographical situations were different. Similarly, while the notifying party indicated that the maritime passenger transport market in New Caledonia was subject to strong competitive pressure from the air sector, the ACNC had concluded that there was a maritime market, particularly in view of the differences in terms of rotation frequencies, journey times and passenger demand[11]. In an opinion on this subject, the APC noted that the breakdown of passenger traffic by mode of transport for 2015 highlighted the importance of air transport for services to archipelagos outside the Windward Islands. For the Windward Islands, inter-island transport is mainly by ferry for residents, with only tourists using air[12]. For the other islands, passenger traffic was mainly by air. Finally, it should be noted that the ADLC considered that the maritime passenger transport market "includes the transport of passengers and tourist vehicles".[13]

2. Freight transport

52. In the freight transport sector, decision-making practice traditionally distinguishes according to the mode of transport: (i) air transport, (ii) sea transport, (iii) land transport[14]. The choice of a freight transport mode would be constrained by certain factors such as the customer's geographical location or the nature of the goods transported. APC has therefore adopted an "origin-destination" approach, and considers that the different modes of freight transport are generally not substitutable. Within maritime freight transport, the APC left open the question of subdivisions according to ship type and type of goods.

53. Nevertheless, it noted that statistical data traditionally distinguish vehicle transport from freight transport, and segment freight transport into food products, building materials, hydrocarbons and miscellaneous.

54. With regard to finer segmentations, the competition authorities distinguish between scheduled and non-scheduled transport of goods[15]. Decision-making practice has also made a distinction between containerized and non-containerized (bulk)

---

10 Decision no. 2017-CC-01 of the Polynesian Competition Authority and see opinion on maritime services between Tahiti and Moorea.

11 ACNC decision no. 2023-DCC-09 of December 11, 2023 concerning the acquisition of exclusive control of Transiles SARL, Marifret SARL and Compagnie Maritime des Iles SARL by Société d'Exploitation Financière SARL.

12 APC Opinion 2017-AO-01 on a draft deliberation on the operating license and public service obligations in maritime and air inter-island transport.

13 ADLC decision n°06-MC-03 of December 11, 2006 concerning maritime transport in Corsica.

14 See in particular CPA decisions, No. 2017-CC-01 of March 9, 2017 on the acquisition of sole control of Compagnie maritime de Tahiti (CFMT) and Vaipihaa by SCP Emar; No. 2020-CC-02 of December 10, 2020 on the acquisition of joint control of the Dubreuil Aéro group by CMA CGM and the Dubreuil group.

15 See, for example, ADLC decisions n°19-D-03 of January 16, 2019 relating to practices implemented in the cross-Channel transport of day-old chicks sector and n°12-DCC-154 of November 7, 2012 relating to the acquisition of exclusive control of SeaFrance assets by Groupe Eurotunnel.

transport[16]. Lastly, competition authorities in metropolitan France and Europe have considered the possibility of segmentation according to the services associated with transport (e.g. refrigerated or non-refrigerated containers), but the question of the relevance of this segmentation has been left open.

55. The CMA CGM / Bolloré case reviewed in parallel by the APC, ACNC and the European Commission (for services to the Caribbean islands and French Guiana) provided a refined definition for containerized freight transport[17]. The traditional decision-making practice of the ADLC[18] and the European Commission[19], examined deep-sea freight market segments on the basis of routes linking two geographical areas defined by a wide range of ports served at both ends. The market surveys carried out by these three competition authorities showed that this approach was not applicable to small, isolated Ilian economies. The Commission's investigation revealed a lack of substitutability between, on the one hand, each of the ports of Martinique, Guadeloupe and French Guyana and, on the other, other ports in the Central America and Caribbean region. Similarly, the APC rejected the possibility of considering the Oceania/Pacific zone as a single geographic destination zone. This was due to the insularity and geographical isolation of French Polynesia, including with regard to its Oceania neighbors (more than 4,000 km from the main metropolises in the Pacific zone: Auckland. Honolulu or Sydney). What's more, the Oceania region is predominantly maritime, and consequently lacks other infrastructures, including short sea links, which would enable continuity from the port of unloading. Furthermore, APC noted that French Polynesia has developed privileged links with metropolitan France and the European Union, and remains liole integrated into the main trade flows in Oceania. Given the volumes imported, only one line serves it directly, from Europe. For the same reasons, ACNC has also concluded a market for the transport of goods by deep-sea containers, based on the binomial geographical zone of departure – port of arrival.

56. As far as the geographic market is concerned, decision-making practice in the maritime transport of passengers or goods has consistently adopted the "origin-destination" principle, according to which any combination of two cities or areas is considered a relevant market: goods must be transported from a point of origin to

---

16 See in particular ADLC decision no. 13-D-15 of June 25, 2013 on practices implemented in the maritime freight transport sector between Northern Europe and the French West Indies and its opinion no. 2018-A-06 of August 29, 2018 on the draft deliberation to amend deliberation no. 173 of March 29, 2006 on the structure of gasoline and diesel prices.

17 APC decision no. 2024-CC-01 of January 31, 2024 on the merger control of the acquisition of exclusive control of Bolloré Logistics and its subsidiaries by CMA CGM SA; ACNC decision no. 2023-DCC-11 of December 27, 2023 on the acquisition of exclusive control of SE Bolloré Logistics by SA CMA CGM; and Commission decision in case M.11143 CMA CGM/Bolloré Logistics presented in: One-way trade to structural remedies in vertical shipping mergersti – Competition Merger Brief No 2/2024.

18 Decision no. 19-DCC-170 of September 17, 2019 concerning the acquisition of exclusive control of Société de Manutention et de Consignation Maritime by Terminal Investment Limited and decision no. 13-D-15 of June 25, 2013 concerning practices implemented in the maritime freight transport sector between Europe and the French West Indies.

19 Commission decisions of July 25, 2022 in case M.10733 – CMA CGM / GEFCO; of April 29, 2022 in case M.10522-HapagLloyd/Eurogate/Eurogate Container Terminal Wilhelmshaven; and of February 6, 2019 in case M.9221 CMA CGM/CEVA.

a point of destination, without any other destination being substitutable[20]. In reality, it essentially concerns the nature of the service provided (I want to move from point A to point B), and does not include information on the geographical nature of the demand. Decisions generally make no distinction according to the origin of passengers or freight customers

3. Related markets

57. In CMA CGM / Bolloré Logistics, the competition authorities left open the question of defining the freight forwarding market. However, it is clear from decision-making practice that the freight forwarding business can include, in addition to transport itself, various other services such as customs clearance or warehousing, on behalf of customers according to their needs. Decision-making practice has envisaged a segmentation of the freight forwarding market according to (i) the national or international nature of the transport and (ii) the mode of transport used (air, sea or land). In geographical terms, the competition authorities concluded that demand was local in nature.

B. *Anti-competitive practices*

58. As far as 'classic' competition cases are concerned, although there is a fairly extensive practice of applying the prohibition of cartels or abuse of dominant position in the transport sector under European or French law, there are relatively few cases of this type in the Pacific Islands. The following descriptions are based on Oceanic and European cases with relatively similar circumstances.

1. Air sector

a) Agreements

59. The ADLC had noted a significant and simultaneous increase in air ticket prices in autumn 2017 on the Pointe-à-Pitre / Fort-de-France route by two airlines, Air Antilles and Air Caraïbes, and had opened an investigation into the behavior of these companies[21]. This case ended with a decision on December 4, 2024, finding the existence of cartels. According to the decision, the companies had fixed prices notably by concluding a "non-aggression agreement", the tariff component of which prohibited each of the two airlines from undercutng the other in terms of fares. They aimed to reduce supply and share slots on inter-island routes within the French and international Caribbean, and once an equilibrium had been reached, to maintain the level of supply

60. In a 2017 decision, Airfreight, the European Commission found that a number of airlines had coordinated their pricing policies for airfreight services from, to and within the EEA, so that the same surcharge and its variations were passed

---

20 See decisions n°13-D-15 by the ADLC, n°2017-CC-01 and n°2020-CC-02 by the APC, and n°2023-DCC-09 by the ACNC.

21 ADLC Decision no. 24-D-10 of December 4, 2024 concerning practices in the inter-island passenger air transport sector.

on in full and in a coordinated manner to customers[22]. Some carriers had also extended their cooperation to refusing to pay a commission to their customers (freight forwarders) on surcharges. By refusing to pay a commission, they ensured that surcharges were not subject to competition through discounts negotiated with their customers.

b) Abuse and concentration

61. There have been no cases of abuse or concentration in French Polynesia or New Caledonia.

62. Airport abuse cases decided by the European Commission concerned discriminatory charges. In several cases, airports were condemned because their charging systems favored one air operator to the detriment of its competitors. Similarly, the Commission found that the operator of Frankfurt am Main airport had abused its position as exclusive supplier of airport facilities for aircraft landing and take-off by not granting airlines the right to provide ground handling services themselves, and by not granting other airlines access to these services[23]. Finally, in another case[24], the Commission concluded that Aéroports de Paris had abused its dominant position by discriminating through its fees for the provision of ground handling services.

63. In the European merger cases that led to remedies, competition problems arose from a reduction in the number of players on routes. In these cases, the remedies consisted in freeing up slots.

64. In the Olympic/Aegean case, which concerned a planned merger between the only two scheduled airlines operating in Greece, the European Commission adopted a prohibition decision[25]. Both Olympic Air and Aegean Airlines had their main base at the same airport (in this case, Athens International Airport). International routes to and from Athens were deemed sufficiently competitive after the merger. On nine domestic routes, however, the merger would have resulted in a virtual monopoly. Ferry services, present on some of the routes concerned, were generally not considered to exert sufficient competitive pressure on the parties' air services, notably due to longer journey times and lower frequencies. Barriers to entry were not so much in the form of slot constraints, but rather in the form of a general difficulty for competitors to establish a base in Athens, due to airport charges and the importance of brand recognition. In this context, the proposed undertakings, which essentially concerned the release of slots, were not considered sufficient to encourage a competitor to set up a base at Athens airport and exert sufficient competitive pressure on the routes concerned. Consequently, the Commission prohibited the merger. Nevertheless, in 2013, the Commission authorized the second aoempted combination between Aegean Airlines and Olympic Air, basing

---

22 Commission decision of March 17, 2017 relating to a proceeding pursuant to Article 101 of the Treaty on the Functioning of the European Union, Article 53 of the EEA Agreement and Article 8 of the Agreement between the European Community and the Swiss Confederation on Air Transport (Case AT.39258 – Air Freight).

23 Commission decision of January 14, 1998 in case 34.801 Flughafen Frankfurt AG.

24 Commission decision of June 11, 1998 in case 35.613 Alpha Flight Services/Aéroports de Paris.

25 Decision of January 26, 2011 in case M.5830 – Olympic/ Aegean Airlines.

its decision on the particular circumstances that Olympic Air was a failing airline that would leave the market anyway if not acquired by Aegean Airlines.[26]

2. Marine sector

a) Agreements

65. If there has been no finding of cartels in this sector by the APC or ACNC, a summary of French and European cases may provide useful information on possible cases.

66. In its decision 13-D-15 of June 25, 2013, the ADLC noted that sea freight transport between Northern Europe, notably French ports, and the West Indies is the main route used for imports and exports. On this route, 90% of trade (excluding fuel) was handled by CMA-CGM, which shared its transport capacity with its competitors. CMA-CGM leased space on its vessels to Maersk, Marfret and WEC Lines to transport their containers. According to the ADLC, the space leasing contracts contained clauses that limited the intensity of competition and the possibility for new entrants to drive the market. These included exclusivities prohibiting the loading of containers on a vessel competing with CMA-CGM, an opaque capacity allocation mechanism, the absence of any possibility for Maersk, Marfret and WEC Lines to resell unused reserved capacity to third parties, and the indefinite duration of the contracts.

67. These clauses reduced the companies' ability to adapt to demand, and may have hindered the entry of new operators into the market. According to the ADLC, the cumulative effect of all the restrictive clauses could result in prices 10% to higher than the average fares charged by airlines operating on similar routes.

68. In its decision of April 15, 2010[27], the ADLC sanctioned four port handling companies for coordinating, in the case of three of them, in order to share berths under construction as part of the ongoing expansion of the Port of Le Havre's capacity, and for sharing, in the case of two of them, the port handling clientele.

69. In a decision dated February 27, 2009[28], the Conseil de la concurrence (the predecessor of the ADLC) ruled that SNCM had abused its dominant position on the Corsica route by submitng an indivisible global offer and refusing to make a firm commitment on the amount of subsidies requested line by line in response to a call for tenders from the public authorities. In fact, given the constraints imposed by the call for tenders in terms of service and fleet requirements, the other competitors were not in a position to submit a global bid within the timeframe set, and SNCM was therefore unavoidable, at least for part of the service to Corsica. By submitng an indivisible bid, SNCM was guaranteed to win all the routes, as the Corsican local authority could not reject it in favor of competing bids in order to preserve the continuity of the entire maritime service between Marseille and Corsica.

---

26 Decision of October 9, 2013 in case M.6796 – Aegean / Olympic II.

27 Decision 10-D-13 of April 15, 2010 concerning practices in the container handling sector at the port of Le Havre.

28 Decision 09-D-10 of February 27, 2009 concerning practices in the maritime transport sector between Corsica and the mainland.

70. Finally, in a decision of December 21, 2004[29], the French Competition Council noted that the three companies operating on the France-Channel Islands route had agreed to avoid a price war after a period of low prices offered by the third player who had recently entered the market.

b) Abuse: APC's opinion on maritime services between Tahiti and Moorea

71. In its opinion (2016-A-01) on competition on the maritime service between Tahiti and Moorea, the APC examined whether a dominant position on the freight and vehicle transport markets could lead to cross-subsidies into the passenger transport market and possibly to predatory pricing.

72. First of all, the APC found that the Degage group held a dominant position (monopoly) in the freight transport market between Tahiti and Moorea, and a dominant position in vehicle transport between Tahiti and Moorea. The APC stressed that the fact that a company holding a monopoly uses its monopoly resources to subsidize a new activity does not in itself constitute "an abuse of a dominant position. It added that this can only be sanctioned as an abuse of a dominant position when it is used to charge predatory prices, or when it has conditioned a commercial practice which, without being predatory, has led to a lasting disruption of the market which would not have occurred without it.

73. The APC emphasized that, in its view, the search for cross-subsidies, like that for predatory pricing, can therefore only be based on an analysis of cost accounting that enables the company's revenues and costs to be allocated to the various activities in an economically correct manner. In the case in point, APC concluded that it was unlikely that the surpluses generated by this activity would be sufficient to subsidize the passenger activity.

74. In a decision dated December 23, 2004[30], the French Competition Council concluded that the Régie du Port Autonome du Havre had abused its dominant position by charging predatory prices. The autonomous port charged different rates for the use of its public unloading facilities at the multivac terminal, depending on whether handling was entrusted to the terminal's storage concessionaire and its subcontractors or, on the contrary, to these companies' competitors. Similarly, the concessionaire had abused its dominant position by offering its customers combined storage and handling services, which had the effect of foreclosing competitors on the handling market. Similar cases had been dealt with by the European Commission in cases where ferry operators also owned and operated port facilities. This gave them the possibility of granting favorable treatment to their own ferry services, either by refusing access to port facilities to competing operators, or by granting them access on less favorable terms than those granted to their own services.[31]

---

29 Decision 04-D-74 of December 21, 2004 concerning practices on the market for maritime links between France and the Channel Islands.

30 Decision 07-D-28 of September 13, 2007 concerning practices implemented by the Autonomous Port of Le Havre, Compagnie industrielle des pondéreux du Havre, Société havraise de gestion et de transport and Havre Manutention.

31 See precautionary measures decisions of May 16, 1995 in the CCI de Morlaix case (port of Roscoff) and of June 11, 1992 in the Sealink/B&I case

3. Conclusion

75. Due to its economic characteristics, the transport sector is relatively prone to anti-competitive practices. These are generally highly concentrated markets, where barriers to entry and exit can be high. The cases reviewed belong to broad categories of issues such as fighting a new entrant (through predatory pricing fuelled by public subsidies, as alleged in the Vendée motorboat case, by relying on exclusive rights, as in the Corsica service case, or by relying on a dominant position in a related market, as in the Port of Le Havre case). Another major category of cases involves concerted practices in the face of economic shocks, such as a rise in the price of an input (in both the maritime and air transport sectors), or the aftermath of a price war that threatened the profitability of both parties (services to the Channel Islands and air transport in the Caribbean).

C. *Merger control*

1. Maritime transport in New Caledonia

76. In the Transiles case[32], the planned transaction involved an acquisition by a private company, but the subsequent acquisition of a minority stake by the Province of the Loyalty Islands in one of the target companies (CMI) was likely to harm competition. This shareholding entailed financial advantages in that any financial aid received by this company from the province of the Loyalty Islands for its passenger shipping activity could be passed on to the competitive freight shipping business. The distortions of competition thus created could, in the long term, lead to the ousting of existing competitors and/or deter the arrival of new entrants to the sea freight transport market. In terms of non-financial benefits, the risks examined concern CMI's easier access to port infrastructures and public contracts in the Loyalty Islands province.

77. The ACNC has authorized the transaction on the basis of a number of undertakings. Firstly, any financial aid or benefit to this company will be subject to prior approval by the Autorité. In addition, the notifying party has undertaken not to receive more favorable treatment from the Province of the Loyalty Islands in respect of CMI's shipping activities than its competitors enjoy for access to port infrastructures.

2. CMA CGM / Bolloré Logistics

78. In the CMA CGM / Bolloré Logistics case[33], the European, New Caledonian and French Polynesian competition authorities had to take a position on similar issues concerning the servicing of the island economies. This transaction essentially raised issues of vertical integration between the upstream market for containerized

---

32 ACNC decision no. 2023-DCC-09 of December 11, 2023 concerning the acquisition of exclusive control of Transiles SARL, Marifret SARL and Compagnie Maritime des Iles SARL by Société d'Exploitation Financière SARL.

33 APC decision no. 2024-CC-01 of January 31, 2024 on the merger control relating to the acquisition of exclusive control of Bolloré Logistics and its subsidiaries by CMA CGM SA; ACNC decision no. 2023-DCC-11 of December 27, 2023 relating to the acquisition of exclusive control of SE Bolloré Logistics by SA CMA CGM; and European Commission decision in case M.11143. CMA CGM/Bolloré Logistics as summarized in: One-way trade to structural remedies in vertical shipping mergersti | Competition Merger Brief No 2/2024

sea freight and the downstream market for the organization of freight transport. Freight forwarders organize the transport of goods on behalf of their customers, and may also provide customs clearance and warehousing services. As intermediaries, ocean freight forwarders are the main source of revenue for ocean carriers.

79. On each of the relevant Europe/territory markets, CMA CGM had a market share in excess of, and faced few competitive constraints. One of its few competitors, Marfret, had signed a ship-sharing agreement and was therefore not considered an independent competitive force. The combined market shares of CMA CGM and Marfret exceeded 90% for French Polynesia, the Caribbean and French Guiana. New Caledonia, on the other hand, had a market share of less than 70%. The three authorities concluded that CMA CGM held a dominant position, notably due to the scale of the barriers to entry. Firstly, due to the asymmetry of trade, a shipping line wishing to serve these territories would not be able to optimize its loading capacities, given the low volumes destined for export to Europe. Secondly, these markets have become increasingly concentrated in recent years, with acquisitions and exits to the benefit of CMA CGM.

80. The three competition authorities concluded that the new entity would have the ability and incentive to partially foreclose inputs by increasing the rates charged to Bolloré Logistics' competing freight forwarders, or by reducing the volumes allocated to competing freight forwarders on the Europe – relevant territory route. Indeed, CMA CGM faced only weak competitive pressure on these routes, with imperfect substitutes (e.g. for New Caledonia, the Europe-Australia route followed by a much longer transshipment than the direct route) and high barriers to entry. In the absence of immediate substitutes, demand would not be able to counteract such a strategy. Incentives to implement this partial foreclosure would be high, since demand from local forwarders has low price elasticity, any forwarders foreclosed would not be able to retaliate, upstream profit losses would be lower than downstream gains, and final demand would have no credible alternative.

81. Faced with these risks of partial foreclosure, the competition authorities finally authorized the transaction on the basis of remedies. The ACNC opted for a behavioral remedy, while the Commission and the APC accepted the divestiture of the commissionaire activities. It should be noted that the respective sales were made to the same buyer. The remedies accepted by the ACNC have a maximum duration of fifteen years and provide that CMA CGM undertakes to (i) guarantee that, on a half-yearly basis, at least 65% of its containerized sea freight volumes originating in Europe and unloaded in New Caledonia are reserved for shippers and forwarders that it does not control, (ii) apply transparent and non-discriminatory pricing and (iii) implement internal measures to ensure the effectiveness of these commitments.

Effective Economic Regulation Independence from the Companies in the Sector and from Political Power

Vincent Jaunet*
Magenta

1. The network industries (telecommunications, transport, media and energy) and competition law have a close relationship.

2. Part of the explanation naturally lies in the fact that these sectors have a natural monopoly, and their liberalization precisely requires the mobilization of principles derived from competition law. Due to their history, they are typically characterized by the presence of a historic operator who, prior to the opening to competition, held a monopoly position and was also likely to own essential infrastructures. In addition, an organized opening usually takes place in stages, with the coexistence of monopolistic markets and markets in a competitive situation.

3. The result is a host of competition issues such as the question of access to infrastructure, possible barriers to entry possible coupling or cross-subsidization between competitive and monopoly sectors, possible price squeezes, etc.

4. Although these sectors are generally subject to the control of a dedicated sectoral regulatory authority, they also give rise to a large body of decision-making practice (whether in the form of penalty decisions or opinions) by the competition authorities.

---

* Vincent Jaunet is a partner and co-founder of Magenta – Société d'Avocats.

5. Players in the competitive game (particularly new entrants) often call for concomitant action by sector regulators (through *ex ante* intervention) and competition authorities, whose considerable powers to impose sanctions and injunctions can ensure that conditions of competition on markets evolve rapidly and satisfactorily.

6. In addition, it issues various opinions on the operation of competition in these sectors, which may be requested by the public authorities, the regulatory authorities concerned or certain market players. These opinions are used in particular to assess potential changes to the legislative or regulatory framework necessary for the development of a given sector.

7. A look at the decisions of the Polynesian Competition Authority shows that Polynesia is no exception to the rule.

8. For example, the first decision issued by the Polynesian Competition Authority concerning anti-competitive practices related to the telecommunications sector.[1] More generally, since its creation, of the six decisions sanctioning anticompetitive practices issued by the Polynesian Competition Authority, three concern regulated sectors (in this case, telecommunications). The situation is identical in terms of opinions: of the 48 opinions issued by the Polynesian Competition Authority since its creation, 20 concern the network industries.

9. The energy sector (by energy, we mean hydrocarbons, gas and electricity) is no exception to these observations, even though, to date, it has not been the subject of any decisions concerning anti-competitive practices. The Polynesian Competition Authority has issued eight opinions on the subject:[2]
   - Opinion No. 2016-A-02 of November 7, 2016, regarding the competitive situation in the hydrocarbon transport sector to French Polynesia;
   - Opinion No. 2018-AO-03 of August 10, 2018, on a draft law of the country establishing an Energy Code for French Polynesia;
   - Opinion No. 2020-AO-02 of September 3, 2020, on a draft law of the country specifying the content of Titles III and IV of the Energy Code of French Polynesia;
   - Opinion No. 2020-AO-03 of September 24, 2020, on a draft law of the country establishing a solidarity scheme in the electricity sector;
   - Opinion No. 2021-A-01 of October 15, 2021, on a draft law of the country regarding the procedures for handling applications for hydroelectric concessions and authorizations;
   - Opinion No. 2022-A-01 of April 21, 2022, regarding the competitive situation in the hydrocarbon supply sector in French Polynesia;

---

1 APC, Decision No. 2018-PAC-01 of 6 June 2018 on practices implemented in the mobile telephony sector aimed at residential customers, see also RONZANO Alain, "Telecoms: The Polynesian Competition Authority issues its first contentious decision and accepts the commitments of the Polynesian incumbent telecoms operator putting an end to practices identical to those already sanctioned by the metropolitan Competition Authority (OPT)", *Concurrences* [online], 6 June 2018, No. 3-2018, art. n° 87221. Available at: www.concurrences.com.

2 The attentive reader of the Polynesian Competition Authority's website will note that the page of the site dedicated to the energy sector also refers to Opinion No. 2019-AO-01 on a draft law of the country relating to the organisation of the vanilla industry.

- Opinion No. 2023-AO-05 of November 7, 2023, on a draft law of the country regarding the deployment of electric vehicle charging infrastructure (IRVE);
- Opinion No. 2024-A-04 of May 30, 2024, on a draft law of the country concerning sectorial regulation in the energy sector.

10. While hydrocarbons (gas and oil) are essential to Polynesia's energy supply (in 2022, 64% of Polynesia's electricity will be generated from hydrocarbons; in 2020, Polynesia's energy dependency rate will be 93%, compared with 45% in France), they have already led to the adoption of two opinions by the Polynesian Competition Authority (the last of which, issued following an ex officio referral from the Authority, identified pricing practices that were not in line with the French market). These opinions identified inefficient pricing practices on the part of operators and issued recommendations likely to result in substantial savings for Polynesia in general and the end consumer in particular. It should be noted, however, that the most significant and recent development for the Polynesian Competition Authority in the energy sector concerns both gas and electricity, as a draft law of the country is currently under discussion to make the Polynesian Competition Authority the regulator of the gas and electricity markets

11. A strategic issue for any country, even more so in the context of the energy transition, the electricity market in French Polynesia is characterized by certain organizational specificities compared to the typical divisions observed in other countries. These particularities have their origins both in history and in the geography of the Polynesian territory (isolation from other territories, the multiplicity of islands making the creation of production, transport, or distribution infrastructures more costly, the absence of domestic hydrocarbon resources, a limited market size while having certain advantages for some renewable energies, notably hydroelectric, photovoltaic, geothermal, and marine)

12. In the electricity value chain, it is customary to distinguish between the following activities (going from upstream to downstream):
    - Electricity generation (in Polynesia, this can be from fossil or renewable energy sources);
    - Transmission, which involves transporting the electricity produced from generation sites to major consumption sites or the distribution network via high-voltage lines;
    - Distribution, which covers the final delivery of electricity via the transmission network or production units directly connected to the distribution network to consumers. This activity also includes connecting sites and supplying and reading meters;
    - Supply/marketing, which involves the sale of electricity to the consumer.

13. In the majority of electricity systems (particularly in mainland France), transmission and distribution activities are subject to a legal monopoly (which may be organised through concession systems), given the significant investment they require and the lack of economic relevance of duplicating the networks that support them.

14. Competition comes from production and supply/marketing activities.

15. French Polynesia has some specificities compared to this model:
    - Transport is not present on all the islands. In fact, there is only a transmission network on the island of Tahiti. On the other islands, the production sites are directly connected to the local distribution network;
    - Distribution and supply activities are not separated: if distribution activities are carried out under different concessions, this organisation means that once the concession has been awardedthere is no competition in the supply/ marketing segment.
16. Key players in the value chain include :
    - The Electricité de Tahiti (EDT)-Engie group, which controls, directly or via its subsidiaries, most of the generation activities and holds a large proportion of the distribution concessions (and, via the latter, the supply to end customers);[3] and
    - Transport d'énergie électrique en Polynésie (TEP), a company majority-owned by the country.
17. In response to the issues raised by global warming, the Polynesian public authorities drew up an Energy Transition Plan 2015-2030 in 2015[4].
18. This plan, which has since been replaced by the Multiannual Energy Programme, had three main objectives (changing the energy model, changing behaviour and changing economic models), with the ultimate aim of achieving a renewable energy mix by 2030. The plan also identified a number of means of achieving these objectives. In addition to clarifying the applicable legal framework, the plan aims to promote competition by focusing on three areas: (i) facilitating access to the public network; (ii) attracting new competitors; and (iii) establishing an independent arbitrator.
19. The aim is to encourage the emergence of more competitive prices and to encourage investors to develop electricity production from renewable energy sources, as the development of such facilities requires major investment.
20. To achieve these various objectives, several pieces of legislation have been passed since 2018, which have been submitted to the Polynesian Competition Authority for its opinion (4 of the 8 opinions mentioned above).
21. Given the technical nature of the subject, the public authorities have opted for codification in stages.
22. As early as the first opinion issued in 2018, when examining the draft law of the country instituting an *Energy Code* for French Polynesia, the French Competition Authority pointed out the main obstacles to the development of competition in the electricity market:
    - the status of the transmission operator ;
    - the framework applicable to production, particularly in regards to hydroelectric concessions; – regulation.

---

3 Until recently, it held all the distribution concessions, but in 2022, several communes, including MooreaMaiao, have decided to take over the management of their electricity networks directly.

4 The 2015-2030 Energy Transition Plan finally came to an end in 2022, and was succeeded by the Multiannual Energy Programme.

23. Despite the progress made regarding the status of the manager (I), the changes made to production activities appear incomplete and could take some time to produce their effects (II). As for the organisation of regulation, it is likely evolve from one moment the next, even if a certain uncertainty remains in view of the recent turbulent parliamentary debates on the subject (III).

24. Incidentally, if the reader wants to get an idea of the progress made in the electricity market over the last 7 years, a comparative reading of the presentation of the electricity sector at the beginning of both Opinion No. 2018-AO-03 and Opinion No. 2024-A-04 is a very useful tool.

I. TEP reform

25. TEP (*Territoire d'Énergie de la Polynésie*) plays a key role in the Polynesian electricity market, as it owns the transmission network.

26. A company with a majority of public capital, it had for a long time a substantial part (39%) of its capital owned by EDT, a situation that raised legitimate questions about its independence.

27. For a long time, TEP's activities were limited to owning transmission network infrastructure: it had no operational responsibility for network maintenance, operation or balancing, and in fact subcontracted these services to EDT.

28. This situation was more problematic given that balancing is a key task for the electricity system: it is ensuring a balance electricity supply and demand (also known as *dispatching*). To do this, the operator may have to mobilise additional generation resources or, on the contrary, interrupt them, just as it may have to relieve certain consumers in the event of consumption that is too high in relation to available generation.

29. Under the Polynesian *Energy Code*, electricity transmission is a public service.

30. In view of the role of the transmission operator, and as the Polynesian Competition Authority has pointed out (repeating the conclusions already drawn by the experts from the Commission de régulation de l'énergie [CRE] who were asked by Polynesia in early 2010) the transmission operator must be independent of any other operator in the value chain in order to guarantee transparent and nondiscriminatory treatment of upstream producers and downstream distributors and suppliers.[5]

31. In 2022, the following two decisions from the Polynesian Authority emphasized the importance of TEP's independence from any other player in the value chain, EDT sold its stake in TEP. To date, 75% of TEP's capital is held by the country and the remaining 25% by RTEi, the international subsidiary of the French electricity transmission system operator (RTE). As a result, the company is now truly independent.

---

5 "A central player strengthened in this way should complete the separation of activities and unify the treatment of producers upstream and distributors downstream, in their relations of injection and extraction of electricity flows, in particular without going through the integrated incumbent operator, present and competing at both levels. Strengthened in this way, such a transmission operator would seem able to play a beneficial role for all players in the chain, by providing neutrality and equal treatment, predictability and confidence in the sector" (APC, Opinion No. 2018-AO-03, pt 120).

32. At the same time, TEP has gradually gained functional independence. While it has long been dependent on EDT for its operations, TEP has internalised maintenance operations in 2019, operations in June 2020, network control functions in December 2020 and dispatching/balance responsibility on the 1st of January 2022.

33. Most of the work has therefore been done in light of the initial assessments of the Polynesian Competition Authority.

34. The only major recommendation from the Polynesian Competition Authority on the issue of the transmission system operator that has not yet been adopted is the one proposing to make TEP the sole purchaser.

35. As a reminder, in a single-buyer system, one player in the electricity system (often the transmission operator) is responsible for buying all the electricity produced and then selling it to distributors/suppliers. This system has the advantage of simplicity and guarantees equal access to electricity production (avoiding the bias that can result from the presence on the market of integrated groups versus *pure players* in the supply sector).

36. If they are to function effectively, the question of tariffs and their duration of application are essential. If set incorrectly, tariffs can lead to investment disincentives or production rents, as well as economic inefficiencies in downstream markets. They are also likely to be subject to strong political influence.

37. In the case in point, the Polynesian authorities put forward other reasons for not favouring this organisational structure, in particular the need to amend TEP's articles of association and its service delegation, but also the lack of sufficient resources to provide TEP with the necessary cash flow to acquire the electricity produced on the Polynesian market.

38. Irrespective of the possibility of setting up a single-buyer type scheme, at present, following the reforms carried out, the stage aimed at creating an independent transmission system operator on the Polynesian market can be considered to have been reached.

II. Organisation of production

39. While a satisfactory competitive structure now exists in the transport sector, the situation is more complex in the other segments.

40. As a preliminary point, it should be noted that while the Energy Code establishes the principle that electricity producers on the island of Tahiti and public network operators are required to manage these two activities through separate entities,[6] this principle, with the exception of the SECOSUD loop, is currently only theoretical as it does not apply to existing contracts. Moreover, the concession contract related to the Tahiti North loop will not expire until 2030. This is a point of concern from a competition perspective

41. Furthermore, the introduction of competition in the supply marketing business will not take place for several years, even if it ever does.

---

6 See *Energy Code*, art. LP 111-8.

42. Consequently, electricity generation is the main field in which competition is likely to exercised.[7] In this segment, the principle is that of free competition. However, there are numerous frameworks and exceptions, so that electricity generation remains a highly controlled activity.

43. Installations with a capacity of more than 500 kW require authorisation. Below that, they are subject only to a declaration.

44. What's more, the generation facilities that contribute to the guaranteed power are allocated as part of a public service delegation or under public management. According to the Polynesian *Energy Code*, the term "guaranteed power" does not refer to a particular form of energy, since it represents:

> *The obligation to respond, in all situations and at all times, except in cases of force majeure, to the electricity demand of consumers connected to the public electricity distribution network, both in terms of power and energy. It helps to ensure the security of electricity supply.*[8]

45. In the light of this definition, which, like the Polynesian Competition Authority and the Economic, Social, Environmental and Cultural Council of French Polynesia (CESEC), is regrettably not more precise, it seems rational to consider that this formula designates, *at the very least,* the largest facilities capable of guaranteeing the territory's security supply. In any event, it is a given that the most powerful hydroelectric facilities do indeed fall within the scope of this system, since the *Energy Code* expressly provides for these facilities (with a capacity of over 2 MW) to be allocated through concessions.

46. This concession system also applies to distribution.

47. According to a 2018 opinion from the Polynesian Competition Authority, the concession regime normally ensures equal access for operators to exploit the granted asset or service. However, for the system to be competitively effective, the duration of the concession must be properly determined (it should be long enough to allow for the amortization of investments while providing prospects for regular renewals so that operators can maintain their activities and apply when the time comes). Furthermore, the implementation of the system must not create an advantage for the incumbent operator due to, for example, information asymmetry.

48. On this last point, in its opinion no. 2021-A-01 on the conditions for awarding hydroelectric concessions, the Polynesian Competition Authority considered that the information mechanisms in place ensured that interested operators were properly informed about potential or current projects (memoranda of intent) and about the hydrological potential of the basins and their current use, without there being any risk of information being stolen.

49. On the other hand, the Authority is more critical of the relationship between concession and authorisation procedures, and of the periods that can be set in this context.

---

[7] Article LP 311-1 of the French *Energy Code* states in its second paragraph: "Everyone is free to produce electricity, in particular for personal consumption".

[8] See *Energy Code*, art. LP 311-2, para. 2.

50. This is all the more important given that hydroelectric generation units are one of the segments where competition could develop and where new generation units could emerge.

51. However, the chosen legal framework raises certain questions from the perspective of the Polynesian Competition Authority.

52. Firstly, the maximum duration of licences has been increased. the previous maximum term of 30 years was already considered long by the Polynesian Competition Authority,[9] it has been increased to 45 years with the possibility of extending it to 60 years (by way of comparison, in mainland France, the maximum term is 75 years, but most licences issued today have a term of 30 years).

53. This question of duration also arises in the context of concessions, whether hydroelectric or distribution.

54. On the other hand, the authorisation procedure requires the agreement of the transmission and distribution system operators concerned, although this issue is not specific to hydroelectric facilities, as all generating facilities are subject to an authorisation procedure.

55. However, as explained above, to date there is not necessarily a separation between the distribution network operator and the generation activity. As a result, this prior agreement raises two competitive risks: a risk of discrimination in favour of generation projects carried out by the distribution operator concerned (or the entity of its group active in the field of generation) and a risk of this same operator capturing privileged information (particularly technical) from competitors for the benefit of its generation activities.[10]

56. For the time being, the Polynesian authorities have not seen fit to correct these two points[11].

57. These are certainly not the only explanatory factors. Financial and land issues – in particular strong opposition from local residents to the development of new water concession projects – are more likely to be the main reasons. For all that, they certainly contribute to the relative sluggishness in the development of competition in the field of production.

58. This situation could ultimately have an impact on the objectives of the energy mix or price competitiveness. In this respect, if all electricity producers, for installations with a power output of 200 kW or more, are required at all times to be able to justify the cost of the energy produced by showing all the contributing components (on this point, they send a detailed statement containing these elements to the competent administrative authority every year), competitive pressure is certainly a better spur than a simple communication obligation.

---

9 See APC, Opinion No. 2020-AO-02, pt YY.

10 In its final observations report of 4 July 2023 on the management of French Polynesia's energy policy, the Chambre territoriale des comptes included lengthy comments on the breaches of the principle of equal treatment and freedom of access observed in the context of call for projects procedure for the construction and operation of photovoltaic installations with storage on the island of Tahiti.

11 In the Marquesas Islands in 2021-2022, when a public service delegation renewal procedure was being considered, EDT obtained a 2-year extension, provoking the ire of potential competitors.

III. The future organisation of regulation

59. In its first opinion issued in 2018, the Polynesian Competition Authority emphasized how crucial regulation and the role of the regulator were in network industries, making it essential to guarantee the independence and expertise of the bodies responsible for regulatory functions. In particular, the Authority highlighted that 'effective economic regulation requires means of independence from the companies in the sector and from political power, notably to ensure the impartiality and legitimacy of its actions' [12].

60. However, to date, despite repeated reminders from the Polynesian Competition Authority, the situation has changed little.

61. Regulatory tasks are shared between the Polynesian Energy Directorate (DPE), which is a department of the Polynesian administration, and the Energy Commission, which is a political body (it has five members, including four ministers and a member of the Polynesian Assembly). So there is no independence.

62. The situation is all the more damaging because, at the same time, the country retains stakes in certain operators in the value chain (TEP but also production companies, in particular 35% of Marama Nui, which manages five of Tahiti's six hydroelectric facilities). This puts the country in the position of judge and jury, particularly in procedures concerning hydroelectric concessions, which may lead it to adopt biased decisions with regard to potential competitors.

63. On this point, the Polynesian Competition Authority has, on several occasions, invited the public authorities, if they intend to retain the regulatory function at the level of the Country, to consider the sale by the latter of its economic and operational holdings in the energy sector[13].

64. This recommendation was not followed. However, the country cannot necessarily be blamed for the fact that factors other than the organisation of sectoral regulation are likely to be taken into account in the decision to sell a stake in electricity generating assets.

65. In any case, the public authorities seem to be aware of the need to organise the regulation of the energy sector differently. A far-reaching reform aimed at making the Polynesian Competition Authority the regulator of the energy market is now being considered, but its fate remains uncertain.

66. The core of the reform, which takes the form a draft law on energy sector regulation, aims to transfer some of the regulatory tasks to the Polynesian Competition Authority.

67. This measure cannot be seen as genuinely new, since it was already included in the 2015-2030 Energy Transition Plan adopted in 2015.[14] The Plan even set a target of implementation by the end of the 2nd half of 2016.

---

[12] APC, Opinion No. 2024-A-04, pt 91.

[13] "Nevertheless, if the government wishes to remove any ambiguity as to its role in this area, the solution is undoubtedly to withdraw from the capital of electricity producers and in particular to sell its shares in Marama Nui", APC, opinion no. 2021-A-01, pt 55.

[14] Specifically, the plan stated: "All players in the energy system (established players and new entrants) will have to be able to rely on an independent 'arbitrator' in the event of disputes. *The handling of such disputes could be entrusted to the new French Polynesia Competition Authority, whose energy expertise would be based on the partnerships established with national regulators (in this case with the Commission de Régulation de l'Energie)*" (emphasis added).

68. In its 2018 opinion, the Polynesian Competition Authority also pointed out the need to set up a regulator, although it did not expressly envisage this function being devolved to it.

69. Aware in the case of Polynesian economy of the need to pool resources, the Polynesian Competition Authority, in its opinion No. 2018-AO-03, recommended the creation a multi-sector regulator. No doubt the Authority also had in mind that other sectors (notably telecommunications) could also benefit from the establishment of a dedicated sector regulator.

70. So this is not the route that is currently being considered.

71. However, a single authority that combines the functions of competition authority and sector regulator raises a number of questions. Admittedly, this is not an original model. It has already been implemented on several occasions in other countries around the world.

72. Among the most notable examples is the Dutch Consumer and Markets Authority (ACM), which combines sector-specific regulatory functions energy, telecommunications, transport and postal services with anti-competitive practices and merger control. The ACM is also responsible for enforcing consumer protection laws. The same organisation also exists in Spain. Closer to Polynesia, in Australia on the one hand, and in New Zealand on the other, the Australian Competition and Consumer Commission (ACCC) and the Commerce Commission (COMCOM) of New Zealand combine the functions of competition authority and sector regulator for numerous network industries

73. (telecommunications, energy and water sector for Australia, airport, restructuring of the dairy sector, groceries, telecommunications, gas, electricity and hydrocarbons for New Zealand).

74. As far as Polynesia is concerned, it makes perfect sense to combine a number of powers within a single institution, particularly with a view to pooling resources. In addition, it would enable the Polynesian Competition Authority to intervene more effectively, since its intervention would be continuous (and not optional and sporadic if it is confined to acting solely on the basis of competition law) and would be carried out *ex ante*. Many emphasise the synergies that can be achieved by combining the functions of regulation and competition under the same authority.

75. However, the transfer of the task of regulating the energy markets to the Polynesian Competition Authority, as in the other countries mentioned above, does raise certain questions. These will have to be taken into account if the planned reform is really to achieve its objectives.

76. Firstly, as the Polynesian Competition Authority pointed out in its opinion, the transfer of powers envisaged by the public authorities is incomplete for the time being.

77. First of all, from a material point of view, it should be noted that while the bill refers to a transfer of regulatory powers for electricity and gas, the country retains jurisdiction over hydrocarbons. Although this division may be debatable given the importance of hydrocarbons in the energy value chain in Polynesia, in any,

the texts seem to need to be amended to clearly specify the scope of each, as gas as such also constitutes a hydrocarbon. It would also seem necessary, as a second step, to consider transferring jurisdiction over hydrocarbons to the Polynesian Competition Authority.

78. The opinions already issued by the Polynesian Competition Authority on the subject hydrocarbons are certainly the best illustration of the relevance that a permanent intervention by the Authority could have in this area.

79. Furthermore, in the field of electricity, the transfer of powers from the administration to the Polynesian Competition Authority is only partial: while it is envisaged that the function of settling disputes or supervising public service delegates and concessionaires will be transferred to the Polynesian Competition Authority, the administration and the Government will retain regulatory powers, particular with regard to connection rules or setting tariffs, in order to achieve a system of shared regulation.

80. Secondly, combining the functions of sector regulator and competition authority can give rise to a number of difficulties, such as:

- *Sometimes contradictory approaches:* sector regulators do have the power to settle disputes, but much of their regulatory power translates into the adoption of *ex ante* measures. This approach can conflict with the principles of a competition authority, which generally favours an *ex post* approach that leaves more room for market forces.

  But the point is not purely hypothetical. Very recently, the French competition authority (Autorité de la Concurrence) and the energy regulator (Commission de Régulation de l'Energie) were asked to carry out an assessment of the future of regulated tariffs for sale of electricity. They came to divergent conclusions, with the former advocating their abolition while the latter was in favour of maintaining them for a further 5 years[15].

- *Difficulties linked to the management of multi-skilling:* risk of diluting priorities or administrative overload, with a consequent risk of reducing the institution's overall efficiency.
- *Difficulties in terms of resources and organisation* and, ultimately, possible problems in ensuring full compliance with the principles applied in their dispute resolution and/or sanctioning activities: case law, in particular that of the Constitutional Council, reminds us that the regulatory and competition authorities are required to respect certain essential principles in procedural terms, in particular the separation of the functions of investigation and judgement. In the event of a dual role, this principle will apply both to the dispute resolution function and to the power to impose sanctions in regulatory matters and as competition authority. Under these conditions, it is not

---

15 See Autorité de la concurrence, *Rapport d'évaluation sur le dispositif des tarifs réglementés de vente d'électricité*, 12 November 2024 and CRE, *Rapport relatif à l'évaluation des tarifs réglementés de vente d'électricité*, 7 November 2024.

certain that the new resources provided for the draft law will enable this requirement to be fully met in the long term (one vice-president and two new rapporteurs, with the Polynesian Competition Authority calling for an additional rapporteur in addition to the two provided for). While closer cooperation with the CRE is certainly to be encouraged, it will not make up for the need have sufficient human resources to ensure strict compliance with the above principles.

81. Criticism is also emerging at Polynesian level. The CESEC, which was consulted on this draft law, was particularly critical, to the extent that it unanimously adopted an unfavourable opinion. In addition to the reservations shared with the Polynesian Competition Authority regarding the scope of the powers transferred, CESEC also believes that the transfer should not be made to the Authority but to another institution, in order to avoid the risk of interference between the functions of competition authority and regulatory authority.

82. Today, no one knows what will happen to this reform. Although the bill was due to be examined by the Assembly, it withdrawn by the government under pressure from certain MPs, who believe that regulation should not be transferred to an independent authority but should remain in the hands of the public authorities. According to media reports, the bill is due to be amended and resubmitted during the next parliamentary session.

83. While there had been a degree of consensus for some ten years on need to transfer the regulatory functions to an independent body, the recent withdrawal of the bill to bring about this reform raises questions.

84. In this respect, the Polynesian Competition Authority emphasised Opinion No. 2024-A-04 that "effective economic regulation requires means independence from companies in the sector and from political power, in order to guarantee the impartiality and validity of its action". This objective cannot be achieved if the regulatory function is maintained within the administration and the Government. On this point, It is revealing to note that although the DPE has been responsible for settling disputes for several years. No procedure has yet been initiated.

85. If the public authorities were to take a step backwards, it would mark a major halt to the process of opening up the energy sector that has been underway nearly 10 years.

86. Although it has not yet borne all its fruit, partly due to the remaining developments to be made, it remains that the opening of the energy sector to competition seems essential to allow for the development of renewable energies and, more broadly, to achieve the energy transition goals of French Polynesia.

87. As for the Polynesian Authority, through its various opinions, it has fully participated in these developments. The Polynesian government's project to also make it a regulatory authority, regardless of the debates this reform generates, is further proof of its legitimacy and the fact that it is now a key player in the Polynesian economy.

The Challenges of Competition Law in the Energy Sector

Elisabeth Moreau[*]
Lawyer at the Paris Bar

1. Energy, a sector of primary importance, includes the production, transformation, storage, transportation, and distribution of electricity, heat, cold, and fuel (liquid or gaseous). By definition, like telecommunications or transport, the energy sector involves networks characterized by the interconnection of infrastructures, resulting in a high level of interdependence between users and suppliers.
2. The main challenge in network industries lies in the balance between the investments they generate, particularly for infrastructure, and the public interest nature of the goods or services provided. Therefore, public authorities naturally intervene in the implementation of these industries. However, driven by competition policies, the liberalization of these activities has allowed them to become more competitive, benefiting economic development that is favorable to consumers.
3. However, the functioning of competition in these industries is not straightforward, especially in small island economies where geographical characteristics sometimes require limiting the liberalization of these activities to specific segments of the value chain. It is clear that French Polynesia is no exception, and the evolution of its public policies is marked by the ongoing tension between economic

---

[*] Lawyer admitted to the Paris Bar (2025), Elisabeth Moreau combines legal expertise with a strategic vision of business. She previously held legal director positions at Vodafone Polynesia (telecom), AMP VISUAL TV Group (audiovisual), and Mobilitas Group (international transport). She also served as an advisor to the President and members of the board of the Polynesian Competition Authority (APC).

development, promoted by competition, and the maintenance of territorial unity through public interest missions.

4. Indeed, French Polynesia is characterized by its double insularity, due to its isolation and its geographical fragmentation. This territory, located in the heart of the South Pac ific Ocean, includes 118 islands and atolls scattered over a maritime area of more than 4 million square kilometers, an area equivalent to that of Europe, with 80% of its population concentrated on the island of Tahiti.

5. Territorial unity is therefore naturally an ongoing issue for the country, which has the responsibility to ensure equitable access for its inhabitants to the goods and services provided by network industries. Thus, in the energy sector, the country initially chose extensive intervention, which has since evolved towards a market liberalization that is not yet fully achieved by 2024.

6. Over the past 10 years, the Polynesian Competition Authority (APC) has almost systematically reminded that competition law 'is a tool in the service of economic efficiency' capable of adapting to the specificities of small island economies. The energy sector in French Polynesia is characterized by an energy mix largely dominated by fossil fuels. In 2022, 92.5% of the energy consumed still came from the importation of various petroleum derivatives.[1] This dependence on fossil fuels exposes the territory to fluctuations in global prices and increases its economic vulnerability. To limit the impact of the inflationary trend of international oil prices on Polynesian consumers, the country intervenes through various price regulation mechanisms.

7. In the face of these challenges, French Polynesia adopted an Energy Transition Plan for 2015-2030, aiming to achieve an electricity mix composed of 75% renewable energy (RE) by 2030. However, in 2022, RE represented only 7.3% of primary consumption,[2] reflecting the difficulties in achieving this transition.

8. Despite these modest figures, notable progress has been made. Hydroelectric production, stimulated by favorable weather conditions, covers one-third of Tahiti's electricity needs. Photovoltaic energy has been growing at a rate of 6% per year since 2017, driven by self-consumption and grid injections from new solar farms developed by local entrepreneurs. Innovative technologies such as Sea Water Air Conditioning (SWAC), a deep-sea cooling system, are also contributing to this diversification.

9. However, in 2023, electricity production increased by 2.1% to reach 501 GWh, but this increase is still largely based on diesel thermal production.

10. The economic organization of the energy market in French Polynesia is based on a centralized structure dominated by a limited number of historical players.

11. In the electricity sector, these players benefit from public service delegations (DSP) or management, which grants them exclusive rights in specific areas. Specifically, French Polynesia has 65 public electricity distribution networks spread across 58 islands. Islands with low populations or non-permanent populations do not

---

1 Polynesian Energy Observatory, *Energy Balance of French Polynesia*, 2022.

2 IEOM French Polynesia, *Annual Economic Report*, 2023.

have public electricity services; their production means are limited to generators or isolated photovoltaic installations.

12. However, the structure of the market limits competition. The weak separation between production, transport, and electricity distribution complicates the entry of new players. This situation is particularly pronounced in remote islands, where high logistical costs require a price equalization financed by the electricity solidarity contribution (CSE), introduced in 2022.

13. Since its creation by the Country Law No. 2015-2 of February 23, 2015, the APC has issued numerous recommendations to best support the economic efficiency of the energy sector in French Polynesia. Competition law plays a crucial role in balancing economic efficiency and public service.

14. The APC has issued eight opinions on the energy sector, relentlessly encouraging the strengthening of competition and sustainable development. Many of the recommendations it has made over the decade have been followed by the country, which is keen to provide operators with the most appropriate competitive environment.

15. French Polynesia must face several challenges to meet its energy objectives. Diversifying production methods and integrating renewable energies (RE) are essential to reduce dependence on fossil fuels. However, this requires increased investment, simplification of regulatory procedures, and improved attractiveness for private players.

16. To meet its energy objectives, French Polynesia must overcome structural challenges related to its remoteness, high logistical costs, and market fragmentation. Diversifying production methods, combined with better integration of renewable energies, is essential to strengthen the energy resilience of the territory.

17. The APC continues to play a key role in ensuring healthy competition adapted to local specifics, enabling its players to optimize costs and improve service quality for the benefit of Polynesian consumers.

I. The Energy Sector in French Polynesia

18. Normative texts often address broader public interest concerns beyond competition and outline public authorities' intervention that impacts the functioning of the economy. For the past decade, the APC has fulfilled its mission of informing the Government and the Assembly of French Polynesia about the effects of public intervention on competition. In its eight opinions on the energy sector, the APC has proposed various measures to reconcile the public interest objectives and economic efficiency related to this sector.

19. Many of its recommendations have been followed by the Polynesian government, notably for the adoption of the *Energy Code* in 2019 and the clarifications made in 2020 and 2021.

20. However, since the country combines the roles of regulator and owner of the historical electricity operator, the APC has consistently warned about the need for independent regulation of the sector. A draft law was submitted to the relevant bodies in 2024, but the issue has been postponed to 2025.

A. *Legislative and Regulatory Framework*

21. French Polynesia is an overseas community whose autonomy, proclaimed in 1984, is governed by Organic Law No. 2004-192 of February 27, 2004. The primary mode of functioning of this autonomy status is to grant French Polynesia general competence, with the French State retaining attributional competence.

22. In accordance with this principle, French Polynesia is competent in all matters except those expressly assigned to the State. It can, through the acts of the Assembly of French Polynesia, define its own rules in most areas, subject to the respect of the general principles outlined in the texts forming the constitutional block or those established by jurisprudence.

23. The energy sector falls under the competence of French Polynesia and has undergone a major regulatory evolution through the Country Law No. 2019-27 of August 26, 2019, adopting an *Energy Code*.

24. The *Energy Code*, a fundamental text for the sector, structured the regulation by defining the guiding principles for production, distribution, and consumption, while embedding the objectives of sustainability and energy transition into a clear legal framework.

25. Aligning with the goals of the 2015-2030 Energy Transition Plan, the *Energy Code* sets a target of 75% renewable energy in the energy mix by 2030.[3]

26. The APC, consulted for its opinion on the *Energy Code* project, acknowledged that it represented "a step forward promoting economic efficiency, market opening for the benefit of businesses and consumers, and more effective, clear, and proportionate public intervention".[4]

27. Indeed, this text requires the separation of production, transport, and electricity distribution activities, which was intended to have the virtuous consequence of facilitating cost transparency and opening the market to other players. The *Energy Code* also entrusts the responsibility for network balance, previously held by the historical operator EDT, to the company Transport d'énergie électrique en Polynésie (TEP), thus promoting competition by removing this role from the historical operator EDT.[5]

28. Furthermore, the code entrusts the regulation of the sector to the Minister of Energy. In this regard, the APC recommended clarifying the existing content on regulation by affirming its legal nature and strengthening it. It also emphasized the need for the regulator's independence while recommending the establishment of an independent authority to assume this role.

29. It issued a favorable opinion, while highlighting potential improvements for better transparency and more effective regulation.[6]

---

3. *Energy Code*, art. LP 111-2
4. APC, press release of August 16, 2018, regarding the opinion issued on the *Energy Code*.
5. *Ibid.*
6. APC, Opinion No. 2018-AO-03 of August 10, 2018, on the draft country law establishing an *Energy Code* for French Polynesia.

30. A year later, the country evolved its *Energy Code* by adopting a new text aimed at specifying the operational modalities of the electricity production, transport, and distribution sectors in French Polynesia, notably to achieve the objectives of the 2015-2030 Energy Transition Plan, which aims to develop renewable energies, reduce energy consumption, and foster the emergence of new players for the benefit of consumers.

31. The APC will issue a favorable opinion on this draft law, which confirms better separation and greater independence between electricity production and distribution functions. It will specify: "The Authority particularly approves that the modalities for the exit of the capital of the transport network manager, whose shareholders are also present in the distribution and production segments, be explicitly provided for."[7]

32. The Polynesian Competition Authority recommends adjustments to ensure a true separation of functions and avoid "creating information capture or blocking power for certain historical players by strengthening the regulator's control role." It also emphasizes the need for clarifications to ensure a stable framework for investors and facilitate market access for new players.

33. In conclusion, the Authority issues a favorable opinion on the project while advising measures to improve regulation and encourage initiatives in renewable energy. The country law No. 2021-6 of January 28, 2021, will amend the *Energy Code* and integrate five of the APC's fourteen recommendations.

34. The *Energy Code* has thus helped to consolidate and update the entire regulatory framework for energy, making it clearer, more readable, and more predictable for the relevant actors. It adopts and adapts organizational principles and public intervention modalities that have been tested for network industries in the context of historical or natural monopolies and vertical integration of the historical operator. It aims to reconcile market opening in the favorable segments of the value chain with the pursuit of public interest objectives.

B. *Sectoral Regulation by the Country*

35. The need for regulation arises in sectors where market conditions favor the formation of monopolies. It is often entrusted to a so-called 'regulatory authority,' which is independent of both public authorities and economic actors to ensure an objective approach. Its mission will be to ensure the effective, fair, and sustainable exercise of competition, and it will have sanctioning power to achieve this.

36. Moreover, the sectoral regulation law for energy, a softer law better suited to the regulated sector,[8] provides complementary tools compared to competition law to ensure the efficient functioning of markets. Under current law, the APC exercises limited control over the energy sector, restricting itself to *ex post* control to sanction

---

7 APC, Opinion No. 2020-AO-02 of September 3, 2020, on the draft country law specifying the content of Titles III and IV of the *Energy Code* of French Polynesia

8 Beatrix Olivier and Coin Rémy, *Energy Regulation Law*, December 2023. APC, Opinion No. 2018-AO-03 of August 10, 2018, on the draft country law establishing an Energy Code for French Polynesia, as mentioned above.

anti-competitive practices and preserve the conditions for effective competition between operators. As part of its advisory functions, the Authority examines the impact that regulation may have on competition and markets in the energy sector.

37. For the energy sector in Polynesia, the situation is clear. In 2024, the country is responsible for defining public policies, normative competence, setting tariffs, managing the FRPH and price equalization, issuing operating permits for production units, the transport and distribution of electricity with TEP, and the distribution of electricity through a concession to EDT.

38. Therefore, the regulation of the energy sector under the control of local authorities could conflict with and impact the proper functioning of the energy sector.

39. As early as 2018, the APC indicated that:

> *The diversity of functions of public authorities, being both regulators, regulators, and operators, leads to situations that generate potential conflicts of interest. These situations can cause competitors and consumers to doubt the legitimacy of regulatory and regulatory decisions made, as well as the behavior of the operator responsible for transport and balance responsibilities in Tahiti, central to the value chain, in relation to upstream or downstream actors.*[9]

40. Therefore, from the adoption of the *Energy Code* in French Polynesia, the APC recommended effective and independent economic regulation, separate from the sector's businesses and political power, to ensure the impartiality and legitimacy of its actions. It has reiterated this recommendation in all its opinions on the energy sector.[10]

41. Recently, the energy sector could have been marked by a major new development with the arrival of an independent sectoral regulator. Indeed, a draft country law from June 2024 proposed transferring part of the regulation of the energy sector (electricity and gas), currently under the Polynesian Directorate of Energy, to the APC, and it was submitted to the local authorities.

42. The explanatory note of this draft law allows us to observe that French Polynesia has a clear vision of the limits of its current model. Indeed, this document reminds that public authorities must balance their various missions, including the regulatory mission of the energy sector. However, the potential contradiction of these roles could impact competitive functioning and investment incentives in the energy sector.

---

9 APC, Opinion No. 2016-A-02 of November 7, 2016, regarding the competition situation in the sector of hydrocarbon transport to French Polynesia

10 APC, Opinion No. 2016-A-02, November 7, 2016, on the competition situation in the hydrocarbon transport sector to French Polynesia; APC, Opinion No. 2018-AO-03, August 10, 2018, on the draft country law establishing an Energy Code for French Polynesia; APC, Opinion No. 2020-AO-02, September 3, 2020, on the draft country law specifying the content of Titles III and IV of the Energy Code of French Polynesia; APC, Opinion No. 2020-AO-03, September 24, 2020, on a draft country law establishing a solidarity mechanism in the electricity sector; APC, Opinion No. 2021-A-01, October 15, 2021, on a draft country law regarding the procedures for reviewing requests for hydroelectric concessions and authorizations; APC, Opinion No. 2022-A-01, April 21, 2022, on the competition situation in the hydrocarbon supply sector in French Polynesia; APC, Opinion No. 2023-AO-05, November 7, 2023, on a draft country law related to the deployment of electric vehicle charging infrastructure; APC, Opinion No. 2024-A-04, May 30, 2024, on a draft country law concerning sectoral regulation in the energy sector.

43. In its opinion on this draft law, the APC specified that: 'The choice of an independent administrative authority is the form of public intervention offering the best guarantees of expertise and independence for the organization and regulation of network industries, to the benefit of businesses and consumers.'[11]

44. On December 12, 2024, the text that was to formalize the transfer of energy regulation to the APC was withdrawn and will be subject to a new proposal in September 2025.

II. The Challenges of Competition Law in the Energy Sector

45. The APC has contributed to major developments in the energy sector through proposals for adjustments to important reforms that have taken place over the past 10 years. It has notably welcomed measures allowing for the gradual liberalization of the public power monopoly in electricity.

46. However, the current energy crisis and the transition to carbon neutrality could lead to an inadequate response by further strengthening public intervention. Yet, in light of the imperative energy transition, sectoral regulation by an independent authority seems more virtuous.

A. *Competition Dynamics*

47. It is clear that the energy sector in French Polynesia is characterized by limited competition dynamics and growing regulatory needs.

48. Vertical integrations are a common phenomenon in the production and distribution of basic products such as energy. From its earliest opinions, the APC has reminded that 'vertical integration can sometimes promote competition, especially in the early stages of a sector's development.'[12] However, safeguards must be put in place to prevent abuses of dominant positions and allow healthy competition, particularly in segments of the value chain that are gradually opened to competition.

49. The energy market in French Polynesia is marked by the dominance of historical players. However, under the influence of competition policies, there has been a liberalization of activities, particularly in electricity distribution, which is a public service that can be delegated to a private operator in the form of a concession or lease. These public service delegation (DSP) contracts, which are subject to mandatory tenders, grant the delegates exclusive rights to production, transport, and distribution in specific geographical areas. The execution of a public service mission also requires them to comply with specific accounting obligations, allowing for effective oversight of the management of the delegated service. Thus, in the specific case of electricity, infrastructures require significant investments and benefit from economies of scale, creating a natural monopoly. It is therefore difficult for other players to enter the market, limiting competition. To address

---

[11] APC, Opinion No. 2024-A-04, May 30, 2024, on a draft country law concerning sectoral regulation in the energy sector.

[12] XXX

this challenge, the APC recommends strengthening the separation of production, transport, network balancing, and distribution functions, and regularly putting transport and distribution networks out to tender.[13]

50. However, these recommendations, though long-standing, are still hindered by the weak separation of production, transport, and distribution functions, which complicates the entry of new players and the diversification of offerings, thus slowing the emergence of a true competitive dynamic.

51. Due to low consumption volumes and high logistical costs related to insularity, private investments remain limited, reinforcing dependence on natural monopolies. Moreover, operators must adapt their business models to marked geographical constraints, where sparsely populated areas require price equalization to ensure equitable access to energy.[14] This structure creates tensions between the need to maintain a quality public service and the objectives of economic profitability.

52. Thus, in the electricity sector, production can be opened to competition, but transport and distribution activities are natural monopolies within a given territory, meaning structures where the significance of fixed costs relative to demand makes it more efficient to have only one supplier. However, the existence of a natural monopoly does not prevent organizing competition 'for the market' among potential companies for a limited period, after which the monopoly is put back up for competition.

53. Specifically, hydroelectric electricity production is a textbook example. In an opinion from 2021,[15] the APC emphasized the need for a clear regulatory framework for hydroelectric installations, considering the size and cost of the installations necessary for local electricity production, their environmental impact, and the effects on local populations downstream, as well as their long operational lifespan, which can extend for decades.

54. The competition law applied by the APC urged the country to pay particular attention to the awarding of hydroelectric concessions to ensure it does not hinder competition among project developers and that it does not create barriers to the entry of new players and innovative projects.

55. Thus, in the case of hydroelectricity, while a tender procedure is indeed carried out for each public service delegation, it is crucial that projects be examined objectively and independently. The APC identified the main issue in the sector: the country holds stakes in production companies, particularly 35% of Marama Nui, which operates all the hydroelectric concessions in Tahiti. This particularity 'is likely to interfere with the assessment of the quality and relevance of a competitor's hydroelectric project.'

56. Therefore, the APC recommended creating an independent regulator in the form of an independent administrative authority to limit any potential barriers to market entry.

---

13 Ibid.

14 APC, Opinion No. 2020-AO-03, September 24, 2020, on a draft country law establishing a solidarity mechanism in the electricity sector.

15 APC, Opinion No. 2021-A-01, October 15, 2021, on a draft country law concerning the procedures for reviewing requests for hydroelectric concessions and authorizations.

57. To maintain healthy competition in a market where public authorities regularly intervene to regulate prices, allowing them to impose transparency obligations on all concerned economic actors.

58. Thus, the APC has examined various aspects of regulating petroleum product imports and has made significant progress in this area. In Polynesia, imported petroleum products are distributed by the three importing companies through four main distribution channels: retail sales at gas station networks for gasoline and through distributor networks for gas, wholesale sales for aviation, wholesale sales for marine, and wholesale sales for major accounts: industries, construction, fisheries, administrations and military, municipalities, and EDT.

59. In recent years, the energy sector has been marked by the inflationary trend of oil prices and the value of maritime freight, which, despite the amortization carried out by public finances, has had a significant impact on the Polynesian economy with a rise in energy prices, as the price of hydrocarbons is regulated.

60. The Directorate General of Economic Affairs (DGAE) is responsible for calculating the CAF (cost, insurance, freight) benchmark value and, more broadly, for calculating and evaluating each of the variables in the price structure of hydrocarbons, which is broken down as follows: the CAF benchmark, duties and taxes, local services, retail margins, and stabilization.

61. To carry out this mission, and in particular to regularly determine the CAF benchmark value, the DGAE must have access to a number of pieces of information held by the transporters and importing oil companies, making a clear need for transparency from these entities.

62. The importation of hydrocarbons also relies on agreements between the country and the importers, which include the conditions for compensating them. In the context of negotiating a new agreement, an opinion from the APC on April 22, 2022, pointed out that the importing companies had applied a uniform tariff of 57.37 dollars per ton for 5 years, in agreement with the country, corresponding to the floor of the agreement signed in 2006. However, the application of this tariff turned out to be unfavorable to the country.[16]

63. Since then, negotiations with the importers have led to Order No. 2638 CM of December 8, 2022, which partially takes into account some of the APC's observations on draft agreements it had been made aware of.[17]This order removes the range that had framed the freight tariffs. The formula now relies on market indices, which provides an objective basis for billing and represents a significant improvement over the previous situation.

64. Furthermore, in the electricity sector, the price equalization planned by the 2015-2030 Energy Transition Plan and adopted in 2022 has helped harmonize costs for consumers but has created tensions regarding the economic viability

---

16 Chambre territoriale des comptes, Final Observation Report of the Collectivity of French Polynesia – Energy Policy, September 4, 2023.

17 APC, Opinion No. 2016-A-02, November 7, 2016, regarding the competition situation in the hydrocarbon transport sector to French Polynesia; APC, Opinion No. 2022-A-01, April 21, 2022, regarding the competition situation in the hydrocarbon supply sector in French Polynesia.

of operators. The APC's analysis recommends revising the tariff calculation mechanisms, which is essential to ensure a balance between fairness and competitiveness.[18]

65. To ensure equal access to the public electricity service throughout French Polynesia, the country has implemented a price equalization system that compensates for the heterogeneity in production costs across all network operators, with electricity production in less populated islands being structurally more expensive than in Tahiti.

66. In practice, to ensure both the financial balance of each concession outside of Northern Tahiti and the uniform pricing of electricity across its entire scope, EDT operates financial flows between Northern Tahiti, a concession that generates a surplus, and the deficit-driven municipal concessions.

67. In addition to this organization specific to EDT, a general regulatory element has been introduced, allowing network operators to benefit from a tax exemption on hydrocarbons used for electricity production/distribution activities. This exemption is conditional on the implementation of a uniform electricity price, so the municipal utilities in remote archipelagos have the same pricing grid as Northern Tahiti, without benefiting from any equalization system to compensate for their higher production/distribution costs.

68. To address this inequality, the polyensian law on price equalization for electricity tariffs came into effect on January 1, 2022.

69. In its opinion on this draft law, the APC will observe that the objective pursued by this text is to:

> *directly ensure, through a solidarity fund financed by a tax, the payment of a flat-rate compensation by the country for the additional costs to each concessionaire, without mutualization between the different concessions. Its stated goal is to place all candidates for the management of a distribution network on an equal footing (level playing field), a sine qua non condition for effective competition.*[19]

70. Specifically, the compensation paid to electricity distribution network operators should compensate for the additional costs induced by the existence of small networks, so that all users benefit from an electricity kWh tariff similar to that practiced in Tahiti, which is much lower than the production cost of the smaller networks.

71. A clear and proactive regulatory framework is essential to encourage innovation, facilitate the entry of new players, and ensure a balance between tariff fairness and economic efficiency. Furthermore, targeted support mechanisms for renewable energies and greater transparency in tariff setting are essential to accelerate the energy transition while promoting healthy competition.

---

18 APC, Opinion No. 2020-AO-03, September 24, 2020, on a draft country law establishing a solidarity mechanism in the electricity sector.

19 *Ibid.*

B. *Opportunities to Strengthen Competition*

72. Island nations and French overseas territories share many common characteristics in the energy sector, typical of isolated systems: absence of local fossil resources, high fuel supply costs, electricity production capacity primarily relying on thermal power plants, small-sized electrical networks, and lack of interconnections.

73. These constraints result in high energy prices, which hinder the economic development of small island economies. However, an alternative is possible: the development of renewable energies and the optimization of energy use. The APC specifies in its 2021 annual report that:

> *several Pacific territories with populations and geographical constraints similar to French Polynesia have successfully developed the share of photovoltaic energy in their energy mix (Guam in Micronesia, from Kaua'i to Hawaii, or from Tongatapu in Tonga), by effectively freeing up production.*

74. It adds that in French Polynesia, the context is specifically that of the gradual opening to competition of a sector that was previously integrated and dominated by a historical operator.

75. While the country law project assigning energy sector regulation to the APC did not come to fruition, it remains clear that regulation by the independent administrative authority is essential to overcome these challenges and create favorable conditions for the growth of renewable energies (RE) by ensuring equitable access to infrastructure, preventing abuses of dominant positions, and facilitating access for new entrants.

76. Energy sector regulators can intervene ex ante, through standards and licenses conditioned on specific obligations, while competition authorities act ex post, sanctioning cartels or abuses of dominant position. This preventive approach by regulators includes tools to limit structural barriers to competition and can be crucial in supporting energy transition objectives.

77. For example, the APC recalls in its opinion on the subject:

> *that the Australian Competition and Consumer Commission (ACCC) and the New Zealand Commerce Commission (ComCom) are already working under a common structure on a variety of missions. They have, in particular, a threefold mission: combating anti-competitive practices; protecting consumers; and regulating network industries.*

78. The APC plays a key role in energy regulation. Responsible for ensuring non-discriminatory access to infrastructure and overseeing public service delegates, it can maintain market balance by pursuing four objectives:

- Strengthening competition: by facilitating the entry of new players, it stimulates innovation and reduces costs for consumers;
- Market stability: rigorous supervision prevents abuses and ensures a balanced framework for investors;
- Support for sustainability: by promoting RE projects, it helps achieve climate goals while reducing dependence on fossil fuels;
- Consumer protection: price transparency and pricing mechanisms guarantee equitable access to energy.

79. Finally, sectoral regulators play a complementary role to competition authorities by proposing mechanisms such as price regulation in specific situations, which illustrates the balance between their distinct but interconnected objectives.

80. Proactive regulation can prevent market distortions and create a stable framework to attract investments in renewable energies (RE).

81. To achieve this, the APC has recommended additional measures to strengthen its effectiveness as a regulator of the energy sector, namely:

- Expanding the APC's competencies to the hydrocarbons sector;
- Ensuring increased transparency in pricing mechanisms;
- Collaborating with the Polynesian Energy Observatory for a rigorous monitoring of energy indicators.

82. In Polynesia, the development of RE primarily relies on hydroelectricity and photovoltaics. Tahiti produces a third of its electricity through hydroelectricity, while solar energy shows an annual growth of 6%. However, the lack of centralized storage and the absence of interconnections are slowing this transition. Strengthened regulation could encourage investments in solar storage and the expansion of networks that are starting to emerge.

83. For French Polynesia, strengthening energy regulation is a crucial step towards a sustainable transition. By providing the APC or any other independent administrative authority with the necessary resources, the country can create an environment conducive to the development of RE and address energy challenges while stimulating the local economy.

84. Ten years of competition law practice in Polynesia have demonstrated that it is an essential lever for modernizing and transforming the economy, especially the energy sector. There is still room for progress regarding the implementation of suitable regulation, supported by an independent authority. This will inevitably lead to virtuous outcomes such as stimulating competition, improving service quality, and accelerating the transition to a more sustainable energy mix. By meeting these challenges, French Polynesia could become a regional model of balance between economic efficiency and environmental responsibility.

Competition and Tourism: Assessment of a Decade of Decision

Nathalie Jalabert-Doury* and Sarah Vidal*
Mayer Brown

1. The Polynesian Competition Authority (APC) has a rich decision-making practice in the tourism sector, and its analysis led to the examination of some fifteen merger control decisions, all of which concerned targets in hotel sector. However, the tourism sector is obviously broader and encompasses travel agencies, transport (air, land and sea), catering, as well as cultural, sporting and entertainment activities.[1] Some of these activities have also been examined in the context of these decisions, given that the parties concerned are active in these neighbouring markets.
2. The number of decisions taken by the Polynesian Authority in this sector comes as no surprise, given that tourism is the country's leading economic activity, accounting on average for 9-10% of annual GDP.[2] Although the sector to a virtual standstill for many months in 2020 and 2021 as a result of the Covid-19 epidemic, it has since gradually returned to normal, reaching a higher number of tourists in 2023 than before the pandemic[3].

---

* Nathalie Jalabert-Doury is head of Mayer Brown's Antitrust & Competition practice in France and co-heads the firm's European Antitrust practice.

** Sarah Vidal is a lawyer at Mayer Brown.

1 See, for example, OECD, *Tourism trends and policies*, study, 2014.

2 Institut d'émission d'outre-mer, *Annual Economic Report*, 2023, p. 100.

3 Institut de la statistique de la Polynésie française, *Le bilan de tourisme de l'année 2023*, n° 1447. *Competition law and the challenges of island economies*

3. Mergers in the tourism sector also declined from the start of the pandemic and do not yet appear to have recovered to a level comparable to the previous period. Be that as it may, the decision-making practice established on this basis provides a solid base of references (I), detailing the assessment of the competitive stakes of change of control transactions in this sector (II), including in terms of commitments, since two of these decisions were conditional on compliance with commitments (III).

I. A sector of activity that plays a significant role in the decision-making practice of the Polynesian Authority

4. The Polynesian Competition Authority has examined a large number of mergers in the tourism sector, taking due account of the control analysis required in the case of hotels, which are generally covered by hotel management contracts.

A. *Overview of transactions subject to the Authority's assessment*

5. The Polynesian Authority's decision-making practice in the tourism sector accounts for almost half of the merger decisions issued by the Authority (48%) between 2016 and 2024, with an average of between one and two decisions per year.

6. Although the pace of decisions has slowed over the most recent period (no decisions published in 2024, and an average of less than 2 decisions per year between 2021 and 2023, compared with 5 published in 2016 and 2017), this level of decisions remains significant. By comparison, in mainland France over the same period, only 36 decisions concerned this sector of activity out of a total of nearly 2,250 published decisions, i.e. less than 2% of merger control decisions.

7. The cases investigated during this period (listed in the appendix) all resulted so called "phase 1" decisions, adopted at the end of a preliminary analysis phase lasting in principle 5 weeks after notification. Thirteen of the 15 mergers were approved without reservation, while in two cases the transactions were authorised subject to the fulfilment of behavioural commitments (*Louis Wane/Tahiti Nui Travel* and *Grey/Tahiti Nui Travel* decisions).[4]

8. All the decisions relate to a similar scenario of planned acquisition of a Polynesian hotel complex by a local investor (i.e., the Grey group or the Louis Wane group), or an international investor (i.e., the Chinese group Dazhong or the fund HNA, a Hong Kong investment company, through the acquisition of a majority stake in the target hotel. The hotels in question were all luxury tourist hotels (4 or 5 stars) located on the islands of Bora-Bora, Moorea and Tahiti (Society archipelago), Rangiroa (Tuamotu archipelago) and Nuku Hiva (Marquesas archipelago).

---

[4] APC, decision no. 2016-CC-04 of 5 December 2016 on the acquisition of exclusive control of the Tahiti Nui Travel group by the Grey group; and APC, decision no. 2022-CC-02 of 8 June 2022 on the acquisition of exclusive control of the Tahiti Nui Travel group (TNT) by Mr Louis Wane.

9. Although targeting the hotel sector, these various transactions enabled the Authority to examine other levels of the tourism value chain in Polynesia, given the acquirer's preexisting activities in all or part of these related markets.

Levels of the tourism value chain (hotel sector) examined by the APC, 2015-2024

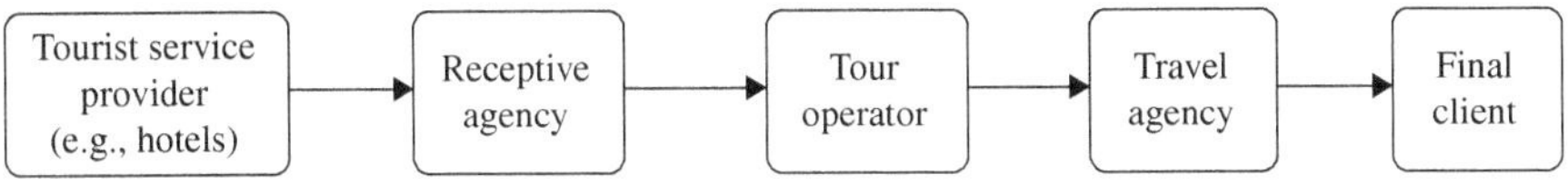

B. *Specific features of the sector in terms of control conditions*

10. The merger control regime[5] applies to "concentration" transactions – a concept defined by Article LP 310-1-1 of the *Polynesian Competition Code* in three main scenarios: a merger of two previously independent companies, the creation of a joint venture performing on a lasting basis all the functions of an autonomous economic entity and/or a takeover (exclusive or joint).

11. Each scenario involves a "change of control", defined by the Polynesian Guidelines on the Scope and Procedure for Merger Control ("Guidelines") as "the possibility of exercising, alone, decisive influence over the business of another undertaking"[6].

12. Most mergers are carried out by acquiring a stake in the target company. While in principle a majority shareholding is sufficient to exercise decisive influence over the acquired company, a minority shareholding may also be sufficient to grant sole or joint control, provided that it is accompanied by rights exceeding those normally granted to a minority shareholder to protect his financial interests. These rights must be such as to demonstrate the existence of a decisive influence over the target company (for example, through the holding of a veto over the strategic plan, the possibility of appointing key managers, investments, the budget, etc.)[7].

13. Like the French[8] and European[9] systems, the Polynesian system also provides that a change of control may result from certain commercial contracts. However, such cases are rare. As explained in the Polynesian Guidelines, for a contract to bring about a change of control over a company, the contract must:

- gives one of the parties control over the management and resources of the business equivalent to that obtained through the acquisition of shares or assets; and
- is characterised by an extremely long duration (with no possibility of early termination by the party granting the contractual rights)[10]

---

5. *Polynesian Competition Code*, art. LP 310-1 to LP 310-10.
6. APC, *Guidelines on the scope and procedure for merger control*, January 2019, pt 23.
7. *Ibid*, pt 37.
8. Aut. conc. *revised merger control guidelines*, 23 January 2020, pt 31.
9. European Commission, February 2009, Consolidated Communication on the competence of the Commission, pt 16.
10. APC, *Lignes directrices relatives au champ d'application et à la procédure de contrôle des concentrations*, *op. cit*, pt 41; Commission européenne, février 2009, Communication consolidée sur la compétence de la Commission européenne, précitée, pts 18 et s.

14. An example of this type of contract is the management lease contract[11] or, applied to the hotel sector, the hotel management contract whereby an owner entrusts the management of the hotel he owns to a hotel operator who accepts the management, despite the fact that the ownership rights or shares have not been transferred to him.

15. In this case and according to consistent decision-making practice,[12] both the European Commission and the French Autorité consider that the provision of this management service on a contractual basis is likely to lead to a situation joint control, to the benefit of the manager. Among the criteria adopted by the Commission is the fact that the hotel management contract gives the operator broad managerial and budgetary control for a long period (contracts concluded for periods of at least 10 years)[13].

16. In practice, the mergers examined by the Polynesian Authority were essentially "classic" in that they involved the acquisition of control through the acquisition of the entire capital of the target hotel company.

17. However, some of the control situations examined included a management contract, which the Autorité took fully into account in determining whether there had been a change of control. For example, the Authority dealt with transactions involving the capital of hotels that were jointly controlled by the outgoing owner and the hotel manager.[14] The hotel thus went from being jointly controlled by former owner to being jointly controlled by the new owner.

18. The Authority analyzed the management contracts in question in light of its Guidelines and, like the European Commission or the French Authority, it considered that the joint nature of the control was established due to the

---

11 Aut. conc. decision no. 09-DCC-46 of 28 September 2009 on the lease management by Distribution Casino France of a hypermarket owned by Dorémi; European Commission, of 5 December 2003 in case M.3136, *GE/AGFA NDT*; see also, RONZANO Alain, "Retail and Consumer Goods Sectors: The French Competition Authority Considers that the Control of a Supermarket Acquired on a Contractual Basis Leads to a Merger (Casino)", *Concurrences* [online], 28 September 2009, n° 1-2010, art. n° 65013.

12 European Commission, Decision of 31 October 2018 in Case M.9099, *Jin Jian/Radisson*, pts 63 et seq.; European Commission, Decision of 27 June 2016 in Case M.7902, *Marriott International/Starwood Hotels & Resorts Worldwide*, pts 192 et seq.; European Commission, decision of 4 January 2018 in Case M.8718, *Starwood Capital Group/Accor/Sofitel Budapest Chain Bridge Hotel*; and European Commission, decision of 26 August 2008 in Case M.5164, *MSREF/IHG/Crowne Plaza Wiesbaden*.

13 European Commission, decision of 31 October 2018 Case M.9099, cited above: "The Commission notes that, under the standardized management agreements of both Jin Jiang and Radisson, 85 the Parties in their function as hotel managers are granted a broad authority by the hotel owner to control all major aspects of the operation of the hotel, in particular setting rates, collecting revenues, preparing books and financial reporting, and performing repairs and maintenance. Furthermore, the Parties' management fees consist of a percentage of the hotel's gross annual revenues and a percentage of the hotel's annual operating profit" (pt 65).

14 APC, decision no. 2016-CC-01 of 6 July 2016 on the acquisition of sole control of South Seas Resort Limited (Louis Wane Group) by HNA Tourism (HNA Group); APC, decision no. 2016-CC-02 of 29 August 2016 on the acquisition of joint control of the three Sofitel hotels in French Polynesia by Lupesina Tahiti Investments (Grey Group) alongside the AccorHotels Group; APC, decision no. 2016-CC-05 of 13 December 2016 on the acquisition of joint control of Société des Nouveaux Hôtels by M. Louis Wane alongside the Starwood Group; and APC, decision no. 2017-CC-02 of 23 March 2017 on the acquisition of sole control of Société d'Investissement de Polynésie (Four Seasons Hôtel & Resort Bora-Bora) by Swansea King Limited (Gaw Hospitality investment fund).

particularly long duration of the management contract (between 10 and 15 years), as well as the existence of clauses allowing the manager to have a determining influence. In each decision examined, the manager had a veto right over the target hotel's business plan and was the exclusive operator of the hotel (allowing them to set room prices, manage human resources, and provide centralized services for the entire hotel group). They also had a right of first refusal in the event of the hotel's sale.

II. Transactions giving rise to examination of possible horizontal, vertical and/or conglomerate effects

19. Traditionally, mergers in the hotel sector give rise to the examination so-called *horizontal* effects of strengthening the acquirer when the parties to the transaction are actual or potential competitors (A). However, in Polynesia, players in the sector often also develop upstream or downstream activities, which leads to the examination of possible *vertical* effects (B) or even on neighbouring markets, which leads to the examination possible *conglomerate* effects (C).

20. In most of the transactions examined, the risk of such effects could be ruled out.

A. *Analysis of horizontal effects*

21. According to the APC's Guidelines, where a proposed acquisition is likely to confer significant market power on the new entity, or is capable of strengthening the market power held by the acquirer prior to the acquisition of control of the target hotel, the notified transaction is likely to generate horizontal effects that should be examined.

22. In this scenario, the parties are direct competitors active on the hotel market, which the Polynesian Authority will first define (1), before addressing the main competition risks identified (2).

1. Hotel

23. The Authority considers that the hotel sector in French Polynesia encompasses three main types of accommodation: international tourist hotels and residences, tourist accommodation in private homes and furnished tourist accommodation. Only the first category (hotels and residences for international tourism) has been examined by the Authority, which envisages several types of segmentation for this type of accommodation:

- a distinction according to the degree of comfort of the hotel: grouping by star pairs (1-2 stars; 2-3 stars; 3-4 stars); grouping considering the category immediately below and the category immediately above (1-3 stars; 2-4 stars); distinction between economy category (1-3 stars) and luxury category (4 stars and more); and
- a distinction according to the way in which the establishments are operated, depending on whether they belong to a hotel chain.

24. This approach is in line with French and European decision-making practice, which consistently envisages[15] a segmentation based on price and the level of comfort of the hotel based on its classification, as emphasised in the French decision *LFPI/LSF6* of 23 June 2015:

> *regarding the distinction between hotel establishments according to comfort level, the decision-making practice has envisaged several segmentation methods [...]: grouping by pairs stars (1-2 stars; 2-3 stars; 3-4 stars) or by taking account of the category immediately below and the category immediately above (1-3 stars, 2-4 stars).*[16]

25. Regarding its geographical delimitation, although recognising that "competition authorities consider that the hotel market can be analysed both at national level [...] and at local level [...]",[17] the Polynesian Authority leaves open the question of whether the hotel markets should be limited to French Polynesia, to each archipelago or to each island.[18]

26. In practice, however, it systematically examines the different levels of appraisal right down to the finest link (i.e., island level), illustrated by its examination of the proposed acquisition of the *Saint Regis Bora-Bora* hotel by the HNA Tourism group, a Hong Kong investment fund that already owned three hotels in French Polynesia[19].

Combined market shares of the parties *HNA/Saint Regis Bora-Bora* decision (Case no. 2016-CC-01)

	All Hotels		4 & 5 stars		5 stars	
	Nb of rooms	Nb Hotels	Nb of rooms	Nb Hotels	Nb of rooms	Nb Hotels
French Polynesia	7,2 %	4,5 %	10,2 %	9,1 %	28,1 %	25 %
Company archipelago	7,6 %	5,1 %	10,7 %	10 %	28,1 %	25 %
Windward Islands	6,8 %	4,8 %	10,8 %	25 %	75,2 %	50 %
Leeward Islands	9,8 %	5,6 %	107, %	8,3 %	16,3 %	16 %
Island of Moorea	17,5 %	10 %	23,1 %	25 %	100 %	100 %
Island of Bora Bora	11 %	9,1 %	12,3 %	11,1 %	18,2 %	20 %

27. The Authority first sought to assess the effects of the proposed acquisition at the level of Polynesia, then at the level of the archipelago, and finally at the level of each affected island, noting, for example, that "in the Windward Islands, the

15 Aut. conc. decision no. 15-DCC-77 of 23 June 2015 on the acquisition of sole control by LFPI of LSF6/Alliance Holding SAS; Aut. conc, decision no. 14-DCC-82 of 12 June 2014 on acquisition of joint control of the Park&Suites group and the GMI group by the M Finance group and the Equistone investment fund, pt 16; European Commission, decision of 31 October 2018 case M.9099, *Jin Jian/Radisson*, pt 30; European Commission, decision of 16 February 2001 in case M.2197, *Hilton/Accor/Forte/Travel Service JV*, pt 26.

16 Aut. conc. decision no. 15-DCC-77, cited above, pt 11.

17 APC, Decision No. 2016-CC-01 of 6 July 2016 on the acquisition of sole control by HNA Tourism (HNA Group) of South Seas Resort Limited (Louis Wane Group), pt 17.

18 *Ibid*, pt 22.

19 *Ibid.*

new entity will account for 6.8% of the supply of rooms and 4.8% of the number of hotels"[20].

28. From this point of view also, the practice of the Polynesian Authority is in line with French practice in mainland France, which seeks to analyse transactions affecting the tourism sector at national, regional and then local level – generally analysed at the level of the conurbation (e.g. Paris, Nice or Toulouse, which seems consistent in the absence of a comparable island precedent).[21] In the case of tourism as practised in Polynesia, the competitive pressure exerted by existing hotels in regions developing tourism based on the same fundamentals could also prove relevant, but it has not been examined by the Authority at this stage.

2. The absence restrictive effects on competition

29. To date, no notified transaction has been considered likely to harm competition through horizontal effects – including in acquisition scenarios with overlaps in the same areas, with substantial market shares, as illustrated by the *HNA/Manava Beach Resort & Spa* decision of 31 May 2017[22].

30. The Polynesian Authority was due to vote on the proposed takeover of the *Manava Beach Resort & Spa* (a hotel in Moorea owned by the Mahana Investment fund and managed by the South Pacific Management hotel group) by the Hong Kong fund HNA Tourism (which owns two other hotels in Polynesia, the *Moorea Lagoon Resort & Spa* and the *Saint Regis Bora-Bora Resort*).

31. The investigating departments first estimated the level of concentration of the parties following the transaction, in order to assess whether or not the integrated group would sufficient competition on the affected market to guarantee satisfactory competitive pressure.

Combined market shares of the parties
Decision HNA/Manava Beach Resort & Spa (decision no. 2017-CC-04)

2017	All Hotels		4 & 5 stars	
	Nb of rooms	Nb Hotels	Nb of rooms	Nb Hotels
French Polynesia	10,6 %	6,8 %	15,2 %	13,6 %
Company archipelago	11,3 %	7,7 %	16,0 %	15,0 %
Windward Islands	12,8 %	9,5 %	20,3 %	25,0 %
Island of Moorea	33,1 %	20,0 %	43,8 %	50,0 %

32. The Authority considered that the transaction did not give rise to any serious competition concerns at these various levels, including the most local, insofar as the group would continue to face "competition from the Pacific Beachcomber

20 *Ibid*, pt 32.

21 Aut. conc. decision no. 24-DCC-191 of 27 August 2024 concerning the acquisition of exclusive control of several hotel businesses by Covivio Hotels.

22 APC, Decision No. 2017-CC-04 of 31 May 2017 on the acquisition of sole control of Compagnie touristique polynésienne by South Seas Resort Limited (HNA Group).

and Grey groups,[23] which account for 31.5% and 24.7% respectively of the room supply"[24] on the hotel market in Moorea.

33. To this was added the fact that HNA Tourism's control over the target would only be joint, thus limiting its power influence: "the formation of the new entity has the effect of only slightly reducing competitive pressure since the hotel remains subject to joint control by South Pacific Management", the manager of the target hotel and remaining in place after the transaction[25].

B. *Analysis of vertical effects*

34. The possible vertical effects of proposed hotel acquisitions were also examined by the Polynesian Authority when the notified transaction involved players present at different levels of the tourism value chain (incoming agency, travel agency, hotel complex, etc.).

35. The *Grey/Tahiti Nui Travel* decision of 5 December 2016[26] concerning the proposed acquisition of Tahiti Nui Travel by the Grey group exemplifies this second risk of anti-competitive effects.

1. The specific organisation of travel agency business in Polynesia

36. In this decision, the Polynesian Authority adapted the analysis of the travel agency market to the specific characteristics of Polynesia, distinguishing between (a) the upstream activity of designing and selling tourist holidays/supplying tourist services, carried out by incoming agencies, and (b) the traditional downstream travel agency activity.

---

23 In 2017, the Grey group owned the *Sofitel Ia Ora Beach Resort* in Moorea (now exclusively owned by the Louis Wane group, since May 2020). The *Pacific Beachcomber* hotel has been closed since May 2020.

24 APC, Decision No. 2016-CC-01 of 6 July 2016 on the acquisition of sole control by HNA Tourism (HNA Group) of South Seas Resort Limited (Louis Wane Group), supra, pt 32.

25 *Ibid.*

26 APC, Decision No. 2016-CC-04 of 5 December 2016 on the acquisition of sole control of the Tahiti Nui Travel group by the Grey group, cited above.

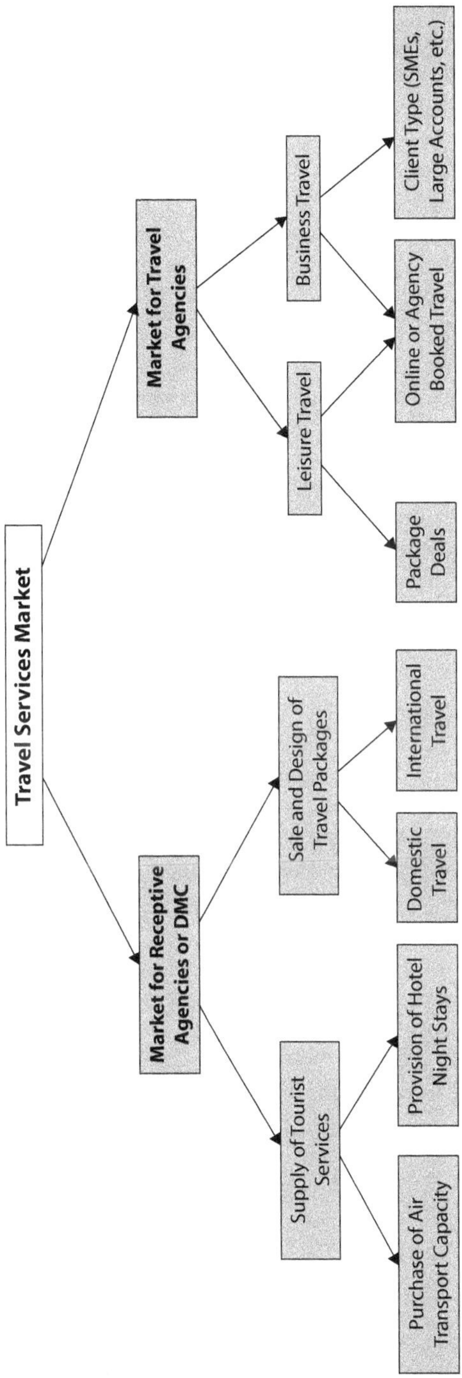
Travel Services Market
Market for Travel Agencies
Market for Receptive Agencies or DMC
Business Travel
Leisure Travel
Sale and Design of Travel Packages
Supply of Tourist Services
Client Type (SMEs, Large Accounts, etc.)
Online or Agency Booked Travel
Package Deals
International Travel
Domestic Travel
Provision of Hotel Night Stays
Purchase of Air Transport Capacity

37. Incoming agencies are local, or even very local, travel agencies specialising organising holidays in French Polynesia. They collect and centralise all the services offered by Polynesian service providers (hotels, restaurants, carriers, tourist guides, etc.), which they then resell to tour operators and/or travel agencies in the travellers' countries of origin (via catalogues).

38. The Polynesian Authority's decision states that they are key players in Polynesia for at least two reasons: (i) the complexity of the tourism offering in French Polynesia, linked to the island nature of the territory (spread over five archipelagos), means that holidays have to be organised on several islands and requires the cooperation of many tourism service providers; (ii) the upmarket positioning of the tourism industry in French Polynesia justifies having recourse to the know-how and expertise of an incoming agency.

39. In the same way as the analysis conducted for the hotel market, and although it theoretically leaves open the scope of its geographical delimitation, the Polynesian Authority analyzes the receptive agency market at the local level, examining the effects that the operation under review is likely to have on each affected island. This is the case in the aforementioned decision, where the Authority first focused on evaluating the effects of the acquisition project (of Tahiti Nui Travel) on the receptive agency market at the level of French Polynesia, then at the level of the Society Archipelago, and finally at the level of the Windward and Leeward Islands (Bora-Bora, Tahiti, and Moorea), highlighting, for example, that "according to the market delimitation adopted, the hotels of the Grey group [will have] a market share between 10 and 50% for the number of hotels"[27] in Tahiti and Moorea.

2. A classic analysis of the risks of market foreclosure

40. The acquisition of a hotel complex by an incoming agency raises the two classic vertical issues of input foreclosure and access to customers, but the Polynesian Authority's analysis of this issue could raise questions given that its Guidelines only cover the scope of the scheme and the procedure.

41. The decision handed down on the proposed acquisition by the Grey group[28] – active in the upstream hotel market and the downstream market for incoming agencies[29] – of sole control of Tahiti Nui Travel – active in the downstream market for incoming agencies and travel agencies, confirmed that the analysis of vertical effects in Polynesia is carried out in the classic manner.

42. According to the guidelines of the French competition authority,[30] a vertical merger may restrict competition by making it more difficult to access to the markets in which the new entity will be active, or even potentially foreclosing competitors or

---

27 *Ibid*, pt 79.

28 APC, Decision No. 2016-CC-04 of 5 December 2016 on the acquisition of sole control of the Tahiti Nui Travel group by the Grey group, cited above.

29 The Grey Group owns five hotels in Polynesia (Le *Méridien*, *Sofitel Moorea la Ora Beach Resort*, *Sofitel Bora-Bora Marara Beach Resort*, *Sofitel Bora-Bora Motu Private Island* and *Manava Beach Resort & Spa Moorea*) and an incoming agency (Samoa Scenic Tours & Inbound Services). [30] Aut. conc. *revised Merger Control Guidelines*, *op. cit.* pts 668 et seq.

30 Autorité de la concurrence, Revised Guidelines on Merger Control, op. cit., points 668 and following.

penalising them by increasing their costs. This is known as "foreclosure". Such a situation increases the market power of the new entity and enables it to increase its prices and/or reduce the quantities offered.

43. There are two different types of lock:

- In the first case, the integrated company refuses to sell an input to its downstream competitors, or provides it under unfavorable conditions or at a degraded level of quality (this is referred to as *input foreclosure).* This foreclosure can be total, when competitors are no longer supplied at all, or partial, when the tightening of pricing conditions leads to an increase in the competitors' costs.
- in the second case, the downstream branch of the integrated company refuses buy or distribute the products of suppliers active upstream, thereby reducing their commercial outlets (*foreclosure of access to customers*).

44. These two competition risks were examined in detail by the Polynesian Authority in the aforementioned case.

a) Input lock-in hypothesis

45. The Authority first examined whether, following the acquisition of Tahiti Nui Travel by the Grey group, the latter could consider foreclosing the downstream market for incoming agencies by refusing to market the hotel nights of the Grey group to competing incoming agencies.

46. This risk – considered low by the investigating services – was quickly ruled out for the following reasons: the integrated group only had joint control over the acquired hotels. Consequently, it could not unilaterally decide to boycott competing receptive agencies. Furthermore, it seemed unlikely that the international hotel chains holding control alongside the Grey group would accept this boycott as a viable business strategy – their interest being, on the contrary, to expand their distribution channels. Finally, even if this had been the case, the strategy could only have been detrimental since it would have deprived these hotels of nearly 70% of the receptive agency market, given the limited market share of the Tahiti Nui Travel group.

b) Assumption of blocked access to customers

47. The investigating departments then examined whether the integrated group could also decide to boycott competing hotels (in favour of Grey group hotels) so that its agencies (incoming and outgoing) would no longer market them to their customers (risk of total foreclosure).

48. Once again, the risk of foreclosure was considered low.

49. In the Authority's view, such a strategy would not make sense from an economic point of view and would have only a very limited effect on the market insofar as it would lead the merged entity's incoming/outgoing agencies to deprive themselves of access to a significant part of the market for the supply of hotel overnight stays in French Polynesia (Grey group hotels representing only 20% of available rooms). Furthermore, such a strategy would not prevent competing

hotels from finding alternative outlets, while retaining 65-75% access to of the affected market.

50. On the other hand, the investigating departments considered it more likely that the integrated group's incoming/travel agencies would decide to give priority to the group's hotels over competing hotels, by selling their overnight stays as a priority.

51. This risk was considered greater due to the presence of a context marked by significant variations in occupancy rates (a substantial decrease during the low season); the ability to implement this exclusion strategy (increased targeted advertising, pricing incentives for travel agencies and tour operators to prioritize selling the hotel group's rooms…); and the potential profit generated by it (acquiring new receptive agencies could provide the integrated group with key information/ competitive advantages on the prices charged by competitors, their occupancy rates, their promotional policies…)

52. As a result, the Polynesian Authority only authorised the Grey group's takeover of Tahiti Nui Travel on condition that it gave behavioural undertakings to reduce the risk thus identified (see 3 below). These undertakings had to be reiterated when the group was sold again to the Louis Wane group, which also had hotel operations.[31]

C. *Analysis of conglomerate effects*

53. A third and final level of risk may have to be analysed when the notified operation is likely to produce conglomerate effects. These may arise where the new entity will hold significant positions on closely related markets, with the ability to use its strong position on one of these markets to strengthen its position on the other.

54. To this day, no decision submitted to the Polynesian Authority for review in the tourism sector has been deemed likely to present such a risk on the markets under review (hotels or travel services), due to the acquirer's presence on other related markets (in this case the air market or the food/beverage supply market).

55. In conducting this analysis, the Autorité systematically examined whether: (i) the acquirer had the possibility of technically or commercially linking the product of the market affected by the merger and that of the related market; (ii) whether it had an incentive to do so; and (iii) whether a foreclosure strategy would have had a significant effect on the relevant markets.

56. In addition to illustrating this reasoning, the proposed takeover of South Seas Resort by the Hong Kong group HNA (decision *South Seas Resort Limited/ Compagnie touristique polynésienne*)[32] means that, as regards conglomerate effects as well as vertical effects, the Polynesian Authority applies a completely standard analysis grid as defined for example in the Guidelines of the French Competition Authority.[33]

---

31 APC, decision no. 2022-CC-02 of 8 June 2022 on the acquisition of sole control of the Tahiti Nui Travel group (TNT) by Mr Louis Wane, cited above.

32 APC, Decision No. 2017-CC-04 of 31 May 2017 on the acquisition of sole control of Compagnie touristique polynésienne by South Seas Resort Limited (HNA Group), cited above.

33 Aut. conc. *revised Merger Control Guidelines*, *op. cit.* pts 718 et seq.

57. As a reminder, the HNA group, in addition to acquiring the assets held by the target (*Moorea Lagoon Resort & Spa*, Motu Ome'e and the Bora-Bora Eden Cruise company), was planning to open a new Beijing-Papeete air route. This route was a potential entrant on the passenger transport market between China and French Polynesia, which had links with the hotel market on which the target was present.

58. No conglomerate risk was ultimately retained by Polynesian Authority for the following reasons. Firstly, the nature of the (joint) control of the target (shared with the South Pacific Management group) could only give the acquirer a limited ability to reserve hotel capacity for passengers on its China-French Polynesia flights.[34] Secondly, and more importantly, Chinese tourists accounted for only 5,202 of the 129,746 tourists staying in French Polynesia, i.e. less than 5% of the total volume. The effects of a foreclosure strategy could therefore only be very limited.[35]

III. Behavioural commitments honoured by the Polynesian Authority

59. When the Polynesian Authority examines a merger likely to create anticompetitive effects, it may only authorise the merger if it is accompanied by "corrective measures to remedy the harm to competition that it has identified"[36].

60. The choice of the most appropriate type of corrective measure depends on the effects of the operation.

61. According to its Guidelines, the Autorité polynésienne considers that: "when the transaction harms competition essentially because of the horizontal overlap of the parties' activities, structural remedies are the most effective".[37] Structural remedies make it possible to rebalance the ownership rights of the target company through a transfer/retrocession of assets belonging to the notifying companies, in order to strengthen a competitor or to enable new entrants to compete with the new entity resulting from the merger.

62. On the other hand, when it is necessary to address the risks of foreclosure in upstream or downstream markets, 'behavioral remedies aimed at ensuring competitors' access to inputs or customers may prove sufficient while preserving the efficiency gains linked to vertical integration. The same applies to conglomerate mergers.[38]

63. These measures aim to preserve or promote competitors' access to the market when it is threatened by the risks of foreclosure in upstream or downstream markets, generated by the vertical effects of the operation. Among the various measures cited by the Guidelines are granting access to networks or infrastructures in a non-discriminatory and transparent manner, granting access to licenses, patents,

---

34 *Ibid*, pt 39.

35 *Ibid*, pt 42.

36 APC, *Guidelines on the scope and procedure for merger control*, *op. cit.* pt.

37 *Ibid*, pt 259.

38 *Ibid*, pt 260.

trademarks, or technologies, terminating or modifying exclusive contracts, and/ or disclosing information on a non-exclusive basis.[39]

64. The French Competition Authority itself regularly uses behavioural commitments in such a context.[40] It may be added that such measures also seem entirely appropriate in island markets where, by their very nature, the same investors are found at different levels of the value chain and at different levels of the economy, and where divestments could prove particularly penalising without, however, any guarantee of finding buyers.

65. Between 2016 and 2024, of the five commitment decisions adopted by the Polynesian Authority, four were based on this type of commitment, including the two that concerned the tourism sector.[41]

66. More specifically, with each new takeover of the Tahiti Nui Travel group by a group with significant activities in the hotel sector, the acquirer (the Grey group in December 2016, then the Louis Wane group in June 2022) has agreed to commit, for a period of 5 years, to:

- renew annually all contracts concluded between the receptive agencies held by the target (Tahiti Nui Travel) and its suppliers (competing hotels) under objective, transparent and non-discriminatory commercial conditions;
- Not to circulate strategic information concerning competing hotels (such as, for example, the prices charged by them) to the hotels of the integrated group and their management bodies. To this end, the acquirer has committed to ensuring the autonomous operation of its receptive agency activities in relation to its hotel activities, by prohibiting its hotel managers or executives from holding a position related to the receptive agency activity in the year preceding and following their appointment; and
- set up a programme to raise awareness and train staff in the incoming agency and hotel business in the commitments made as part of the operation.

67. According to the Polynesian Authority, these undertakings were designed to prevent the purchaser from using its newly acquired position on the incoming agency market to drive out or discriminate against competitors on the hotel market.

68. By renewing an authorisation subject to the same commitments in the event of a subsequent acquisition of the group by another player, the Autorité also confirmed that its 2016 analysis remained fully relevant after several years of commitments.

---

39 *Ibid*, pt 287.

40 Autorité de la concurrence, *Les engagements comportementaux*, La Documentation française, Les Essentiels series, 2020, p. 64.

41 APC, Decision No. 2016-CC-04 of 5 December 2016 on the acquisition of exclusive control of the Tahiti Nui Travel group by the Grey group, cited above; and APC, Decision No. 2022-CC-02 of 8 June 2022 on the acquisition of exclusive control of the Tahiti Nui Travel group (TNT) by Mr Louis Wane, cited above.

N°	Date	Wording
1.	2 November 2023	Decision 2023-CC-04 of 2 November 2023 relating to the acquisition of joint control of the Hilton Moorea Lagoon Resort & Spa hotel by Louis Wane alongside the Hilton Group
2.	8 June 2022	Decision no. 2022-CC-02 of 8 June 2022 on the acquisition of sole control of the Tahiti Nui Travel group (TNT) by Mr Louis Wane
3.	19 January 2022	Decision No 2022-CC-01 of 19 January 2022 concerning the acquisition of sole control of Moorea Lagoon Resort and BoraBora Eden Cruise by Dazhong Transportation (Dazhong group) and the acquisition of joint control of Société hôtelière Motu Ome'e by Dazhong Transportation (Dazhong group) alongside the Marriott group
4.	15 November 2021	Decision No. 2021-DREC-01 of 15 November 2021 on compliance with the commitments made in Decision No. 2016CC-04 of 5 December 2016 on the acquisition of exclusive control of the Tahiti Nui Travel group by the Grey group
5.	6 May 2021	Decision no. 2021-CC-01 of 6 May 2021 concerning the acquisition of joint control of the Tahiti hotel by Hilton Worldwide Manage Limited (Hilton group) alongside SAS Hôtel Tahiti (Wane group)
6.	25 May 2020	Decision no. 2020-CC-01 of 25 May 2020 concerning the acquisition of joint control of the Sofitel Moorea Ia Ora Beach Resort hotel by Mr Louis Wane, who will be replaced by Eimeo Holding SAS (in the process of being incorporated) alongside AAPC-NZ Pty. Ltd (Accor group)
7.	16 April 2019	Decision No. 2019-CC-01 of 16 April 2019 on the acquisition of joint control of the Le Méridien Tahiti hotel by AAPC-NZ Pty. Ltd Accor group) alongside SAS Société hôtelière Rivnac (Grey group)
8.	18 December 2018	Decision No. 2018-CC-01 of 18 December 2018 on the acquisition of sole control of Hotel Kia Ora SA by SAS Ranginui
9.	31 May 2017	Decision No. 2017-CC-04 of 31 May 2017 on the acquisition of sole control of Compagnie touristique polynésienne by South Seas Resort Limited (HNA Group)
10.	27 April 2017	Decision No. 2017-CC-03 of 27 April 2017 on the acquisition of exclusive control of Société financière hôtelière polynésienne by Société Brasserie de Tahiti
11.	23 March 2017	Decision No. 2017-CC-02 of 23 March 2017 on the acquisition of sole control of Société d'investissement de Polynésie (Four Seasons Hôtel & Resort Bora-Bora) by Swansea King Limited (Gaw Hospitality investment fund)
12.	13 December 2016	Decision no. 2016-CC-05 of 13 December 2016 on the acquisition of joint control of Société des Nouveaux Hôtels by Mr Louis Wane alongside the Starwood group
13.	5 December 2016	Decision No. 2016-CC-04 of 5 December 2016 on the acquisition of exclusive control of the Tahiti Nui Travel group by the Grey group
14.	6 October 2016	Decision No. 2016-CC-03 of 6 October 2016 on the acquisition of joint control of the Manava Beach Resort & Spa hotel (Compagnie touristique polynésienne) by Lupesina Tahiti Investments (Grey group) alongside the SPM group
15.	29 August 2016	Decision no. 2016-CC-02 of 29 August 2016 on the acquisition of joint control of the three Sofitel hotels in French Polynesia by Lupesina Tahiti Investments (Grey group) alongside the AccorHotels group
16.	6 July 2016	Decision No. 2016-CC-01 of 6 July 2016 on the acquisition of sole control by HNA Tourism (HNA Group) of South Seas Resort Limited (Louis Wane Group)

Not Every Cloud Brings a Storm: When the Winds of Competition Blow Across the Polynesian Tourism Sector

Yannick Lecornu* and Hironui Johnston**

1. During the preliminary examination of the future Competition Code by the Assembly of French Polynesia in 2015, the government behind the text endeavoured to explain the expectations of a text on which all would quickly project their hopes and fantasies. Thus, one of the representatives of the deliberative body declared his approval of the project on the grounds that it would put an end to an "*incestuous relationship between private companies and the public*".
2. With this objective in mind, it was natural for former public servants with a proven masochistic bent to take part in the celebration of the tenth anniversary of the entry into force of the Competition Code in French Polynesia.
3. Even after a decade, it's still amusing to note that elected officials are ever quicker to point the finger at the relationship between the private and public sectors, forgetting in the process that, in the Polynesian economic system, the weight of public companies in strategic sectors is preponderant... and their positioning is far more incestuous than that of their private counterparts. As Confucius said, when a wise man points at the moon...
4. This being said, it is true that the implementation of Competition law represented a major step in the transformation of a territory called upon to move from an

---

* Yannick Lecornu is a civil servant, former Chief of Staff for the Ministry of Economy and Finance, and former General Director of the Chamber of Commerce and Industry of French Polynesia.

** Hironui Johnston is a consultant and former technical advisor in charge of tourism and international air transport to the government of French Polynesia.

administered economy to a market economy based, ultimately, on independent regulation.

5. This was not necessarily expected by all, and many voiced opposition from the very beginning of the project. After all, wasn't our territory too small and too specific to adopt rules devised in latitudes where the unit of measurement for population is *at least* one million inhabitants and for wealth one billion dollars? What's more, in our part of the world, interpersonal relations generally take precedence over institutions, and everyone knows everyone else, so getting along seems consubstantial with living together. In essence, these are the arguments that were once used to refute the value of introducing Competition law in our latitudes.

6. Ten years on, no one in public decision-making circles – with the possible exception of a few doctrinaires in search of a differentiation strategy – would dispute the relevance of Polynesian Competition law. At most, they insist on the need to take into account the specific features of the island context. Most economic players agree with this double postulate: Competition law is beneficial, notwithstanding the legitimate primacy given to the most elementary common sense. This shared conviction is of the utmost concern to the tourism industry.

7. Before explaining what we're talking about, we feel it's essential to set out a few considerations about the tourism sector in French Polynesia, particularly with a view to guiding the potentially uninformed reader through the characteristics of our small island economy.

I. Between island challenges and tourism opportunities

8. French Polynesia is an autonomous overseas collectivity within the French Republic, made up of five archipelagos covering an area the size of Europe, with 118 islands, 76 of which are inhabited, and a total population of 280,000.

9. Because of its geographical location away from the major development hubs, the constrained nature of its space, the problems of transport and load breakage, and the high spatial dispersion of its population, the area is generally referred to by economists as a region with structural handicaps. It should be noted that the plural is used here.

10. These specific geographical features – an extremely vast territory with a small, relatively unconcentrated population and scattered, remote islands – have an impact on the structure of the Polynesian economy. At the same time, French Polynesia faces the challenge of integrating its workforce, which is still far in excess of the needs of the modern sector. This integration is the only way to redistribute the benefits of economic growth, without purely welfare-based policies. So much for the rough outline of the global panorama.

11. With a contribution of almost 10% to the local economy, tourism is one of the growth drivers of the Polynesian economy. By way of illustration, in 2023, exports, of which tourism accounts for the largest share (nearly 85%), will contribute one-third of annual GDP growth.

12. Yet the volumes are surprising. In a good year, the total number of tourists hardly exceeds 260,000, a rather meagre figure for a country that has made tourism one of

its main growth priorities. However, the level of expenditure per tourist makes up for the small number of tourists. Indeed, each of these people consumes far more than in other latitudes, so that the average income per room on Bora Bora stood, in October 2024, at 120,000 francs per night, or 1,065 USD. These prices are within the reach of the executives, liberal professionals and retirees who make up the vast majority of holidaymakers. Unsurprisingly, they come from the high-paying regions of North America (45%) and Europe (42%, with over 70% from France).

13. What's more, the region's geographic isolation favours lengths of stay, which range from 11 to 14 days for market accommodations (broken down by type: 80% land-based vs. 20% floating), all this with an annual occupancy rate of over 80%.

14. Tourism also makes a major contribution to regional planning and the spatial distribution of tourism-related income. With accommodation facilities on 40 islands, 34 of which have airports, the tourism sector provides work for more than 4,500 businesses and employs 5,500 people in the accommodations sector alone.

15. In recent years, an increasing concentration of tourism on American and French customers has revealed both the strength of the local offering in relation to these outbound markets, and the great fragility of a sector struggling to diversify its customer base, particularly from Asia, and thus exposed to potentially strong market ups and downs.

II. Rules of the game that patiently transform players' behaviour

16. According to orthodoxy, competition fosters a healthy economic environment in which companies compete to offer the best products and services at the best prices, and thus remain competitive and innovative. On the other hand, an overly lax competition policy generally provides fertile ground for cartels and abusive practices, the germination of which quickly leads to sluggish economic growth, declining service quality and amorphous innovation.

17. In this anniversary year, it is therefore appropriate to consider the impact of the introduction of Competition law in French Polynesia on the tourism sector. In other words, has this innovative legal framework stimulated innovation, improved the quality of offers and strengthened the competitiveness of tourism-related businesses?

18. A short while ago, some pessimists remarked, with disconcerting fatuity, that Competition law had failed on the grounds that merger control rulings concerning tourist resorts had all been favourable.

19. This type of reasoning is hardly new. The Greeks, who placed man at the heart of the universe, already believed that the sun and stars revolved around the Earth. Faced with the stubborn refusal of the planets to revolve with the regularity of a metronome around the Earth, the Greeks christened these planets "wandering stars". This was the counter-example to Ptolemy's astronomical model, and it wasn't until the genius of Copernicus some twenty centuries later that they realised that this counter-example simply called into question the explanatory system itself.

20. Similarly, as far as Competition law is concerned, the regularity of mergers declared over the last ten years in no way attests to the uselessness of the procedure, unless you consider that the absence of fines for speeding in the vicinity of an elementary school constitutes proof of the uselessness of speed regulation in this type of zone.

21. The very existence of a body of standards designed to prevent competitive distortions has enabled local companies to intensify their legal and economic approach to merger issues, prompting executive committees to think at a much higher level than under the previous legal framework. This move upmarket has also produced positive externalities in the relationship between economic players and public decision-makers. The introduction of an objective frame of reference and an impartial arbitrator has provided both parties with a basis for a more enlightened discussion, free from subjective considerations.

22. This impact should not be underestimated. In French Polynesia, the public authorities play an important role in the economy, particularly in the tourism sector, where they define strategic orientations, which translate into multi-year infrastructure construction programs, regulatory changes and financial support for investment.

23. From this point of view, the emergence of an impartial arbitrator, the formalisation of the rules of the game, and the appropriation by the parties of this new framework constitute long-term advances in favour of the objectification of exchanges in this major sector.

24. So, while Competition law may not have revolutionised the Polynesian tourism economy in the truest sense of the word, the gradual development of a competition culture has undeniably had an impact. But to understand them properly, we need to shorten the focus and look at the Polynesian tourism sector in relation to its direct competitors and its playground: the world of high-end tourism.

25. The attractiveness of a tourist destination depends on three major factors: price, level of service and identity. While French Polynesia is easily able to hold its own against international competition on the identity factor, notably by riding the wave of the "mana" concept, it has to be said that it is lagging behind on the other two. And with good reason. Since the beginning of the 21st century, new tourist destinations have been marketing "paradise-like" services similar to those found in Polynesia: transparent, turquoise bathing waters, white sand beaches, bungalows on stilts, and so on. And all at lower prices than here. So, with a structurally very high price for a stay, French Polynesia lacked differentiation and therefore competitiveness.

26. This international competition prompted French Polynesia to rethink its positioning and move upmarket. As mentioned above, this trajectory was not driven by economic players alone. By defining an initial sectoral tourism strategy for the 2015-2020 period, the public authorities have helped to raise the profile of the destination. The inscription of the Marae Taputapuatea complex, soon followed by that of the Marquesas Islands, on the UNESCO World Heritage List was a strong signal sent to players in the industry and to tourists from all over the world. Similarly, the last decade has seen the development of numerous certifications and labels aimed at structuring this trajectory towards quality.

27. In addition to the "cash cow" Bora Bora, positioned in particular in the strategic honeymoon sector, French Polynesia has developed other destinations within the destination, such as Raiatea and the Marquesas Islands for the quest for authenticity, or the Tuamotus for diving activities or Robinson Crusoe-type experiences. The nautical tourism sector has also benefited from considerable public investment, enabling service providers to guarantee travellers a high level of quality and safety.

28. In this segment, small local companies have specifically benefited from the clarification of the competitive environment. In a small economy, the increased risk of concentration can have a lasting impact on the negotiating power of suppliers and customers, and on the freedom of challengers to innovate. However, since the introduction of Competition law, local multi-trade groups, particularly those involved in the tourist accommodation sector, have integrated the consideration of small players into their strategies. Admittedly, this has not always been the case, but both parties are now aware that the same matrix applies to all.

29. The impact of Competition law on the sector's dynamism deserves to be both emphasised and qualified. While it cannot, on its own, constitute the sole solution to the problem of the sustainable and balanced development of Polynesia's tourism sector, it will have helped to introduce private and public players to a renewed economic culture, taking account of side effects in a long-term perspective.

III. Local consumers and world travellers: who benefits from competition?

30. Competition law also postulates the defence of the interests of the consumer, that humble layman unaware of implacable economic rationality who quickly falls prey to the voracious company driven by its sole short-term interest. Nevertheless, this is a crude dual portrayal that has little real-world relevance.

31. While the ultimate aim of competition policy is to protect consumers, this term must be understood in a broader sense: it includes not only end consumers, but also companies that are customers of other companies. Thus, agreements concluded to the detriment of companies in intermediate markets are just as harmful as agreements targeting end consumers.

32. In this sense, the introduction of Competition law benefits all consumers, individuals and professionals alike, especially those in the tourism sector. After all, if you think about it, a hotel, whether a five-star resort or a guesthouse, is also a formidable intermediary consumer likely to be impacted by cartels on the markets on which it relies for its supplies. As a result, their price structure may be affected, their quality of service altered and their competitiveness compromised.

33. From this point of view, compliance with competition rules on services that are essential to the functioning of the tourism sector, especially network activities, is a key success factor for the entire ecosystem. We'll come back to this point later.

34. With regard to the final consumer, i.e. the customer of tourism services in French Polynesia, we need to distinguish between two market segments: local customers, who mainly frequent small hotels and guesthouses, and international customers, who mainly stay in hotels flying the flag of the world's major brands. These two

segments are so different in terms of capital, customers, products and approach that it is difficult to agree on one single consumer profile.

35. As we saw above, our non-resident consumer is a senior executive, a liberal professional or an affluent retiree from Europe or North America. We might therefore question the relevance of Polynesian Competition law intervening to protect consumers who do not fall within its geographical jurisdiction. Similarly, the local taxpayer might resent the mobilisation of public funds to protect non-nationals. After all, evaluations left on networks of all kinds already make it possible to penalise companies that show little regard for their customers. According to this logic, Polynesian Competition law should, above all, protect Polynesian consumers, their purchasing power and their freedom of choice.

36. But there is an objection to the objection. Firstly, because our international consumer may frequent a boarding house, and our local tourist may venture into a luxury hotel complex. Secondly, because we're in a global market, where competition rules similar to our own apply for the most part. On this point, it's important to emphasise that the upscale hotel business here is the result of partnerships between local investors and international hotel chains, which ensure that competition rules are applied by both their own teams and those of their competitors. The path of Competition law is inseparable from the trajectory of the internationalisation of trade. Finally, because Competition law is not limited solely to the borders of the sector in question, and has an impact on the entire local economic fabric. For example, a company controlling too large a share of high-end tourist accommodation would have disproportionate bargaining power over the other economic players in the ecosystem, which could have a negative impact on overall prosperity.

37. At the very most, this differentiation of two markets according to their majority clienteles may justify a different definition of the relevant market, with international brands competing more with the above-mentioned paradise destinations than with boarding houses. This is the position adopted by the Polynesian Competition Authority in its decisions on mergers in the tourism sector.

38. A final category of accommodation still escapes our analysis: furnished tourist accommodations. Here, the risk of concentration, collusion or anti-competitive practices is virtually nil, given the sheer number of players. However, the rapid emergence of this type of competition to the conventional hotel sector calls into question the limits of application of Competition law. By benefiting from a much lower level of regulatory constraints and an advantageous tax system, vacation rentals introduce a distortion of competition likely to harm, in the long term, a structured sector guaranteeing long-term employment. Between defending the interests of the consumer, sometimes in a short-termist logic, and protecting an economic ecosystem that remains, in many respects, cacophonous, temporality is the most appropriate reading grid, and a source of discord between the public decision-maker and the electorate. Unfortunately, Competition law is not currently concerned with this parameter, and legislators are still struggling to take it into account, allowing deregulation to produce effects that are already highly perceptible in several sectoral policies, tourism and housing in particular.

IV. Open skies and air turbulence

39. In an archipelagic system, a final group of players must not be forgotten in this reflection: airlines. An essential pillar of the Polynesian economy, the aeronautical sector operating out of the country's only international airport has in the past been characterised by a high degree of concentration. The recent development of competition has provoked strong reactions and is still the subject of much debate. Although the arrival of new airlines on the Tahiti-Faa'a hub is the result of the "treaty on open skies" and not of local Competition law, protests generally lead to a challenge to the entire edifice as a whole.

40. The arrival of French Bee, for example, led to lower prices and a more diversified product range, which in turn boosted tourism in the region. This was followed by the entry of other operators, including United and Delta Airlines, or the strengthening of existing players such as Air France. At the same time, this relative increase in competitive intensity revealed the fragility of the local airline Air Tahiti Nui, whose annual accounts are now balanced only thanks to public intervention via balancing subsidies.

41. On this subject, the rhetoric of defence is often more moral than practical, opposing the values associated with market competition – freedom of action, consumer purchasing power and economic efficiency – with the social values of social solidarity and security, embodied by what remains perceived as a quasi-public service. This argument is emotionally reinforced by the local character of the victim, opposed to predators from outside. On this last point, it should be emphasised, if it were necessary, that the latter companies have never harboured the secret intention of damaging the local airline.

42. The same opposition can be seen in the domestic air transport sector. This monopoly has recently been challenged by a new entrant. Here again, as with every opening to competition of a sector hitherto subject to a monopoly, voices have been raised about the risks of destabilising the market – it's amusing to note that a sector with a single player cannot constitute a real market – and about the need to protect a natural monopoly. What's more, certain players, blinded by a common fatuity, were quick to use this textbook case to predict the apocalypse in the event of the generalisation of Competition law, and to denounce the advocates of a reasonably open market.

V. Efficiency for course and common sense for compass

43. As we said at the outset, common sense remains the best guarantee that the principles of competition are properly adapted to the Polynesian context. It is this compass of discernment, lucidity and temperance that has governed the fair application of competition rules, which have already had an impact, particularly in terms of corporate behaviour.

44. Admittedly, there is still room for improvement, and clouds are gathering here and there, putting stress on certain economic activities and calling into question models that were once thought immutable. However, the winds of competition, far from undermining the tourism sector, have, on the contrary, energised it,

accompanying it in its inevitable adaptation to the standards of high-end tourism with the world as its only frontier. It is, moreover, because of this planetary scope of the market that cooperation between competition authorities must be encouraged as quickly as possible. In a multipolar world faced with the challenge of global warming and the preservation of natural resources, a Competition law enriched with environmental and social concerns could, in the long term, contribute to the harmonious development of business, satisfying both producer and consumer, while avoiding all forms of dumping, particularly social dumping.

45. Finally, if Polynesian Competition law has been positively received in the tourism sector, this is probably due to the absence of public authorities as shareholders. If it had had a direct interest in the hotel or cruise industries, as it does in the airline sector, it's a safe bet that the deployment of a competitive scheme would have been significantly altered, and certainly vilified as the source of all the ills of our time. It's also a safe bet that, in such a scenario, regulation would have been accommodating to the interests held, directly or through an intermediary, by the public authorities. If Competition law is to be fully effective, public decision-makers need to be ambitious enough to tackle another incestuous relationship: that between publicly-owned companies and the public.

46. As an advisor to the government and the courts, and likely to be consulted on texts or cases falling within its remit, the Polynesian Competition Authority can become this lever for the gradual transformation of the Polynesian economy, and participate in the renovation of erroneous conceptual frameworks that still hamper the decision-making process at many levels. In this way, to quote Confucius' aphorism, we may one day be able to turn our gaze to the moon.

PART IV

The Proper Use of Cooperation to Break Structural Isolation

The French and Polynesian Authorities Will Continue to Unite their Efforts to Promote the Vitality of the Metropolitan and Polynesian Economies

Stanislas Martin*
Autorité de la concurrence

1. The French Competition Authority is responsible for applying competition law on national territory, including the overseas regions (Guadeloupe, Guyane, Martinique, Réunion, Mayotte, Saint-Barthélemy, Saint-Martin, Saint-Pierre-et-Miquelon, and the Wallis and Futuna Islands), with the exception of New Caledonia and French Polynesia, which have their own legal framework and competition authorities.
2. However, there is a strong proximity between the three French competition authorities. There is, of course, linguistic proximity, legal proximity, as the applicable texts are relatively similar, and shared challenges, with all three authorities facing the issues encountered by island economies.
3. From the creation of the Polynesian Competition Authority, this proximity was materialized by the signing in Papeete on July 23, 2015, by Presidents Bruno Lasserre and Jacques Mérot, in the presence of the President of French Polynesia, Edouard Fritch, of a framework agreement for technical assistance. This agreement was renewed and enhanced on May 4, 2022, in Berlin, on the sidelines of the annual conference of the International Competition Network (ICN), by President Benoît Cœuré and President Johanne Peyre.

---

* Stanislas Martin is the General Rapporteur at the French Competition Authority in Paris.

4. The first aspect of these agreements focuses on training. The Competition Authority regularly hosts agents from the Polynesian Competition Authority, who participate in initial training seminars for new agents of the Competition Authority. Ad hoc training sessions have also been organized for the senior staff of the Polynesian Authority, who were able to engage with their Parisian counterparts on various aspects of their roles.

5. From the outset, the framework agreement included the assistance of the Competition Authority in the deployment and updating of the "Pegase" application, which is the software used to manage procedures (digitizing and indexing documents, managing business confidentiality, handling the adversarial process, and providing access to case files for the parties involved).

6. As part of this deployment, the head of the Procedure Service traveled to Tahiti to train the agents of the Polynesian Authority on using and operating this software, and more broadly, on procedure management. Polynesian procedural agents were later hosted in Paris to maintain and further develop their skills.

7. The 2022 framework agreement also includes a "technical cooperation on personnel" component, which strengthens a practice established earlier. To encourage the mobility of experienced rapporteurs from the Competition Authority to assist their Polynesian counterpart, the framework agreement stipulates that an agent on a permanent contract who undergoes mobility with the Polynesian Authority will be granted a mobility leave for a period of up to six years, allowing them to return to a position at the Competition Authority after gaining experience with the Polynesian Competition Authority.

8. The human relations between the two authorities are particularly close, reflecting a level of cooperation that is unparalleled. Of the three general rapporteurs who have succeeded one another at the Polynesian Authority, two come from the Competition Authority, as well as the deputy general rapporteur and several other rapporteurs. In a different context, two vice-presidents of the Competition Authority are alternate members of the board of the Polynesian Authority, further strengthening the proximity between the two institutions. These organic links illustrate the mutual trust between the two authorities and enhance the exchange of best practices.

9. Cooperation between the two authorities is not limited to training and human or IT resources, but also includes an operational dimension.

10. The framework agreement allows for "mutual consultations and information exchanges," enabling informal consultations on legal or principled matters. This informal cooperation is particularly strong across all areas and is facilitated by the fact that the rapporteurs from both institutions are well acquainted, either because Polynesian rapporteurs are former members of the Competition Authority or because they have been trained with their Parisian colleagues and established connections during that time.

11. However, when the needs of the investigation justify it, and when elements must be added to a procedure, this informal cooperation can become more formal. In this regard, the framework agreement specifies that the two authorities may 'exchange information related to an ongoing investigation or inquiry, subject to

the compliance with procedures and confidentiality rules to which each authority is bound.'

12. This enhanced cooperation is framed by Ordinance No. 2017-157 of February 9, 2017, which extends and adapts certain provisions of Book IV of the *Commercial Code* relating to controls and sanctions in competition matters to French Polynesia. Article 9 bis of the Ordinance provides that:

> *The Competition Authority referred to in Article L. 461-1 of the [Commercial] Code and the Polynesian Competition Authority may, within their respective competencies, mutually communicate the information or documents they hold or collect.*

13. The Ordinance also provides for the possibility for each authority to carry out investigations on its territory on behalf of the other authority:

> *The Competition Authority may, under the same conditions, according to the same procedures, and under the same sanctions as those provided for carrying out its mission, conduct investigations or take investigative actions at the request of the Polynesian Competition Authority. The minister responsible for the economy may also conduct investigations or take investigative actions at the request of the Polynesian Competition Authority. The information and documents thus collected are communicated to the Polynesian Competition Authority.*
>
> *The Competition Authority and the minister responsible for the economy may request the Polynesian Competition Authority to conduct investigations or take investigative actions. The information and documents thus collected are communicated to the authority that made the request.*

14. These provisions have not remained idle and have been successfully implemented on two occasions.

15. In a case related to the air freight transport of pets in French Polynesia, which led to Decision No. 22-D-05 of February 15, 2022, sanctioning for abuse of a dominant position the company operating the only authorized metropolitan quarantine station built and operated by the GIP company at Grais in Orne, the Competition Authority's investigative services requested the assistance of the General Rapporteur of the Polynesian Competition Authority in October 2020. They carried out various investigative actions and provided the General Rapporteur of the Competition Authority with essential information and documents that were crucial for the successful conclusion of the case.

16. Conversely, in June 2021, the General Rapporteur of the Polynesian Competition Authority requested the investigative services of the Competition Authority to conduct investigative actions with wholesalers based in mainland France.

17. Finally, the two authorities also cooperate in a multilateral framework, at the OECD, within the International Competition Network, and more recently within the Pacific Island Network of Competition Consumer and Economic Regulators (PINCCER), created in November 2023 at the initiative of the Polynesian Competition Authority. This network brings together authorities from New Caledonia, French Polynesia, Australia, New Zealand, the Cook Islands, Kiribati, the Solomon Islands, Fiji, Papua New Guinea, Samoa, the Kingdom of Tonga,

and Vanuatu. The Competition Authority, which is also a Pacific authority due to its jurisdiction over Wallis and Futuna, participates in this network.

18. The celebration of the 10th anniversary of the competition regime in French Polynesia gives us the opportunity to reflect, through these few pages, on the quality of the relationship between our two authorities, but also to acknowledge the remarkable work accomplished by the Polynesian Competition Authority and its agents. Thanks to this remarkable cooperation, our two institutions will continue to unite their efforts to promote the vitality of the mainland, overseas, and Polynesian economies.

Building Competition in the Pacific: Seven Years of Cooperation Between the Polynesian and New Caledonian Authorities

Stéphane Retterer* and Chloé Racine**
New Caledonian Competition Authority

1. In honour of the 10th anniversary of the Polynesian Competition Authority (APC), the New Caledonian Competition Authority (ACNC) would like to look back over the 7 years of cooperation between these two young institutions.
2. At the outset, the two Pacific authorities emerged in a historical context marked by major economic challenges. In New Caledonia, the report by the French Competition Authority (Autorité de la concurrence métropolitaine) on the import and distribution mechanisms for consumer products[1] raised awareness of the challenges of competition. Against a backdrop of protests over the high cost of living, the report led the local authorities to introduce a legal framework dedicated to competition. Thus, a year and a half later, loi du pays no. 2014-7, adopted on 14 February 2014, created a New Caledonian competition law, followed by the establishment of the ACNC by law no. 2014-12 of 24 April 2014. Similarly, the APC was instituted by loi du pays no. 2015-2, adopted on 23 February 2015,

---

* Stéphane Retterer is the President of the Competition Authority of New Caledonia.
** Chloé Racine is a paralegal in the legal department of the Competition Authority of New Caledonia.

1 Autorité de la concurrence, *Rapport relatif aux structures de contrôle en matière de concurrence en Nouvelle-Calédonie*, 21 September 2012.

in response to growing concerns about consumer protection and the need for a competitive market. These creations have also been accelerated by political reasons, some of which are unspoken.

3. Although the timeframes for Polynesian and New Caledonian competition law are similar, it should be noted that delays, particularly in the recruitment process for the Chair and the General Rapporteur, have delayed the start of the ACNC's activities in March 2018.

4. Since then, cooperation between the APC and the ACNC has naturally developed and gradually intensified, drawing on ongoing dialogue and joint initiatives (I).

5. This anniversary nevertheless comes at a time of turmoil, marked by the economic and social crisis that New Caledonia has been experiencing since the riots that began in the territory on 13 May 2024, described by some as "cataclysmic events" for the local economy. This unrest has had a profound effect on the ACNC, which has had to navigate through major uncertainties, highlighting the need for competition law to be both robust and flexible in times of crisis.

6. Throughout this period, the collaboration with the APC, as well as with other competition authorities, even if reduced, allowed the ACNC to adjust its responses to emerging needs and to envisage a more competitive economic model for the reconstruction of the Caledonian economy (II).

I. Long-term cooperation between the competition authorities in New Caledonia and French Polynesia

A. *Framework and challenges of cooperation between New Caledonia and French Polynesia*

7. Cooperation between the New Caledonian and Polynesian competition authorities has been developing since 2018 on the basis of institutional and economic similarities between the two territories. Although geographically distinct, the two authorities share an almost identical population (around 270,000 inhabitants) and administered economies with similar characteristics. This context has encouraged regular exchanges of expertise, close collaboration and the gradual construction of a solid inter-institutional framework.

8. However, the specific nature of these two island economies is based on marked differences in terms of economic structure and protectionist policies. In New Caledonia, the economic model is more self-centred and administered, reinforced by a significant local industry, while in French Polynesia, relative openness to external markets, particularly the United States, tempers market protection. These economic differences are also reflected in market protection measures: while the local development tax (TDL) and import quotas protect Polynesian companies, in New Caledonia, the quantitative STOP (or QTOP) restrictions on imports of competing products mainly benefit New Caledonian industrial and processing companies. These protections, which affect around 400 local companies, are designed to preserve and develop the productive capacity of local industry in the face of external competition. New Caledonia's assertive protectionism and

barriers to entry illustrate a more marked approach to island markets than in French Polynesia, reflecting different economic models.

9. The economic differences between these two island territories are also reflected in price trends. According to statistics from the Institute of Statistics and Economic Studies (ISEE),[2] price differences between mainland France, French Polynesia and New Caledonia are particularly marked, and generally to the disadvantage of New Caledonia. For example, in the telecommunications sector, where there is a legal monopoly in New Caledonia, prices are 77% higher than in mainland France, compared with in French Polynesia, where the market is open to competition. In the food sector, the difference with mainland France is in New Caledonia, despite the territory's high level of local production, compared with in French Polynesia, where production is relatively low. These disparities highlight the impact of protectionist policies and the economic structures in place in these territories.

B. *International cooperation and regional competition networks*

10. Despite these differences, the two competition authorities have succeeded in establishing a long-term framework for cooperation, marked by a series of joint initiatives. The ACNC's participation in the APC's "Competition Days", starting in 2018, has been an important milestone in the development of this cooperation. These meetings have enabled officials from both authorities to share their respective experiences, both on regulatory mechanisms and on best practices for implementing competition law in island economies. For example, during the 2023 edition of the "Competition Days" in Tahiti, ACNC representatives took part in debates on key subjects, such as competition in public procurement and distribution, or mergers and commercial developments, bringing their expertise on the specificities of competition law in New Caledonia.

11. The APC's "Competition Days" were expanded in 2024, with a twofold objective: to increase regional expertise and strengthen cooperation between Pacific authorities, even beyond the New Caledonian and Polynesian entities. Indeed, these events have also recently seen the participation of members of the Pacific Island Network of Competition Consumer and Economic Regulators (PINCCER), which brings together competition or multi-sector authorities from countries such as Australia, New Zealand and Fiji.

12. The launch of the PINCCER network in 2023 marked a new stage in cooperation in the Pacific. Working with authorities across the region, the ACNC and the APC are pooling their resources and expertise to address common challenges related to competition, the high cost of living and consumer protection in small island economies. The aim of the network is to strengthen the capacity of Pacific competition authorities by providing them with a platform dedicated to promoting competition in regional markets. PINCCER enables the authorities to speak with one voice on regional issues while developing their collective expertise.

---

2 ISEE, "Enquête de comparaison spatiale des prix", New Caledonia, 2022.

13. In addition, the two authorities regularly participate jointly in the conferences of the International Competition Network (ICN), demonstrating their desire to be involved on a global scale in discussions on the challenges of competition regulation, and thus strengthening their cooperation beyond their respective territories.

C. *Exchanges of expertise and best practice*

14. The staff of the two territories can also consult each other in a very practical way on specific issues, which brings a concrete dimension to this cooperation. For example, ahead of the "Competition Daysorganised by the Polynesian Authority in 2023, the head of the ACNC's Merger and Retail Bureau met with her Polynesian counterparts to discuss the practicalities of handling cases and the challenges of this activity for the small Pacific island territories. This exchange provided an opportunity to share best practices on the management of mergers in often restricted markets, while highlighting the specific characteristics of island economies.

15. At the same time, the APC has recently provided valuable support to the ACNC regarding the implementation of independent regulation in the telecommunications sector in New Caledonia (see *below*).

D. *Sharing legal knowledge through training and technical meetings*

16. Meetings and collaborations have increased over the years, through joint conferences, co-authored legal articles,[3] and joint participation in international forums. Joint training courses also illustrate the wealth of exchanges between the two authorities. For example, in 2018, in partnership with the chambers of commerce and industry of the two territories, the APC and ACNC launched a training course entitled "Practising competition law in New Caledonia and French Polynesia". The aim of this initiative was to make the rules of competition law accessible to local businesses and their legal advisers, while offering a practical framework based on concrete cases. This type of educational cooperation familiarised local economic players with the subtleties of a legal framework recently introduced in New Caledonia and French Polynesia.[4]

17. The APC has also always played a key role in conferences organised by the ACNC. For the first ACNC colloquium in March 2019, devoted to the practice of competition law in New Caledonia and the other overseas collectivities, Jacques Mérot, then Chairman of the APC, for example, presented the authority's decision-making practice since 2016, which offered valuable comparative perspectives.[5]

---

3 See for example Stéphane Retterer, Merot Jacques, Sims Rod, Zoude-Le Berre Aurélie, Healey Deborah, Marchal Tehono, Simpson Robin, Troianiello Antonino, and Raimana Lallemant-Moe Hervé, "Antitrust Regimes in the Pacific Region," Concurrences, November 2018, n° 4-2018, art. n° 88123, p. 19-54, www.concurrences.com/*88089*

4 For example, the two authorities also took part in a workshop with the journal *Concurrences* in 2020 in Paris on "New Caledonia and French Polynesia: New challenges for competition law".

5 Similarly, at a second colloquium organised by the ACNC in July 2022 on the application of competition law in overseas France, a rapporteur from the APC was invited to speak, testifying to the continuing close collaboration between the two authorities.

18. Alongside these numerous direct exchanges, the "APC + ACNC Meetings" are another essential forum for exchange between the two authorities. These meetings, which have been held regularly for several years, give the rapporteurs the opportunity to talk to leading experts in competition law. Thanks to these videoconferences, figures such as Olivier Guersent, Director General of the European Commission's Competition Directorate General, and representatives of the US Department of Justice have shared their knowledge and expertise with the ACNC and the APC. This initiative, which provides an opportunity to immerse oneself in international practices and thinking, contributes to refining the application of competition law in the two island territories, as well as bilateral cooperation between the two authorities.

E. *Synergies and cross-influence in the authorities' decision-making practice*

19. The results of this cooperation are not limited to meetings or conferences, but are also reflected in the opinions issued by the two bodies, which often draw on the experiences of the other territory. For example, the opinion issued by the ACNC on the spare parts market in New Caledonia[6] was based on a similar study carried out by the APC.[7] Conversely, the APC mentioned the ACNC's economic note on the regulation of prices and margins[8] in its opinion on a draft law of the country relating to the regulation of the prices of certain products and services,[9] highlighting common perspectives and testifying to the reciprocal influence between the two authorities.

20. This inter-institutional collaboration creates a fertile exchange of views, in which certain opinions of the two authorities become permeable, or even interchangeable. For example, the ACNC's opinion on the price formation mechanism[10] and the APC's opinion on imports[11] provide a comprehensive and accurate view of production, import and distribution mechanisms in the two territories.

---

6 ACNC, Opinion No. 2023-A-03 of 31 October 2023 on the request for an opinion on the draft decision amending the regulatory part of the *Commercial Code* applicable in New Caledonia, relating to car spare parts; see also *Stéphane Retterer, Enguerrand Simminger, Nouvelle-Calédonie : L'Autorité de la concurrence de la Nouvelle-Calédonie recommande de laisser le jeu de la concurrence s'opérer librement sur le marché des pièces détachées automobiles, 31 October 2023, Concurrences N° 1-2024, Art. N° 116988, pp. 18, concurrences.*

7 APC, Opinion No. 2021-A-04 of 23 December 2021 on the competitive operation of the motor vehicle spare parts repair and trade sector.

8 ACNC, *La Réglementation des prix et des marges en Nouvelle-Calédonie : quand et comment réglementer*, Economic Note, No. 2, June 2024.

9 ACNC, Opinion No. 2024-AO-05 of 29 July 2024 on a draft local law amending Book Ier of the *Competition Code* and relating to the regulation of the prices of certain products and services benefiting from a special tax or customs regime.

10 ACNC, Opinion No. 2020-A-07 of 28 December 2020 on the price formation mechanism for consumer products in New Caledonia; see also VITALIS Nils, "New Caledonia: The New Caledonian Competition Authority issues an important opinion on the price formation mechanism for mass market products in New Caledonia, which is an opportunity to carry out a comparative approach between the opinions of the metropolitan, Polynesian and New Caledonian competition authorities on this issue", *Concurrences*, 28 December 2020, no. 2-2021, art. n° 100463, p. 219-222, www.concurrences.com/100463

11 APC, Opinion No. 2019-A-02 of 19 September 2019, on import and distribution mechanisms in French Polynesia.

21. In such highly administered economies, the competition authorities of New Caledonia and French Polynesia have made major contributions to improving the effectiveness of uncompetitive regulatory frameworks. Mainly through the notice procedure, these authorities seek to introduce competitive mechanisms to stimulate innovation and improve the competitiveness of local businesses. Their recommendations aim to replace current systems with more effective solutions that are conducive to competition.

22. Exchanges of expertise between the two authorities also took the form of collaboration on specific cases. For example, as part of the review of the merger involving CMA CGM's acquisition of sole control of Bolloré Logistics, the two authorities worked in close coordination to ensure an in-depth competitive analysis of the impact of this transaction in the Pacific.[12]

23. Cooperation between the ACNC and the APC is therefore not limited to a simple juxtaposition of good practices. It is a lever for efficiency, enabling the two authorities to learn from each other's experience, while contributing to the development of a competitive framework better adapted to the realities of island economies. This collaboration, both institutional and practical, is set to be strengthened in the years to come, in response to the growing economic and legal challenges in the Pacific.

II. Cooperation in times of economic reconstruction in New Caledonia

24. The year 2024 left a lasting impression on New Caledonia. From 13 May onwards, the territory was shaken by an unprecedented social and economic crisis, giving rise to riots that devastated the local economic fabric. The economic repercussions were striking: 750 businesses destroyed or damaged, a contraction in GDP, a loss of tax revenue for all local authorities, and 25,000 jobs affected (of which around 10,000 were lost). The estimated cost of the crisis is in excess of €2 billion.

25. Against this backdrop, the ACNC has had to adapt its methods of intervention. This has resulted in a reorganisation of resources and priorities within the investigation department, with a refocusing of activities on *advocacy* and the targeted suppression of abusive behaviour. This reorganisation drew on lessons learned from other competition authorities, which provided valuable support to the ACNC in terms of exchanging expertise, sharing best practice and strategic coordination.

A. *Adaptation of merger control and retail trade procedures*

26. Fully aware of the difficulties faced by many businesses, the ACNC demonstrated its adaptability in the area of merger control and retail trade. Indeed, as many

---

[12] ACNC, decision no. 2023-DCC-11 of 27 December 2023 on the acquisition of sole control of SE Bolloré Logistics by SA CMA CGM; APC, decision no. 2024-CC-01 of 31 January 2024 on the merger control of the acquisition of sole control of Bolloré Logistics SE and its subsidiaries by CMA CGM SA; see also SIMMINGER Enguerrand, "Nouvelle-Calédonie: L'Autorité de la concurrence de la Nouvelle-Calédonie éclaire sur sa pratique décisionnelle en matière d'engagements", *Concurrences*, 27 December 2023, no. 2-2024, art. n° 118411, www.concurrences.com/118411

shops were destroyed or damaged during the riots, the New Caledonian authority introduced temporary measures aimed at facilitating the procedures for businesses. It has introduced a simplified procedure to speed up notifications of mergers and retail transactions, and has reiterated the possibility of waiving the suspensive effect normally applicable to these procedures.

27. However, the ACNC was facing pressure from certain players who wanted to abolish merger and retail notification procedures altogether because of the crisis. The New Caledonian authority nevertheless firmly reaffirmed the need to maintain rigorous control. This control in no way hinders the ability of companies to rebuild, since the ACNC was able to issue authorisation decisions, and even derogation decisions, within tight deadlines. The Chairman of the ACNC had also made a public commitment on this subject, making the quotation from the United Nations Conference on Trade and Development (UNCTAD) his credo vis-à-vis local institutions:

> *In times of crisis, even more than in normal times, it is important to be able to rely on a sound competition policy to help overcome the difficulties and ensure that the recovery from the crisis is as rapid and sustainable as possible. Competition law helps to ensure that businesses compete on a level playing field and encourages investment, innovation and efficiency, so as to promote job creation and economic recovery. Full economic recovery is not possible without competition law and policy.*[13]

28. The simplification of formalities has therefore made it possible to speed up the examination of applications, particularly for companies wishing to rebuild or refurbish damaged premises. For example, the notifying party was able to take advantage of this simplified procedure in connection with the decision to open a Mr.Bricolage shop[14] in Dumbéa.

B. *Supporting businesses and rebuilding the business model*

29. At the same time, support for businesses has also led to increased consultancy activity, with both private players and public institutions. Very early on, the ACNC sought to take part in the debate on the overhaul of New Caledonia's economic model as part of its reconstruction. It has published several economic notes to contribute to these debates, alongside the New Caledonian government, local businesses and the State.

30. In particular, the ACNC warned of the anti-competitive risks associated with the reconstruction, stressing the need to review certain issues that are particularly detrimental to competition, such as market protection. Indeed, the crisis has revealed inherent weaknesses in New Caledonia's protectionist system , as demonstrated by the shortages observed in May and June 2024 of consumer products subject to

---

13 UNCTAD, "Redefining competition law enforcement: lessons from the pandemic, with a focus on socially important markets – effective responses to the pandemic and post-pandemic economic recovery: challenges and opportunities", 11 May 2022.

14 Decision no. 2024-DEC-03 of 3 September 2024 relating to the opening of a 904 m² "Mr.Bricolage" shop in the "Green Retail shopping centre in Dumbéa.

import restrictions, such as rice, pasta and flour. In an economic note, the ACNC therefore calls into question this development model, which until now has been based on market protection.[15] It proposes two scenarios for economic development, as well as the conditions for their success.

31. In this perspective, the analyses conducted by the ACNC could serve as inspiration for other authorities in the Pacific, such as French Polynesia, whose TDL reform project could benefit from these reflections.

C. *A Foresight Committee to overcome the economic and competitive challenges of the crisis*

32. In addition, the Caledonian Authority has reaffirmed that business aid schemes, which are essential in times of crisis, must respect the principles of competition. In a note on business aid,[16] , it proposed transparent and effective mechanisms to avoid any distortion of the market as regards aid to compensate for damage suffered by businesses and aid for restructuring. This note was drawn up with the help of Henri Piffaut, a member of the APC college, who has joined the ACNC's Foresight Committee created in response to the exceptional economic crisis New Caledonia is experiencing.

33. The need for openness, as part of the reconstruction of New Caledonia's economic and competitive model, led to the creation of this voluntary Foresight Committee, which reports to the President of the ACNC. This Committee facilitates exchanges on economic issues and helps to reflect on the New Caledonian economic model of tomorrow and the necessary competition and regulatory tools. The participation of Henri Piffaut and Vivien Terrien, who are also members of the APC, brings valuable expertise, thanks to their experience of the Pacific and the specific economic features of the islands, to support New Caledonia in this critical period and enable the ACNC to propose appropriate and resilient solutions.

34. Collaboration between the APC and the ACNC has thus been strengthened with the inclusion of these APC figures on the Foresight Committee, in addition to the appointment of Johanne Peyre, President of the APC, as a non-permanent member of the ACNC college in 2023. These exchanges of expertise and this institutionalisation of relations testify to the mutual trust between these two Pacific authorities.

D. *Inter-institutional cooperation and regulation of strategic sectors*

35. The crisis has undeniably accentuated the importance of cooperation between competition authorities. The close relations maintained by the ACNC with other competition authorities, in particular the Polynesian authority, constitute an essential lever to face the economic and social challenges generated by the crises. A key

---

15 ACNC, *Modèles de développement économique et protectionnisme en Nouvelle-Calédonie*, Economic Note, No. 3, October 2024.

16 ACNC, *Note de sensibilisation des pouvoirs publics en matière de soutien aux entreprises en période de crise*, 6 September 2024.

issue is the establishment of independent regulation for the telecommunications and energy sectors.

36. The institutional trajectories of the ACNC and the APC bear witness to a shared view of the need to establish such regulation in these strategic sectors, dominated by de facto or de jure monopoly operators. The imperative need for independent regulation to guarantee access to essential services at competitive prices has become even more fundamental during the crisis.

37. As such, the APC is in the process of acquiring partial regulatory powers in the energy sector.[17] This progress has fuelled constructive exchanges between the two institutions, reinforcing discussions within the ACNC and sparking discussions with the local government on the need to gradually introduce independent regulation in the field of telecommunications, particularly in the light of the opinion issued by the ACNC on connectivity in New Caledonia in 2024,[18] but also in the field of electricity.

E. *Increased vigilance against anti-competitive practices in times of crisis*

38. Finally, while flexibility was the order of the day in assisting companies, the ACNC also demonstrated increased vigilance with regard to crisis "profiteers". From the outset, the ACNC reiterated that its mission to protect economic public order remained fully in force and that anti-competitive practices, particularly those involving market sharing, concerted price fixing or abuse of market power, would only exacerbate the already fragile economic situation and would be severely punished.

39. The ACNC has naturally had to deal with attempts to form "crisis cartels" and attempts to organise import monopolies on a regulatory basis, against a backdrop of supply shortages. Yet even the most open-minded and pragmatic economists view crisis cartels with great suspicion.[19] The CNCA's controls could not therefore be relaxed.

40. In addition, the Caledonian Authority has benefited from enriching exchanges with other competition authorities beyond the Pacific, particularly on the subject of anti-competitive practices in times of crisis and the advisability of pursuing them. In particular, fruitful discussions took place with rapporteurs from the Chilean Competition Authority, allowing the ACNC to draw valuable lessons on the management of economic crises and social unrest. Chile, faced with massive protests in 2019, has had to adjust its competition policies to deal with market disruption.

41. The ACNC was again able to count on the support of the APC and the French Competition Authority through a new tripartite cooperation established in June 2024. This annual meeting promotes the exchange of best practice between

---

17 See APC, Opinion No. 2024-A-04 of 30 May 2024 on a draft law on sectoral regulation of energy.

18 ACNC, Opinion No. 2024-A-01 of 11 March 2024 on the Authority's referral of the preliminary draft law for better connectivity in New Caledonia.

19 COMBE Emmanuel, Did you say crisis cartels?", *Les Echos*, 18 June 2022.

the three authorities, particularly in crisis management, merger control and the regulation of strategic sectors.

42. In conclusion, the Polynesian Competition Authority and the New Caledonian Competition Authority have, over the last seven years, written their own competition stories. The experiences shared by the ACNC and the APC make them strategic partners in the promotion of competition in their respective economies, but also sources of mutual inspiration.

43. Through exchanges of expertise and regular collaboration, they are working to continuously improve the regulatory frameworks and commercial practices in these island territories. This approach encourages greater integration of competition in these administered economies.

44. What's more, in times of crisis, cooperation with the outside world has enabled the ACNC to transcend the day-to-day and engage in more detailed economic thinking and construction.

45. Thanks to this cooperation, the role of the ACNC has become all the more essential in the post-crisis reconstruction phase, with the primary mission of guaranteeing respect for competition while supporting businesses in the resumption of their activities. The ACNC contributed to the local government's "Plan de Sauvegarde, de Refondation et de Reconstruction" (S2R) plan to map out a different economic model, in partnership with State services.

46. The ACNC would like to express its gratitude to all the people and institutions outside Caledonia, both well-known and lesser-known, who have shown their support, in particular the APC staff and the various authorities of the PINCCER network.

47. Let us therefore wish our two Pacific competition authorities an ever richer and more fruitful cooperation, in the service of competition and economic prosperity in these two magnificent territories.

PINCCER: A New Era of Collaboration and Market Competitiveness in the South Pacific

Fostering Unity, Innovation, and Growth Across the Pacific Islands

Joel Abraham[*] and Vinitesh Kumar[**]
Fijian Competition and Consumer Commission

1. For many living outside the region, the Pacific Ocean may seem inscrutable in its vastness. Despite the miles of blue that separate us, the Pacific Island nations share common threads woven through our histories, cultures, and economic challenges. As the Chief Executive Officer (CEO) of the Fijian Competition and Consumer Commission (FCCC), I have first-hand experience with the unique hurdles faced by our small island economies – challenges that cannot be effectively addressed in isolation. It was this realisation that led to the birth of the Pacific Island Network of Competition, Consumer Protection, and Economic Regulation (PINCCER).

2. The journey behind the creation of PINCCER holds a special place in my heart. This idea was born from a conversation I had with Mr Marcus Bezzi, the Chief Advisor to the Competition Taskforce of Australia's Commonwealth Treasury, who was then serving with Australian Competition and Consumer Commission. The idea of creating

---

[*] Joel Abraham is the Chief Executive Officer of the Fijian Competition and Consumer Commission.
[**] Vinitesh Kumar is the Director General of Human Resources, Culture, and Corporate Services at the Fijian Competition and Consumer Commission.

the Pacific network was further discussed during the first meeting of competition authorities in the region that took place in Tahiti, during the Tahiti Competition Days 2023, at the initiative of the APC during a panel led by myself and Mr Bill Kovacic.

3. And little did we know how this conversation would lead to the creation of PINCCER.

4. The specific challenges confronting our Pacific nations such as the high costs of living, limited market access, monopolistic practices, and the increasing sophistication of fraudulent schemes were the initial focus for the Pacific island agencies and developing countries in the Oceania region. These issues are not just isolated incidents but systemic problems affecting over *2.7 million*[1] people across the South Pacific. While our islands are separated by vast distances, the economic struggles we face are remarkably similar.

5. While we conversed, the idea began to crystallise around a unified network – a platform where regulatory bodies across the Pacific could collaborate, share knowledge, and develop strategies tailored to our unique contexts. Not as an abstract concept but a *tangible* solution to the pressing issues that impacted the livelihoods of our people. Organisations like the OECD were proof that such a venture had merit, demonstrating the value in multilateral collaborations between nations.

6. Similar initiatives in other regions provide valuable lessons as well, such as ASEAN's collaboration on competition policy which fostered market integration, reduced barriers to entry, and improved consumer outcomes. In Africa, the Common Market for Eastern and Southern Africa (COMESA) Competition Commission has successfully addressed cross-border anti-competitive practices, benefiting millions of consumers. These examples highlight the potential for regional cooperation to dismantle monopolistic practices and promote economic growth. By tailoring these lessons to the Pacific's unique context, PINCCER can accelerate its impact.

7. Our goal in creating the Pacific network became clearer through a finer discussion at the International Consumer Protection and Enforcement Network (ICPEN) Pacific side event in Sydney 2023 hosted by the Australian Competition and Consumer Commission (ACCC), where agencies and representatives in charge of Consumer Protection, Economic Regulation and Competition from the Pacific Island were gathered together for the very first time.

8. We agreed that Pacific Island Network will be created to foster cooperation, mutual support, and shared learning among our Pacific Island nations, bearing in mind that our respective nations are like different strands woven into the rich tapestry of the South Pacific. Each is unique yet contributes to a shared history and culture that defines our beautiful region. Our challenges are also unique at times, resulting from factors like geographic isolation, ongoing economic development, and political uncertainties.

9. These challenges present opportunities for us to work together towards, creating solutions tailored to our specific needs. The economy affects each and every one of us, impacting our quality of life in profound ways.

---

1 https://data.worldbank.org/indicator/SP.POP.TOTL?locations=s2&utm_source

10. The cost of living, for example, is at the forefront of everyone's mind, which is why the work we do is so crucial. Many of the issues we face are not confined to a single border. They are shared challenges that require shared solutions.

11. By collaborating, we can leverage our collective expertise and resources to address these issues more effectively. Our network aims to build a sustainable framework that addresses our current challenges while also preparing us for future ones.

12. Upon returning to Fiji, the vision of the Pacific Network remained vivid and compelling. The FCCC, with unwavering commitment from the ACCC, reached out to fellow regulatory bodies responsible for competition, consumer protection, and economic regulations across the Pacific region. This task took considerable time and resources, and I would like to acknowledge the ACCC team for the part they played in organising this with the rest of the team.

13. The response was overwhelmingly positive. Regulatory authorities from Australia, the Cook Islands, French Polynesia, Kiribati, New Caledonia, New Zealand, Papua New Guinea, Samoa, Solomon Islands, Tonga, and Vanuatu agreed to join us, united by a shared purpose and able to see the far-reaching potential.

14. Our primary goal was clear: to enhance our collective expertise and work towards establishing fair market conditions that favour both consumers and traders throughout the Pacific. We aimed to synchronise our efforts, fostering increased collaboration, exchanging vital information, and implementing best practices among regulators. The journey was not without its challenges – coordinating across different time zones, languages, and regulatory frameworks required dedication and mutual respect. Yet, the shared commitment to improving the lives of our people kept us steadfast.

15. After a mix of spirited brainstorming and strategic deliberation, the network proudly emerged with the name "PINCCER" reflecting both our collective vision and determination. As an initiative born out of necessity and ambition, PINCCER is a testament to the power of collaboration in transforming our region's economic landscape.

16. PINCCER was envisaged to contribute significantly to building agency capabilities, fortifying the collective voice of competition and consumer protection authorities in Pacific Island economies, and providing a focused forum to advocate for well-functioning markets. It unifies our efforts and embracing the wealth of knowledge and experience from our Pacific neighbours.

17. PINCCER is the manifestation of our collective aspirations for the region, and the establishment of this network signifies a commitment to mutual support, knowledge sharing, and the development of best practices tailored to our unique context.

18. "PINCCER is not just about collaboration; *it's about shaping the future of our markets*. We aim to set new standards for competition, consumer protection, and economic regulatory aspects across the Pacific, strengthening regulatory practices and promoting fair business."

19. In small island economies like ours, challenges to competition are amplified by limited economies of scale, market concentration, and barriers to entry. Only a few nations in our region have fully operational competition laws, leaving significant gaps in consumer protection and market fairness.

20. Geographical isolation contributes to shipping costs that are significantly higher than the global average. According to industry reports, the average shipping cost to Pacific Island countries can be up to five times higher[2] than in other regions. For example, shipping a standard 20-foot container to Pacific Island countries can cost between $5,000 and $7,000, depending on the destination and shipping route. In contrast, shipping the same container between major Asian ports or within Europe can cost less than $1,000 due to higher shipping frequencies and more intense competition.[3] Such barriers demand innovative and collaborative regulatory approaches to reduce market inefficiencies.

21. By fostering regional collaboration, we can work towards reducing these costs, enhancing market access, and stimulating economic growth. Initiatives such as joint procurement, shared shipping routes, and collaborative negotiations with shipping companies are potential strategies that could emerge from our collective efforts.

22. The lack of fully operational competition laws leaves significant gaps in consumer protection and competition promotion. Several Pacific Island countries have not yet enacted comprehensive competition legislation, leaving consumers and businesses without protection against anticompetitive business practices within their countries.

23. Without effective competition regulation, monopolies and oligopolies persist, leading to consumer prices that are higher by an estimated 20% to 50% than they would be in competitive markets. This situation disproportionately affects low-income households, exacerbating inequality and limiting access to essential goods and services.

24. By uniting our efforts through PINCCER, we aim to address these challenges head-on. Regional collaboration is key to enhancing competition because it allows us to pool resources, share expertise, and coordinate policies that can stimulate market dynamics. The network serves as a platform for aligning our regulatory approaches, thereby reducing inconsistencies that could hinder cross-border trade and investment.

25. Aligning key regulatory standards could save Pacific nations millions of dollars annually, freeing up resources for other development priorities. Studies suggest that harmonising regulations can reduce compliance costs for businesses operating across borders, this not only encourages regional trade but also attracts foreign investment by providing a more predictable and stable business environment.

26. Moreover, PINCCER aligns with the broader objectives of fostering economic integration within the Pacific. By harmonising competition laws and regulatory practices, we can create a more cohesive market environment.

---

[2] World Bank. (2022). *Pacific Possible: Long-term Economic Opportunities and Challenges for Pacific Island Countries*. Washington, D.C.: World Bank Group.

[3] Pacific Islands Forum Secretariat. (2022). *Maritime Transport Challenges in the Pacific Region*. Suva, Fiji: PIFS.

I. The Inaugural PINCCER Conference: A Catalyst for Change

27. FCCC proudly hosted the inaugural PINCCER conference in Fiji, marking a significant milestone in regional collaboration. This landmark event brought together competition authorities, policymakers, and experts from across the Pacific to strengthen consumer protection and competition enforcement. Through dynamic discussions and shared strategies, the FCCC reaffirmed its leadership in driving innovative solutions to address common challenges and fostered a unified approach to ensuring fair markets and consumer welfare across the region.

28. The PINCCER conference was held from 21 to 23 July 2024 with delegates from the thirteen Pacific nations participating, either in person or remotely, representing a rich tapestry of cultures, languages, and experiences. The countries in attendance included Fiji, Papua New Guinea, Australia, Cook Islands, Kiribati, Nauru, New Caledonia, New Zealand, Samoa, Solomon Islands, Tonga, and Vanuatu. Each delegation brought unique perspectives and insights, reflecting the diverse economic landscapes and regulatory frameworks of their respective nations.

29. PINCCER serves as a bridge, facilitating dialogue and understanding among these varied contexts, a unifying platform for aligning economic strategies while respecting local contexts.

30. The presence of government officials and lawmakers added a profound dimension to the discussions, bridging the gap between regulatory bodies and policy-making institutions. Outside of the financial support provided by the Fiji government, its involvement highlighted the political will necessary to drive reforms and implement effective competition policies. It also underscored the recognition at the highest levels of government that collaboration is essential for tackling the complex economic challenges we face.

31. The energy and enthusiasm at the conference were remarkable and gratifying to see, as the success of such endeavours is not guaranteed. From the moment the event was opened by a video message from Fiji's Deputy Prime Minister and Minister for Trade, Co-operatives, Small and Medium Enterprises, and Communications, Honourable Manoa Kamikamica, it was evident that PINCCER represented more than just a gathering of regulators. It was the beginning of a transformative journey toward regional collaboration and shared prosperity.

32. The Deputy Prime Minister spoke at length about the Pacific's shared challenges and opportunities, describing PINCCER as a "united front" for tackling the unique economic realities of our region. He emphasised that regional collaboration is essential for enhancing competition, which in turn is critical for combating the high cost of living.

33. He stated, "Our Pacific region is unique, with its own set of challenges and opportunities. PINCCER is our response – a united front to address these issues head-on, sharing knowledge and strategies that are specifically suited to our local contexts."

34. His message highlighted that by working together, we can create larger, more competitive markets that benefit consumers and businesses alike. He also addressed the importance of sustainable development, noting that our efforts to enhance

competition must be aligned with environmental stewardship. The Pacific region is particularly vulnerable to the impacts of climate change, and our regulatory frameworks must reflect a commitment to sustainability.

35. Fiji's Permanent Secretary for Trade, Co-operatives, MSMEs (Micro, Small and Medium Enterprises), and Communications, Mr Shaheen Ali, who joined us in person, further emphasised the importance of a regional approach to competition and regulation. He spoke about how collaborative efforts can break down barriers to entry, encourage new market participants, and stimulate innovation.

36. He stated, "A regional approach to competition is essential to foster a fair and open market environment across the Pacific. By aligning our competition policies and regulations, we can create a level playing field for businesses, ensuring that no single entity can dominate the market unfairly."

37. His insights reinforced the idea that enhancing competition is not just about enforcing laws but about creating an environment where businesses can thrive, and consumers have choices. Mr Ali also highlighted the critical role of small and medium enterprises (SMEs) in our economies. By fostering a competitive environment, we enable SMEs to enter markets, compete effectively, and contribute to economic diversification. This, in turn, can lead to job creation, innovation, and greater economic resilience.

38. The conference agenda was set up to reflect the diverse and complex challenges faced by Pacific regulators. Over three days, we delved into issues such as competition law enforcement, market dynamics, consumer protection, and economic regulation. The sessions were designed to encourage open dialogue and the development of actionable strategies that could be implemented across different national contexts.

39. One of the most inspiring moments was the launch of the PINCCER Fiji logo – a symbol of a new era of regional cooperation. The Fiji logo, featuring interconnected waves and island motifs, represents unity, collaboration, and a shared vision for the future. Its unveiling was a moment of collective pride, capturing the spirit of the conference and our shared belief in the power of working together to enhance competition and improve consumer welfare.

40. Another significant highlight was the signing of two Memorandums of Understanding (MOUs), one with Papua New Guinea's Independent Consumer and Competition Commission (ICCC) and the other with the Bureau of Price Monitoring and Consumer Affairs (BPMCA) of Vanuatu. These agreements formalised our commitment to collaborate on enhancing competition, conducting cross-border investigations, and building regulatory capacity.

41. At the signing, FCCC Chairperson Mr Isikeli Tikoduadua remarked, "By joining forces with our counterparts in Papua New Guinea and Vanuatu, we are strengthening our bilateral ties and reinforcing our shared commitment to creating fair and competitive markets that benefit all consumers in our respective nations."

42. The MOUs outlined specific areas of cooperation, including information sharing, joint training programs, and coordinated enforcement actions. By establishing these formal partnerships, we took concrete steps toward creating a unified regulatory front capable of addressing anti-competitive practices that transcend national borders.

43. One of the most valuable aspects of the conference was the opportunity to share experiences and learn from each other. Representatives from countries like Samoa and Tonga shared their journeys in developing competition laws, highlighting the importance of stakeholder engagement, the challenges of limited resources and shared insights on overcoming market concentration, reducing barriers to entry, and promoting fair trading practices.

44. Enhancing competition is fundamental to building resilient economies, because competitive markets are more adaptable to economic shocks and can stimulate innovation and efficiency.

45. Small island economies are uniquely vulnerable to price volatility – making robust competition policies essential for economic resilience. We recognised that by fostering competition we can reduce dependency on a limited number of industries or companies. This diversification enhances economic resilience and provides more opportunities for employment and growth.

46. We recognised that in our contexts enhancing competition often requires innovative approaches tailored to our unique market conditions. For example, we discussed the challenges of enforcing competition laws in markets dominated by a few large players. Strategies such as promoting entry by reducing regulatory burdens for new businesses, providing incentives for SMEs, and implementing targeted regulations to prevent abuse of market power were explored.

47. Another workshop examined the role of consumer advocacy in promoting competition. We explored how informed consumers can drive competition by making choices that reward competitive behavior. This highlighted the need for consumer education programs and transparent information about products and services.

48. We also engaged in discussions about the digital economy and its implications for competition. With the rise of e-commerce and digital services, there are new opportunities and challenges for competition regulation. The significant growth of e-commerce offers immense opportunities for competitive markets but also requires updated regulatory frameworks to address emerging behaviors. According to the United Nations Economic and Social Commission for Asia and the Pacific (UNESCAP), e-commerce in the Pacific has grown significantly in recent years.

49. The digital economy offers transformative potential for small island nations, but it also presents challenges such as platform dominance and limited digital infrastructure. PINCCER can lead efforts to modernize regulatory frameworks for the digital age.

50. We considered how to adapt our laws and enforcement strategies to address issues such as platform dominance, data privacy, and cross-border digital transactions. Adopting digital tools could enhance regulatory efficiency, enabling regulators to do more with limited resources.

51. Technology and innovation were recurring themes throughout the conference. We explored how digital tools can enhance regulatory efficiency, improve market surveillance, and facilitate communication with stakeholders.

52. We considered the development of centralised digital platforms for PINCCER to facilitate information sharing, training, and collaboration. Such platforms could

host databases of regulatory best practices, legal precedents, and market data, accessible to all member agencies.

53. Moreover, we discussed the use of data analytics and artificial intelligence in detecting anti-competitive practices. Advanced tools can help regulators identify patterns of behavior indicative of collusion or abuse of dominance, enabling more proactive and effective enforcement.

54. Protecting consumers is also intrinsically linked to promoting competition. We explored strategies to enhance consumer awareness and enforce consumer rights effectively.

55. Consumer awareness remains a significant challenge, with a significant percentage of Pacific Island consumers are unaware of their rights, pointing to the critical need for consumer education initiatives. We discussed the importance of consumer education campaigns to inform the public about their rights and the benefits of competition. Empowered consumers can drive demand for better products and services, which in turn stimulates competition among businesses.

56. In addition to competition and consumer protection, the conference also highlighted the growing threat of scams and fraudulent activities in the Pacific – and how a weak competitive market landscape provides fertile ground for such activity to thrive, as anti-competitive behavior plays a part in scams such as price fixing.

57. Integrating sustainability into competition policies presents immense opportunities for the Pacific. By incentivising renewable energy projects, such as solar farms and wind turbines, PINCCER can catalyse green investments that benefit both the environment and the economy. Sustainable fisheries, eco-tourism, and climate-resilient infrastructure are other areas ripe for development.

58. By fostering a regulatory environment that encourages sustainable practices, we can attract green investments and stimulate economic growth in sectors such as renewable energy, sustainable agriculture, and eco-tourism, while ensuring that economic growth does not come at the expense of future generations.

59. The MOUs we signed are just the beginning. We plan to initiate exchange programs, joint investigations, and shared learning initiatives.

60. Cost savings from collaboration are significant. Regional alignment of competition standards can save Pacific Island nations millions annually in reduced trade compliance costs. Aligning key regulatory standards frees resources for other development priorities.

61. We also discussed the potential for harmonising certain regulatory standards and procedures. Increased cross-border trade creates more dynamic and resilient markets. Harmonised policies could boost intra-Pacific trade substantially, fostering greater regional integration and economic growth.

62. Furthermore, we intend to establish regular communication channels among member agencies. This includes quarterly virtual meetings, shared newsletters, and collaborative projects.

63. The inaugural PINCCER conference was more than an event; it was a statement of intent. It demonstrated that the Pacific is ready to take control of its destiny by

leveraging collaboration to enhance competition and stimulate economic growth. We left the conference with new knowledge, strengthened partnerships, and a renewed sense of purpose.

64. I extend my heartfelt thanks to everyone who contributed to the success of the conference – the delegates, government officials, organising committee, and support staff. Your dedication and enthusiasm were instrumental in achieving the conference's objectives.

65. As I reflect on the conference, I am filled with a deep sense of fulfilment and hope. The support from government leaders, the collaborative spirit among member nations, and the shared vision for a better future have galvanised our efforts.

66. Standing on the shores of Denarau at the close of the conference, watching the sun set over the tranquil waters, I felt a profound sense of optimism. We had not only laid the foundation for PINCCER but also ignited a movement that would drive positive change across the Pacific.

II. Moving Forward with Confidence

67. The road ahead is filled with potential and promise. We must remain steadfast in our commitment to collaboration, innovation, and excellence. By doing so, we will not only improve our economies but also enhance the quality of life for our citizens.

68. We are excited about the possibilities that lie ahead participating in events like the "Competition Days" organised by the Polynesian Competition Authority, continuing our partnerships, and building on the foundations we have laid.

69. Our commitment extends to supporting our fellow regulators through PINCCER, recognising that our collective success depends on the strength of each member. We understand that excellence is not a destination but a continuous journey.

70. As we chart the path forward for PINCCER, the establishment of dedicated workstreams will be central to achieving the network's long-term objectives. These workstreams are the backbone of our mission, each addressing critical aspects of competition, consumer protection, and economic regulation. The Competition Workstream focuses on dismantling monopolistic structures and ensuring fair market practices. The Consumer Protection Workstream is dedicated to empowering consumers by addressing misleading advertisements, unfair trade practices, and fraud. Lastly, the Economic Regulation Workstream aligns regulatory standards to facilitate cross-border trade and investment. By prioritizing these areas, PINCCER aims to create a more equitable and competitive economic environment for all Pacific nations and provide targeted platforms for collaboration and capacity building, tailored to the unique challenges faced by Pacific Island economies.

71. To ensure focus, capacity and leadership, the following streams were assigned inaugural coordinators, as follows:

Consumer Protection

Papua New Guinea is currently leading the efforts in this critical area, focusing on safeguarding consumer rights and enhancing public awareness.

Competition

New Zealand and French Polynesia are the co-leads to harmonise competition laws, share best practices, and promote a level playing field for businesses across the region.

Economic Regulation

Fiji and Tonga are leading the stream's activities, addressing issues such as pricing policies, natural monopoly regulation, and the impact of infrastructure costs.

72. This collaboration among member agencies through knowledge sharing, joint action, and capacity building helps leverage collective expertise and promoting shared learning and innovation. Coordinated responses to regional challenges, such as monopolistic practices, price volatility, and unfair trade behaviors, ensure a united approach to common issues. Additionally, training programmes and resource sharing equip member agencies with the tools and knowledge needed to effectively navigate complex regulatory landscapes.

73. By opting into these workstreams based on their interests and capacities, member economies can contribute meaningfully while benefiting from targeted support. This flexible approach ensures inclusivity and maximises the network's impact.

74. Looking ahead, PINCCER plans to build on its momentum with follow-up conferences, capacity-building workshops, and further MOUs to deepen collaboration. A critical focus will be on enhancing digital regulatory tools to increase efficiency and transparency. By fostering knowledge-sharing and building institutional capacity, PINCCER aims to ensure that the benefits of competition reach even the most remote Pacific communities

III. Final Reflections

75. The South Pacific represents a vibrant mosaic of cultures, languages, and traditions. Over 20 official languages[4] – and 1,200 dialects and sub-languages[5] – are spoken across our member nations, and this diversity, while a source of strength, presented challenges in policy harmonisation and regulatory alignment. PINCCER became the bridge that facilitated dialogue and understanding among these varied contexts.

76. To all stakeholders' governments, businesses, consumers, and international partners – I extend an open invitation to join us on this journey. Your support and engagement are crucial to the success of our collective efforts.

77. Together, we can create competitive markets that drive innovation, reduce costs, and improve the quality of life for all our people. By embracing collaboration and innovation, we can overcome the challenges we face and unlock the immense potential of our region.

---

4 **Pacific Islands Forum Secretariat**. (2018). *Pacific Regional Cultural Strategy: Investing in Pacific Cultures 2010–2020*. Suva, Fiji: Pacific Islands Forum Secretariat. Retrieved from *https://www.forumsec.org/wp-content/uploads/2018/10/Pacific-Regional-Cultural-Strategy-2010-2020.pdf*

5 **Eberhard, D. M., Simons, G. F., & Fennig, C. D. (Eds.)**. (2022). *Ethnologue: Languages of the World* (25th ed.). Dallas, Texas: SIL International. Retrieved from *https://www.ethnologue.com*

78. At the FCCC, we remain unwavering in our commitment to upholding the highest standards of regulatory excellence. We will continue to work diligently to promote competition, protect consumers, and contribute to the sustainable development of our nation and the region.

79. Our dedication to professionalism and integrity will guide us in all our endeavours. We will strive to improve our practices, embrace innovation, and adapt to changing market conditions.

80. PINCCER represents a new chapter in fostering Pacific market competitiveness. It is more than an organisation; it is a movement – a collective commitment to unity, innovation, and growth.

81. The establishment of PINCCER is a testament to what we can achieve when we unite behind a common purpose. It symbolises our shared aspirations and our determination to create a better future for all Pacific peoples.

82. As we move forward, let us keep the spirit of PINCCER alive in all our endeavours. Let us remain open to learning from one another, to innovating, and to embracing the opportunities that collaboration brings.

83. Together, we can create a legacy of collaboration and progress that will benefit generations to come. The Pacific region is poised for a new era of prosperity, and PINCCER stands ready to lead the way.

84. "Our vision is clear: a Pacific region where fair markets, informed consumers, and sustainable practices drive prosperity for all. Together, we are charting a course toward a brighter, more inclusive future."

85. In closing, I would like to extend my thanks to **Concurrences** for giving us the space to highlight PINCCER and its work. Your dedication to promoting understanding and dialogue in competition law has been an invaluable resource to practitioners and scholars alike. We are honoured to contribute to this milestone publication and look forward to continued engagement with the global competition law community.

The Role and Achievements of the OECD Competition Committee in Promoting Good Practices and International Cooperation

Frederic Jenny*
ESSEC Business School
OECD

1. Over the years, the Organisation for Economic Co-operation and Development (OECD) has expanded its membership and broadened its perspective. In line with this development, the OECD Competition Committee has evolved, reinforcing its dialogue with competition authorities in non-member countries and expanding its agenda to include reflections on issues of high relevance for new and young competition authorities in developing countries. The international dialogue and cooperation on competition undertaken in the context of the OECD has contributed to the convergence of Competition law enforcement principles and the dissemination of good practices in a policy field that was new and rapidly expanding in several countries worldwide. The Competition Authority of French Polynesia has participated in the work of the OECD Competition Committee, and this work offers relevant insights into a number of the challenges it faces.

*
* *

* Frédéric Jenny is professor emeritus of economics at ESSEC Business School and chairman of the OECD Global Forum on Competition.

2. The origins of the Organisation for Economic Co-operation and Development (OECD) are linked to the Marshall Plan created to rebuild Europe after the Second World War. The Organisation for European Economic Co-operation (OEEC), which preceded the OECD, was established in 1948 to administer Marshall Plan aid.

3. In 1961, the OECD was created through a transformation of the OEEC whereby the scope of OECD was extended beyond Europe and its membership expanded to include North American countries and other industrialised nations.

4. Initially, the goals of the OECD were, first, to promote economic growth through the promotion of policies designed to improve the economic performance of its member states, to increase productivity, and to raise standards of living; second, to provide a forum for governments to coordinate policies, exchange information, and agree on solutions to global challenges, thus promoting multilateral cooperation among European nations to pacify the European continent, and, third, to promote sustainable economic development, particularly in less-developed countries, through policy dialogue and the transfer of knowledge and expertise.

5. In their article "From the Marshall Plan to Global Governance: Historical Transformations of the OEEC/OECD, 1948 to Present", M. Leimgruber and M. Schmelzer[1] describe the OECD in the following way:

> *"(..)the OECD can be described both as a "forum organisation", providing a framework in which member countries exchanged views, negotiated common initiatives and agreements, and collectively legitimated their policies, and a "service organisation", which itself conducted services important to member countries such as the collection, standardisation, and dissemination of information and data."*

6. In its early years, the OECD focused heavily on fostering economic growth in member states, especially as the postwar boom began to wind down. This included activities related to trade liberalisation, the promotion of free markets, and coordination on monetary and fiscal policy.

7. Over time, the focus of OECD has evolved from the promotion of market liberalisation and neoliberal ideas in the 1970s to the globalisation of the economy and the cooperation with non-members in the 1990s–2000s and to the promotion of sustainable development, digital transformation, and addressing global challenges like climate change and inequality since the 2010s.

8. Simultaneously, the geographical scope of the OECD has become wider. Initially, the OECD comprised 20 countries, primarily European countries with the United States and Canada. It now includes 38 member countries, representing a significant portion of the global economy. Membership has gradually expanded to include countries outside the Western world, such as Japan (which joined in 1964) and South Korea (which joined in 1996), among others. Furthermore, several non-European developing countries from Latin America have joined the OECD

---

[1] M. Leimgruber and M. Schmelzer "From the Marshall Plan to Global Governance: Historical Transformations of the OEEC/OECD, 1948 to Present". Available from: https://www.researchgate.net/publication/321727444_From_the_Marshall_Plan_to_Global_Governance_Historical_Transformations_of_the_OEECOECD_1948_to_Present#fullTextFileContent [accessed 19 January 2025].

since 1994 (Mexico in 1994, Chile in 2010, Colombia in 2020, and Costa Rica in 2021). Several Eastern European countries, former members of the Soviet bloc, also joined the OECD (notably the Czech Republic in 1995, Hungary and Poland in 1996, Slovakia in 2000, Estonia and Slovenia in 2010, Latvia in 2016, and Lithuania in 2018) reflecting both the upheaval in Eastern Europe and the enlargement of the European Union.

9. The OECD is thus a very different organisation than it was thirty years ago, with a stronger focus on economic diversity and development.

10. Not only did the membership of the OECD diversify, but while initially established to serve its member countries, the OECD has increasingly engaged with non-member countries and international organisations. In particular, its cooperation with non-members, aimed at integrating non-members into the global economic system and promoting best practices in governance, economic policy, and development, intensified in the 1990s after the fall of the Berlin Wall.

11. Over time, the number of non-member countries with which the OECD cooperates has increased. It now works with over 70 non-member countries, through committee participation, adherence to OECD instruments, and integration into statistical reporting systems.

12. This cooperation of the OECD with non-members takes a variety of forms: the policy dialogues allow the sharing of expertise and the promotion of reforms in the non-member countries, and the peer reviews allow the OECD Member countries to assess the economic and regulatory frameworks of the countries reviewed (which can both be OECD members or non-members) and give the reviewed countries a blueprint to improve their policies or legal framework. Finally, the fora between OECD members and non-members (or the participation in OECD committees of non-members as observers) addresses issues of common interest to the OECD members and the non-members.

13. These different forms of cooperation take place in a variety of contexts.

14. The policy dialogues and the sharing of experience occur mainly when the OECD works with countries interested in joining as full members. Candidates for membership undergo a rigorous accession process where they must align their policies with OECD standards on governance, anti-corruption, and economic policies (including competition policy). The accession process provides a platform for dialogue and the sharing of best practices.

15. The OECD has also engaged in specific programmes to deepen cooperation with some countries. Such "Enhanced Engagement" programmes have been launched focusing on significant emerging economies such as China, India, Brazil, Indonesia, and South Africa. These partnerships allow these non-member countries to participate in some OECD activities, gain access to research, and adopt OECD best practices. In return, the OECD can incorporate the perspectives of these countries into its analyses and policy recommendations.

16. In addition, the OECD has launched some regional programmes (e.g., Latin America, Southeast Asia, and the Middle East). These programmes aim to promote market-oriented reforms, enhance economic governance, and facilitate the adoption of OECD standards.

17. Through the Development Assistance Committee (DAC), the OECD coordinates member countries' aid and development policies with non-member countries. The DAC supports efforts to improve the effectiveness of foreign aid, including monitoring how development assistance is used and promoting transparent aid practices.

18. Finally, the OECD Development Centre was established in 1961 as an independent platform for knowledge sharing and policy dialogue between Organisation for Economic Co-operation and Development (OECD) member countries and developing economies, allowing these countries to interact on an equal footing. The OECD Development Centre is a forum that contributes expert analysis to the development policy debate to help decision-makers find policy solutions to stimulate growth and improve living conditions in developing and emerging economies with the participation of 25 OECD member countries and 29 non-OECD member countries.

19. One consequence of the broadening of the membership of the OECD and the expansion of its cooperation with a wide variety of developing countries has been the expansion of its mandate beyond economic growth.

20. This mandate now includes environmental sustainability, education, social policy, innovation, and the digital economy. For example, the OECD's work on environmental sustainability grew mainly in the 1990s as climate change became a global priority. However, the mandate of the OECD also expanded in the 2010s, when it began to focus more on inclusive growth, examining issues like inequality, education disparities, and social mobility. This shift partly responded to the 2008 global financial crisis, highlighting the need to address inequality's social and economic impacts. Finally, the technological revolution has led the OECD to engage in new areas of governance, such as the digital economy, the sharing economy, and the regulation of emerging technologies like artificial intelligence.

*

* *

21. The OECD Competition Committee was initially established in 1961[2] as the "Competition Law and Policy Committee" under the OECD framework. Its creation was part of the broader efforts to promote economic cooperation and development among member countries. It provided a platform for member countries to discuss and share best practices in Competition law and policy.

22. In 1991, the Committee's name was changed from "Competition Law and Policy Committee" to "Competition Committee", and its role was further solidified with the adoption of the Communiqué [C(91)91], which stated:

> *"17 Looking beyond the Uruguay Round to the trade issues of the 1990s, Ministers emphasised the need to address the new dimensions of trade policy. This includes a range of issues arising because of the increasing globalisation of the world economy and the closer relationship between trade policy and competition, investment, technology and innovation, and*

---

2 Resolution of the Council concerning the Competition Committee and amending its name and terms of reference [C(87)138(Final)]

environmental policies. The increasingly international scope of economic activity has seen the emergence of areas in which the needs of private agents and governments run ahead of the existing "rules of the game". There is a perceived need for a better understanding of these issues and, where appropriate, convergence of policy approaches and consideration of fresh rules. Many issues, traditionally viewed largely from a domestic policy perspective, have taken on an international dimension, affecting the setting of trade and investment policies. Hence, widening the consideration of trade policies in the 1990s to take account of new developments will go hand-in-hand with efforts to avoid conflict with other policy spheres."

"23 The increasing international scope of economic activity has resulted in a situation in which the existing 'rules of the game", as defined by national or regional competition policies, might be usefully complemented. Ministers ask the Organisation to continue its work on the international dimension of competition policies and their interaction with policies in other areas, such as trade and industry. They note that recent work in the Organisation on Competition law and policy provides the foundation for greater policy convergence and progress towards updating and strengthening the existing rules and arrangements (including policy principles and procedures) for international cooperation in this area. They invite the relevant committees actively to pursue these matters, including the effectiveness of trade rules in facilitating international competition."[3]

23. Thus, the necessity for the Competition Committee to promote Competition law and policy and to promote policy convergence in this area was linked to the increasing globalisation of economic activities, which was a hallmark of the 1990s.

24. Further to the OECD-wide engagements with non-members, it should also be mentioned that the OECD Committees can have non-members attend their meetings. The OECD distinguishes four categories of countries attending a Committee meeting. The Associates are the OECD member states. The Participants have a standing invitation to participate in all meetings for an open-ended period based on the Revised Resolution of the Council on Partnerships in OECD[4] and the Committee's Participation Plan. The Key partners can also be invited to participate in Committee meetings. Finally, Invitees do not have a standing invitation to attend meetings, but a decision by consensus from the committee is required to invite Partners listed as Invitees in its Participation Plan to specific meetings.

25. In the case of the Competition Committee, it is worth noting that two countries (Brazil and Romania) are associates (i.e., permanent members) of the Competition Committee (even though they are not members of the OECD at large). The other four OECD Key Partners (South Africa, China, India, and Indonesia) regularly participate in the Competition Committee meetings with about ten invitees

---

3 The current mandate of the Competition Committee adopted in 2024 states: "1. The main objective of the Committee is to protect and promote competition as an organising principle of modern economies, based on the knowledge that vigorous market competition boosts growth and employment and makes economies more flexible and innovative."

4 [C(2012)100/REV1/FINAL, paragraphs 2 b) and c)]

for each session (such as Argentina, Chinese Taipei, Tunisia, the United Arab Emirates, etc.).

26. The Competition Committee has always had a very open policy concerning non-members. It has, in recent years, extended an invitation to the Competition Authority from French Polynesia, which has been able to see firsthand how the Competition Committee worked and to contribute to this work.

27. In addition to the participation of some non-members in the Competition Committee meetings, since 2001, the Competition Committee yearly holds the OECD Competition Forum, which is a meeting between the OECD member states competition authorities and the non-member states competition authorities (as well as some international organisations such as the United Nations Conference on Trade and Development (UNCTAD), the World Trade Organization (WTO), the World Bank etc….). The Global Forum on Competition, where competition topics of interest to the OECD members and non-members are discussed, usually gathers-more than 100 delegations.

28. The programmes of the Global Forum sessions include OECD-style roundtable discussions, presentations from notable experts, and peer reviews. Discussion topics benefit from the input of the OECD Competition Committee, whose work has already generated substantial results in many countries and economies, such as the voluntary adoption of 'best practices', substantial analytical convergence, the establishment of strong networks of enforcement authorities, and enhanced cooperation. The Forum is also an opportunity for high-level officials from Latin America, the Caribbean, the Middle East, Africa, and the Asia-Pacific region to hold meetings in preparation for regional annual forums.

29. The OECD Competition Committee also oversees three Regional Centres for Competition, providing capacity-building assistance and policy advice through workshops, seminars, and training programmes on Competition law and policy for countries in each region regardless of their OECD membership status.

30. In the early 2000s, as many Eastern European and Central Asian countries were transitioning from centrally planned to market-based economies, there was a growing recognition that a sound competition policy was vital for their economic development. While undergoing significant reforms, many countries lacked the institutional capacity, technical expertise, and legal frameworks to enforce Competition laws effectively. As a result, anti-competitive practices such as monopolies, cartels, and unfair practices were becoming barriers to market efficiency and consumer welfare.

31. The OECD established the Regional Centre for Competition (RCC) in Budapest, Hungary, in 2005 to address these challenges. The Centre is a joint venture between the OECD and the Hungarian Competition Authority (GVH). It was created to help disseminate the region's OECD competition standards and best practices. The Centre's mission was to provide capacity-building assistance and technical and policy advice to competition authorities in countries in Eastern Europe, Central Asia, and the South Caucasus through workshops, seminars, and training programmes on Competition law and policy for officials in competition enforcement agencies, other parts of government, sector regulators and judges. The centre also works to strengthen Competition law and policy in Hungary and the GVH itself.

32. The OECD RCC in Budapest has successfully tailored its activities to the specific economic and political contexts of the countries in the region. This flexibility has allowed the centre to respond effectively to the needs of different countries, some of which have unique challenges related to their political structures, economic conditions, and stages of market development.

33. The OECD GVH RCC in Budapest collaborates closely with national competition authorities, international organisations (such as the World Bank and UNCTAD), and regional organisations (such as the European Union and Eurasian Economic Union), and it works to align regional practices with international standards and supports local capacity-building through training, seminars, and peer exchanges.

34. The OECD GVH RCC in Budapest has played a pivotal role in helping countries in the region develop and modernise their Competition laws. This includes advising on the design of competition frameworks, assisting in drafting Competition laws, and providing guidance on best practices for implementing those laws.

35. Many countries in the region, including Georgia, Kazakhstan, and Ukraine, have adopted or updated their Competition laws with technical assistance from the RCC, leading to stronger regulatory frameworks and more effective enforcement mechanisms. Altogether some 17 countries[5] in the region have benefited from technical capacity-building activities for competition officials, regulators, and judges delivered by the OECD RCC in Budapest.

36. The OECD GVH RCC in Budapest has also fostered greater regional cooperation and coordination on competition policy. This has been particularly important in a region where competition authorities often face similar challenges, such as dealing with state-owned enterprises, dominant market players, and monopolistic structures.

37. A significant outcome of the OECD GVH RCC's activities in Budapest has been an increased focus on the consumer welfare standard in competition enforcement. The centre has emphasised the importance of competition in terms of economic efficiency and in delivering tangible consumer benefits, such as lower prices, better quality products, and more significant innovation.

38. The OECD GVH RCC in Budapest has also worked to raise awareness about the importance of competition policy among governments, businesses, and civil society. Through advocacy campaigns and public outreach, it has contributed to the creation of a more competitive business environment in the region.

39. By supporting the development of an "antitrust culture", the OECD GVH RCC in Budapest has played an essential role in changing attitudes toward anti-competitive behaviour, making it less socially acceptable and more likely to be challenged.

40. The East Asian Region comprises rapidly growing economies such as China, Japan, India, Indonesia, and Australia as well as developing countries like Vietnam, Thailand, Cambodia, and Laos. As the region became more integrated into the global economy in the 1990s and 2000s, there was a growing need

---

5 Including: Albania, Armenia, Azerbaijan, Bosnia and Herzegovina, Bulgaria, Croatia, Georgia, Kazakhstan, Kosovo, Kyrgyzstan, North Macedonia, Moldova, Montenegro, Romania, Serbia, Ukraine and Uzbekistan.

for a coordinated effort to support effective competition policies. These policies could ensure markets remained competitive, that businesses did not engage in anti-competitive practices like cartels and abuse of dominant positions, and that consumers were protected.

41. In 2010, the OECD established the OECD Regional Centre for Competition in Seoul, South Korea, in partnership with the Korean Government and the Korean Fair Trade Commission (KFTC), South Korea's national competition authority, which has been one of the most effective and influential competition authorities in Asia and has long been recognised for its vigorous enforcement of Competition laws and its efforts to foster market competition. Establishing the OECD KFTC RCC in Seoul marked a strategic decision to build on Korea's advanced competition regime and promote regional cooperation and capacity building.

42. In the context of the OECD/Korea Policy Centre in Seoul, the KFTC actively collaborates with the OECD in hosting events, sharing expertise, and providing technical assistance to other countries in the region, many of which are still in the early stages of developing their competition frameworks. The contribution of the KFTC to this joint project is beneficial in three areas. First, the KFTC's expertise and well-developed competition framework constitute a guide and a reference for other countries. Second, the South Korean government has provided financial resources and institutional support to help establish and sustain the OECD KFTC in Seoul. Finally, South Korea has played a crucial role as a regional leader in promoting market-based reforms.

43. The OECD/Korea Policy Centre in Seoul has played a significant role in regional capacity building. It organises training programmes, workshops, and conferences to strengthen the technical skills of competition authorities and officials. These training sessions cover various topics, including merger control, cartel detection, antitrust enforcement, and sector-specific competition issues such as telecommunications, energy, and digital markets.

44. By facilitating knowledge-sharing and peer learning, the OECD/Korea Policy Centre has helped countries in the East Asian region adopt a Competition law or improve their legal and institutional frameworks, enabling more effective enforcement of Competition laws.

45. The OECD/Korea Policy Centre has offered technical assistance to governments in drafting and revising their Competition laws and regulations, offering expert opinions on cases, and advising on enforcement strategies. Countries such as Indonesia, Vietnam, and India have benefited from these support services, which have enabled them to build more substantial competition authorities and tackle anti-competitive practices more effectively. This effort complemented the effort of the ASEAN Economic Commission to push the competition agenda among its members by ensuring that they all adopt a Competition law.

46. The Centre has also promoted cooperation on cross-border anti-competitive practices, such as international cartels and abusive market practices by multinational corporations.

47. Finally, it is worth mentioning that the OECD RCC in Seoul has increasingly focused on digital markets, e-commerce, and technology sectors, which have

become prominent in East Asia's economic landscape. It has provided guidance on how competition policy should adapt to the challenges of these sectors, such as addressing monopolistic behaviour by large tech platforms, ensuring fair competition in digital markets where network effects and data control can lead to dominant positions that harm competition and regulating online platforms and promoting consumer protection in the digital age.

48. Altogether, the OECD/Korea Policy Centre in Seoul has reached competition officials, regulators, and judges from around 26 competition agencies in the region.

49. The OECD and the Inter-American Development Bank decided to join their efforts to promote effective Competition law and policy in Latin America and the Caribbean in 2003 by launching the Latin American Competition Forum. The Forum was positioned as a concrete means for both organisations to promote dialogue, consensus building, and networking among policymakers and enforcers in a region where the notion that economic competition was good for economic development was not widely accepted. In 2015, competition authorities decided to change the official title of the Forum to "Latin American and Caribbean Competition Forum" to reflect the involvement of Caribbean countries in this annual event.

50. Besides promoting international cooperation and disseminating good practices in Competition law enforcement, two activities of the OECD InterAmerican Development Bank are more specifically geared toward the needs of Latin American countries. One of them is peer reviews. Indeed, as progress toward competition is slow in many Latin American countries because of the lack of a strong domestic competition culture, because of a high level of economic concentration, and because competition authorities are under-resourced, the peer reviews organised under the auspices of the OECD and the Inter-American Development Bank give international legitimacy to reform proposals designed to strengthen Competition law regimes. So far, 14 of the 25 countries participating in the Latin American Forum have been peer-reviewed.

51. A second dimension of the activities of the OECD/Inter-American Development Bank Latin American Forum on competition is the comparative examination of competition issues in specific sectors of the Latin American economies which are heavily regulated or dominated by state-owned enterprises and where pro-competition reforms are both necessary but complex to implement (such as air transport and electricity).

52. Finally, in 2019, the OECD launched the OECD Regional Centre for Competition in Latin America and the Caribbean, a joint venture between the OECD and the Peruvian Competition Authority (Indecopi). The objective was to have a local permanent presence to help disseminate OECD competition standards and best practices on Competition law and policy in the countries of the region that face challenges related to monopolistic practices, insufficient market regulation, and the lack of expertise in handling complex antitrust issues. This centre provides regular capacity-building activities to competition officials, regulators, and judges from the region.

53. The "Instituto Nacional de Defensa de la Competencia y de la Propiedad Intelectual", the Peruvian National Institute for the Defense of Competition and

Intellectual Property (Indecopi), has played a leading role in the creation and operation of the RCC, positioning Peru as a regional leader in competition policy. The Peruvian authority supported the initiative and provided expertise in designing and implementing regional capacity-building programmes.

54. Recognising that robust competition policies are integral to economic development, the government's support of Indecopi's role in the RCC is part of a broader strategy to promote sustainable growth, attract investment, and ensure consumer welfare in Peru and across the region.

55. The Centre's activities have reached some 25 of the region's countries, including Argentina, Brazil, Chile, Colombia, Mexico, Costa Rica, Guatemala, Dominican Republic, and Ecuador. These countries have benefited from training workshops and seminars designed for competition officials to strengthen their technical and analytical capacities, case study sharing through which countries can learn from the experiences of others, identifying successful enforcement strategies and best practices, and tailored advisory services on implementing and improving their competition policies and laws.

56. For countries with less developed competition frameworks, such as those in Central America and the Caribbean, the RCC also offers guidance on starting or improving their Competition laws and fostering better market conditions.

57. Altogether, these three OECD regional RCCs have engaged with 68 of the 100 non-OECD member countries with a Competition law.

58. More recently, the annual Arab Competition Forum (ACF), a joint initiative by the OECD, UN-ESCWA, and UNCTAD, was established in 2020 as the first competition network for the MENA region. The Arab Competition Forum aims to help strengthen Competition law and policy across MENA countries, which are characterised by the prominent role of the public sector.

59. Indeed, many of these countries aim to diversify their economies and attract foreign private investments. They need a practical Competition law framework for their pro-business climate reforms.

60. The existing competition policy frameworks are very diverse across the region, with a combination of mature regimes (e.g., in Egypt, Morocco, and Tunisia) and younger regimes (e.g., in Saudi Arabia and the Arabian Gulf states). The ACF provides a platform for knowledge-sharing on competition policy and enforcement for the Middle East and North Africa (MENA) region, bringing together high-level competition officials, policymakers, regulators, and the broader competition community in a unique venue to facilitate coordination and collaboration among the region's competition authorities and discuss ways to reform and strengthen their competition frameworks.

61. Each of the three founding organisations brings its unique experiences and expertise to the initiative:

   - The OECD leverages its storehouse of rigorous competition research and analysis that draws on the peer exchanges that characterise the OECD and the expertise of the Secretariat garnered through bilateral projects.
   - Since 2014, the Economic and Social Commission for Western Asia (ESCWA) has undertaken a combination of research, advisory, and capacity-building

activities on competition policy in the Middle East and North Africa region through the lens of the Sustainable Development Goals (SDGs).

- UNCTAD draws on its extensive consumer protection and competition expertise both in and outside the MENA region to help foster regional economic development as a prerequisite for facilitating regional and international trade by addressing the intricacies inherent in the institutional setup at the local and regional levels.

*

* *

62. As this presentation suggests, the OECD has long been interested in how Competition law should be designed in many different environments and the relationship between competition, growth, and economic development.

63. Early on in the history of the OECD Global Forum on Competition, the OECD competition committee and non-member countries focused on what has become the increasingly relevant issue of small economies. Whereas ninety years ago, there were only 62 countries in the world; there are almost 200 today, 87 of which have populations below five million.

64. Indeed, competition in small economies was a theme of the OECD Global Forum on Competition in 2003. As the background paper for this discussion suggests[6], the unique characteristics of small economies shape the need for tailored competition policies. The background paper presents an analytical framework to address key issues, focusing on economic, political, and enforcement challenges specific to these economies.

65. Small economies are traditionally defined as "independent sovereign economies that can support only a small number of competitors in most of (their) industries when catering to demand" because of the small size of their market. Market size is influenced by three main factors: "population size, population dispersion, and the degree of economic integration with neighbouring jurisdictions".[7]

66. First, small economies often experience high levels of market concentration and limited domestic demand, forcing firms to operate below the minimum efficient scale (MES), and the OECD Background note suggests that "This tendency may mean that economies should adopt competition rules that are more tolerant of mergers or other agreements that may increase efficiency." However, at the same time, the limited number of firms due to the low level of demand increases the risks of monopolistic practices.

67. Second, concerning antitrust enforcement against anticompetitive practices or abuses of market power, small size often creates enforcement challenges, including:

   - limited financial and human resources, making it challenging to establish and maintain effective competition agencies,

---

6 OECD Global Forum on Competition, Competition Policy And Small Economies, Note by the Secretariat, 10-11 February 2003.

7 Michal S. Gal, Competition Policy For Small Market Economies (2003).

- difficulties in preventing collusion among small business elites and risk of close ties among business elites and policymakers leading to tacit collusion or influence over Competition law enforcement,
- difficulties addressing the harm caused by firms outside their jurisdiction, as well as
- difficulties obtaining evidence and enforcing remedies, especially when dealing with multinational enterprises (MNEs).

68. Third, the OECD Background note suggests that developing small economies face additional hurdles such as weak financial markets, corruption, and a lack of competition culture.

69. Concerning policy recommendations, the background note suggests, first, that small economies should consider local conditions, balancing static efficiencies (e.g., cost savings) with dynamic efficiencies (e.g., innovation); second, that pooling resources through cooperation or the creation of regional competition authorities can reduce costs and increase enforcement capacity of each agency; and third that promoting a competition culture can mitigate political and social resistance to enforcement.

70. This analysis and several debates held either within the OECD Competition Committee or in the context of the OECD Global Forum on competition are highly relevant to the situation of the Polynesian Competition Authority, thus suggesting that such a young authority can gain many benefits from participating in the activities of the OECD and drawing on its work.

71. In various articles, Johanne Peyre, the head of the Polynesian Competition Authority, has described the main determinants of the landscape for competition and Competition law enforcement in French Polynesia[8].

72. She has emphasised, inter alia, first, how "competition promotes innovation and productivity growth, thus, fostering competition enhances economic growth and promoting Competition law enforcement will enhance the growth prospects of French Polynesia", adding that: "In this way, consumers, especially the poor, can get value for money. Competition, therefore, empowers the poor; it creates opportunities for new firms, including small businesses, to enter markets and grow; it pressures existing firms to innovate and ensures the lowest possible prices for consumers and better-quality products."

73. The relationship between innovation and competition and between competition and poverty has been repeatedly debated at the OECD Committee or in the Global Forum on Competition[9 10].

---

[8] Johanne Peyre "Competition Law In French Polynesia: Enforcement Challenges From A Young And Small Competition Authority" see also Johanne Peyre (French Polynesian Competition Authority): "The challenges of a small, young jurisdiction in applying competition law", Concurrences, May 2023 and Contribution from French Polynesia by Johanne Peyre, Bill Kovacic and Alejandro Ibarra-OECD Global Forum on Competition, session "From Globalisation To Regionalisation", December 2023.

[9] See for example: OECD Competition Committee, Competition Patents and Innovation, 08 January 2008, Competition and Innovation: A Theoretical Perspective OECD Competition Policy Roundtable 2023, Competition and Innovation: View from Competition Authorities Perspective 2024 and Competition and Poverty Reduction, OECD Global Forum on Competition 28 February 2013.

[10] As early as 2014, the OECD Competition Division produced a factsheet on how competition policy affects macro-economic outcomes where it discusses the relationship between competition productivity, growth, innovation and inequality .

74. Concerning the relationship between competition and poverty, Eleanor Fox, Emeritus Professor of Antitrust Law at New York University, speaking during the OECD Global Forum on Competition in 2013, acknowledged that "there is no such thing as competition law for the rich (well-off; enabled) and competition law for the poor" and that the goal of competition law was not poverty reduction in itself even though a competitive economy is likely to better able to grow and reduce the number of poor people than a non-competitive economy. However, she has explored how one could create "a competition system that is more sympathetic to people without power than to people with power and connections; more sympathetic to outsiders than to incumbents, especially incumbents upon whom privileges have long been showered"[11]. She states:

> *"What do poorer populations and outsiders need the most regarding good competition law? First, access to markets means not being frozen out by the pervasive restraints that attend statism and cronyism and those bound to result from wide exemptions. (…) Second, there is a pro-poorer perspective on competition laws, procedurally and substantively. (…) (i) Thought should be given to procedural vehicles that make the justice system accessible to people experiencing poverty. (ii) It is important to seek out simpler rules that make economic sense and that avoid the need for armies of lawyers and economists. When the opportunities for simple rules arise, authorities and courts should take them, lest we create a paradox that recovery for antitrust offenses is a luxury of those who are better off. (iii) How to get efficient, innovative, and dynamic markets is indeterminate with a range, and within this range, there is a more pro-poor perspective and less pro-insider. That perspective values open markets, rivalry, and freedom of firms to charge sustainably low prices (…)."*

75. The Polynesian Competition Authority is a young agency. It faces the challenges typical in the first years of enforcement – mainly related to advocacy, regulation powers, and economic specificities in decision-making. Johanne Peyre also observes that "Fostering a culture of competition is key" and that

> *"Many businesses appear unaware of the benefits of competition. This appears to be entrenched in the wider community. (…) A culture of competition among stakeholders and the wider business community is necessary for the effective enforcement and promotion of competition law and policy. A culture of competition in this context refers to the awareness of the business community, governmental agencies, non-governmental agencies, the media, the judiciary, academia, and the public of the rules of competition law and their overall responsibility to ensure that such rules are observed in the interest of competition and overall economic development."*

76. The OECD Competition Committee (together with other organisations such as UNCTAD and the ICN) has long recognised that competition advocacy is especially critical in general and for developing countries. As early as 2002, the OECD Competition Committee debated "Communication by Competition Authorities".

---

11 Eleanor Fox, "Imagine: Pro-Poor(er) Competition Law", OECD Global Forum on Competition, 2013.

The Second Latin American Competition Forum, jointly sponsored by the OECD and the Interamerican Development Bank, held in Washington in June 2004, discussed the challenges for developing countries associated with competition advocacy. Since then, the OECD Committee and its Regional Centres have held regular discussions both on the necessity of advocacy and on the techniques of communication that can be used by Competition Authorities to make their communication more effective and on the assessment of the effectiveness of its communication[12]. It is frequently noted that there is a complementarity between vigorous enforcement and effectiveness of advocacy and that sectoral studies or collaboration with sector regulators on the design or reform of regulatory frameworks can be effective ways to advocate for competition[13]. This observation is closely related to Johanne Peyre's observation that: "Lessons learned from more mature competition authorities' experience show a common ramping-up trend from issuing multiple opinions and recommendations (some of them becoming milestones to governmental and regulatory reforms toward free competition) to sanctioning anti-competitive behaviour (from horizontal or vertical collusion to more sophisticated cases related to abuse of dominance). The starting point is that the importance of sectoral opinions and recommendations issued by competition agencies should not be underestimated. They often play a major structural role in the economy."

77. The Polynesian Competition Authority is also faced with institutional issues. On the one hand, it needs to be independent from the executive and private interests to build the trust necessary for the Authority to sanction anticompetitive practices and guarantee its credibility in its advocacy function. On the other hand, Johanne Peyre states:

> *"Often competition issues have huge implications for other regulators and institutions. Competition enforcement cannot happen in isolation and should be considered part of a complex system and process. In addition to sector regulators, other institutions would need to be taken into confidence by the competition regulator to ensure efficiency in the process of competition enforcement. Such necessary cooperation must nevertheless be carefully managed, especially in small insular economies where the business and political elites are often intertwined."*

78. Such problems also arise in other countries, and the OECD Competition Committee has spent much time thinking about the optimal design of competition authorities and the relationship between them and sectoral regulators over the years. For example, it discussed the "Institutional Design of Competition Authorities" in 2014. Another roundtable on the "Independence Of Competition Authorities - From Designs To Practices" during the Global Forum on Competition held in December 2016, and another discussion on "The Optimal Design, Organisation,

---

12 See, for a recent example: Communication by Competition Authorities: Objectives and Tools, OECD Competition Policy Roundtable, OECD (2023); also in May 2024, OECD Korea Regional Centre held a Competition Workshop on Advocacy.

13 See, for example the Follow-up to the Nine Peer Reviews of Competition Law and Policy of Latin American Countries by the InterAmerican Development Bank and the OECD published in 2013.

and Powers of Competition Authorities" during the December 2023 session of the OECD Competition Committee's Working Party No. 3 on Co-operation and Enforcement[14]. Previously, it had held a roundtable discussion in 2019 exploring the roles of existing and future independent sector regulators and their formal and informal relationship with competition authorities[15]. The "Interactions between competition authorities and sector regulators" issue was again examined during the OECD Global Forum on Competition on 2 December 2022.

79. This discussion and the background note[16] showed that, concerning antitrust, the same conduct might frequently be scrutinised both under Competition law and sector regulation. Cooperation between the competition authority and the sectoral regulators may be conducted informally or, when formally provided, may take different forms: notification and consultation, information sharing, or, more rarely, the establishment of working groups.

80. Co-operation concerning merger control follows more structured procedures than cooperation on antitrust cases. It is usually regulated in the legal framework. There are two main models: parallel reviews by the competition authority and the sector regulator and the model where full responsibility for merger control is assigned to the competition authority, which requests an opinion on the transaction from the regulator.

81. The background note[17] [18] draws some initial conclusions from its examination of the various Competition law frameworks:

- "Clarity of roles and mandates as set out in competition law and sector legislation matters. When they are not clear, cooperation can be difficult.
- Competition law and sector legislation should include provisions that encourage cooperation and encourage cooperation.
- While public officials have a general duty to notify each other of any matter of interest to other public authorities, the legal framework should emphasise this requirement to promote cooperation
- Informal cooperation appears familiar and could pave the way for more formal cooperation. At the same time, it has some limitations, as it does not allow for sharing confidential data and information."

82. Another area of interest within French Polynesia is government interventions in strategic sectors. Johanne Peyre states:

> *"Local government regulates strategic economic sectors. The government is, therefore, the pivotal authority fixing prices or deciding which actor can enter the market. This is especially the case in the energy and telecommunication sectors. This can prove problematic due to historical operators*

---

14 See also "The Optimal Design, Organisation and Powers of Competition Authorities" OECD Policy paper, 31 October 2023.

15 See "Independent Sector Regulators" OECD Policy paper, 22 October 2019 which was prepared as a background note for a discussion held at the OECD in December 2019 on independent sector regulators.

16 OECD (2022), Interactions between competition authorities and sector regulators.

17 OECD Competition Policy Roundtable Background Note, www.oecd.org/daf/competition/interactions-between-competition-authorities-and-sector-regulators-2022.pdf.

18

controlled by the local government, which could theoretically benefit from an information asymmetry."

83. Again, the OECD has worked on several related issues.

84. First, it has long been interested in implementing competition law on state-owned enterprises, a complex issue in many developing countries or small economies. It held a roundtable discussion on "Competition Law and State-Owned Enterprises" at the OECD Global Forum on Competition in November 2018.

85. Second, the OECD Competition Committee has done a lot of work to promote the importance of competitive neutrality (a "principle" according to which all enterprises are provided a level playing field concerning a state's (including central, regional, federal, provincial, county, or municipal levels of the state) ownership, regulation or activity in the market). The underlying idea is that competitive neutrality fosters competition by eliminating or reducing undue competitive advantages that some players may enjoy over their competitors, such as support granted by the state or regulations that favour incumbents. Therefore, Governments should ensure a level playing field between state-owned and privately-owned enterprises, different privately-owned enterprises, and domestic and foreign enterprises. Ensuring a level playing field is key to enabling competition to work correctly and benefit consumers and the broader economy.

86. The OECD Competition Committee debated applying competition rules to state-owned enterprises and the principle of competitive neutrality in October 2009 and also during a discussion on "Competition Policy and Competitive Neutrality" in October 2015.

87. Subsequently, the OECD Council adopted a Recommendation of the Council on Competitive Neutrality in May 2021. This recommendation urges its members (and other interested jurisdictions) to ensure competitive neutrality to the maximum extent practicable unless overriding Public Policy Objectives requires otherwise. This recommendation followed several previous recommendations, including one on the Guidelines on Corporate Governance of State-Owned Enterprises, which had been adopted in 2015.

88. That same year, 2021, the OECD Competition Committee held a roundtable on "the promotion of competitive neutrality by competition authorities" at the virtual meeting of the 2021 Global Forum on Competition on 6-8 December 2021, thus reaching out to non-OECD members to alert them to the importance of ensuring competitive neutrality.

89. In 2024, a Competitive Neutrality Toolkit was developed to support the implementation of the competitive neutrality principles set out in the Recommendation. It provides a set of good practice approaches based on examples drawn from international experience on competitive neutrality measures. It covers the legal framework, including competition law and enforcement, the regulatory environment and public procurement, and measures that may enhance a competitor's performance, such as state support and compensation for public service obligations.

90. Third, the OECD Competition Committee which had held a roundtable on "Industrial Policy and the Promotion of Domestic Industry" during the 2018 Latin American and Caribbean Competition Forum in Argentina, recognising the fact

that more and more governments are tempted to intervene in the sectors that they deem strategic also held a roundtable on "Pro-Competitive Industrial Policy" on 12 June 2024, thereby outlining the types of government interventions which could be consistent with a pro-competition policy.

91. The Italian contribution to this last debate is worth mentioning, which detailed how the Authority has used its advocacy power to promote a pro-competitive industrial policy. The contribution states:

> *"Relying on its advocacy powers, the Authority has provided the Government with guidance on designing efficiency-enhancing industrial policies and pro-competitive reforms. These recommendations target traditional supply-side instruments and include the following key policy strategies: i) public investments in projects, focusing on projects directly aimed at creating conditions conducive to economic activity development or accelerating investments in specific areas, such as large infrastructure projects; ii) the Italian Government support at the level of individual firms: they consist of financial incentives or subsidies designed to achieve public interest objectives. Boosting transparency in subsidy allocation and selecting the least disruptive and proportionate responses is crucial to preserve a level playing field and promote genuine competition. Ensuring that this kind of financial support is given without unfairly benefiting certain players over others limits the competitive distortions these targeted incentives may introduce; iii) public direct investment or ownership: this involves government participation in business sectors, either through direct investment or ownership of enterprises. The Authority suggested careful management to avoid undue market distortions and maintain competitive neutrality. In some cases, the Authority highlighted the importance of facilitating a demand-driven push for contributing to industrial transformation, digitalisation, and sustainable development."*

92. Concerning the intensity of competition in markets, French Polynesia, composed of small islands with a limited population, suffers from low demand, high levels of domestic concentration, and import bottlenecks. This structural situation is problematic for competition. As Johanne Peyre points out:

> *"Production and exports (In French Polynesia) are concentrated on a few major industries (e.g., tourism, fishing, pearls) and thus depend on a narrow range of products. On the distribution side, products are mainly produced elsewhere and imported. In addition, some markets create bottlenecks for other markets (e.g., transportation services, telecommunications, or warehousing). (....). Almost all markets are highly concentrated, with few players operating in them. Although high concentration is often needed to realise economies of scale and produce efficiently, in small economies such as French Polynesia, the challenge in decision-making is increased when deciding on mergers.*
>
> *In addition, several large business entities often control a large part of the market's economic activity, and their business and political elites are frequently intertwined. In such markets with high aggregate concentration, the*

risk is that firms might prefer to operate at sub-optimal levels rather than grow internally, to avoid modification to the status quo, thereby engaging in oligopolistic coordination with direct consequences affecting social welfare."

93. A number of the underlying issues have been discussed in the context of the OECD Competition Committee. Regarding the bottlenecks, the OECD Competition Committee discussed the Access to Key Transport Facilities in February 2006 and debated competition in ports and port services in June 2011.

94. Concerning the concentrated economy, the OECD Competition Committee devoted much of its work to various aspects of enforcement in concentrated environments with oligopolies or dominant firms.

95. In February 2006, the Competition Committee debated "Prosecuting Cartels Without Evidence of Agreement", and in June of that year, it debated issues related to "Proving Dominance/Market Power" and "Remedies and Sanctions in Abuse of Dominance Cases". The following year, in June 2007, the OECD Competition Committee held a roundtable on "Facilitating Practices in Oligopolies". In 2011, it held a roundtable on "Economic Evidence in Merger Analysis", another one on "Economic Analysis and Evidence in Abuse Cases" in 2020, and yet another on the "Use of Economic Evidence in Cartel Cases" in the Global Forum on Competition in 2021. These are just a few examples of the numerous debates at the OECD on enforcement practices.

96. To complete this quick review of the extent to which the work of the OECD Committee is valuable for all competition authorities, including competition authorities of small developing countries, I would like to quote Johanne Peyre again on the importance of international cooperation for the Polynesian Competition Authority. Johanne Peyre states in an interview she gave to Concurrences[19]:

> *"The emerging cooperation amongst competition authorities in the Pacific and the creation of the Pacific Island Network of Competition Consumer and Economic Regulators (PINCCER) is a shining example of useful regional cooperation that can help tackle the challenges faced by new competition agencies in small economies in the region".*

97. She also developed this theme in her article "Competition Law In French Polynesia: Enforcement Challenges From A Young And Small Competition Authority"[20] where she stated: "Closer agency cooperation would benefit more robust, efficient, and consistent enforcement in the region. APC team members have already benefited from training and fellowship with counterparts in mainland France, Australia, and New Caledonia. The cooperation encompasses practical feedback and resources on methodology, conducting investigations, market analysis tools, market test questionnaires, etc."

98. The OECD has actively encouraged the development of bilateral and regional cooperation between competition authorities.

---

19 Johanne Peyre (French Polynesian Competition Authority): The challenges of a small, young jurisdiction in applying competition law , Concurrences, May 2023 https://www.concurrences.com/en/review/issues/no-2-2023/interview/johanne-peyre-the-challenges-of-a-small-young-jurisdiction-in-applying.

20

99. Early in 2012, the OECD and the International Competition Network joined forces to survey cooperation between national competition authorities. This report was discussed in the Global Forum on Competition 2012 Improving International Co-operation in Cartel Investigations and was the source of an OECD report. In 2021, the OECD and the ICN produced a second report on "International Cooperation Enforcement", which outlines key aspects of the current state of international enforcement cooperation between competition authorities. It describes the drivers of international enforcement cooperation, a high-level review of the main OECD and ICN initiatives to support international enforcement cooperation, the results and analysis of the survey conducted by OECD and ICN members in 2019, and comparisons with the 2012 survey results.

100. A central finding of the report is that if international enforcement cooperation is increasing, and while significant work has been undertaken to improve it, there is significantly more to address the long-term and well-known limitations of enforcement cooperation.

101. Among other things, the report identifies five key categories of challenges that limit enforcement cooperation: resourcing; co-ordination/timing; legal limitations, especially relating to sharing confidential information, investigative assistance, enhanced cooperation; trust and reciprocity; and practical issues (such as language, or time differences).

102. The Report provides four key areas of focus to attempt to address these limitations:

103. First, further enforcement cooperation work products and networks should be developed. The report suggests that

> *"involving more case-handlers in understanding the basics of international enforcement co-operation will likely help authorities to promote the benefits of enforcement cooperation internally, and help them establish stronger relationships of trust between authorities, to scale-up their enforcement co-operation".*

104. Second, transparency and trust between competition authorities should be improved. The report notes that

> *"(...) a number of authorities noted that a lack of transparency and trust around the ability of other authorities (and the rules and protections that existed about this co-operation) limited and slowed potential cooperation. In some instances, these concerns about trust and transparency (or the ability to resolve them in a timely way) prevented potential cooperation".*

105. The report then suggests that it would be helpful to

> *"consider mechanisms that create improved transparency and trust around the ability of jurisdictions to co-operate, in particular about issues such as the ability to share confidential information and how confidential information from a counterpart would be handled in a co-operating jurisdiction; whether leniency or merger parties must notify if they have engaged with another authority on the same matter; what is the ability of the co-operating jurisdiction to provide investigative assistance and to engage in enhanced cooperation or its ability to enter into second generation style agreements with other authorities.*

106. Third, policy and practical support should be provided to develop effective regional enforcement cooperation further. Indeed, the Survey revealed that regional co-operation was highly valued by authorities of varying sizes and across jurisdictions. (…) "The OECD to consider work-streams that will promote dialog and understanding to facilitate regional enforcement co-operation and improve wider international enforcement co-operation. In particular, the OECD could consider building on the work undertaken in 2018 about regional cooperation and using the RCCs to promote improved models for regional cooperation further."

107. Fourth, remove substantive and legal barriers to cooperation by considering possible models to resolve key legal obstacles to improve the ability to cooperate on certain types of enforcement cooperation activities, such as sharing confidential information, enhanced cooperation, and investigative assistance (such as the cooperation arrangement used by International Organization of Securities Commissions (IOSCO), an update to the 2014 OECD Recommendation, an OECD Decision, an OECD model bi-lateral/multi-lateral agreement, an OECD facilitated international treaty, with the possibility of (bi-lateral or multilateral) competent authority agreements on specific topics within a sub-set of parties).

108. The OECD committee also organised a "Hearing on Thinking out of the Competition Box: Enforcement Co-operation in Other Policy Areas" at the June 2022 session of the OECD Competition Committee's Working Party No. 3 on Co-operation and Enforcement. A report on this hearing contains a description of the legal models and instruments for international cooperation, including enforcement against corruption and cybercrime, police cooperation, financial and tax cooperation, and patent law. It provides background information and suggests ways to promote deeper cooperation between competition authorities.

Conclusion

109. This review has shown the increasing interest of the OECD Competition Committee in promoting a dialogue with and between an ever more extensive set of countries as the organisation saw its membership increase significantly and the number of countries adopting Competition laws skyrocketed.

110. The dialogue established has contributed to the convergence of Competition law enforcement systems around good practices but has also contributed to the increasing acceptance of the fact that if national Competition laws shared the common goal of promoting competition in markets to improve consumer welfare and efficiency, they can differ depending on the history, the level of economic development, the legal and political systems of the countries concerned.

111. The dialogue and the cooperation that have resulted from the development of Competition law and policy throughout the world and the ever more profound and broader exchanges between authorities from different countries under the auspices of international organisations such as the OECD have allowed newly created competition authorities, as well as competition authorities in developing and/or small countries to benefit from analysis helping them to overcome some of the challenges they were confronted with due to a hostile or indifferent economic or political environment, high level of market concentration, and a weak institutional framework.

112. Several factors have contributed to developing a shared culture of understanding and cooperation among competition authorities, which stands to benefit not only the members of the OECD but also, as exemplified by the case of the Competition Authority of French Polynesia, newly created competition authorities and competition authorities in developing countries which participate in its activities. The most important of these factors are the openness of the exchanges between competition authorities under the auspices of the OECD, the maintenance of the high standard of quality of economic thinking by this organisation as well as its commitment to helping its members to identify "better policies for better lives", the rapidly increasing diversity of its membership pushing the organisation to fully integrate in its perspective the diversity of economic and legal situations of its members, the fact that the OECD as an international organisation can only rely on soft power to promote its views and therefore must build trust and understanding among its members and earn the respect of all countries that participate in its activities, the fact that the economic globalisation movement of the final two decades of the 20th century has meant that national economies are profoundly interdependent and that markets overlap national boundaries, thus giving an incentive to trading countries to find ways to avoid or solve potential competition conflicts.

113. Open dialogue and cooperation are a win-win proposition.

PART V

Issues, Challenges, and Future of Competition in French Polynesia

Fighting the High Cost of Living in French Polynesia: The ISLE Initiative

Jérôme Philippe*
Freshfields

1. Like other French Overseas Departments and local authorities, French Polynesia faces a recurring cost-of-living issue, which has been recognised by numerous official reports[1] but remains unresolved.
2. It was against this backdrop that the ISLE research institute was created in 2023 as a non-profit association, on the initiative of the President of the Polynesian Competition Authority, Ms Johanne Peyre.
3. ISLE is dedicated to the in-depth study of Competition law and economics, taking into account the unique challenges of small and island economies. Its mission is to contribute to the development of effective and sustainable competition policies to promote fair and competitive markets, while tackling cost of living issues for the benefit of consumers.
4. ISLE's activities focus on three 5 areas:
   1. Research
      - Specific studies on competition dynamics in small economies.
      - Analysis of the links between Competition law, intellectual property and innovation in island economies.

---

* Jérôme Philippe is a partner at Freshfields Bruckhaus Deringer, based in the Paris office, where he leads the antitrust, competition, and commerce team.

1 National Assembly report No. 1549 of 20 July 2023, Senate report No. 620 of 9 July 2020, Opinion of the Economic, Social and Environmental Council No. 2023-023 of 13 October 2023. See also National Assembly Report No. 698 of 4 December 2024 on a proposed law, which does not concern French Polynesia.

- Identification of anti-competitive practices and consumer protection challenges in these territories.

2. Economic policy
   - Study of the impact of competition policies on island markets.
   - Assessment of regulatory frameworks to propose appropriate improvements.
   - Drafting and review of legislative and regulatory texts.
3. *Advocacy*
   - Making governments, businesses and citizens aware of the benefits of competition.
   - Promoting a culture of competition in island economies.
4. Training
   - Development of customised training courses for local governments and institutions.
   - Organisation of interactive workshops and educational programmes to strengthen operators' skills.
5. Community development
   - Creation of networks of researchers and advisors specialised in island economies.
   - Sharing results and running conferences and workshops to stimulate collaboration.

5. ISLE's first action is a project to study the causes of and solutions to the high cost of living in island economies, starting with French Polynesia. The aim is then to apply this work and methodology to other island economies.

6. The aim of this analysis is to understand the multidimensional causes of high prices in French Polynesia (transport, taxes, standards, market structure, etc.), then to formulate concrete proposals to improve local competitiveness, reduce import and transport costs, and encourage price transparency.

7. Our analysis is based on four pillars:
   - Identification of existing data and their quantitative study in order to carry out an economic diagnosis
   - Analysis of applicable law and the functioning and governance of institutions
   - A study of the many existing reports
   - Interviews with the main stakeholders: economic operators, government departments, French Polynesia's statistical institute

8. There is a strong convergence between quantitative economic studies and the feelings expressed in interviews, which emphasise the following factors:
   - Transport costs and other related costs (e.g. port handling costs)
   - Taxes and quantitative restrictions (quotas, bans)
   - Small market size preventing local economies of scale, often resulting in high local production costs
   - Local production deficit
   - Demand structure (two highly polarised demands and levels of purchasing power)

- Applicable standards (often incompatible with regional trade needs)
- Highly concentrated and vertically integrated import and distribution structures

9. Based on these findings, which are largely consistent with existing reports, ISLE has formulated interim proposals, which were presented to local stakeholders in 2024. This consultation process is set to continue with a view to producing final proposals.

10. The intermediate proposals are as follows:

I. Strengthen local competition

11. Strengthen local Competition law by:
    - Introducing the possibility of structural injunctions in the event of a definitively confirmed infringement.
    - Imposing mandatory consultation of the Polynesian Competition Authority (APC) prior to any limitation of the principle of freedom of pricing and trade, or prior to any regulatory measure impacting competition.
    - Lowering the burden of proof for exclusive import agreements: a total prohibition or prohibition in principle is excessive, as it applies uniformly to very different situations and leads to sub-optimal results in certain sectors or situations; conversely, competition authorities, which are small in size in small economies, find themselves having to make considerable efforts to provide evidence in law of the economic harmfulness of some of these agreements, which leads them to select only very few agreements and sectors, and undermines the effectiveness of their action; the proposal is therefore to find an intermediate solution that would apply to exclusive import agreements for operators holding more than 30% of the market concerned, by introducing above this threshold an obligation for prior written self-assessment, which would have to be substantiated and made available to the competition authority on request; this solution would take into account the economic situation of the sectors concerned, while lightening the burden of proof incumbent on the competition authority.
    - Strengthening civil chambers to rule on anti-competitive practices: the appropriation of Competition law by operators is not only achieved by and through competition authorities, but also through direct, private actions between operators based on Competition law, and which enable direct application; these include claims for the nullity of clauses and contracts and claims for damages based on Competition law, in cases where the facts are sufficiently simple or established not to require investigation by the public authorities.
    - Increasing cooperation with competition authorities in the Pacific region: many Pacific island territories share common concerns, and experience in other parts of the world shows that cooperation between competition authorities increases the effectiveness of Competition law enforcement. This mainly involves exchanges of know-how and information on cases of common interest (sometimes on the basis of waivers requested from the parties), and, where appropriate, coordination in certain actions (choice of

remedies, investigations, etc.). The establishment of the Pacific Competition Authorities Network (PINCCER) between Pacific competition authorities is a first step in this direction.

II. Facilitate "go to market" and increase retail price transparency

12. Price transparency is not always conducive to greater competition, far from it. It all depends on market conditions. For example, when there are few players on wholesale markets, it is essential that prices and commercial conditions not be transparent on these markets, otherwise situations of price parallelism are created, which can have harmful effects on competition.

13. On the other hand, to develop local production and make distribution more efficient, it is important to facilitate market access and public detection of the most attractive local offers.

    - Local products often go through the artisanal stage before being able to develop further. However, this lively artisanal micro-economy has no access to distribution. It therefore needs to find its way to its customers without the help of distribution before, for the most efficient, it can develop ("scalability") and reach a sufficient stage to be distributed.

      Today, most market access is via Facebook, whether for products (vanilla, fruit, etc.) or for certain pensions or activities. From this point of view, Facebook offers an effective solution for micro-producers, giving them easy and inexpensive access to the market. The limit of this solution is that each offer remains relatively invisible (unless you invest in advertising on the platform, which most players do not have the means to do) and it is difficult to grow the offer in this way.

      Similarly, a small distributor who chooses to lower a price will not necessarily have the means to make this easily known.

      The proposal is therefore to create a platform (website and/or mobile application) to display retail prices and product availability, opening it up not only to distributors but also to local producers.

      Unlike existing sites, offers on this site would not be entered by the administration. This would be done by the producers or distributors themselves. A dual system of rating by customers and control by the authorities would prevent abuse of communication.

      The primary aim of this proposal is for the most efficient suppliers to become better identified, and increase their demand, so as to set up a virtuous circle enabling them, at least in certain cases, to move on to the next stage. The other objective is to enable all operators, distributors and producers alike who charge lower prices to be easily identified and to increase their sales, thereby strengthening competition in distribution and access to the market.

    - Another proposal: for comparable products, display for information purposes the average price of the comparable product in mainland France.

III. Reduce transport and import costs

- Increasing the capacity of the port of Papeete to accommodate larger vessels
  The limited depth of the port of Papeete does not allow the entry of large vessels (over 2,400 TEU). This places considerable constraints on shipowners, who are unable to serve the port with the usual deep-sea vessels. For many, this requires transshipment, and therefore higher costs. The result is a barrier to entry, and competition would likely be stronger if larger vessels could also dock. The proposal is therefore to increase the depth of the pass to enable these vessels to dock at Papeete.
- Reduce port handling costs, which are much higher than in all other regional ports (excluding New Caledonia).
- Ensure sufficient competition in the services required for imports.

IV. Revise the tax and quota system

- Reform the Local Development Tax (TDL) and import quotas to make them incentive-based. The aim is to return the tax to its original purpose as an incentive, rather than an instrument for contributing to the budget. This means focusing it on products for which local production would really be possible, and adapting the rate to the level needed to enable such local production.
  What's more, in order to avoid the creation of rents that are ultimately paid by consumers, it would be necessary to make it temporary: it would be instituted for a limited period, at the end of which its necessity and rate would be re-evaluated. There could be two reasons for not maintaining it: either local production has developed sufficiently and can now subsist without tax or with a lower tax; or, conversely, the attempt at local development has failed and there is no need to continue penalising consumers with higher prices for local production that is not going to develop.
  Periodic reassessment is therefore essential. This also implies that, at the time of each introduction, a sufficiently precise objective is stated (what development, for what volume, at what price, etc.).
  Finally, it would be useful to introduce an absolute ceiling for all taxes on a product.
  The same periodic, justified and conditioned approach would be adopted for quotas.
- Simplify and increase the transparency of all taxes on each product.
  As taxes are incentives, they must be easy for operators to understand.
  With this in mind, it would be useful to merge the TDL with equivalent or similar taxes, and to publish a summary of taxes on each product.
- Ensure that all tax regulations, including rates and terms and conditions, are easily accessible in Polynesia and for foreign operators.
- If it is confirmed that distribution tends to focus on higher value-added products to the detriment of basic necessities, consider a tax incentive to counterbalance this trend.

V. Strengthen regional trade

- Create a label to identify purely local production, excluding products for which only a limited part of the added value is local.
  - This label could be based on the existing "Made in Fenua" or "Eat local" labels, adapting or extending them.
  - Adopt the "black diamond" branding model in Chile as a criterion for presence in schools and social welfare systems.
- Develop additional designations of origin (such as "Monoï de Tahiti") to encourage local consumption and exports (rum, noni, vanilla, pineapple, etc.).
- Explore the possibility of developing joint purchasing with New Caledonia for certain imports, in order to increase order volumes.
- Explore the creation of a Pacific common market.

VI. Align standards with needs

- Enable certain standards from the Pacific region, which have the same quality and safety requirements as European standards (e.g. Australian and New Zealand standards), to be used concurrently with French and European standards.
- Promote the development of "Pacific" standards.
- Adapt labelling requirements to avoid creating artificial barriers to entry.

VII. Better identify needs and better target economic support

- Enable the Institute of Statistics of French Polynesia (ISPF), the Polynesian Competition Authority (APC), the Department of Agriculture (DAG) and the Directorate General of Economic Affairs (DGAE) to have better access to customs data (subject to statistical confidentiality) and DICP tax data.
- Introduce an obligation to provide the APC with relevant excerpts from tax returns (sales, EBITDA, gross margin, etc.).
- Enable the DAG to gain a better understanding of the sharing of added value in vertical agricultural production and supply chains, either by providing it with investigative powers and resources, or by enabling it to request an inquiry from the DGAE.
- Examine ways to obtain better visibility of import margins (which are often not realised within the territory of French Polynesia, but are nonetheless essential in the value chain).
- Implement an electricity price cap regulation and increase the share of hydropower, to reduce the costs of this essential input for the Polynesian economy.
- Boost the development of SOFIDEP and improve bank financing for the Polynesian economy.

Increasing Competition to Moderate the Cost of Living in French Polynesia: The ISLE Initiative

Benoît Durand*
RBB Economics

Sean Ennis**
University of East Anglia

I. Introduction

1. The cost of living in French Polynesia is significantly higher than in mainland France, while the median income is lower. This is mainly due to a high dependence on imports and a protectionist policy aimed at supporting local production. However, these measures have a significant impact on prices, competition and consumer purchasing power. This article explores the causes of the high cost of living in French Polynesia, analyses the effects of tariff and non-tariff barriers, and suggests ways of improving the economy to make it more dynamic and competitive.

---

* Benoît Durand is a partner at RBB Economics.

** Sean Ennis is Director of the Centre for Competition Policy and Professor of Competition Policy at Norwich Business School.

A. *A structurally high cost of living*

1. Comparison with metropolitan France and other territories

2. Residents of French Polynesia pay on average 55% more than residents of mainland France for an equivalent basket of goods and services, and up to 81% more for food products. This gap widened between 2010 and 2016, despite extensive price regulation. In 2022, prices were on average 31% higher in French Polynesia than in mainland France.

3. However, this difference in the cost of living must be considered alongside the income gap between French Polynesia and mainland France. In 2018, the median income in French Polynesia was about 18% lower than in mainland France. This income disparity further limits the purchasing power of Polynesian households, making the high cost of living even more pronounced for a large portion of the population.

4. The cost of food is a key factor explaining this gap, but it is not the only sector affected. Imported food products are experiencing price increases due to high transport costs and import taxes. In particular, basic necessities such as meat, dairy products, and cereals are significantly more expensive than in mainland France. The food price index rose by nearly 60% in French Polynesia between 2006 and 2022, which is a growth rate faster than general inflation. This increase is primarily due to dependence on imports, logistics costs, and the structure of the local market, which limits competition in the distribution sector.

5. An important point to note is that the high cost of living is not necessarily the result of an increase in companies' profit margins. Margins have remained relatively constant between 2008 and 2022 in many sectors, according to data from the Statistical Institute of French Polynesia (ISPF) (see Figure 1). However, some sectors, such as real estate, agriculture, fishing and financial services, have seen a substantial increase in margins.

Figure 1: Margin ratio by sector, 2008, 2022

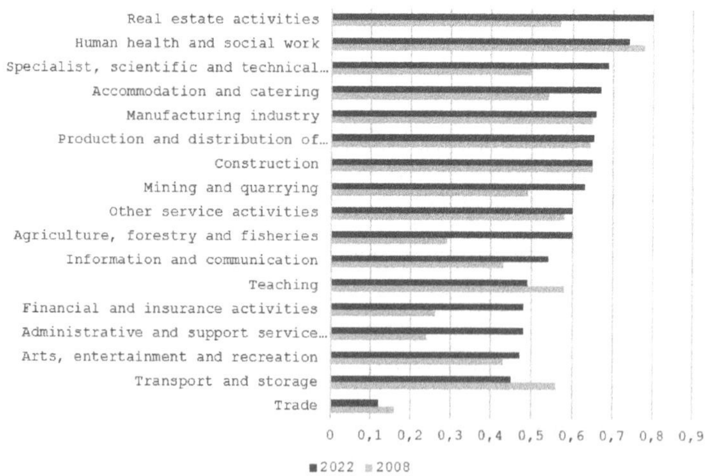

2. An island economy heavily dependent on imports

6. Like many island economies, French Polynesia has a largely negative trade balance: in 2019, imports amounted to 2 billion euros, or 35% of GDP. Certain sectors are highly dependent on imports, notably hydrocarbons (100% imported) and agri-food products (60% imported). In 2021, more than 80% of industrial and food products were imported.

7. A notable feature of Polynesian imports is their geographical remoteness.[1] A significant proportion of imported goods come from mainland France, but also from other distant regions such as the EU, Asia, the USA and Oceania. This dependence on distant markets results in high logistical costs, particularly due to sea freight costs and long delivery times. Freight costs, influenced by the lack of competition on sea routes to Polynesia, are a major contributor to consumer price inflation.

8. In the agri-food sector, French Polynesia is heavily dependent on imports from Europe. In 2022, around *36% of agri-food imports came from the EU, including directly from France*. This is due to the lack of sufficient local production to cover the population's needs. Most processed products, including canned goods, dairy products and certain cereals, are imported from Europe, where production standards and consumption habits are similar to those of the Polynesian market.

9. The import of agri-food products is also influenced by the structure of trade and the customs agreements in place. French Polynesia applies preferential tariffs for certain products from the EU (Source: Opinion of the Polynesian Competition Authority, 2019), but these advantages do not fully offset the high costs of freight and logistics. This situation thus contributes to *maintaining higher prices on the local market*, particularly for necessities.

3. The various sources of the high cost of living in French Polynesia

10. There are three main reasons for the high cost of living in French Polynesia: structural factors, regulatory barriers and market power.

- *Structural factors:* Insularity means high transport costs for shipping and storage. The small size of the economy limits the number of viable businesses in certain sectors, limiting the emergence of competition. The structure of demand is influenced by unequal income distribution and consumption that is sometimes oriented towards European products, which are more expensive to import. Finally, commercial links with French retailers favour imports from France, limiting the diversification of suppliers.
- *Regulatory barriers*: Numerous protectionist measures, such as customs duties, exclusions, import quotas and differential taxes, increase the cost of goods. Local competition is further restricted by licences, business permits and training requirements for businesses.

---

1 Like many Pacific islands, Tahiti is far from the main economic centres of gravity. Distances are much greater for the Pacific islands than they are for the Caribbean islands, for example. This handicap contributes to the high cost of imports.

- *Market power*: The absence of entrepreneurship could be a factor, but there is no evidence to support this. Other sources include natural monopolies in certain sectors, barriers to entry due to high vertical integration that excludes new entrants, and dominant market shares of the main economic operators.

B. *A historically rooted protectionist policy*

1. Official justifications for protectionism

11. Protectionism in French Polynesia is based on a rationale of supporting the local economy and safeguarding jobs in strategic sectors. This policy was introduced in the 1970s in response to the territory's heavy dependence on imports and the need to secure more autonomous economic development.

12. One of the main objectives of this policy is to *promote import substitution*, i.e. to encourage local production in order to reduce dependence on foreign products. This approach has been justified by the need to strengthen the region's economic autonomy in the face of the vagaries of international trade and fluctuations in world prices.

13. Another argument put forward is the *protection of local employment*. By limiting the entry of imported products, local businesses benefit from a protected market, which enables them to maintain and create jobs. This measure is particularly crucial in sectors where foreign competition could rapidly dominate the local market, such as agriculture, agri-food and certain manufacturing industries.

14. The Polynesian government also defended these measures, highlighting the need for *stability in tax revenues*. Import duties and taxes are a major source of revenue for the territory, enabling it to finance infrastructure and public services. Although this customs tax has an impact on the price of imported goods, it is seen as a means of guaranteeing a balanced budget for the territory.

15. Finally, protectionism was conceived as a tool for *regulating trade flows*, allowing imports to be controlled according to local needs and production capacity. Certain products are therefore subject to quotas or restrictions to ensure fairer competition between local players and importers.

16. However, despite these justifications, numerous studies have highlighted the perverse effects of this policy, particularly an increase in consumer prices, limited supply for consumers and market distortions that harm innovation and the competitiveness of local businesses in the long term.

17. It should be noted, however, that certain constraints on imports, such as limited port infrastructure and the high cost of sea freight, while contributing to higher prices, are not directly the result of a protectionist policy. Rather, these factors are the result of the geographical configuration of the territory and the choices made in terms of public investment, which further complicates the issue of the cost of living in French Polynesia.

2. The tools of protectionism

18. The protectionist policy implemented in French Polynesia is based on a set of tariff and non-tariff barriers designed to restrict imports and encourage local production.

19. Tariff barriers include particularly high import duties and taxes on certain products that compete directly with local industries. Among these, the *Local Development Tax (LDT)* plays a key role, applying variable rates ranging from 2 to 82% of the CIF (cost, insurance and freight) value of imported goods.

20. The TDL has been justified as a means of offsetting the structural disadvantages faced by local businesses, particularly due to the high cost of inputs and the small size of the local market. However, several studies, including those carried out by the Polynesian Competition Authority (APC) (Source: Opinion of the Polynesian Competition Authority, 2019), have shown that this tax contributes directly to the increase in consumer prices and limits the diversity of products available on the market.

21. A striking example of this protectionist policy is the beer sector. Duties and taxes on beer imports exceed 200%, leading to a drastic fall in imports and favoring local production. In 2017, imported beer accounted for only 4.8% of total sales by value, whereas its share was much higher before the application of these taxes. In addition, the raw materials used to make beer locally, such as unroasted malt, benefit from lower taxes, making local breweries even more competitive with imported products.

22. Non-tariff barriers include quotas on certain foodstuffs and necessities, as well as import licences that limit the number of authorised importers. These quotas are defined according to local consumption forecasts and adjusted periodically to maintain a balance between supply and demand. However, they can limit the entry of new importers and so restrict competition, indirectly contributing to higher prices. Certain products are also subject to import bans to protect local production. These bans apply to foodstuffs for which a local alternative exists, such as certain types of meat and agricultural products. This measure aims to promote food self-sufficiency but can also lead to shortages and price rises when local production fails to meet demand. This regulation applies to fresh fruit and vegetables, meat products and certain agri-food products.

23. In addition, the administrative procedures associated with imports are often complex and costly. Obtaining import licences involves a validation process that can be lengthy and discouraging for new entrants.

24. Finally, the limited port infrastructure in French Polynesia considerably increases maritime transport costs, a key factor in the price structure of imported goods.

C. *Effects of protectionism on prices and competition*

1. A documented inflationary impact

25. In theory, free trade is beneficial to economic development. The work of Arvind Panagariya analyses trade openness and economic growth, showing a correlation between trade growth and economic growth.[2]

---

2 Panagariya A., "Miracles and Debacles: In Defence of Trade Openness", *The World Economy*, August 2004, Vol. 27, Issue 8.

26. Unsurprisingly, the impact of protectionism on prices has also been widely demonstrated. According to a study by Poirine and Gay, the net welfare loss associated with import taxes and quotas is estimated at of the value added of industry excluding construction and energy.[3]

27. At the very least, the New Caledonian Competition Authority raises the question of how protectionist measures can be assessed, at least in the short term, and in particular whether losses for consumers are offset by gains for producers and the government in the form of tax revenue.[4]

28. Price controls on essential products were introduced in the 1990s to limit the inflationary effects of protectionism on consumers. The system is based on strict regulations that set price ceilings on certain products deemed essential. This system is based on strict regulations that set price ceilings on certain products deemed essential. The aim is to ensure affordable access to these goods for low-income households and to contain inflation in the most sensitive sectors.

29. However, despite these intentions, several analyses show that price controls can also have undesirable effects. On the one hand, it can reduce the incentive for importers and distributors to supply the market in sufficient quantities, which can lead to shortages. On the other hand, capping margins can limit the ability of economic players to invest and improve their supply, thereby maintaining the sometimes-inferior quality of the products available.

30. The Polynesian Competition Authority has noted that in some cases, price controls act as a factor of price rigidity, limiting competition between distributors and leading to a high level of price homogenisation. In other words, while the measure is supposed to protect purchasing power, it can paradoxically lead to prices stagnating at a higher level than would have prevailed in a more competitive market.

31. Finally, it should be noted that the price control system for PPNs is applied differently in different geographical areas. In remote archipelagos, where the cost of transport is higher, prices often remain above regulated levels, making the system less effective for these populations who would need it most.

2. Distortions of competition and economic inefficiencies

32. Protectionism in French Polynesia has led to a high concentration of economic players, particularly in the import and distribution sectors. This observation was noted in the opinion of the Polynesian Competition Authority (2019), which stresses that import restrictions and administrative barriers favour established players to the detriment of new entrants, thereby limiting competition. This concentration limits competition and allows certain companies to exert considerable influence over prices.

---

[3] Poirine B. and Gay J.-F., "Le coût du protectionnisme dans une petite économie insulaire : le cas extrême de la Polynésie française", *Région et Développement*, n° 42-2015. The observation that prices are high in French Polynesia due in particular to a protectionist policy is not new. See POIRINE B., Tahiti: une économie sous serre, Paris: L'Harmattan, 2011.

[4] Modèles de développement économique et protectionnisme en Nouvelle-Calédonie, Notes économiques de l'Autorité de la concurrence, n° 3, October 2024.

33. The tariff and non-tariff barriers put in place have the effect of restricting the entry of new players into the market. The need to obtain import licences, combined with strict quotas on certain products, *favours established companies and hinders the diversification of supply*. As a result, *competitive pressure is reduced*, which can lead to artificially high prices and limited supply for consumers.

34. The distribution market is also highly concentrated, as documented in the opinion of the Polynesian Competition Authority (2019). This study highlights the small number of chains controlling food retailing and their power to set prices. A small number of large chains dominate food retailing, which gives them greater pricing power. The Polynesian Competition Authority has pointed out that this lack of competition leads to *higher margins for retailers* and limits the potential benefits for consumers.

35. Another effect of protectionism is *the rigidity of price structures*. In a more competitive market, companies have an incentive to innovate and optimise their costs to offer more attractive prices. In French Polynesia, trade restrictions and regulated margins on certain products often prevent such a dynamic, which *limits the modernisation of businesses and the natural lowering of prices through innovation and process optimisation*.

36. Finally, high logistics costs, although independent of protectionism, exacerbate the situation. Limited access to modern port infrastructure and heavy reliance on a few shipping lines make freight costs particularly high. This economic reality, combined with protectionist measures, *exacerbates the overall costs of imported goods and hampers the development of a more open and competitive market*.

D. *Outlook: recommendations for reforming certain aspects of the business model*

37. Based on our analysis, we propose several reforms to reduce the high cost of living in French Polynesia. The main strategies include:

    1. *Redirecting imports by modifying customs duties and differential taxes and by partially or totally abolishing certain measures*, with these changes being limited in time.
    2. *Remove import exclusivities and limit exclusivity contracts* to resolve bottlenecks and increase access to scarce resources and vertical supply chains.
    3. *Reassess protectionist measures that restrict competition and encourage the creation of monopolies*.
    4. *Revise regulations to relax restrictions on competition in high-margin sectors*.

38. These recommendations have several objectives.

1. Supporting more competitive local production

39. To reduce its dependence on imports without resorting excessively to protectionism, French Polynesia needs to promote an economic model based on the development of local businesses and job creation. This requires *targeted investment in infrastructure*, particularly to improve logistics, transport and local production capacity.

40. The development of *support programmes for local businesses*, including aid for business start-ups, training for entrepreneurs and financial support schemes, could encourage more dynamic and innovative production. Promoting *local initiatives* and encouraging exports would make Polynesian companies more competitive on regional and international markets.

2. Towards a more balanced trade policy

41. Economic regulation and protectionist measures in French Polynesia, while aimed at protecting local production, also generate significant costs for consumers and stifle competition. A more balanced approach could be to gradually ease certain restrictions while maintaining targeted measures to support local industries that really need it.

42. Among the avenues for improvement, a *gradual reduction in import quotas and taxes on certain everyday consumer goods* could help to mitigate the inflationary effects observed. In addition, a trade policy more open to free trade agreements with strategic economic partners could promote better access to external markets while guaranteeing more competitive prices.

3. Import diversification and regional integration

43. At present, a large proportion of French Polynesia's imports come from mainland France and the EU. This choice is partly explained by trade preferences (reduced customs duties), consumer habits and the compliance of European products with local standards. However, this dependence on distant suppliers results in high logistics costs and a lack of supply flexibility.

44. A policy of opening up more to regional imports, by encouraging greater trade with nearby countries such as New Zealand, Australia and certain Asian countries (Singapore, South Korea, Japan), could help to:

- *Reducing import costs*: Exchanges with regional partners reduces transport costs, which make up a significant proportion of the final cost of imported products.
- *Diversifying the product offering:* Greater access to regional markets would enable Polynesian consumers to benefit from cheaper products that are better adapted to local conditions.
- *Improving the competitiveness of suppliers:* At present, the structure of trade favours importers with privileged links to France, which can limit competition. Greater openness could intensify competition and reduce margins on certain everyday consumer goods.

45. Opening up to regional imports represents an interesting alternative for moderating the cost of living in French Polynesia, particularly in the food and everyday consumer goods sectors.

4. Strengthening the role of the Competition Authority

46. The Polynesian Competition Authority (APC) plays an essential role in analysing anti-competitive practices and market distortions. To improve the effectiveness of the regulatory framework, *strengthening the APC's control powers* would enable

stricter monitoring of abusive practices, with particular emphasis on the *agri-food and distribution sectors*, which are critical to the cost of living in French Polynesia.

47. The APC could also introduce *price transparency mechanisms*, in particular through more detailed monitoring of the margins applied by importers and distributors. This would help to limit the risks of collusion and abuse of dominant positions that have been identified in some recent studies. Particular attention could be paid to the structure of the mass retail market, where a small number of players can limit competition and keep prices high.

II. Conclusion

48. French Polynesia faces a high cost of living. Sectoral regulations and protectionist measures in French Polynesia have a significant impact on the cost of living and the structure of the local market. Although they may offer advantages to certain local industries, their inflationary effects and distortions of competition need to be better controlled. A more balanced approach, combined with a strengthened role for the Competition Authority and a policy to support competitive local production, could ensure more dynamic and sustainable economic development for French Polynesia.

An Overview of Competition Law and Policy Challenges in the Pacific Islands: The Case of French Polynesia[1]

By Johanne Peyre[*], William E. Kovacic[**] and Alejandro Ibarra[***]

[1] The original version of this article was presented at the 2023 OECD Global Competition Forum and subsequently published in the Comparative Law Journal of the Pacific, Vol. 30, 2024.

[*] Johanne Peyre, is currently the President of the French Polynesian Competition Authority. She previously led the competition practice with a global remit for GSK Healthcare (New York), Pearson, a major publisher of educational solutions (New York) and Michelin, a leading tyre manufacturer (Clermont-Ferrand, France). She also worked in major Law Firms (Baker & McKenzie, Paris; and Cleary Gottlieb, Brussels) and was Concurrences Special Adviser on competition law trends and project development. Elected by 40 in their 40s Notable Women Competition Professionals in Europe, the Americas and Africa, and featured as an influential lawyer by several expert publications including Concurrences, Modern Legal Practice and GCR, Johanne has an unwavering commitment to ensuring innovative change in the antitrust compliance management.

[**] William E. Kovacic, is Professor of Global Competition Law and Policy at the George Washington University Law School. He was Director General of the FTC from 2001 to 2004, Commissioner from 2006 to 2011, and Chairman of the FTC from March 2008 to March 2009. From August 2013 to March 2022, he was Deputy Director of the UK Competition and Markets Authority (CMA).

[***] Alejandro Ibarra, is a fellow at the George Washington University Center for Antitrust Law, directed by William E. Kovacic, and a partner at Ibarra Rimon in Bogotá, Colombia. He is a Juris Doctor (SJD) candidate at George Washington University, a lawyer and specialist in Competition and Free Trade Law at Pontificia Universidad Javeriana, and a Master of Laws (LL.M.) in International and Comparative Law at George Washington University.

I. Introduction

1. Competition enforcement is often thought of as a uniform body of theory aiming to attend to the same needs through the same methods. However, the experience of many jurisdictions, along with the findings of different scholars, primarily from or about developing countries, have shown that this is not the case. In fact, we could say that competition policy, theory and application, have evolved over time at two different paces.

2. On one hand of the spectrum are the developments for and from mature economies that got on board early. Currently, these jurisdictions benefit from robust antitrust regulations, case law, and enforcement agencies that are well established and whose primary purpose is to preserve allocative efficiency or consumer welfare.[2] Their current priorities are often related to the digital economy and high technological industries, which have led them to focus on the surveillance of Big Tech companies, where most of the antitrust debate is concentrated right now.

3. On the other hand of the spectrum remain smaller economies and developing countries, which is the case of the majority of the 151[3] competition authorities created around the world by 2023[4], as well as other developing states that have not enacted Competition laws. As is well known, these jurisdictions have different market structures, especially regarding the size, and struggles compared with developed ones.[5] Many of them face profound inequality and poverty issues where competition policy could make a difference. Such policy – when correctly developed – becomes part of the engine to boost the development process, creating the necessary incentives to enhance growth, innovation, and distributive effects. Therefore, it could contribute to solving the high living cost crisis existing in some of these nations.

4. However, developing countries have a weak voice in the international antitrust arena[6] despite the fact that they constitute a majority worldwide, and the challenges

---

2 The authors recognise that there are currently ongoing debates regarding the goals of Competition law. However, from a historical point of view, it is possible to affirm in general terms that the main objective of this branch of law for the past decades has been consumer welfare. For more about the tension between the goals of Competition law, see William E. Kovacic Antitrust, Vol. 35, No. 3, Summer 2021. © 2021 by the American Bar Association. Reproduced with permission available at: https://www.americanbar.org/groups/antitrust_law/resources/magazine/2021-summer/root-and-branch/ . See Fox, Eleanor M., Economic Development, Poverty, and Antitrust: The Other Path. Southwestern Journal of Law and Trade in the Americas, Vol. 13, p. 211, 2007, NYU Law School, Public Law Research Paper No. 07-12, NYU Law and Economics Research Paper No. 07-26, Available at SSRN: https://ssrn.com/abstract=1002637

3 This information is drawn from the George Washington University Competition Law Center Database, which reports a total of 151 Competition authorities including regional supranational authorities and the Lebanon National Authority in the process of creation after the enactment of the national Competition law in March 2022. Of these 151, 130 are part of the ICN, while 21 are not; 6 are regional international authorities and the rest are national competition authorities which can be an agency itself or part of another government entity.

4 According to the IMF, only 37 countries were considered advanced economies by 2015, while the rest of the world was classified as emerging or developing economies, and some countries were not even included In the tables. See *https://www.imf.org/external/pubs/ft/weo/2015/02/weodata/groups.htm#cc*

5 Budizinski, Oliver, Beigi Maryam H.A., Generating instead of protecting competition, The economic characteristics of developing jurisdictions, (2015) Edward Elgar Publishing

6 See Guidi, Mattia, Tavares, Mariana, Twonly, Christopher, Considerations for a "top-to-bottom review" of the ICN: Legitimacy, effectiveness and efficiency (2022) available at: https://awards.concurrences.com/en/awards/2023/academic-articles/considerations-for-a-top-to-bottom-review-of-the-icn-legitimacy-effectiveness. *"Despite the*

derived from their market structure similarities (size, in particular) could be the most common across jurisdictions. In many cases, they have no interest in or have been discouraged from taking a leading role in global discussions, and their challenges capture the attention and resources of only a small group of scholars and research institutions.

5. Thus, there is a need for these countries to learn from experience, from the successful and failed attempts of their peers in similar economic and structural conditions, which can shed some light on the path and enhance the learning curve and implementation of a proper competition and enforcement policy. The sharing and building of this collective set of knowledge can help resolve some questions that have been posed by one of the authors of this article*: How can a competition agency leader find winning policies? What techniques could improve the likelihood of good policy results?*[7]

6. The emerging cooperation amongst competition authorities in the Pacific and the creation of the Pacific Island Network of Competition Consumer and Economic Regulators (PINCCER) is a shining example of useful regional cooperation that can help tackle the challenges faced by new competition agencies in small economies in the region.

7. This article focuses primarily on French Polynesia. Therefore, in section 2 we start with an overview of the Polynesian market and its particular challenges; in section 3, we propose possible approaches to solve the competition challenges it faces, and finally in section 4 we draw our conclusions.

II. Overview of the Market and Economic Challenges Faced by French Polynesia

8. Developing economies are often equated with small market economies, due to their common features. Normally, the size of the market in these jurisdictions is influenced by three main factors: size, dispersion of the population, and openness to trade.[8] These factors usually translate into the three main characteristics of small economies: high industrial concentration, high barriers to entry, and suboptimal levels of production[9], and may be reinforced by the toll on competition pressure

---

ICN's "consensus rule" for accepting new work products, NCAs and NGAs from advanced industrialised economies often have more influence. So, ICN work tends to focus on issues of interest to them (even at the expense of others). The same is true for the focus of the resulting work products". See Fox, Eleanor M., Linked-In: Antitrust and the Virtues of a Virtual Network (8 July 2009). International Lawyer, Vol. 43, p. 151, 2009, NYU Law and Economics Research Paper No. 09-27, Available at SSRN: https://ssrn.com/abstract=1431560 *"[I]n spite of great efforts of inclusiveness, the ICN agenda is principally set and the norms principally forged by the developed world, although consensus when reached involves give-and-take on all sides.*

7 Kovacic, William E., Leading a Competition Agency, Great Competition Enforcers Lessons from Regulators, (September 2023) Concurrences.

8 Gal, Michal, Size Does Matter: General Policy Prescriptions for Optimal Competition Rules in Small Economies (1 April 2001). Southern California Law Review, Vol. 73, 2001, NYU Ctr for Law and Business Research Paper No. 01-004, Available at SSRN: https://ssrn.com/abstract=267070 or http://dx.doi.org/10.2139/ssrn.267070

9 Gal, Michal, Merger Policy for Small and Micro Jurisdictions (January 18, 2013). More Pros and Cons of Merger Policy (2013), Available at SSRN: https://ssrn.com/abstract=2202718

imposed by remoteness or isolation[10], as is the case for French Polynesia. In this regard, Evans and Hughes concluded that:

> *"Particularly in small economies, there is a trade-off between numbers of firms and economies of scale that competition policies should reflect. The tension between scale and numbers of firms is aggravated by geographic isolation. Further tension can occur where economies are widely dispersed within national borders, resulting in even smaller geographical markets within the small economy (...)."*[11]

9. In this sense, we will now describe the French Polynesian market, analysing how those factors and characteristics have affected it.

A. *What Policy Challenges Does the NCA Face?*

10. French Polynesia is located in the Pacific Ocean, more than 4000 km from the principal cities of the Pacific.[12] According to the World Bank, its GDP was around 6 billion USD in 2021[13] and its population rose to 306,279 inhabitants by 2022[14], distributed in 5 archipelagos grouping a total of 118 islands spread along 500.000 km^2.[15] Most of the population is concentrated in the archipelago of Barlovento (around 75%), primarily in Papeete, the capital, where access to land is also affected by scarcity due to physical limitations inherent to an island.

11. Given the small market size, internal production is not sufficient to supply the demand and therefore the country is highly dependent on imports.[16] A major part of the goods are mainly transported by sea (99% by volume and 83% by value of imports). However, the only port in a condition to accept international trade is the port of Papeete, which can handle medium-sized ships. Therefore, all foreign goods must arrive first in Tahiti for shipping off to other locations inside the country. Also, the port operation suffers from inefficiencies and high prices, due to the regulatory framework applicable to the stowage sector, which makes the loading and unloading process more expensive than in other countries of the region.[17]

12. Regardless of the country's remote location, most importations (measured by value) come from France (27.2%) and from the rest of the EU (15.4%).[18] This could be a direct result of the preferential treatment French Polynesia grants to EU

---

10 Gal, Michal, The Effects of Smallness and Remoteness on Competition Law - the Case of New Zealand. NYU, Law and Economics Research Paper No. 06-48, Competition and Consumer Law Journal, Vol. 14, No. 3, 2007, Available at SSRN: https://ssrn.com/abstract=942073

11 Evans, Lewis. (2004). Competition Policy in Small Distant Open Economies: Some Lessons from the Economics Literature, available at: https://www.treasury.govt.nz/publications/wp/competition-policy-small-distant-open-economies-some-lessons-economics-literature-wp-03-31#abstract-01

12 French Polynesian Competition Authority, Opinion No.2019-A-02, Import and Distribution Mechanisms on French Polynesia, September 2019, available at: https://autorite-concurrence.pf/avis-n2019-a-02-du-19-septembre-2019/

13 Statistics can be found at The World Bank Database, available at: https://data.worldbank.org/indicator/NY.GDP.MKTP.CD?locations=PF

14 Statistics can be found at The World Bank Database, available at: https://data.worldbank.org/indicator/SP.POP.TOTL?locations=PF

15 Op cit. French Polynesian Competition Authority, Opinion No.2019-A-02

16 Ibid.

17 Ibid.

18 Ibid.

imports in comparison with the ones coming from the rest of the world, including from its closest neighbours.

13. Moreover, despite the high dependence on imports, the country possesses a complex system composed of tariffs, taxes, and non-tariff barriers designed to protect the national industry. Nonetheless, in most cases, the national industry cannot supply all of the demand and sometimes it does not produce the goods covered by the aforementioned measures. If we analyse the tariff rate individually, it does not raise much concern; however, if it is considered along with the rest of the taxes designed as protectionist measures, the rates go up around 30%[19], a highly concerning value in terms of competitive pressure.

14. Furthermore, the amount collected through customs duties and substitute taxes represents an important source of income for public finances.[20] This is concerning given that, in modern trade, the role of customs duties is to regulate the flow of trade through transparent and clear incentives. But when the finances of the state are structured in ways that depend on the money collected in customs, the government loses the ability to use them as a proper incentive to promote or decrease the flow of international goods into the national market.

15. The local development tax (TDL), imposed as a transitory tax to replace custom duty reductions, appears to be of special concern given its particularly punitive effect on essential products (coffee, toilet paper, apparel, beer, among others).[21] It also appears to be too broadly based, since it also applies to imported goods that have no equivalent in local production, or protects goods that have scant local added value (e.g. only packaging or assembly activities).

16. It is also necessary to consider the local tax exemptions that favour already incumbent and powerful players to the detriment of new entrants, and the old sanitary regulations in need of re-evaluation, which have some anti-competitive effects (e.g. French-language labelling, etc.).

17. On the side of non-tariff barriers, French Polynesia imposes a ban on some imports of consumer goods, such as fish, sausages, soaps, and juices, among others – some of the bans apply only to products that are not from the EU. Other products are also affected by import quotas, such as rice, sugar, flour, fruits, and meat, among others. The system for setting import quotas for fruits and vegetables by the Agricultural Conference also appears to be ineffective. Demand forecasts are underestimated, supply forecasts are overestimated, and quotas allocated are unpredictable. This limits the ability of importing wholesalers to buy at lower costs, leads to price increases and frequent shortages, and has no positive effect on meeting local production needs.

---

19 Ibid.

20 Ibid. According to the Competition Authority's opinion, the revenue from these tariffs and taxes could represent 40% of the government's fiscal income.

21 According Opinion 97-24 APF, Article 11: "Art. 11. - *As of 1 October 1997, local products shall enjoy special customs protection.- As of 1 October 1997, a local development tax (T.D.L.) shall be introduced to protect local processing industries, in charge of the customs service, whose base, rates and modalities of payment and collection shall be defined by decision of the Assembly of French Polynesia no later than 2 months before its implementation.*" (Authors´ translation)

18. As a result of the aforementioned conditions, consumer good prices as a whole are 40% higher than in metropolitan France and the other French overseas territories. This situation has a greater impact on the purchasing power of the poorest households, for whom these goods represent a significant proportion of their budget (more than 30% compared with 12% for the richest households). The final price paid by consumers is composed of: (i) the initial purchase price, that represents only 27% of the total price of a product; (ii) transport, 8%; (iii) import duties and taxes, also 8%; (iv) VAT, 13% on average; and (v) the remaining 44% corresponds, most likely, to the commercial margin of the distributors (importers-wholesalers and retailers).

19. One obvious conclusion is that distance or remoteness alone does not explain high prices. Transport and duties only represent 8% each of the consumer's final price. Rather, we conclude that the regulatory barriers and the framework established by the country over time, along with the size and structure of the markets concerned (routing, production, import, and retail distribution), and the fact that such markets are often not competitive enough, are the factors driving up the prices that take such a high toll on the country's population.

20. The French Polynesian Competition law was introduced in 2015, and the authority started to function in 2016. Therefore, it is a young authority in its first stage of existence[22], that faces big challenges derived from the landscape described above. Among those, the smallness dilemma[23], which implies that the size of the market cannot hold many producers efficiently, but the high levels of concentration to achieve economies of scale could reinforce and incentivise oligopoly coordination or market power abuses that can come back to bite consumers, and overall, worsen the current situation. The Polynesian Competition Agency has mentioned in this regard that:

> *"First, the small size of the Polynesian market means that, for many products, domestic demand is insufficient for local companies to reach a minimum optimal production size. This has a negative impact on production costs and investments, as the tightness of the market reduces the utilisation rate of production capacity and weakens the return on invested capital. Second, the tightness of the market leads local firms to concentrate their production and marketing resources in order to increase their production efficiency. However, this concentration process can be detrimental to competitive intensity (...) As the OECD points out, the limited number of players in most narrow markets can also facilitate the maintenance of cartels and collusive agreements: the repeated interactions between this small number of players reduces the need for the detailed contractual arrangements necessary to support the establishment of a cartel."*[24] *(Authors´ translation)*

---

22 Kovacic and Lopez-Galdos studied the different stages that a Competition agency passes through in order to achieve successful maturity or failure, along with the rates at which the competition policy is implemented, a whole complex process which the authors have called "*Competition systems´ lifecycles*". See Kovacic William. E and López-Galdos Marianela, *Lifecycles of competition systems: Explaining variation in the implementation of new regimes*, Law and Contemporary Problems Vol 79, 2016, Duke University.

23 Op cit. Gal. The Effects of Smallness and Remoteness on Competition Law - the Case of New Zealand.

24 Op cit. French Polynesian Competition Authority, Opinion No. 2019-A-02

21. This dilemma deepens when the youth of the agency and the protectionist measures implemented by the government, reinforcing the restrictive effects derived from the market´s natural structure, are added to the equation.

22. Ennis and Piffaut have identified six challenges faced by the French Polynesian Authority: i) creating a competition culture and training officials; ii) setting appropriate standards; iii) developing a proper prioritisation system that results in the right cases being picked; iv) ensuring a proper budget; v) dealing effectively with the bargaining power of multinational companies; and vi) ensuring political independence.[25]

23. At this point, the authority does not address capacity building or structural challenges; it concentrates mainly on policy and market structure concerns.

1. Lack of competitive pressure, exclusivities, and supply model

24. As mentioned above, 44% of the final price offered to the consumer remains a distributor´s surplus (importers-wholesalers and retailers), probably due to a detrimental lack of competitive pressure.

25. While the small size of the market already favours a certain concentration of local producers, this phenomenon is accentuated by the high level of protection they enjoy (particularly in the food industry). This leads to rent-seeking behaviour and high prices. In other words, producers and distributors are not encouraged to improve the quality, diversity, or price of their products.

26. Competition law generally focuses on competition in a market. However, as economic studies have shown, one of the main sources of competition concerns for small jurisdictions is the impact of high levels of aggregate concentration in their markets.[26] In particular, oligopolistic coordination within and across markets, along with barriers to entry, may increase.

27. In the case of French Polynesia, concentration is reinforced by the vertical integration of the main importers, producers, and distributors. Goods are imported in one of two ways: on the one hand via what is called the "*short channel*", in which a retailer is supplied directly by the foreign manufacturer on its warehousing platforms, possibly via its own central purchasing office; this channel is mostly used in the commercialisation of the distributors´ own brands; on the other hand, via the "*longer channel*", which involves a broker, or brand agent that is the one who negotiates the terms and supplies the Polynesian distributor; this is the most common way in which goods are supplied. The latter channel allows economies of scale and provides services to distributors (supply, shelving, advertising, promotions, after-sales service).

28. Importers often benefit from exclusive import rights for one or more brands, either *de jure* (formalised by a written contract) or *de facto* (without a formal agreement, but with the supplier selecting a privileged distributor who alone has access to

25 Ennis, Sean, Piffaut, Henri, Insular Economies: An overview of the national case law (September 2023) Concurrence, available at: https://www.concurrences.com/en/bulletin/special-issues/insular-economies-research-program/insular-economies-an-overview-of-the-national-case-law.

26 Micha S. Gal. Competition Policy for Small Market Economies. Harvard University Press (2003).

the brand's entire product range, its advertising budget or product training). This limits intra-brand competition between importers.

29. However, in a small, concentrated economy where inter-brand competition is structurally weak, the incentive to pass on economies of scale is also limited. Importers benefiting from such exclusivity have little incentive to exploit inter-brand competition.

30. Their market power is even greater if the exclusive importer is also a retailer, which is mostly the case in the Polynesian market. This is why, as a precautionary measure, there is a general ban on this type of exclusive agreement in all French overseas territories. However, French Polynesia is an exception. Since 2018, such agreements have not been covered by the ban.

31. In the retail sector, the leading operator can take advantage of this to set high reference prices for the market as a whole, based on the consent of the most affluent consumers. The other brands match these prices and therefore have no incentive to compete on price.

32. The aforementioned vertical integration, along with the exclusivities, poses different challenges to the authority. First, even though the exclusivities could represent some efficiencies or cost savings while increasing the buying power of the distributor, allowing it to get better deals, they could also impose a block on the few existing distribution channels, stalling the incentives and ability of other competitors brands to enter the market. Therefore, absent a ban, the agency is loaded with the burden of investigating and proving the anti-competitive nature of the agreements in each case, which in practice may prove difficult. The authors recognise that there is no point in a blind ban on exclusivities. Nonetheless, as we explain below, in a small market, especially in one so remote as the Polynesian, policymaking shall defer any measure that aids in maintaining open markets and eliminating unnecessary barriers. So, despite the efficiencies that could be generated, these agreements could imply a contractual or *de facto* closing of the distribution channels, eroding the chances to foster inter-brand and intra-brand competition.

2. Creation of proper and applicable standards for the jurisdiction

33. We have already mentioned that the remoteness and size of the market are reflected in a set of features, which create the need to tune the applicable standards and analyses to the particular needs and characteristics of these types of economies. In other words, the standards and analyses applied in mature jurisdictions cannot be directly transplanted to French Polynesia without a prior refining and adjusting process.

34. The above is especially true in the merger review process, where an improper threshold can lead the authority to spend already scarce resources on reviewing necessary transactions. Where the risk of a false negative can cause great harm, given that the self-correcting force of the market is weaker than in big and developed economies[27], but also where the risk of a false positive can deprive the market

---

27 Op cit. Gal, Michal, Merger Policy for Small and Micro Jurisdictions.

of the dynamic efficiencies necessary to move forward in the development process. Simply put, an error of judgment can have a longer-term and more profound impact on the Polynesian economy in comparison with developed ones.

35. Thus, the Polynesian Authority decision-making process has become very complicated. On the one hand, it must be careful not to block deals that increase concentration and are necessary to achieve beneficial economies of scale. On the other hand, it must block or impose conditions on deals that are likely to create unrepairable damage or a profound risk of competitive harm to the market.

36. It is also important to consider that the existing regulatory barriers deepen the impact on competitive pressures already affected by the connatural features of the Polynesian market. Therefore, a proper and assertive assessment requires a complex dynamic analysis, balancing, and also consideration of up- and downstream markets, along with the possible conglomerate effects when applicable.

37. The French Polynesian law introduced an uncommon instrument in its toolbox: the *ex-ante* control of retail outlets. In order to maintain a sufficiently competitive environment in the retail sector, the agency has the power to control the creation and modification of commercial space. Any creation, extension, or modification of a commercial outlet of more than 300 square metres requires prior authorisation from the authority.

38. The instrument aims to examine whether the transaction is likely to create or strengthen a dominant position. Following this analysis, the agency may approve, prohibit, or condition the transaction to measures protecting competition.

39. To limit this risk of error and improve the process, the agency has a tool that allows the parties to submit and negotiate commitments at the assessment stage of the procedure. If the authority identifies competition concerns, it invites the parties to propose remedies to address them before the decision phase in order to achieve the best outcome for the market.

40. In a recent decision, the agency blocked the construction of a Carrefour hypermarket of more than 1,800 m^2 in Pao Pao, on the island of Moorea. This was the first ban issued by the authority in the retail development sector. According to the agency, the transaction raised competition concerns. It was likely to crowd out several competing projects, thereby affecting the competitive landscape in the area, and to strengthen the Wane group's leading position in the food retail market. In addition, the operator's vertically integrated structure and the fact that its buying centre also supplied competing retailers in the area raised, in the agency´s opinion, concerns regarding discrimination and risks of self-preferencing. In this case, the remedies that were offered did not meet the expectations of the Polynesian Competition Authority (ACP). This a tool that raises sensitives issued, and the authority needs to find the balance on a case-by-case basis.

3. Oligopolist coordination and social ties

41. Another big challenge is addressing oligopolistic coordination. In this sort of behaviour, in principle, the prohibition on restrictive agreements does not apply. Given the interdependent relationship among oligopolistic agents, parallel practices

without a prior agreement is not *prima facie* forbidden.[28] However, despite its apparent legality, such behaviour, which is very common in small, marginal economies[29], could discourage entrance and impact competition, driving the prices up without rendering any particular benefits to the consumer or society itself.

42. In that sense, this type of behaviour represents a difficult issue that competition agencies must deal with primarily in three manners: i) through merger control; ii) through regulation (directly or through advocacy and promotion of proper measures before the competent authority); and iii) through close scrutiny that prevents illegal behaviour, facilitating coordination or restrictions on entrance. Finding regulatory solutions to overcome such threats to competition is no easy task, but lowering barriers to entry is a must to increase competitive pressure and the health of the Polynesian market.

43. Strong social ties and interest groups connected to political power are another problematic feature derived from a small population and even smaller business and political classes. While such links are a normal and important aspect of social life, they can also serve to dampen competition. Social and family links between competitors or conglomerates increase even more the risk of coordination and illegal behaviour and can stall agency tools or initiatives. For example, leniency programs are often ineffective where market participants are linked in more than economic ways. Also, these ties foster and strengthen the lobbying activity and the rent-seeking behaviour of these privileged groups towards the imposition of protectionist measures and barriers by the government.[30]

III. Possible solutions

44. The first concern reflected in all of the challenges mentioned above, and generally in small market economies, is the creation of competition[31], or in other words, increasing output. It cannot be ignored that competition is not an end but a means to maximise living conditions for the public, which, in the case of developing countries, is equal to growth or development. Thus, competition policy and enforcement in those jurisdictions should aim to promote growth, innovation, and allocative efficiency or redistribution effects in the long run.[32]

45. With that in mind, it is important to emphasise that, given the complex situation already described, the implementation and improvement of a successful

---

28 *See. Donald F. Turner. Definition of Agreement Under The Sherman Act: Conscious Parallelism And Refusals To Deal. 75. Pp 5. Harvard Law Review 1962.* The authors recognise that there is some discussion on the matter; however correctly there is now a thesis about interdependent behaviour at the moment that, in our opinion, could be administrable as a theory of harm for a competition agency. There must be other elements in addition to the parallel behaviour, that renders the coordinated behaviour illegal. See *William E. Kovacic, Rober C. Marshall, Leslie M. Marx, Halbert White. Plus Factors And Agreement In Antitrust Law.110. Pp. 6. Michigan Law Review. 2011.* .Also, see *William H. Page. Objective and Subjective Theories of Concerted Action. 79. Pp2. Antitrust law Journal 2013.*

29 Op cit. Gal. Competition Policy for Small Market Economies.

30 A. E. Rodriguez & Mark D. Williams, *The effectiveness of proposed antitrust programs for developing countries* 19 N.C. J. INT'L L. 209 (1993). Available at: https://scholarship.law.unc.edu/ncilj/vol19/iss2/1

31 Op cit. Budizinski and Beigi, Generating instead of protecting competition.

32 Kovacic, Willia E. Competition Seminar Pontificia Universidad Católica de Ecuador, 22 November 2023.

competition policy does not rest exclusively on the shoulders of the French Polynesian Competition Authority. It requires profound fiscal and customs policy reforms along with an investment in basic infrastructure, such as the Papeete port, to maximise conditions in the market. However, this does not mean that the agency is powerless before the challenges it faces. On the contrary, there are concrete actions that the authority can take to push the necessary shifts and improve the competition conditions.

A. *Aggressive policy advocacy*

46. At this early stage of the competition system, probably the most important task for the agency is to build widespread knowledge around Competition law and its benefits. Not only among the general public and business community, but also, and especially, inside the government. It is extremely important to generate awareness among high and senior public officials; decisionmakers and policy makers must take the subject into consideration. Along with this, the authority must identify problematic regulations that could be stalling the competition process, especially those posing unnecessary barriers, and then push for reforms.

47. It could be persuasive for the heads of government if the agency showed them the high cost that society has to bear in terms of prices (especially in public procurement), lack of quality, and on the development process, due to inefficient regulation. Naturally, this a burdensome task that requires time and persistence, but it is of the outmost importance.

48. In this respect, the Polynesian authority has been very active. It has issued important opinions analysing the structure of the national markets and identifying courses of action to be taken to improve conditions on imports and distribution mechanisms in the agricultural, industrial, oil, and energy sectors.[33] The authority has very successfully raised the interest of the government, much so that it incorporated most of the recommendations presented by the agency to an inter-ministerial committee in its negotiations with oil companies. The dialogue between the government and the competition authority increases the chances of the agency to succeed in achieving the structural shift needed. The quality of the opinions also helps build the authority's legitimacy and establish its brand as a technical body.

49. In this respect, the Polynesian authority has been very active. It has issued important opinions analysing the structure of the national markets and identifying courses of action to be taken to improve conditions on imports and distribution mechanisms in the agricultural, industrial, oil, and energy sectors. What has raised the interest of the government, which incorporated most of the recommendations presented by the agency to an inter-ministerial committee, in its negotiations with the oil companies. The dialogue between the government and the competition authority increases the chances for the agency to be successful in achieving the structural shift need. The quality of the opinions also helps to build the authority's legitimacy and establish its brand as a technical body.

---

33 Available at: https://autorite-concurrence.pf/avis-liste/

50. Ties with the international community are important too. In January 2023, the agency organized the Tahiti Competition Days, which brought together local stakeholders, practitioners, international experts and, for the first time, representatives of competition authorities from Pacific countries. It was a successful three-day training and exchange focused on Competition law in French Polynesia and the Pacific region. It helped to strengthen the expertise of local lawyers in this field, with the long-term aim of reducing the need for local companies to hire expensive lawyers from abroad.

51. The aforementioned is encouraging. Nonetheless, it is important to build persistence and resiliency, not only because there is much road ahead but also because once the authority starts to generate successful changes, it is only natural that many powerful groups and individuals will oppose bluntly when they see threatened their comfortable business position.

B. *Lenient merger review*

52. Once the authority has achieved some of the necessary regulatory shifts, incumbent players will be exposed to international competition, forcing them to improve in terms of price and quality. In the interim, it is advisable for the agency to allow national players to grow and achieve scale economies. In this perspective, merger review should focus on identifying the mergers that represent a high risk for the market and spare the resources that would be consumed in a broader review, to use them in other areas that could render more benefits, such as enforcement procedures and market studies, essential for effective advocacy.

53. In this sense, the thresholds triggering the notification process must be tuned to address only meaningful transactions that can pose a competitive risk to the market. In the same way, as Gal has explained[34], to avoid the unnecessary consumption of resources, only problematic transactions must pass on to the second stage of the analysis procedure. This means that, in principle, structural indexes should not play a major role in the decision to pass the transaction to the second stage unless it represents an unacceptable level of concentration, which is especially tricky given that measures such as HHI must be tuned to the realities of a small market.

54. The dynamic analysis must take into account the size and resources available in the market. Thus, when assessing the entry possibilities, it is worth considering that this process is longer in remote and small economies, and if there is a likelihood of entry, it is possible to be more lenient or tolerant towards the levels of concentration.[35] Also, it is convenient to apply a balancing approach that "*recognises that a merger should be permitted if the benefits resulting from a merger are greater than its disadvantage and offset its anti-competitive effects.*"[36] Conglomerate effects should also be considered, as they can play a much more important role than in big jurisdictions.

---

[34] Op cit. Gal, Merger Policy for Small and Micro Jurisdictions

[35] Ibid.

[36] Ibid.

55. Finally, it is also important to include in the analysis foreign subsidies that could be affecting imports and driving the prices artificially down. When this is the case, achieving economies of scale and efficiencies that help the producers drive the cost down could be the only way to stay in the market and to overcome this kind of market distortion.

C. *Aggressive enforcement policy*

56. The enforcement policy is key to the success of the system. There should be and special focus on detecting any legal conduct discouraging entry, either agreement or unilateral conduct. Hardcore cartels directly on prices, of course, are important. However, we emphasize on exclusionary and rising rival cost conducts given that the priority of the authority should rest on keeping the market open and fostering innovation.

57. Aggressive is also important to create incentives for the leniency program to work, particularly in such small jurisdictions as the Polynesian one in which close social and family ties can strongly discourage this tool.

58. In this aspect, the French Polynesian Competition Authority has given important steps. In the telecom sector, for example, there is a precedent in which the authority investigated on the grounds of abuse of dominant conduct the biggest provider; the procedure was closed by accepting the commitments presented by the company. This procedure was extremely important since the sector was historically dominated by state-owned monopoly enterprises, and the entry of new operators represented a significant price fall.[37]

59. More recently, the agency investigated and sanctioned a cartel in the numerary industry during the pandemic, which increased the prices of funeral services for people who died from COVID-19. More than a thousand families, most of them in vulnerable conditions, were affected by this agreement.[38]

D. *The new Pacific Island Network of Competition* Consumer and Economic Regulators (PINCCER) – can help

60. In November 2023, the competition agencies of Australia, Cook Islands, Fiji, French Polynesia, Kiribati, New Caledonia, New Zealand, Papua New Guinea, Samoa, Solomon Islands, Tonga, and Vanuatu created the Pacific Island Network of Competition Consumer and Economic Regulators (PINCCER). The network "*is designed to enhance the capabilities of competition authorities by allowing them to speak with one voice in the Pacific region, and providing them with a forum for exchanging experiences dedicated to promoting competition in the markets under their jurisdiction*".[39]

---

37 https://autorite-concurrence.pf/decision-n-2018-pac-01-du-6-juin-2018/

38 https://autorite-concurrence.pf/decision-n2022-pac-01-du-5-septembre-2022/

39 New Caledonian Competition Authority, Pacific competition authorities create collaborative network to promote the competitive functioning of markets, Press Release, November 2023, available at: https://www.concurrences.com/IMG/pdf/communique_pinccer.pdf?115477/c8c1cff4f1c6c101cb88db4517ad24eccc1e004322f7cf2d9636330266bb71aa

61. The establishment of PINCCER has at least three potential advantages for the authority. The first is that the collective efforts of PINCCER participants can enable the authority (and other PINCCER members) to achieve results that may be unattainable through the work of individual national competition authorities. The resource constraints discussed above require ingenuity in devising alternative approaches to carrying out the mandate of the competition laws of each jurisdiction. For example, rather than having each national competition authority undertake a market study or perform other research projects the PINCCER network could pool resources in ways to upon the capabilities of each and share costs that might be unbearable for a single authority. The PINCCER network also could supply a platform for developing common strategies – in advocacy and law enforcement – to address phenomena that affect many or all of the network's members. Regional networks have a special capacity to enable members to focus in a single minded way on issues of distinctive importance to the region – something that often is generally not possible in the context of participation in multinational networks with a diverse global constituency.

62. A second potential advantage comes from the network's capacity to accelerate learning by each member. Learning from experience, good and bad, is a vital means for organizations to progress. Mastering the cycle of experimentation, assessment, and refinement is fundamental to the success of institutions in competition policy and other fields of endeavour. Networked collaboration enables each member to benefit from the experience of all members – to reach beyond the experience base of an individual national competition authority and absorb learning from multiple organizations. For a competition authority, the common learning can take the form of pooling knowledge about economic problems, investigation and enforcement techniques, and solutions for management challenges (e.g., methods of setting priorities and selecting projects to carry them out). The network also supplies a forum in which members can discuss how to cope with political pressures and interagency frictions that arise in every jurisdiction.

63. The third advantage is to enable the PINCCER members to have a more effective voice in dealing with the rest of the competition policy world. Smaller economies – including the island states of the South Pacific – can easily be overshadowed by the larger economies and jurisdictions that figure most prominently in the development of competition policy. The PINCCER network provides a means to amplify the voice of the member authorities and draw attention to their programs and their views on competition policy.

Assess and Incorporate Comparative Experience

64. As noted above, comparative learning is one of the main benefits that the Polynesian Competition Authority can receive from the PINCCER. Among the network's members, there are agencies that have already collected a great amount of experience, especially, in dealing with the size and remoteness concerns. New Zealand is a good example worth considering.

65. By 2022, it had a population of around 5 million[40], much bigger than French Polynesia but still small, its location is very remote, even from Australia, its principal commercial partner, and its markets are highly concentrated.[41]

66. New Zealand, has embraced this situation by opening its economy to foreign trade, reducing barriers to imports and exports[42], along with applying competition policy and enforcement. They have adjusted the law and standards to face the challenges posed by the particular features of the jurisdiction, for example, Section 1A of the Commerce Act recognises as one of the main goals the promotion of competition for the long-term benefit of the consumer.[43] This implies the recognition of dynamic efficiency as a preponderant objective. In the same way, they have tuned their merger review standard, recognizing that high concentration is a connatural situation of their jurisdiction. Thus, they have created safe harbours that tolerate a HHI higher than the traditional markers used in the US or the EU, and they have even allowed mergers to monopoly when verifying the existence of potential competition that can discipline the merged entity.[44]

67. This experience could become very handy for French Polynesia to make the necessary adjustments to improve competitiveness in its market.

IV. Conclusions

68. Small and remote economies possess inherent features that have to be taken into account when designing and applying their competition law. Due to their size, they cannot support many agents producing efficiently, which often makes them highly concentrated. Thus, lowering barriers and openness are extremely important, given that help to increase the output, create competitive pressure, and protect the consumer welfare in the long run.

69. French Polynesia is facing a high cost of living condition, which is probably caused not only by its size and location but also by the high regulatory barrier that shields its industry from foreign trade. Therefore, its competition agency has great work ahead to successfully implement a competition poly that can properly address the situation. Even though it has made important achievements in the six years since it was created, the agency still needs to persuade the government to undertake profound shifts in fiscal, customs, sanitary, and phytosanitary policy in order to effectively improve the competition conditions in the market.

70. The experience of other countries could play a very important role in that process. In that sense, the creation is a great step that could help the agency learn from comparative experience and address effectively as a group common problematics and concerns across the region.

---

40 Statistics can be found at The World Bank Database, available at: https://databankfiles.worldbank.org/public/ddpext_download/POP.pdf

41 Op. cit. Evans, Lewis. (2004). Competition Policy in Small Distant Open Economies.

42 Ibid.

43 Op. cit. Gal. The Effects of Smallness and Remoteness on Competition Law - the Case of New Zealand.

44 Ibid.

The Prohibition of Exclusive Import Agreements in French Polynesia: A Plea for the Return of a Missing Law

Walid Chaiehoudj*
New Caledonian Competition Authority

1. **A controversial subject.** Is there a more controversial issue than the prohibition of exclusive import agreements in French Polynesia?[1] When one looks at overseas competition law, it's immediately noticeable that the topic provokes very contrasting, opposing, and often visceral reactions.

2. **Antagonistic positions.** On the one hand, part of the doctrine is satisfied with the legal death of this prohibition. It should be noted that the majority of the critics of the former article LP 200-3 of the French *Competition Code*, which stipulated that "agreements or concerted practices having the object or effect of granting exclusive import rights to a company or group of companies are prohibited", played an active part in the disappearance of this provision[2] and are still campaigning vigorously

---

* Walid Chaiehloudj is Vice-President of the New Caledonia Competition Authority and is also board member of the French Competition Authority. He is also a professor at the University of Perpignan. The author's opinions are personal.

1 It seems to us that the emphasis placed on the "structural injunction" as a weapon is also highly controversial and lacks consensus.

2 See in particular Montet Ch., "Accords exclusifs d'importation : en finir avec le régime d'exception", *in Le droit de la concurrence en Polynésie française et dans les petites économies insulaires du Pacifique (dir. S. Cabon, Ch. Montet et F. Venayre)*, LexisNexis, 2018, p. 57 et seq. This text is a contribution to a symposium held in 2017 in Fenua, which led to a very rapid reaction by the legislator.

for the removal of this prohibition from the metropolitan legal system.[3] On the other hand, there are the disappointed and those who consider that loi du pays n° 2018-31 du 9 août 2018 portant modification de la partie législative du *Code de la concurrence* is a bad blow to the protection of competition in Fenua and to the well-being of the Polynesian consumer. In a February 28, 2018 memo to the members of the French Polynesian Assembly's Committee on the Economy, Finance, the Budget and the Civil Service, the former chairman of the Polynesian Competition Authority (hereinafter the APC) had pointed out vehemently that the abolition of, among other things, the prohibition on exclusive import agreements would deprive the APC of a tool to combat the high cost of living. It added that "the opinion of academics (referred to in the explanatory memorandum) who met at a colloquium in Tahiti last November should not be taken as 'revealed truth', since the academic world, lawyers and economists alike, is so divided on the subject".[4] In an important opinion, the APC once again defended the prohibition of exclusive import agreements, considering that the arguments for maintaining inter-brand competition were hardly convincing, given the well-known characteristics of island territories, namely the small number of substitutable products from competing brands.[5]

3. **Law of August 9, 2018 and the Polynesian exception.** In any case, the disappearance of the prohibition on exclusive import agreements is surprising, as it runs counter to the dynamics of metropolitan France and New Caledonia. Admittedly, the "principle of legislative speciality"[6] allows legislators in the French overseas territories to legislation to meet and take into account the territory's specific economic and social needs, which are very different from those in mainland France. That said, the Polynesian legislator's haste to abolish a text that came into force on February 1·2017 can only come as a surprise.[7] It should be remembered that the country's competition law No. 2014-2 of February 23, 2015 stipulated that:

> *within one year of the entry into force of the present code, the Polynesian Competition Authority shall rule on the admissibility of agreements or concerted practices in progress whose object or effect is to grant exclusive import rights and which have been submitted to it.*

---

3 See, for example, Venayre F. Exclusive import rights overseas. Se poser les bonnes questions avant d'interdire?", *RLC*, 2018, n° 71, p. 22. Very recently, see Vogel L. and Vogel J., "Interdiction des droits exclusifs d'importation dans les DROM-COM : Quels risques ? Quelles solutions?", *BRDA*, 2024, n° 4, p. 24.

4 APC, *Note aux membres de la Commission de l'économie, des finances, du budget et de la fonction publique de l'Assemblée de la Polynésie française sur le projet de loi réformant le* Code de la concurrence, February 28, 2018, p. 4.

5 APC, opinion No. 2019-A-02 of September 19, 2019 on import and distribution mechanisms in French Polynesia, § 391 et seq.

6 V° "Spécialité législative", *in* GIRAUDEAU G. and MAISONNEUVE M. (dir.), *Dictionnaire juridique des Outre-mer*, LexisNexis, 2021, p. 504: "the principle of legislative speciality means the existence of a specific law applicable in the territories concerned. They are subject either to a specially developed regime, or to metropolitan laws and regulations, provided the latter expressly mention their applicability. In other words, metropolitan law does not apply as of right, but only by way of exception and following the expression in this sense of the will of the normative power, in the initial text or on the occasion of the explicit extension of its application".

7 The *Polynesian Competition Code* came into force on February 1st 2016.

To this end, Polynesian companies were granted a "pedagogical period",[8] not only to acculturate themselves to a new, more demanding regulatory environment, but also to apply to the APC for its approval, in much the same way as the old comfort letters from the European Commission. In this respect, three points deserve particular attention. Firstly, from a temporal point of view, the lifespan of the prohibition was very short. Between the entry into force of the prohibition on exclusive import agreements and the adoption of the country's law of August 9, 2018, a mere 18 short months have elapsed... Is this really enough time to draw definitive conclusions about the effects of legislation? Secondly, the pedagogy of competition has hardly worked, since no company has notified exclusive import agreements to the APC.[9] Finally, no condemnation decision was handed down during the period when the text prohibiting exclusive import agreements was in force. Under these conditions, how can it be said without reservation that the prohibition had negative effects on the Polynesian economy?

4. **Market concentration in Polynesia.** The cost of living in the French overseas territories deserves to be more rigorously measured, especially as in some territories with Polynesian characteristics, such as New Caledonia, the prohibition of exclusive import agreements is applied, enabling open markets to be maintained.[10] What's more, several factors need to be taken into account when looking at the high cost of living in overseas France, such as taxation, like the famous "octroi de mer" inherited from colonial times, but above all market concentration, which can be described as hyperconcentration in the case of Polynesia.[11] This concentration "refers to the density of companies, which is usually measured by the share of supply held by them".[12] As the Organisation for Economic Co-operation and Development (OECD) recently pointed out, "the smaller the number of companies operating in a market, or the higher the share held by a relatively small number of companies, the more concentrated the market".[13] Such concentration has deleterious effects for consumers in terms of price, product quality and innovation, but also from a democratic point of view. In such a context, the risk of capture by the legislator is great, since through lobbying, the economic power of companies with a monopoly or operating in an oligopolistic market can be transmuted into political power.[14] Doesn't a distributor's exclusive right to import reinforce this economic power, regardless of any efficiency gains?

---

8 Venayre F., "Prohibition des exclusivités d'importation à Tahiti : Fin de la (discrete) période pédagogique", *RLC*, 2017, n° 64, p. 14.

9 *Ibid.*

10 Even in small markets such as electronic cigarettes. See ACNC, decision No. 2023-PAC-01 of March 1 2023 concerning practices implemented in the import and distribution of electronic cigarettes in New Caledonia.

11 A recent commission of inquiry, which interviewed us, noted that "In French Polynesia, four groups of supermarket chains own almost the entire market: the Carrefour banners (Carrefour, Champion and Easy Market) are managed by the Wane group, a major player in mass retailing, which holds 52% of the market, the U banners (Hyper U, Super U and U Express) represent 34% of the market, followed by the LS Proxi banner (almost 8%) and the newly-created Happy Market banner, a partner of Intermarché at 5.6%". See Vuilletet G. and Hajjar J., *Rapport fait au nom de la commission d'enquête sur le coût de la vie dans les collectivités territoriales régies par les articles 73 et 74 de la Constitution*, submitted on July 20, 2023, p. 380.

12 OECD, *The Interaction between Competition and Democracy*, OECD Competition Policy Roundtable Papers, No. 316, 2024, p. 16.

13 *Ibid.*

14 *Ibid*, p. 18.

5. **The usefulness of prohibition in the light of antitrust history.** In fact, we need to go back to the essence of antitrust law to understand the usefulness of prohibiting exclusive import agreements. In a famous speech, Senator Sherman, father of the Sherman Act, declared that :

> *If we don't want a king to rule our country, we can't allow a king to rule our production, our transport or the sale of our products. If we don't want to submit to an emperor, we must not submit to a trade autocrat with the power to prevent competition and fix the price of any commodity.*[15]

Since exclusive import rights make the elected distributor an "autocrat of the trade", i.e. the only entity able to sell the product in the territory, the prohibition of the agreement does not appear to be meaningless, at least in terms of competition policy.

6. **A plea.** This contribution proposes a plea, defined by the Académie française as "writing in support of an idea or a cause". This plea is intended to be free and sometimes "without rigor" in its Carbonian sense. It supports the cause of prohibition with arguments of unequal value, but which all point to the resurrection of the defunct text. On the one hand, the return of the prohibition on exclusive import agreements would enable Polynesian consumers to benefit from intra-brand competition (I). On the other hand, it would free up limited resources so that the APC could focus its action on practices that are more difficult to detect and sanction (II). Finally, it is necessary to experiment with a ban in order to draw conclusions (III).

I. The benefits of intra-brand competition

7. **Genealogy of prohibition.** The belief that an exclusive import agreement is less serious than a cartel or abuse of a dominant position stems from an unfortunate position that was expressed during the parliamentary debates prior to the adoption of Law No. 2012-1270, known as the "Lurel Law" of November 20, 2012. In its opinion of October 3, 2012, the Commission des lois constitutionnelles, de la législation et de l'administration générale de la République had stated without justification that:

> *practices involving exclusive rights in overseas France are not as serious as cartels and abuses of dominant positions, and are not subject to the same criminal penalties, since the infringements of competition rules and economic public policy are less serious.*[16]

8. In its first decision to impose sanctions[17] , the French competition authority (Autorité de la concurrence métropolitaine) took up this argument – which has

---

[15] Senator Sherman John, 21 Cong. Rec. 2515 (1889): "If we will not endure a King as a political power we should not endure a King over the production, transportation, and sale of the necessaries of life. If we would not submit to an emperor we should not submit to an autocrat of trade with power to prevent competition and to fix the price of any commodity".

[16] Commission des lois, opinion No. 243 of October 3, 2012.

[17] Aut. conc. decision No. 16-D-15 of July 6, 2016 concerning practices implemented in the distribution of massmarket products in overseas France, § 46.

since become a familiar refrain[18] – but once again, without justifying itself as to the less damaging nature of the practice in comparison with that of cartel and abuse of a dominant position. This assessment runs somewhat counter to its original analysis. Indeed, it is important to remember how the prohibition came about. In adopting the Lurel law, the legislator relied on the work of the French Competition Authority, and in particular on a 2009 opinion which stressed the importance of maintaining intra-brand competition in the French overseas territories, and the weakening of this competition in the retail sector, which would in turn weaken inter-brand competition.[19] In this respect, she pointed out that :

> *Depending on the characteristics of the market and of the exclusivity(ies) in question (duration and terms of the exclusivity(ies), termination procedures, market share of customers bound by the exclusivity(ies), market share of manufacturers using the exclusivity(ies), cumulative nature of the exclusivity(ies) in question, existence of barriers to entry on the markets in question, etc.), a supply exclusivity may be such as to prevent the entry of competing manufacturers, while the reduction in intra-brand competition resulting from a customer exclusivity may also extend to inter-brand competition. The French Competition Council stated [Decision No. 05-D-49 relating to the franking machine sector] that these infringements [on competition] are all the more serious in that the economic and legal context of the market in question is highly unfavorable to competition, and that they are the result of a significant number of similar contracts covering almost the entire market concerned, and producing a cumulative effect.*[20]

---

18 Aut. conc. decision No. 17-D-14 of July 27, 2017 relating to practices implemented in the FMCG distribution sector in Overseas France, § 48; Aut. conc. decision No. 18-D-03 of February 20, 2018 relating to practices implemented in the marketing of biocidal termite traps in Réunion, the West Indies and Guyana, § 123; Aut. conc.., decision No. 18-D-21 of October 8, 2018 relating to practices implemented in the FMCG sector in the islands of Wallis and Futuna, § 79; Aut. conc.., decision No. 19-D-11 of May 29, 2019 concerning practices in the marketing of reagents and consumables for hospital laboratories in French Guiana, § 94; Aut. conc.., decision No. 19-D-20 of October 8, 2019 relating to practices implemented in the perfumery and cosmetics distribution sector in the West Indies, French Guiana and Reunion, § 110; Aut. conc. decision No. 20-D-16 of October 29, 2020 relating to practices implemented in the champagne marketing sector in the West Indies and French Guiana, § 151; Aut. conc.., decision No. 21-D-23 of October 7, 2021 concerning practices in the champagne and spirits marketing sector on Reunion Island (Cattier), § 70; Aut. conc.., décision n° 23-D-02 du 8 mars 2023 relative à des pratiques mises en œuvre dans le secteur de la commercialisation du champagne Canard-Duchêne aux Antilles et en Guyane, § 179, see also, *French Competition Authority, The French Competition Authority fines several companies which have implemented exclusive import agreements (Materne / Sodibel), July 27, 2017, e-Competitions July 2017, Art. N° 84545, concurrences.com/84545, see also Michel Debroux, Exclusivité d'importation : L'Autorité de la concurrence sanctionne à nouveau des accords exclusifs d'importation et de distribution dans les collectivités d'outre-mer et précise le champ d'application de la loi Lurel (Commercialisation de pièges à termites à base de biocides à La Réunion, aux Antilles et en Guyane), February 20, 2018, Concurrences N° 2-2018, Art. N° 86863, pp. 73 – 74.*

19 In this opinion, after presenting the structure of "long circuit" distribution, the Autorité noted that "To a certain extent, this limitation of intra-brand competition can affect inter-brand competition: in the presence of territorial exclusivity, a price increase by a manufacturer or wholesaler is more likely to be followed by competing wholesalers". See Aut. conc. avis n° 09-A-45 du 8 septembre 2009 relatif aux mécanismes d'importation et de distribution des produits de grande consommation dans les départements d'outre-mer, § 102, see also, *Alain Ronzano, Santé - Réseaux de professionnels de santé : L'Autorité de la concurrence dit tout le bien qu'elle pense des réseaux de professionnels agréés par les complémentaires de santé (Affaire réseaux de soins agréés), September 9, 2009, Concurrences N° 4-2009, Art. N° 55848, www.concurrences.com/55848*

20 *Ibid*, § 135.

All this argumentation shows how detrimental the practice is to the free play of competition in a territory characterized by the narrowness of its market. There is therefore a dissonance between the severity of the repression and the claim that these practices are less prejudicial to economic public policy. What's more, adopting an *in abstracto* approach rather than an *in concreto* one seems irrelevant. What does this mean? It means that the Autorité currently adopts a case-by-case approach and remains indifferent as to the market concerned when applying the severity criterion. However, seriousness is all the more important in sensitive sectors such as healthcare, . For, in addition to economic damage, there is also obvious social damage. Doesn't public order suffer when medical equipment is sold at a higher price because of a lack of competition due to exclusive import rights?

9. **A barrier to entry.** What's more, in territories dominated by a culture of non-competition and where market concentration is high, it seems to us that there is little reason to consider that the practice is less serious than an agreement or an abuse of a dominant position. So, if the legislator has considered that the practice should be sanctioned *per se*, and has therefore lightened the burden of proof for the Autorité de la concurrence, it is because he believes that the practice closes off overseas markets to competition. In other words, it is a legal barrier to entry, since a well-known or attractive product subject to import exclusivity cannot be offered by a new entrant. Isn't this blatant economic damage?

10. **Competition.** In fact, members of the French Competition Authority (Autorité de la Concurrence Métropolitaine) recently stated that "the ban on exclusive import agreements has made it possible to introduce *more competition* into relations between importing wholesalers and suppliers, through the generalization of competitive bidding procedures".[21] What's more, under the impetus of the French Competition Authority,[22] , the French legislator introduced a new provision in Article L. 420-2-1 of the French *Commercial Code*, by the DDADUE Act of December 3, 2020,[23] , which prohibits integrated distributors, i.e. distributors who are both present upstream as importing wholesalers and downstream in retail sales, from favoring intra-group stores to the detriment of competing stores. In other words, it is now a punishable offence for an integrated player to discriminate between its third-party customers and its intra-group customers.

11. **Protection of intra-brand competition.** In any case, the prohibition of exclusive import agreements protects intra-brand competition. And to this day, it is hard to understand why some legal writers remain hostile to this defense of intra-brand

---

21 Kerguelen E. and Piffau H., "Distribution", *Concurrences*, 2023, n° 2, p. 19 (Journées Concurrence Tahiti [Papeete, January 23-25, 2023]).

22 Aut. conc. avis n° 19-A-12 du 4 juillet 2019 concernant le fonctionnement de la concurrence en outre-mer, see also *ean-Philippe Kovar, Outre-Mer : L'Autorité de la concurrence dresse un état des lieux de la concurrence dans les départements et régions d'Outre-Mer et recommande un renforcement de ses pouvoirs (Fonctionnement de la concurrence en Outre-Mer), July 4, 2019, Concurrences N° 4-2019, Art. N° 92374, pp. 191-193, www.concurrences.com/92374*

23 Law No. 2020-1508 of December 3, 2020 containing various provisions for adapting to European Union law on economic and financial matters.

competition.[24] Comparisons with certain countries are not always convincing. For example, the comparison with the island of Malta, where exclusive import agreements are not prohibited, does not allow us to draw any conclusions. The data provided by many entities show that the cost of living in Malta is lower than in other European countries such as Germany or France[25] , while the gap between Polynesia and mainland France is estimated at 30.8%.[26]

12. **The Caledonian example.** In any case, the Caledonian example offers a tangible way of opening the eyes of the Polynesian legislature and its misconduct. In a recent decision, the New Caledonian Authority intervened in the telecommunications sector,[27] a sector of vital importance for the archipelago's connectivity to the rest of the world. In this case, Ericsson sold telecommunications network equipment exclusively to a distributor. As a result, the end customer, mainly the Office des Postes et Télécommunications de Nouvelle-Calédonie (OPT), could not benefit from intra-brand competition for Ericsson products, as the distributor enjoyed a monopolistic position for the distribution of Ericsson solutions in New Caledonia. This meant that lower prices for these products were completely illusory. What's more, if a new entrant wished to offer Ericsson products, the exclusive import rights would definitively close the doors to the market. Of course, it's impossible to know at this stage whether or not competitors will be able to enter this market in the short, medium or long term, given the high level of technical expertise required. That said, isn't it the role of a competition authority to ensure that market access is not foreclosed?

13. **Weak economic argument.** Finally, it seems to us that the economic efficiency argument is weak when it comes to exclusive import agreements. Firstly, the former text of the French *Competition Code*, as well as the equivalent texts in mainland France and New Caledonia, authorize companies to save an exclusive import agreement provided they can demonstrate efficiency gains in the form of economic progress. To date, however, no company has been able to demonstrate this since the adoption of the Lurel law and the installation of the New Caledonian Authority in 2018. Secondly, there is no reliable economic literature on the subject, so authors in favor of deleting the text often cite the same studies. Finally, deleting the text is not in line with history. There is currently intense debate about the real contribution of the more economic approach.

---

24 Montet Ch. and Venayre F., "Coût de la vie en outre-mer et politique de concurrence en Polynésie française", *in Mélanges offerts à Louis Vogel*, LexisNexis e.a., 2024, p. 303 et seq.

25 And above all, much lower than in French Polynesia. For example, EURopean Employment Services reports that the average cost of many consumer goods is much lower than in Polynesia. For example, a salad costs an average of 1.63 euros in Malta, whereas the average price in Tahiti at the beginning of 2025 is 4.19 euros. For further comparison: https://eures.europa.eu/living-and-working/living-and-working-conditions-europe/livingand-working-conditions-malta_fr (consulted 08/01/2025). What's more, Malta hardly suffers from the problem of distance from mainland Europe, being only 2 hours by plane from Barcelona or Milan and 2 hours 50 minutes from Paris. This is a far cry from the twenty hours or so that separate Tahiti from the metropolitan capital of Paris. This necessarily leads to a much lower cost of importing products.

26 Institut de la statistique de la Polynésie française (ISPF), coll. Point Etudes et Bilans, 2023, quoted by Montet Ch. and Venayre F., "Coût de la vie en outre-mer et politique de concurrence en Polynésie française", *op. cit.*

27 ACNC, decision No. 2024-PAC-04 relating to practices implemented in the telecommunications network equipment sector in New Caledonia.

Nobel Prize-winning economist Jean Tirole himself urges the authorities not to be tetanized by the risk of error.[28]

II. Freeing up resources

14. **APC's limited resources.** It is hardly original to point out that the resources of competition authorities are limited and weak in comparison with the means held by certain companies. The APC's budget is only around one hundred million Pacific francs, and its staff is very small. As for the investigation department, which is the heart of a competition authority's reactor, it is made up of just 6 rapporteurs, including 1 general rapporteur and 1 deputy general rapporteur.[29]These figures don't carry much weight when put into perspective with the sales figures achieved by Fenua's major companies. Local newspapers and radio stations[30] reveal that the Wane group generates sales of 53 billion Pacific francs[31], Air Tahiti Nui 35.4 billion, Carrefour Polynésie 28.9 billion and the EDT-Engie group 28.5 billion. Clearly, with such huge companies, not only do information asymmetries come into play, but above all, financial and economic resources make investigations more difficult. Put another way, detecting anticompetitive practices is not easy. Firstly, competition investigations take time. The French Competition Authority, for example, which has a much larger staff and immense experience in the field, takes an average of 2 to 3 years to reach a decision on conviction. And some cases take even longer! Secondly, the culture of non-competition in French overseas territories leads to difficulties in deterrence and detection. Whether in French Polynesia New Caledonia, the clemency procedure has so far not met with the expected success.[32] The last major cartel case, that of the undertakers, dates back to 2022 and was not detected thanks to a leniency application.[33]Consequently, the low rate of anticompetitive practice cases is not due to a lack of will on the part of the APC, but to the requirement of standards

---

28 Tirole J., *Competition Policy in Digital Age, Keynote Speech at the "Shaping Competition Policy in the Era of Digitization"*, conference, January 17, 2019, quoted by Prieto C., "Sources économiques du droit de la concurrence: quelle efficacité?", *CCC*, 2020, n° 6, dossier 3.

29 See APC, *Annual Report 2023: A level playing field for sustainable growth*, 2024, p. 10.

30 These eloquent figures were disclosed in 2019 in the general press to which we refer, for lack of access to the accounts of the companies mentioned. See https://www.radio1.pf/atn-carrefour-et-edt-engie-restent-les-poidslourds-de-leconomie-locale/ (accessed 08/01/2025).

31 By the end of 2010, this group accounted for almost 12% of Polynesian GDP. See https://la1ere.francetvinfo.fr/polynesie/combien-pese-groupe-wane-polynesie-501389.html (consulted on 08/01/2025).

32 The difference with the EU is striking. For example, in 2020, 8 out of 10 cases were identified and judged thanks to the leniency procedure. Today, half of all cases continue to come from the leniency procedure. See Guersent O., " Le droit de la concurrence est très efficace, mais trop lent dans le contexte du digital ", *Décideurs magazine* [online], December 16, 2024. Available at: https://www.decideurs-magazine.com/regulation-juridiques/60054olivier-guersent-le-droit-de-la-concurrence-est-tres-efficace-mais-trop-lent-dans-le-contexte-du-digital-ce-quine-veut-pas-dire-qu-on-arrete-de-l-appliquer.html (consulted on 08/01/2025). See for the Caledonian case: Chaiehloudj W. Le droit des pratiques anticoncurrentielles calédonien : des procédures diversifiées pour rétablir le jeu de la concurrence", *Concurrences*, 2022, n° 4, n° 109579. For a broader perspective: Chaiehloudj W., "Réguler la concurrence : contexte insulaire et expérience calédonienne", *CCC*, 2025, forthcoming.

33 APC, decision No. 2022-PAC-01 of September 5, 2022 relating to practices implemented in the funeral services sector, *see also, Alain Ronzano, Polynésie française : L'Autorité polynésienne de la concurrence fait le ménage dans le secteur des pompes funèbres en sanctionnant sévèrement une entente horizontale de prix (HPP Funéraire...), September 5, 2022, Concurrences N° 4-2022, Art. N° 110025, www.concurrences.com/110025*

of proof to arrive at the qualification of a practice and a decision that will not be censured by the reviewing courts. What's more, abuse of dominance cases, which require the delimitation of a relevant market, the carrying out of precise econometric studies and the implementation of complex economic tests, are also very difficult to handle.[34]

15. **David versus Goliath.** In view of the above, the argument that

> *if some officials support this type of per se sanction [the prohibition of exclusive import agreements], it's probably because they are less demanding in terms of case processing and ['] they give the impression of sustained administrative activity in the service of the public[s]".*[35]

16. seems to us to be a very harsh and somewhat ideological argument. For this argument is totally reversible and, above all, ignores the reality of an authority's institutional life. Above all, it overlooks the fact that, in this agonistic world, a competition authority is a David trying to expose the illegal practices of many Goliaths! It's also forgetting that, in a world where information asymmetry benefits companies, ways have had to be found to make them more accountable. Wasn't it because of the limited resources of competition authorities – and not to give a sense of activity – that companies were required to self-assess and carry out their own diagnosis of the behaviors they plan to adopt on the market?[36] What's more, in the case of exclusive import agreements, the now-defunct text did not disarm companies, since they were still able to provide evidence of the efficiency gains generated by the disputed agreement. If companies in mainland France and New Caledonia have so far been unable to demonstrate such gains, isn't this an important indication of the harmfulness of the practice?[37]

III. Lack of experience

17. **Common sense.** The last argument does not require very substantial development, since it appeals to simple common sense. How can we draw a lesson from the harmfulness of the prohibition of exclusive import agreements for the Polynesian economy when the text has never been applied and it is therefore impossible to know what impact it would have had in terms of free competition?

---

34 The last abuse of dominance case to date is one that has not yet been dealt with on the merits. See APC, decision No. 2023-PAC-01 of March 31, 2023 relating to a request for protective measures submitted by Viti for practices implemented in the telecommunications sector, concerning roaming services in remote archipelagos. This decision was confirmed by the Paris Court of Appeal. See CA Paris, Pôle 5, Ch. 7, July 6, 2023, No. RG 23/06177.

35 Montet Ch. and Venayre F., "Coût de la vie en outre-mer et politique de concurrence en Polynésie française", *op. cit.* p. 312.

36 Lasserre B., "Concurrence et bien public à travers la *compliance*", *Frison-Roche* M.-A. (dir.), *Régulation, Supervision, Compliance*, Dalloz, 2017, p. 35.

37 For our part, we consider that the rise of "meta-interests", such as sustainability, could lead to an agreement being saved. For example, if an exclusive import agreement leads to environmental protection or positive social effects for employees, such an agreement could be saved. See Chaiehloudj W., "Les avancées du droit européen de la concurrence et des droits étrangers à l'aune de la durabilité", *in* Chaiehloudj W., Mestre J. and Dupouy S. (dir.), *La durabilité et le droit économique*, LexisNexis, 2025, forthcoming.
Cass. 1re civ, May 17, 2023, No. 21-24106, *Monster Energy*.

18. **Monopolistic position of the distributor.** Clearly, import exclusivity is very similar to "territorial exclusivity", which is monitored by the competition authorities.[38] In the insular context, this import exclusivity is bound to lead to a monopolistic position for the distributor, since intra-brand competition is totally foreclosed by the agreement. What's more, as explained above, inter-brand competition is often very weak, making it impossible to compensate for the loss of intra-brand competition. In view of these factors, shouldn't we leave room for experimentation? Wouldn't a return to prohibition allow new competitive pressures to emerge in Polynesia?

*

* *

19. **Conclusion.** In the final analysis, the decision to remove the prohibition of exclusive import agreements from the Polynesian legal system is a poor political decision, incomprehensible in several respects. Incomprehensible, firstly, because the lifetime of the text will not have allowed it to be applied, nor the effect it would have had on Fenua's economy and consumer well-being to be known. Secondly, it is incomprehensible because this choice ignores the constraints of competition authorities. Deciding to sanction these agreements *per se* seems to us to be a sound competition policy in view of the ultramarine context, and allows us to take into account the reality of APC's financial resources. Lastly, it is incomprehensible because the *per se* prohibition did not close the door to economic analysis, insofar as companies remained free to justify the conclusion of agreements by proving efficiency gains.

20. Last but not least, there may well be an additional, more or less anecdotal argument based on the notion of public policy. In one case, *Monster Energy*,[39] the Cour de cassation recently overturned a ruling by the Paris Court of Appeal for lack of legal basis, holding that in rejecting the exequatur of an award, the Paris court had not given sufficient reasons for its decision. Specifically, the Court of Appeal had not sufficiently explained how the award was contrary to public policy, i.e. competition law, and specifically in this case article L. 420-2-1 of the French *Commercial Code*. Should this article be recognized as a component of French public policy in the international arena, the Polynesian exception would appear even more as an anomaly that the legislator of Fenua would be well advised to remedy. *Errare humanum est perseverare diabolicum...*

---

38 Buy F., "Clause d'exclusivité territoriale", *in* Buy F., Lamoureux M., Mestre J. and Roda J.-Ch. (dir.), *Les principales clauses des contrats d'affaires*, LGDJ, 2018, p. 349.

39 Cass. 1re civ, May 17, 2023, No. 21-24106, *Monster Energy*.

Integrating Sustainable Development into Polynesian Competition Law: Between Uncertainty and Opportunity

Hervé Raimana Lallemant-Moe[*]
University of French Polynesia
International Law Centre Lyon 3

E'ere roa atu te Nātura i te hō'ē faufa'a mate, e ao rā e tuatāpapa, e ao māramarama, te puna o te 'ite iā 'oe iho 'e ia vetahi 'ē. E tuatāpapa i te Nātura, nō te 'ite ïa iā 'oe – For Polynesians, nature is not an inert, inanimate object but, on the contrary, a world to be deciphered, a world of meaning, the source of a better understanding of oneself and others. To decipher nature is to understand ourselves.[1]

1. This excerpt from a speech by the Vice-President of French Polynesia, Eliane Tevahitua, on the 21st June 2023 shows just how important the environment is to Polynesians. The situation is different for competition law, a subject introduced very recently and of an exogenous nature for Polynesians, as demonstrated by the stormy debates that followed its contemporary introduction.[2]

2. The combination of the two is obviously out of the ordinary for Polynesian law, although it should be pointed out that regardless of recent developments in national

---

* Hervé Raimana Lallemant-Moe is doctor in public law and associate researcher at the Governance and Island Development Laboratory (University of French Polynesia) and at the International Law Centre (Lyon III)

1 For speeches by members of the government of French Polynesia: https://www.presidence.pf/.

2 Cabon Sarah Marie. *Le Droit de la concurrence en Polynésie française et dans les petites économies insulaires du Pacifique : Bilan et perspectives*, ed. LexisNexis, 11 November 2018.

and European law, the question of the interaction between competition and sustainable development has been considered by legal writers for a very long time.[3] It is clear, however, that at first sight the market logic seems difficult to reconcile with the achievement of general interest objectives such as environmental protection. It is for this reason that we need to take a closer look at the territorial collectivity of French Polynesia and its particularities in terms of competition law and environmental law.

3. French Polynesia is an autonomous overseas collectivity (COM), a category of territorial collectivity created by constitutional law No. 2003-276 of 28 March 2003 on the decentralised organisation of the Republic[4]). Its current autonomous status was established by the amended Organic Statutes Act No. 2004-192 of 27 February 2004. The main consequences of this regime are the application of the principle of legislative speciality, a specific internal normative system and a division of powers between the State, the collectivity of French Polynesia and the communes.[5] It has also been an Overseas Country and Territory (OCT) since the 1957 Treaty of Rome, and is now governed by articles 198 to 204 of the Treaty on the Functioning of the European Union (TFEU). The main effects are that Polynesians are granted European citizenship (because of their French citizenship), that Polynesia is not part of the European territory, and that secondary European Union legislation does not apply there.[6] In general international law, it is a non-self-governing territory attached to the French "administering power". This designation is based on United Nations General Assembly resolutions 66/265 (I) of 14 December 1946 and 67/265 of 17 May 2013. This status leads to an annual report by the Special Committee on the Situation with regard to the Implementation of the Declaration on the Granting of Independence to Colonial Countries and Peoples, as well as an annual resolution by the United Nations General Assembly.[7] Although other territorial collectivities are also COMs, French Polynesia is the most autonomous collectivity within the Republic, alongside New Caledonia, which benefits from a specific constitutional regime. French Polynesia has jurisdiction in principle, whereas the other two entities have jurisdiction by virtue of their status, which can be found in articles 14 and 43 of the aforementioned 2004 organic law.

4. With this law, competition law – with the exception of the provisions of criminal law, criminal procedure, contentious administrative procedure, those relating to the guarantees of public freedoms and foreign policy – comes under the jurisdiction of the country. Articles 7 and 14 of the 2004 statutory organic law confirm that the country has jurisdiction in this area. In French Polynesia, competition law has taken shape through the creation of a Polynesian Competition Code by

---

[3] Idot L., "Environnement et droit communautaire de la concurrence", *JCP G*, 1995.

[4] Art. 74 of the Constitution

[5] Moyrand Alain and Lallemant-Moe Hervé Raimana, *Introduction à l'étude des institutions politiques et administratives de la Polynésie française*, 2e éd. ed. Créaprint, September 2020.

[6] Pastorel Jean-Paul, "Les relations entre l'Union européenne et son outre-mer : entre intégration et spécificité juridique", *Revue du droit public*, 2018, n° 3, p. 823.

[7] Lallemant-Moe Hervé Raimana, "Clearing the Path to Decolonization with Pragmatism and Agility in a Global Pandemic Context: the Case of French Polynesia", *CLJP*, 2022, No. 27, p. 13 et seq.

local laws No. 2015-2 of 23 February 2015[8] and No. 2015-4 of 14 April 2015.[9] Inspired by the national model, Polynesian competition law,[10] the aforementioned Law of the Country No. 2015-2 entrusted the Polynesian Competition Authority[11] (APC) with the implementation and management of Polynesian competition law, designed to ensure the proper functioning of markets for the benefit of consumers, through three types of missions: an advisory role (competitive diagnosis of draft regulations and analysis of the operation of any economic sector, at the request of the Polynesian public authorities or on its own initiative, in order to propose the necessary improvements); preventive control of structures (industrial and commercial mergers and control of commercial development); and control of the practices implemented by economic players with repressive powers to punish anti-competitive practices (illegal agreements and abuse of dominant position).[12]

5. Since the entry into force of law No. 77-772 of 12 July 1977 relating to the organisation of French Polynesia, French Polynesia has had full jurisdiction over environmental law – with the exception of provisions relating to criminal law, criminal procedure and contentious administrative procedure, those relating to the guarantees of public freedoms and foreign policy (including the application in domestic law of international commitments) reserved for the State by article 74 of the Constitution and by article 14 of the statutory organic law No. 2004-192 of 27 February 2004 on the autonomous status of French Polynesia[13] – the country adopted an *Environmental Code for French Polynesia* in 2003.[14] The *Environmental Code* in force at national level is therefore not applicable on Polynesian territory, subject to the powers of the State in matters of defence, contentious administrative procedure, criminal law and procedure, public safety and order (in particular the police and safety of maritime traffic), foreign policy and its own administrative organisation.

6. Although Polynesian law – including competition law and environmental law – remains subject to the hierarchy of national standards, the overseas collectivities (COM), including French Polynesia, are organised in a special way. As a result, the legal regime applicable to them is different, in part, from that which governs France. The special nature of the COMs is justified by the fact that these entities have their

---

8 Loi du pays n° 2015-2 du 23 février 2015 relative à la concurrence, published in extenso in the *Journal officiel*, 2015, n° 8 NS du 23 février 2015, p. 234, in the "Lois du pays" section.

9 Loi du pays n° 2015-4 du 14 avril 2015 portant réglementation des pratiques commerciales, published in extenso in the *Journal officiel*, 2015, n° 17 NS du 14 avril 2015, p. 450, in the "Lois du pays" section.

10 Moyrand Alain, "Polynésie : La révolution concurrentielle serait-elle en marche ?", *Concurrences*, 2014, n° 4-2014, art. n° 69133 ; Retterer Stéphane et Troianiello Antonino, " Antitrust Regimes in the Pacific Region - Le droit polynésien de la concurrence : un premier bilan de l'Autorité polynésienne de la concurrence ", *Concurrences*, 2018, n° 4-2018, art. n° 88089, p. 19-54 ; CABON Sarah-Marie, MONTET Christian. et VENAYRE Florent (éd.), *Le Droit de la concurrence en Polynésie française et dans les petites économies insulaires : Bilan et perspectives*, LexisNexis, 2018, 270 p.

11 Available at: https://www.autorite-concurrence.pdf/.

12 Merot Jacques, Sims Rods, Zoude-le-Berre Aurélie, Healy Deborah, Marchal Tehono and Simpson Robin, "Antitrust Regimes in the Pacific Region", *Concurrences*, 2018, n° 4-2018, art. n° 88089, p. 19-54.

13 Peres Jean, "Application des lois et règlements en Polynésie française", *RJP/NZACL YEARBOOK*, 2004.

14 Order No. 1843 CM of 15 December 2003 codifying territorial environmental regulations, creating the *Environmental Code of French Polynesia* and amending the *Planning Code of French Polynesia*.

own "specific interests".[15] This is why each COM has its own specific legal system, bringing together standards tailored to its needs. This difference is perceptible at all levels of the hierarchy of norms. Although the constitutional framework applies throughout the territory of the French Republic, it is clear that in the overseas territories certain provisions of the Constitution are organised differently and therefore produce legal effects that are not identical to those prevailing in national law.[16]

7. Coming back to the combination of sustainable development and competition, as demonstrated in the Autorité de la concurrence's press release of 27 May 2024 on the Authority's informal guidelines on sustainable development, the relationship between competition law and environmental protection is not necessarily antithetical. However, the situation is very different in French Polynesia, where competition law only came into being in 2015 and is still struggling to be fully understood by public authorities, economic players and users, almost 10 years after its introduction, and it is questionable whether incorporating the concept of sustainability into Polynesian competition law is realistic.

8. While the APC could already take this into account in its guidelines and decision-making practice (I), regulatory integration within the *Competition Code* seems essential to produce real effects in terms of environmental protection and virtuous management of competition (II).

I. The Polynesian Competition Authority as a potential driving force for the integration of sustainable development into Polynesian competition law

9. While the APC, a body separate from the Autorité nationale de la concurrence (A), can theoretically incorporate sustainable development into its decision-making practice, the step has not yet been fully taken by Polynesia's only independent administrative authority (AAI) (B).

A. *A player distinct and autonomous from the Autorité nationale de la concurrence (ADLC) and its guidelines*

10. The APC is a Polynesian AAI and is therefore distinct from national AAIs. These local AAIs are not subject to Organic Law No 2017-54 of 20 January 2017 on independent administrative authorities and independent public authorities, or to Law No 2017-55 of 20 January 2017 on the general status of independent administrative authorities and independent public authorities, or to the jurisdictional decisions relating thereto, unless one undertakes an arbitrary negation of Article 74 of the Constitution and the Statutory Organic Law of 2004. The Constitutional Council reiterated this in particular in its decision No. 2017-746 DC of 19 January 2017 on the aforementioned organic law, clearly differentiating the category of an: "independent administrative authority or an independent public authority created by the [E]tat".

---

[15] French Constitution, art. 47 C.

[16] For example, derogations from articles 34 and 37 of the Constitution; territorial preference in terms of employment and protection of land ownership.

11. The Polynesian AAIs are thus exclusively governed by Article 30-I of the aforementioned Organic Statute Law, which states that :

> *I. – French Polynesia may, for the exercise of its powers, create independent administrative authorities, with or without legal personality, for the purpose of carrying out regulatory missions. / The act provided for in article 140, known as the "loi du pays" creating an independent administrative authority, defines the guarantees of independence, expertise and continuity. / It may grant it, by way of derogation from the provisions of Articles 64, 67, 89 to 92 and 95, a regulatory power as well as the powers of investigation, control, recommendation, dispute resolution and sanction, strictly necessary for the accomplishment of its missions. / It determines the budgetary and accounting system of the independent administrative authority, in compliance with the guarantees set out in the second paragraph of this I. / II. – No person may be appointed as a member of an independent administrative authority if, during the year prior to his appointment, he has held the office of President or member of the Government of French Polynesia or the office of representative to the Assembly of French Polynesia. / III. – The accounts of the independent administrative authority are submitted for audit to the territorial audit chamber. They are communicated to the Assembly of French Polynesia and to the President of French Polynesia.*

12. The APC is currently the only AAI in French Polynesia and is mainly based on the *Competition Code*. This source was created pursuant to the aforementioned Article 30-I (para. 2) through the amended Local Law No. 2015-2 of 23 February 2015 on competition and the amended Order No. 1347 CM of 10 September 2015 creating the "Orders" section of the *French Polynesia Competition Code*. The rules of procedure approved by the Council of Ministers by Order No. 107 CM of 23 January 2019 are also in force.

13. With regard to the State's powers under Article 14 of the 2004 Statutory Organic Law – in particular as regards the investigation of offences and the organisation of the courts – reference may be made to Order No. 2017-157 of 9 February 2017 extending and adapting to French Polynesia certain provisions of Book IV of the *Commercial Code* relating to competition controls and sanctions, Law 2018-643 of 23 July 2018 on competition controls and sanctions in French Polynesia and New Caledonia and Decree 2018-880 of 11 October 2018 implementing Articles 10 and 11 of Order 2017-157 of 9 February 2017 on appeals against decisions of the Polynesian Competition Authority.

14. The APC is therefore quite distinct from the National Competition Authority (ADLC). The fact that the National Authority has passed unharmed under the control of the Constitutional Council, which has validated its organisation, procedure and sanctioning powers,[17] in no way implies that the organisation of the APC must be

---

17 Cons. const. 12 October 2012, No. 2012-280 QPC. See also Sorinas Sergio and Colmet Daage Grégoire, "QPC - Retrait autorisation : Le Conseil constitutionnel confirme la constitutionnalité du pouvoir de retrait des autorisations de concentration et valide l'organisation interne de l'Autorité de la concurrence (Canal Plus)", *Concurrences*, 12 October 2012, No. 1-2013, art. No. 50592, p. 140-141.

identical to that of the National Competition Authority or be subject to national law. These authorities are not governed by the same legal foundations, and the study of the principles specific to the AAI must always be carried out through the prism of article 74 of the Constitution and article 30-I of the statutory organic law of 2004. It should also be noted that the *national Code of Civil Procedure* is not applicable in French Polynesia, as the local authority has primary jurisdiction in this case.[18]

15. The APC is thus different from the ADLC, it is not subject to the regulations that apply to this national AAI, is not obliged to follow its decision-making practice (particularly in relation to sustainable development), but a contrario can draw inspiration from it, especially as the APC's legal system leaves it considerable room for manoeuvre.

B. *Environmental integration through the APC's residual regulatory powers possible but not yet achieved*

16. Under national law, there is a residual regulatory power attributed to the AAIs. The Constitutional Council has stated that it is possible for "the legislature to entrust to an authority other than the Prime Minister the task of laying down [...] standards enabling a law to be implemented " [19] if they "concern only measures of limited scope in terms of both their scope and their content"[20] . A similar mechanism can be found in the 3e paragraph of article 30-I of the 2004 statutory organic law for the Polynesian AAIs, which specifies, however, that these derogations must be established in a law of the country. The aforementioned paragraph stipulates that: "It may grant it, by way of derogation from the provisions of articles 64, 67, 89 to 92 and 95, a regulatory power as well as the powers of investigation, control, recommendation, dispute resolution and sanction, strictly necessary for the accomplishment of its missions".

17. In French Polynesia, the APC may adopt its own rules of procedure, guidelines and press releases. However, in accordance with Article LP 610-11 of the French *Competition Code*, the APC's rules of procedure must be approved by an order issued by the Council of Ministers. This amendment stemming from Law 2018-31 of 9 August 2018 amending the legislative part of the *Competition Code* has considerably reduced the autonomous regulatory power of the APC by making the adoption of this AAI's internal regulations subject to the will of the Government of French Polynesia.

18. However, the guidelines remain. They are based on Article LP 630-1 of the French *Competition Code*, which states that :

> *The Polynesian Competition Authority draws up guidelines which specify, in particular, with a view to informing economic players, the scope and procedures for proceedings brought before it and, within this framework, the definitions and criteria for analysing the situations submitted to it,*

---

18 Gourdon Pascal and Marchand Johan, *Code de procédure civile de la Polynésie française*, ed. Polydroit, 2017.

19 Cons. const., 18 Sept. 1986, No. 86-217 DC.

20 Cons. const. 17 Jan. 1989, No. 89-248 DC.

as well as the methods for determining the penalties that may be imposed by it. / These guidelines are discussed by the college and then published. Any interested party may invoke them in a meeting with the AMF.

19. These guidelines currently only exist for mergers[21] and for the leniency procedure.[22] Logically, they do not include any elements relating to sustainability, sustainable development or environmental protection. In addition, there are still no guidelines for sanctions within the APC, which could potentially include environmental criteria. Within the European Union, on 21 December 2021, the European Commission adopted new guidelines on State aid for climate, environmental protection and energy, setting out the conditions under which State aid granted by Member States in the fields of climate, environmental protection and energy may be considered compatible with the internal market and the criteria applied by the Commission when examining aid provided by Member States in these fields.[23] It is true that an overly strict application of competition law can potentially handicap projects from economic players that are nevertheless of strong general interest, particularly in terms of environmental protection.[24]

20. In terms of *soft law*, the APC has not produced a specific press release on sustainable development or environmental protection, like the ADLC and its press release on the Authority's informal guidelines on sustainable development of 21 December 2023. It is true that it is often in this way that the notion of sustainable development or environmental protection is incorporated into decision-making practice in competition law. For example, on 18 November 2021, the Commission adopted a Communication entitled "A Competition Policy Fit for New Challenges"[25] , which focuses on supporting the recovery from the health crisis, the contribution of competition policy to a green and digital single market and improving the resilience of the single market.[26]

21. Although the APC has not adopted a communiqué directly linked to the integration of the environment into its decision-making practice, there are signs of this in the Polynesian AAI's most recent activity reports. For example, in the 2021 report, the President of the APC emphasises that: "In addition to the dematerialisation of our referral and notification procedures, the APC is committed to taking into account the environmental dimension and issues in its opinions and decisions", including in the same report an article dedicated to "Polynesian competition law and environmental considerations".[27]

---

21 Deliberation No. 2017-DC-06 of 4 October 2017 on amending the rules of procedure of the Polynesian Competition Authority and the guidelines on the scope and procedure of merger control; Deliberation No. 2019-DC-08 of 9 May 2019 amending the guidelines on the scope and procedure of merger control.

22 Deliberation No. 2019-DC-11 of 27 August 2019 adopting the guidelines for the Polynesian leniency programme.

23 Ronzano Alain, "Réforme : La Commission européenne révise les lignes directrices concernant les aides d'Etat au climat, à la protection de l'environnement et à l'énergie, et accorde un sursis au gaz naturel", *Concurrences*, 21 December 2021, No. 1-2022, art. No. 104201.

24 Silicani Jean-Ludovic, "Environnement et développement durable - Comment concilier le droit de la concurrence et le développement durable", *Energie - Environnement - Infrastructures*, April 2024, No. 4, reference 4.

25 COM(2021) 713 final, 18 Nov. 2021.

26 Idot Laurence, "Une politique de concurrence adaptée aux nouveaux défis", *Europe*, January 2022, No. 1.

27 APC, *Rapport annuel 2021 : Relever les potentiels, Autorité polynésienne de la concurrence*, 2022.

The aforementioned sentence from the APC chairwoman is reproduced identically in the 2022 report[28] but disappears from the 2023 report,[29] without having been followed up in any case.

22. This reluctance to unilaterally incorporate environmental criteria into the APC's decision-making practice seems to be directly linked to the fact that this Polynesian AAI is seeking above all to ensure that the rules of competition law are fully understood within a territory with a historically highly administered economy. As the APC's annual *advocacy campaigns* demonstrate,[30] competition law is not yet fully understood in Polynesia. Furthermore, with six decisions on anti-competitive practices in 10 years, only one of which resulted in sanctions, it can be considered that the APC's decision-making practice and guidelines are not yet fully stabilised.

*

* *

23. Although the APC is theoretically capable of incorporating environmental considerations into its decision-making practice, it is nonetheless extremely cautious about doing so in practice. Its relative youth and its difficulties in gaining full acceptance of the basic rules of competition law in French Polynesia certainly motivate its desire to concentrate, for the time being, on the hard core of the rules applicable in this case. It therefore seems that the quickest way to make non-economic factors such as sustainable development applicable is through legislation.

II. The need to amend the Polynesian Competition Code to truly integrate environmental protection

24. While it is possible to rely on interpretations of provisions already existing in Polynesian competition law (A), salvation seems to come above all from an explicit amendment to the *Competition Code* (B).

A. *The unused interpretation of existing provisions of the Competition Code*

25. Although competition law does not necessarily include explicit references to the environment in its rules, there is still room for interpretation. For example, Article 101 of the Treaty on the Functioning of the European Union (TFEU) states that, regarding cartels, agreements or concerted practices may be declared valid provided that they: "contribute to improving the production or distribution of goods or to promoting technical or economic progress, while allowing consumers a fair share of the resulting benefit [...]".

---

28 APC, *Annual Report 2022: Ensuring a level playing field for business*, 2023.

29 APC, *Annual Report 2023: A level playing field for sustainable growth*, 2024.

30 "Trois jours pour comprendre la concurrence", *Tahiti Infos*, 11 January 2023.

26. For some authors, the interpretation of the article may already make it possible to integrate possible environmental considerations, attached to "non-economic" policy factors, into competition law, because environmental benefits can be included in consumer welfare.[31]

27. In French Polynesia, although the creation of the *Competition Code* was not intended to take account of the environmental perspective, certain provisions – following the example of European Union law – potentially make it possible to link environmental protection to the notion of economic progress. Article LP 200-5 of the aforementioned Code states that the following measures are excluded from the scope of prohibitions relating to cartels and abuses of dominant positions:

> *Can justify that they have the effect of securing economic progress, including the creation or maintenance of employment, and that they allow consumers a fair share of the resulting benefit, without affording the undertakings concerned the possibility of eliminating competition in respect of a substantial part of the products in question. Such practices shall impose restrictions on competition only to the extent that they are indispensable to the attainment of this objective of progress.*

28. The notion of "economic progress" could be linked to the need to avoid negative externalities. A negative externality occurs when economic activity imposes costs on stakeholders who are not directly involved. For example, a factory's polluting emissions can affect air quality and the health of neighbouring residents, which can engage the liability of the company in charge of the factory. The risks of infringement of human rights and the environment constitute a problem of negative externality, in other words a debt without spontaneous compensation.[32] It might therefore be thought that article LP 200-5 of the *Competition Code* is a way of introducing an environmental aspect, if it contributes to economic progress.

29. In addition, and in the same vein, in the context of in-depth reviews of mergers (art. LP 310-6) or commercial development operations (art. LP 320-3-1), it is specified in both cases that the Polynesian Competition Authority: "shall assess whether the operation contributes to economic progress in a manner sufficient to offset the harm to competition". Here again, the provisions are sufficiently broad to make it possible to include environmental protection as a sufficient contribution to offsetting expectations about competition. The inclusion of this environmental aspect for the merger mechanism in French Polynesia is realistic in the sense that non-economic elements had already been considered by the APC in the past, during the Covid-19 pandemic in terms of public health. In a press release dated 16 April 2020, the APC stated that:

> *French Polynesia already has derogation rules provided for in the Competition Code, which could, moreover in these exceptional circumstances, be implemented in the interests of the economy, businesses and*

---

[31] Holmes Simon, Middelschulte Dirk and Snoep Martin (eds.), "Competition Law, Climate change & Environmental sustainability", *Concurrences*, 2021, 466 p.

[32] Deffains Bruno, "Pour une lecture économique du devoir de vigilance", *La Semaine juridique - Entreprise et Affaires*, 3 August 2023, nos. 31-35, p. 1242.

> *citizens/consumers. The Autorité encourages companies to inform it of any plans they may have in this area, to ensure that they are compatible with competition rules and the general interest.*

30. A transposition in terms of sustainable development would thus be entirely possible, even if it should be pointed out that despite the aforementioned communiqué, no merger decision has taken this opening into account in terms of public health and the fight against the Covid-19 pandemic. While incentives often give way to a tougher approach to integrating non-economic criteria,[1] has not yet taken this first step in French Polynesia.

31. It should also be noted that based on article LP 620-4 of the French *Competition Code:*

> *The Authority may issue an opinion on any matter concerning competition. It may also recommend that the Government of French Polynesia implement the measures necessary to improve the competitive operation of the markets. The Authority's opinions and recommendations are published in the Official Gazette of French Polynesia and on its website.*

32. This power of self-referral could be used to better define the integration of environmental issues into the law in French Polynesia and, a fortiori, to push for certain regulatory reforms.

B. *The efficient solution offered by explicitly incorporating sustainable development into the* Competition Code

33. While most of the world's competition authorities have made the political choice of vehemently attacking the anti-competitive behaviour most damaging to sustainable development by mobilising the entire procedural and repressive arsenal at their disposal,[2] is still not the case in French Polynesia. Regardless of the context and the willingness or lack of willingness of this AAI to act, it should be pointed out that the Autorité nationale de la concurrence, the other competition authorities in Europe, or quite simply the competent bodies in this area within the European Union have much more freedom in the interpretation of texts and their application.[3] The autonomous regulatory power of the APC is in fact only residual and is very much framed by the institutions of French Polynesia and by the provisions of the *Competition Code.*

34. One way of ensuring the integration of environmental criteria into procedures falling within the remit of the APC is quite simply to amend the *Competition Code.* It is clear that this type of amendment – particularly in the area of substantive legislation – requires particularly close cooperation with Polynesian institutions, and more specifically with the ministry responsible for the economy and the

---

1 Chaiehloudj Walid, "Environnement et développement durable - Les incitations des autorités de concurrence", *Energie - Environnement - Infrastructures*, July 2024, No. 7, dossier 15.

2 Bettoni Lucas, "Droit de la concurrence - Les accords de durabilité ou la promotion du développement durable par le droit des ententes", *Contrats, concurrence, consommation*, March 2024, No. 3, study 3.

3 Bosco David, "Pratiques anticoncurrentielles - 'Porte ouverte' à l'Autorité de la concurrence pour les projets en lien avec le développement durable", *Contrats, concurrence, consommation*, juillet 2024, n° 7, comm. 118.

ministry responsible for the environment. In any event, it would be possible to incorporate the environmental criterion by means of a local law amending the following provisions of the *Competition Code*:

35. 1° Article LP 200-5 could be amended insofar as it distinguishes between practices that are not subject to articles LP 200-1 and LP 200-2 (anti-competitive practices). It could be provided a little more explicitly that certain public interest objectives, such as environmental protection, may be linked to the notion of economic progress.

36. 2° With regard to mergers, article LP. 310-1 states that: "Mergers likely to have a substantial effect on competition or to create a monopoly situation prejudicial to the interests of consumers are prohibited". An additional paragraph relating to the consideration of objectives of general interest – such as the environment – could be added, provided that an exception is not created making it too easy to escape this type of *ex ante* administrative control.

37. 3° The control of commercial developments – the Polynesian and New Caledonian exceptions only – is widely contested as a competition law mechanism[4] and is instead presented as regulation (at best), or even interventionism (at worst).[5] It is hard to see how the notions of sustainable development or environmental protection could be quickly and usefully integrated into this tool, unless the fact that: "The Authority may also ensure that the projects referred to in article LP. 320-1-1 meet spatial planning requirements" (art. LP 320-3-1, para. 3) by adding environmental requirements. As these aspects are not directly linked to the competitive analysis, this addition is not recommended, as APC officers are not intended to become experts in planning or environmental law in the strict sense of the term.

*

* *

38. The integration of environmental protection guidelines or the notion of sustainable development within Polynesian competition law is therefore largely feasible, with or without explicit normative amendment. However, French Polynesia, and more specifically the APC, will have to go beyond mere window-dressing, which could be likened to "*competition-washing*", aimed at making competition law more attractive to Polynesians by incorporating notions that are generally supported, such as environmental protection.

39. But it is undeniable that in competition law, the integration of sustainable development or the environment – or more generally of non-economic elements – cannot be considered as a simple fashion effect. Economic progress can indeed be found beyond the boundaries of market power, and even if the APC must

4 Venayre Florent, "Quelques interrogations relatives à la première sanction d'un défaut de notification d'aménagement commercial à Tahiti", *Revue Lamy de la concurrence*, n° 127, 1er mai 2023.

5 Destours Stéphane, "L'impossible contrôle juridictionnel des autorisations d'aménagement commercial par les autorités de concurrence du Pacifique au regard des principes du droit de la concurrence", *Revue Lamy de la concurrence*, 1er juillet 2023, n° 129.

continue to assert itself as a key player in French Polynesia, it is reassuring to note that this young AAI is part of global movements in the evolution of competition law.

40. We must now put our money where our mouth is. *A rave i te ohipa i te arutaimareva e te ture tata'ura'a mātete.*

Balancing Competition and Sustainability in Island Economies is Not Simply a "Greening" Exercise of Existing Policies

Dr Léopold Temoana Biardeau*
Government of French Polynesia
Member of the College of the Polynesian Competition Authority

Introduction

1. March 2025 marks the tenth anniversary of the competition law regime in French Polynesia, a major milestone in the history of competition policy in the Pacific. To mark the occasion, the Polynesian Competition Authority (APC) intends to take stock of achievements and challenges, while opening up the debate on cross-cutting issues, including the crucial issue of sustainable development. This theme is particularly relevant in island economies, which are subject to both structural constraints – dependence on imports, small markets, risks associated with climate change – and often concentrated issues of economic power.

2. This chapter aims to examine both the tensions and potential synergies between sustainable development and the notion of economic competition, by examining them in the context of island economies, with a particular focus on French Polynesia. To do so, it adopts a critical approach to these two concepts. Some

* Dr Léopold Temoana Biardeau is Interministerial Delegate for Climate and Sustainable Development and a member of the College of the Polynesian Competition Authority.

people believe that sustainable development is self-evident, or that all that is needed to stimulate 'green innovation is to focus on the dynamics of competition. However, certain analyses highlight the ambiguities and contradictions that characterise these concepts. The aim is therefore to explain why it may be necessary to deconstruct these concepts and to identify the possible misuses, instrumentalities or political compromises that restrict their effectiveness. The reservations expressed about sustainable development and competition are not intended as a blanket rejection of these two concepts, but as a means of gaining a better understanding of how they can be articulated, reinvented or, where necessary, reoriented.

I. Critical approaches to sustainable development and competition

A. *The concept of sustainable development: theoretical and critical foundations*

3. The concept of sustainable development was widely popularised by the 1987 Brundtland Report, *Our Common Future*, written by the World Commission on Environment and Development.[1] The report defines sustainable development as a process that "meets the needs of the present without compromising the ability of future generations to meet their own needs". Two principles are highlighted:
    1. priority to be given to the essential needs of the poorest;
    2. taking into account the ecological limits of technology and social organisation.
4. This functional definition was subsequently taken up in the Millennium Development Goals (MDGs), then in the Sustainable Development Goals (SDGs or SDG) adopted by the UN in 2015.
5. Despite this international recognition, analyses highlight the multiplicity of interpretations of the term "sustainable development". On the one hand, reformist approaches focus on technological innovation and green growth; on the other, more radical approaches denounce the fundamental unsustainability of the capitalist growth model. According to Redclift,[2] the tension between "development" (often associated with economic growth) and "sustainability" (referring to planetary limits) has never been satisfactorily resolved, making the concept difficult to apply.
6. Numerous studies have criticised the excessive semantic flexibility of sustainable development, which lends itself to a variety of rhetorical uses. Redclift[3] stresses the apparent incompatibility between the principles of ecological sustainability and the classic paradigm of industrial development. Brown[4] goes so far as to describe sustainable development as an "oxymoron", believing that capitalist economies,

---

1 UN WCED, *Our Common Future*, Oxford: Oxford University Press, 1987.

2 Redclift M., *Sustainable Development: Exploring the Contradictions*, Routledge, 2002.

3 *Ibid.*

4 Brown K., "Sustainable Adaptation: An Oxymoron?", *Climate and Development*, 2011, Vol. *3*, No. 1, pp. 21-31.

based on the perpetual quest for profits and increasing consumption, cannot truly integrate ecological constraints.

7. Moreover, this semantic flexibility opens the way to forms of recuperation by governments or companies seeking "green legitimisation without any real desire for transformation.[5] Büscher and Fletcher[6] describe this phenomenon as a strategy of "accumulation through conservation", where nature becomes a new field of economic valuation and legitimisation of potentially damaging practices. The rise of mechanisms such as carbon offsetting or "green finance" illustrates this possibility of *greenwashing*: private or public players put forward symbolic environmental actions, even though their business models or policies remain fundamentally extractive and, as a result, precarious.

8. Policies and projects described as "sustainable" are often based on market instruments, such as carbon markets or public-private partnerships aimed at "green growth". However, by commodifying natural resources, these instruments can have perverse effects: companies may prefer to buy "rights to polluterather than reduce their emissions at source.[7] Hickel[8] believes that the SDGs endorse economic growth and technological innovation as fundamental levers for development, without really taking into account the planet's physical limits and the urgent need to reduce energy consumption in rich countries.

9. Conceptually, Daly[9] distinguishes between "weak sustainability" and "strong sustainability": the former assumes that natural capital is substitutable for manufactured capital (e.g. planting trees or creating green roofs to compensate for deforestation), while the latter requires the preservation of essential ecosystem processes, which are deemed irreplaceable. In practice, the major institutional frameworks such as the SDGs are more akin to "weak sustainability",[10] since they rely essentially on economic growth and innovation as drivers of the transition, without however calling into question the very model of growth and consumption[11] inherent in capitalist productivism.

10. Finally, the geopolitical dimension is crucial: Escobar[12] shows that the discourse on sustainable development sometimes reproduces North-South asymmetries of power, where the expertise of the North is supposed to 'solve' the underdevelopment of the South, without taking full account of indigenous knowledge or past

---

5 Lohmann L., *Carbon Trading - A Critical Conversation on Climate Change, Privatisation and Power*, 2006.

6 Buscher B. and Fletcher R., "Accumulation by Conservation", *New Political Economy*, 2015, Vol. *20*, No. 2, pp. 273-298.

7 Lohmann L., *Carbon Trading - A Critical Conversation on Climate Change, Privatisation and Power*, *op. cit.*

8 Hickel J., "The Contradiction of the Sustainable Development Goals: Growth Versus Ecology on a Finite Planet", *Sustainable Development*, 2019, Vol. *27*, No. 5, pp. 873-884.

9 Daly H, E., "Toward some Operational Principles of Sustainable Development", *Ecological Economics*, 1990, Vol. 2, No. 1, pp. 1-6.

10 Spash, C. L, "Bulldozing Biodiversity: The Economics of Offsets and Trading-in Nature", *Biological Conservation*, 2015, Vol. *192*, p. 541-551.

11 Hickel J., "The Contradiction of the Sustainable Development Goals: Growth Versus Ecology on a Finite Planet", *op. cit.*

12 Escobar A., *Encountering Development: The Making and Unmaking of the Third World*, Princeton University Press, 1995.

and present colonial dynamics. Shiva[13] criticises, for example, the technocratic approaches of the "green revolution", which marginalise peasant farming practices. In this logic, sustainable development can sometimes be used as a cover for dispossession or concentration of land for the benefit of large industrial groups.[14] The result is that, in the absence of greater vigilance, "sustainable developmentcan be reduced to a consensual slogan supporting an essentially productivist model, to which a green varnish is applied.

11. Faced with the ambiguities we have just highlighted, adopting a critical approach to sustainable development is not just a theoretical exercise: it involves exploring the real conditions under which the concept is implemented and measuring the gap between its promises and its tangible results. While some believe that it is enough to adjust market mechanisms to reconcile growth and environmental preservation, others consider that critical examination is essential to avoid a form of political naivety and to reflect on other avenues for transformation. This does not prevent us from recognising that part of the sustainable development agenda remains useful, particularly when it comes to mobilising resources or developing indicators. But this agenda needs to be refined and supplemented by alternative approaches.

B. *The limits of sustainability driven by competition and the market*

12. In neoclassical economics, competition is often presented as a vector of economic efficiency and, by extension, as a potential lever for sustainability. In theory, "green innovation is stimulated by competition between firms, consumer pressure and regulation. However, a number of analyses point to structural contradictions between the competitive logic practised in market economies and environmental protection.

13. The work of Hickel and Kallis[15] shows that to date there is no empirical evidence of an absolute decoupling on a global scale between growth and its environmental impacts thanks to technological progress and efficiency gains. If this had been the case, we would have seen an overall reduction in greenhouse gas emissions or resource extraction concomitant with an increase in GDP. Even if certain industries turn out to be less polluting (renewable energies, digital economy), the rebound effects[16] – sometimes referred to as the Jevons Paradox – can lead to an increase in overall consumption, offsetting the efficiency gains.[17]

14. By stimulating production and consumption, market competition tends to reinforce this race for growth. Profit-maximising companies are constantly seeking to expand, gain market share and cut costs, even if this means outsourcing environmental costs. In the interests of short- or medium-term profitability, sustainability is often relegated to second place if it does not immediately contribute to the company's profitability.

---

13 Shiva V., *The Violence of the Green Revolution: Third World Agriculture, Ecology and Politics*, Zed Books, 1991.

14 Buscher B. and Fletcher R., "Accumulation by Conservation", *op. cit.*

15 Hickel J. and Kallis G., "Is Green Growth Possible?", *New Political Economy*, 2020, Vol. *25*, No. 4, pp. 469-486.

16 When a technology becomes more efficient (for example, a more fuel-efficient car), the cost of using it falls. This can encourage consumers to increase their use, leading to an overall increase in consumption and emissions.

17 Sorrell S., "Jevons' Paradox Revisited: The Evidence for Backfire from Improved Energy Efficiency", *Energy Policy*, 2009, Vol. *37*, No. 4, pp. 1456-1469.

15. Market mechanisms therefore require a strict regulatory framework to guide economic players towards more sober production and consumption patterns[18] and to internalise these negative externalities. A negative externality occurs when the activity of an economic agent imposes a cost on the community without being compensated. For example, an industry discharging its polluting effluent into a lagoon does not pay for the degradation of the marine ecosystem (pollution, damage to biodiversity, etc.).

16. In a globalised economy, competition encourages companies that can afford it to relocate their polluting activities where environmental regulations are less stringent, a phenomenon known as *pollution havens* or "environmental comparative advantage".
    - For example, a tuna processing company may choose to locate its production units in a country with lax discharge standards at sea, rather than in a jurisdiction with high wastewater treatment standards.
    - Pistor[19] notes that the flexibility of legislation and the possibility of regulatory arbitrage reduce the effective scope of climate and environmental protection policies. So even when one country or region adopts ambitious standards, emissions or environmental damage can simply be transferred elsewhere, eroding the effectiveness of regulation on a global scale.

17. This international mobility of capital and industrial activities complicates the implementation of coordinated sustainability policies. Island countries, often with limited administrative resources, find it difficult to impose and enforce binding standards in the face of multinationals capable of moving their investments to other territories. Conversely, when an island, country or region adopts more stringent environmental requirements, it risks seeing its attractiveness called into question in international competition based on cost reduction.

18. Faced with a growing demand for 'green products and services, companies may resort to misleading marketing strategies or weak labels in order to position themselves as 'sustainable' without significantly changing their production processes.
    - This is what is known as "competitive *greenwashing*": companies claim to have a superficial ecological commitment ("*eco-friendly* packaging, environmental slogans, etc.) to improve their image and win market share, while their actual activities continue to emit large quantities of pollutants or destroy ecosystems.
    - This phenomenon distorts competition to the detriment of players genuinely committed to reducing their environmental footprint (for example, using solar energy or circular economy practices), who see their efforts diluted by the overuse of green communication.

19. In the island tourism sector, for example, a hotel may advertise its "green certification" while continuing to overuse drinking water on an island subject to water stress, or failing to manage its waste properly. Without public control or rigorous labelling standards, this type of practice maintains an illusion of sustainability and misdirects demand, hindering the emergence of more virtuous models.

---

18 Spash C. L., "Bulldozing Biodiversity: The Economics of Offsets and Trading-in Nature", *op. cit.*

19 Pistor K., *The Code of Capital: How the Law Creates Wealth and Inequality*, Princeton University Press, 2019.

II. Competition and sustainability in island economies: prospects and renewal

A. *Competition, sustainability and the specific characteristics of island economies: the case of Polynesia and the Pacific*

20. Island economies, such as Polynesia and many Pacific nations in general, have structural characteristics that exacerbate the difficulties encountered in the areas of competition and sustainable development:

- Tightness of markets: A small market limits the scope for economies of scale and tends to encourage concentration.
- Heavy dependence on imports: Food, energy and the majority of consumer goods are often sourced from outside the region, exacerbating the problem of the cost of living and transport-related emissions.
- Increased exposure to climate risks: Atolls and low-lying islands are particularly vulnerable to rising sea levels, cyclones and climatic variations.[20]
- Fragile biodiversity: Island ecosystems are often endemic and highly sensitive to the introduction of invasive species or the over-exploitation of resources.

21. In this context, promoting sustainable development is as urgent as it is complex. The negative externalities are more obvious (overfishing, marine pollution, etc.), and the budgetary and regulatory room for manoeuvre may be limited.

22. Since 2015, Polynesia has had a competition authority, which has worked to combat anti-competitive practices (cartels, abuse of dominant position) and promote better market regulation. One of the stated objectives is to help reduce the cost of living (a major social issue), while promoting innovation and quality.

23. Yet environmental issues are not explicitly part of the CPA's traditional remit, which is primarily focused on maintaining healthy competition and protecting consumers in terms of price and choice. Some competition authorities around the world, however, are moving towards the explicit integration of sustainability objectives:

- France's Competition Authority, for example, issued a statement in May 2024 to support companies in their sustainable development projects, providing informal guidance on the compatibility of these projects with competition rules.[21]
- At European level, the guidelines on agreements between competitors now include a chapter devoted to the assessment of agreements pursuing sustainability objectives.[22]

---

20 IPCC, *Sixth Assessment Report*, Geneva: IPCC, 2022.

21 Autorité de la concurrence *L'Autorité publie son communiqué relatif aux orientations informelles qu'elle pourra donner aux entreprises qui s'interrogent sur la compatibilité de leurs projets poursuivant un objectif de développement durable avec les règles de concurrence [on line]*, 2024. Available at: https://www.autoritedelaconcurrence.fr/fr/communiques-de-presse/lautorite-publie-son-communique-relatif-aux-orientations-informelles-quelle.

22 European Commission,*Guidelines on the Applicability of Article 101 of the TFEU to Horizontal Co-operation Agreements,* 2021.

24. However, in Polynesia, as in small island economies in general, the oligopolistic structure of many markets (import, distribution, transport) can hinder the development of more environmentally-friendly solutions. For example, if a few large companies dominate the import of goods, they may favour low-cost products with a high carbon impact, rather than encouraging more sustainable (but potentially more expensive) local or regional supply chains.

25. In Europe, a number of 'shared sustainability' initiatives have been judged to be in breach of competition law when they involved an agreement on prices or production standards. The emblematic example remains the Dutch agreement on *Chicken of Tomorrow*, which aimed to improve animal welfare and the environmental quality of poultry production, but which was rejected by the European Commission on the grounds that it limited price competition.

26. In the same way, the promotion of competition defined too restrictively could prevent economic players in Polynesia from agreeing to set strict environmental criteria that would increase the selling price, even if they contribute to reducing the local ecological footprint, as this attempt at agreement could be perceived as an anti-competitive practice.

27. Conversely, competition can encourage innovation in favour of sustainability, provided that it is framed by clear rules and incentives (subsidies for renewable energies, ecological taxation, standardisation of serious labels, etc.). Healthy competition, combined with a proactive public policy, can also help to diversify supply (e.glocal agricultural production, ecotourism) and reduce dependence on imports with a high carbon footprint. In island economies such as Polynesia, where the cost of living is high, this approach to supporting local production can be an opportunity to promote traditional know-how and more environmentally-friendly production methods (small-scale fishing, agroforestry, etc.).

28. Competition authorities can play a more proactive role, provided that their mandate evolves or that their interpretation of the law takes greater account of environmental objectives. A number of avenues can be explored:

    1. Examine environmental effects when analysing mergers: when examining mergers or acquisitions, the APC could consider not only the impact on prices and consumer choice, but also the consequences in terms of sustainability (emissions, impact on biodiversity).
    2. Encourage environmental cooperation: under certain conditions, agreements between competitors aimed at reducing the ecological footprint or setting common environmental standards could be authorised, provided that the collective benefits and environmental gains outweigh the restrictions on competition.[23]
    3. Combating greenwashing and misleading advertising: abuses by companies that present themselves as "greenwithout any real proof of sustainability constitute a misleading practice that can distort competition to the detriment of genuinely committed players. The competition authorities could step up their vigilance, in conjunction with other regulatory bodies.

---

23 *Ibid.*

4. Inter-institutional collaboration: between competition authorities, ministries in charge of ecological transition and environmental protection agencies, in order to pool skills and develop coherent policies. In a post-colonial context, it is also worth remembering that certain monopolies or highly concentrated structures are inherited from the colonial era. Challenging them, by spreading the economic benefits to as many people as possible rather than to a restricted elite, can help to bring about a process of institutional decolonisation.

B. *Beyond competition and "classic" sustainable development*

29. Without claiming to be exhaustive, we present below a few avenues that could enrich the reflection on Polynesia and island economies in the field of sustainable development and competition, despite the conceptual limitations raised at the beginning of the chapter.

30. The degrowth movement advocates a planned reduction in material production and consumption in industrialised societies, in order to preserve ecosystems and redistribute resources fairly. Hickel[24] stresses that it's not just a question of putting the brakes on economic activity, but of rethinking it in favour of well-being, relocation, solidarity and voluntary sobriety. In island contexts where demographic pressure and external dependence pose acute challenges, degrowth could mean supporting circular economies, enhancing cultural heritage and food sovereignty.

31. Escobar[25] and Shiva[26] also stress the need to decolonise the very notion of 'development', which is too often defined according to Western criteria of growth and productivity. In certain regions of the Pacific, cosmovision and indigenous knowledge (for example, customary management of fishing zones) can form a solid basis for the sustainable management of resources, provided that this knowledge is recognised and supported by public policies.

32. In island societies where communities share a strong sense of solidarity, cooperation between producers can be perceived as a form of collusion from the perspective of a strict interpretation of competition law (where each firm acts on the basis of the conditions it faces, without coordinating with its competitors). In reality, these co-operations often reflect a strong social bond and lead to positive spin-offs for the community: better production conditions, risk-sharing, preservation of local know-how, etc. A competition approach adapted to island realities should therefore take account of these socio-cultural specificities and recognise that maximising collective well-being can involve desirable agreements which, although they restrict competition "on paper, bring wider benefits to society.

33. One of the flaws often identified in the *top-down* model of sustainable development is the lack of democratic participation by the populations concerned.[27] Beyond

---

24 Hickel J., "The Contradiction of the Sustainable Development Goals: Growth Versus Ecology on a Finite Planet", *op. cit.*

25 Escobar A., *Encountering Development: The Making and Unmaking of the Third World*, *op. cit.*

26 Shiva V., *The Violence of the Green Revolution: Third World Agriculture, Ecology and Politics*, *op. cit.*

27 Kothari A., Demaria F. and Acosta A., "Buen Vivir, Degrowth and Ecological Swaraj: Alternatives to Sustainable Development and the Green Economy", *Development*, 2014, Vol. 57, No. 3, pp. 362-375.

a strictly competitive approach, we need to rethink economic and environmental governance by actively involving local communities. In an island context, this participation can take the form of :

- Local ecological planning committees: including public authorities, economic players, associations and representatives of traditional communities;
- Co-management mechanisms: for the preservation of marine resources, involving artisanal fishermen and the inhabitants of the archipelagos;
- Transparency in the setting of prices and tariffs: so that consumers can make informed choices, including whether to pay a "fair price" that takes full account of environmental and social costs. In competition theory, it is assumed that the price reflects the real cost of production and the value placed on it by consumers; in practice, numerous distortions (subsidies for fossil fuels, failure to account for environmental costs, etc.) prevent this price signal from being complete and encourage over-consumption.

34. Reflections on the 'sustainability' of competition are gaining momentum, particularly in countries where the climate emergency has become inescapable.[28] Several courses of action are emerging:

 1. Integrating environmental and social objectives into the definition of consumer well-being: this would mean going beyond typical criteria such as price alone to include the total cost of production (emissions, depletion of resources, health risks). In theory, the price is supposed to indicate the 'true' cost of production and the value for the consumer; in reality, it is often distorted by externalities that are not taken into account.
 2. Creation of targeted exemptions for agreements aimed at reducing the carbon footprint or pollution, where the positive effects on the environment and society outweigh the restrictions on competition.
 3. Greater powers to investigate sustainability: enabling the competition authorities to penalise *greenwashing* practices that mislead consumers and distort competition to the benefit of unscrupulous players.
 4. Inter-institutional collaboration : between the competition authorities, the ministries in charge of environmental issues (in Polynesia, in January 2025, this will be the Ministry of Agriculture and the Environment [MPR]), working across the board with other ministries such as the Ministry of Economy and Finance (MEF), with the possibility of logistical support from the Interministerial Delegation for Climate and Sustainable Development, and environmental protection agencies (such as the Environment Directorate [DIREN] in Polynesia, attached to the MPR), in order to pool skills and develop coherent policies. In former colonial territories, it may be crucial to dismantle historical rents and disseminate economic benefits more widely to the population, thereby pursuing an objective of decolonisation.

35. In an island economy like Polynesia, these institutional innovations could help to reduce the cost of living while strengthening ecological and social resilience.

---

28 European Commission, *Guidelines on the Applicability of Article 101 of the TFEU to Horizontal Co-operation Agreements, op. cit.*

For example, by promoting sustainable local food production, we could reduce dependence on imports, preserve biodiversity and create local jobs. However, this requires us to rethink the very notion of competition, so as to enable sustainable cooperation between local economic players.

Conclusion

36. Sustainable development, as it is commonly defined in international agendas such as the SDGs, is based on an apparently attractive synthesis of economics, ecology and equity. However, certain analyses[29] have highlighted the contradictions, ambiguities and potential co-optation of the concept by vested interests. In a neo-liberal capitalist context, the logic of competition and growth all too often tends to result in the expansion of resource extraction, the maximisation of short-term profit and the externalisation of socio-environmental costs.

37. However, competition is not necessarily incompatible with sustainability, provided that substantial changes are made to the methods of regulation, governance and evaluation of economic performance. This implies promoting socially desirable innovation practices, preventing *greenwashing* and rehabilitating cooperation for environmental and social purposes. The authorities responsible for ensuring compliance with competition rules, including in Polynesia with the APC, can play a decisive role in this respect by rethinking their methods of analysis (integrating environmental criteria), encouraging good practice ("virtuous cooperation) and penalising abuses (market distortions to the detriment of sustainability).

38. In island economies, marked by high import dependency, high climate vulnerability and fragile biodiversity, the urgency of rethinking the development model cannot be underestimated. The Polynesian example gives us hope that it is possible to consolidate competition to combat the high cost of living, while at the same time creating a sustainable dynamic. However, this requires going beyond a limited vision of sustainable development, and considering new paradigms that place the preservation of the biosphere, social justice and citizen participation at the heart of the economic model's priorities.

39. Ultimately, reconciling competition and sustainability in island economies is not simply an exercise in "greening existing policies. It involves an in-depth reconfiguration of economic, institutional and socio-cultural logics, so as to ensure the long-term viability of ecosystems and the well-being of populations. The tenth anniversary of competition policy in Polynesia thus provides an opportunity to rethink the role and objectives of competition in the ecological transition, and to place Polynesia and the Pacific as a whole on a truly sustainable and equitable development path.

---

29 Redclift M., *Sustainable Development: Exploring the Contradictions*, *op. cit*; Daly H. E., "Toward some Operational Principles of Sustainable Development", *op. cit*; Escobar A., *Encountering Development: The Making and Unmaking of the Third World*, *op. cit*; Hickel J., "The Contradiction of the Sustainable Development Goals: Growth Versus Ecology on a Finite Planet", *op. cit*.

Warren Dexter

Minister of Economy and Finance of French Polynesia

"Greater focus on anti-competitive practices"[*]

For Warren Dexter, Minister of the Economy and Finance, it is vital to "support the development of competition", and the Polynesian Competition Authority (APC) is "one of the essential levers" for achieving this, in line with the government's objective of fighting the high cost of living. But 10 years after the creation of local competition law, the time has also come to reflect on the budgetary, human and regulatory resources that the country should give to the APC.

March 2025 marks the tenth anniversary of Polynesian competition law. What does this anniversary mean to you?

Competition law established the Polynesian Competition Authority in 2015, and I consider this a great step forward. It's true that the Authority's record over the past 10 years has been satisfactory. It started modestly, because it had limited resources, but has gone from one success to the next. Its ranks include "big names" such as Vivien Terrien and Henri Piffaut, and it has forged links with competition authorities in neighbouring countries. Today, the Polynesian Competition Authority is more influential than ever in terms of public policy: the government's priority is to fight the high cost of living, and one of the main levers for remedying this is to support the development of competition. This is where the Authority can play its full role.

My ambition for the French Competition Authority is for it to place greater emphasis on combating anti-competitive practices, because, from what I hear in the business world, such practices are common.

How do Polynesian economic players see the APC today?

The Authority has carved out a place for itself, notably through the workshops it organises every year. I attended some last year, and saw that, indeed, big business leaders take part. This has helped to demystify the work of the French Competition Authority. This doesn't necessarily mean that the APC's actions are accepted; the latest reports from the Polynesian Competition Authority show that there are more and more disputes over its decisions. This obviously increases costs, especially lawyers' fees.

---

[*] Interview conducted by Caroline Perdrix, Editor-in-Chief at Radio1 Tahiti.

There's a kind of fear on the part of business leaders of turning to the Authority. We need to find a way to democratise the process of referring cases to the Competition Authority, and then give it the means to combat these practices.

How can the APC's tools be strengthened to achieve the goal you've set?

This is a vast topic. When we worked on the competition code, we had two tools at the disposal of the Polynesian Competition Authority: the ban on exclusive import agreements and structural injunctions. And then, as if by a miracle, two or three years later, they disappeared...

So the debate today is: do we put them back? I have to tell you that I'm very dubious. In another life, as a consultant, I saw abuses. But by nature, I'm a liberal, so I don't like bans. The worldwide trend among manufacturers, especially for small markets, is to not bother and go through an exclusive agent. So I'm not sure it's a good idea to ban exclusive agreements for our small market. On the other hand, we need to give the Competition Authority the means to track down anti-competitive practices.

You seem to be torn between the need for regulation in general and your liberal convictions. Doesn't this risk weakening the Polynesian Competition Authority?

We need to make it more present in the economy, because dominant positions are a real problem in this country, and not just here. I think it's an issue for building Polynesia's economic future. When you see that half the economy – to put it simply – is in the hands of a few, it scares me. I recognise that they feed thousands of families, I don't like to force it, but we have to make sure that the APC is a real counterweight to these hegemonic wills. We have to give the smallest a chance to become big.

The APC has lost two jobs. Will the president, who has called for their return, be heard?

We will need to reexamine this issue. Otherwise, the alternative would be to review the scope of the Polynesian Competition Authority's missions, by carrying out a diagnostic. Some could perhaps be lightened or abolished, so that it can concentrate more on the missions that the country wishes to prioritise.

I'm thinking of certain missions, such as controlling the location of supermarkets. Is it worth giving the Polynesian Competition Authority the power to block projects upstream? Can't we just let things happen? On the other hand, it will need to be very careful about how new entrants enter the market.

In December, in the middle of a session of the assembly, you suspended the draft law that would have given the Polynesian Competition Authority the role of regulator of the energy sector. Why did you do this?

Because I want to see the impact it could have on human resources first. The budget we pushed through the Assembly highlighted the country's major payroll problem, which represents over 27% of operating costs. But I'm not convinced by the opposition's argument that, if you let the APC regulate public service delegations for energy, it's going to set the national strategy. Here, we're getting our brushes mixed up. Just because it's going to control doesn't mean it's going to tell the country what to do. But I had supported the project, because I had started from the idea that the Authority has this culture of control.

We need to act quickly, because the draft text of the law provides for implementation on the 1st of September. I will discuss with the members of the Authority again, and we will be revising the provisions.

Will the Polynesian Competition Authority undergo any more changes?

In any case, what is certain is that if there is to be any reform, it will happen in close consultation with the President. I would never do things behind her back, because I know, and regret, that decisions on both the vocation of operating budgets and human resources have been taken without consultation in some cases. I'd like us to be able to do things together.

Moetai Brotherson

President of French Polynesia

*"I am a strong advocate of competition and an equally strong defender of the Polynesian Competition Authority"**

Mr President, what do you see as the main economic challenges and objectives for Polynesia in the years ahead?

First and foremost, the region faces structural challenges:

- its geography, since French Polynesia has a population equivalent to that of a city like Montpellier, but covers an area the size of Europe. In such conditions, it's not easy to ensure that inhabitants are treated equally everywhere, even though this is necessary to our social contract.
- its remoteness from major markets, which creates export difficulties due to cost, and also makes imports more expensive.
- the legacy of the CEP, the Centre d'Expérimentations du Pacifique (Centre for Pacific Tests), which transformed Polynesia's economy. Before the CEP, Polynesia was self-sufficient, and was also an exporter of certain products. For example, it was the world's leading exporter of vanilla. But the CEP transformed the population, which became predominantly blue-collar and civil servant, and triggered a mass exodus to Tahiti. For two generations, Polynesians overwhelmingly wanted their children to become civil servants, and my generation is the first since the CEP that doesn't think that way. As far as the exodus is concerned, in Rapa, for example, there are only around 450 people left on an island that used to have over 2,000. Today, 70% of the Polynesian population lives on the island of Tahiti. Generally speaking, the CEP has transformed the Polynesian economy from a largely self-sufficient one into a counter economy, in which most consumption is imported.

Another challenge is economic and social development

- we have real economic opportunities. Polynesia's 118 islands offer an unrivalled range of tourist attractions. And we're located far away, sheltered from all the world's conflicts, so visitors to Polynesia can enjoy true peace and quiet. This makes for a very favourable ecosystem.

---

* Interview conducted by Jérôme Philippe, partner at the Paris office of Freshfields Bruckhaus Deringer, where he leads the Antitrust, Competition, and Trade team.

- on the other hand, because our population is so small, our domestic market is miniscule. So we can only conceive of economic development through exports.
- energy is also a challenge. The region has no choice but to be self-sufficient in energy. Today, 93% of our energy comes from fossil fuels, although this figure is falling.

Finally, the environment, and in particular global warming, is also a major challenge.

Clearly, given its size, Polynesia will have no effect whatsoever on the global warming trajectory. On the contrary, it is likely to suffer the full consequences of this warming. I'm thinking in particular of the Tuamotu archipelago, which is almost entirely located just above sea level and is therefore very exposed. Depending on the future trajectory, the question arises of remedial action. But these actions could become increasingly costly, and ultimately impossible, if ocean levels rise too much. We would then have to evacuate these atolls, which would be a major trauma, both for the population, who have lived there for generations, and economically, as these atolls concentrate the bulk of the pearling industry and a major part of the fishing industry. The question that will arise is how much we can afford to spend if we want to continue living there in the future.

Faced with these challenges, what are your priorities?

I have defined four priority sectors.

First priority: sustainable tourism

Today, tourism is Polynesia's leading "export". We receive around 300,000 tourists a year in Polynesia, mainly from North America, then Europe, and finally Asia, although the latter segment is growing.

My goal is to double income from tourism. This doesn't necessarily mean doubling the number of tourists, but both increasing the number of tourists and increasing their spending in Polynesia, so that total income doubles. This means developing high-quality, environmentally-friendly tourism, both through hotels and guesthouses. We're also seeing significant growth in Airbnb, which is positive but can sometimes pose difficulties locally for Polynesians looking for lodging.

Today, most tourist spending takes place on Bora-Bora, which is overbuilt and cannot continue to grow.

It is therefore necessary to develop other destinations in Polynesia, while respecting the choices of the local population. For example, in the Austral Islands, the population has chosen not to have hotels, and to limit itself to guesthouses. Similarly, in the Tuamotus, local residents seek to maintain a certain ratio between hotels and guesthouses.

This is why I have already modified the aid scheme to encourage the development of boarding houses. They are eligible for a level of aid that depends on their remoteness.

Over the 2019-21 period, we have experienced hotel closures, and we now have a number of hotel wastelands, often in very beautiful locations. It's important that we reopen hotels in these locations.

And of course, there are also plans for new hotels, which are supported by both Polynesia and France. In this respect, we are currently working on an accommodation scheme with KPMG Hospitality, and have identified 18 interesting sites owned by Polynesia. Next year, it will launch a call for projects for several sites it owns. As land generally accounts for between 15% and 25% of the cost, the assistance provided will be significant.

In addition to accommodation, we also need to develop our transport offering. Under my leadership, we have gone from an Air France / Air Tahiti Nui duopoly to a much broader offering, adding United Airlines, Delta and French Bee, which means we now have over 400,000 seats.

Second priority: the primary sector

As I have already mentioned, for three generations the primary sector has been largely neglected in favour of the secondary and tertiary sectors, with the result that we've lost both our self-sufficiency and our exports.

It is essential to rebuild our food crops so that we are less dependent on imports, and less affected by imported inflation. This also requires action on the demand side, notably through education in schools. Furthermore, exporting is essential in terms of revenue.

However, Polynesia's land surface is 4,500 km^2, of which around one third is exploitable. The exploitable agricultural area is therefore limited, and this is compounded by high transport costs. As a result, apart from food crops, only high value-added production is relevant to the Polynesian economy.

We therefore need to research and develop these high value-added products once again:

- Vanilla, for example: in 1952, vanilla production stood at 330 tonnes, and as I said, we were the world's leading exporter. Today, this production has fallen to just 20 tonnes. We need to redevelop this production.
- For example, we have sea cucumber, which not only cooks well, but also has essential properties for joint health. It has been part of Chinese pharmacopoeia for centuries. As the species is endangered, it cannot be fished at sea. However, we have a start-up in Polynesia that breeds sea cucumbers, and can therefore market and export them.
- In the same way, we're trying to develop Noni, which is part of the local pharmacopoeia.
- Another example is aquarium clams, which are very high value-added products.

Third priority: energy

As I said, 93% of our energy is fossil fuel, even if this rate is falling. And the region has no choice but to be self-sufficient in energy, given its remoteness.

- Solar energy works well in Polynesia, but requires batteries to store the electricity, and we have neither batteries, which have to be imported, nor recycling facilities. We are therefore very dependent, but solar energy is nevertheless an important area of development for us. We already have 4 solar farms in operation.
- Onshore or offshore wind power doesn't work well in Polynesia given the wind regimes, and it's also very poorly accepted, so it's not a solution.

- Thermal energy from the seas is a major source of development. Today's technology enables us to harness the difference in sea temperature between cold deep water and warm surface water. The idea is to extract cold water from deep below the surface and use a heat exchanger to create energy. This source of energy is particularly well-suited to the fact that we have no continental shelf, so it's possible to draw water from deep within the immediate vicinity of the islands. We already have three sea water air conditioning (SWAC) installations in operation, one for the hospital in Papeete, another for the hotel on Teti'aroa and the third for a hotel in Bora Bora, and others are planned. In the long term, this is probably the ideal energy source for Polynesia.

Fourth priority: digital and audiovisual technologies

Digital technology currently accounts for 2% of Polynesia's GDP, and I have set a target of 25% within ten years.

This is an ideal asset, since it doesn't need to be shipped. It's easy, and often optimal, to work in a time zone that's out of sync with North America and even Europe. The beauty of Polynesia, and its gentle lifestyle, make it an ideal place to settle for designers, developers, or virtually any other digital or audiovisual profession. It's the American "*follow the sun*" approach, and it's more pleasant to work in Polynesia than in most other parts of the world, as long as the work allows it.

To achieve this, we obviously need a high level of connectivity, and this has now been achieved with the five new intercontinental cables that will be added to the two existing to better connect Tahiti to the world. The contract I signed with Google will increase the international bandwidth available in Polynesia by a factor of 50, at no cost to the country whatsoever, which is remarkable. We're also going to create a Kanēa school to train young Polynesians in digital professions, and we're launching a partnership with the CNAM, the Conservatoire National des Arts et Métiers (French National Conservatory of Arts and Crafts).

This will enable us to develop new professions in the digital sector, as well as in the audiovisual, medical and many other fields

This agreement, which I was able to initiate thanks to contacts I had previously made with Google in the United States, is a tremendous development opportunity for Polynesia, and will open up new prospects locally for Polynesian youth.

What role do you think competition regulation should play lowering the cost of living and increasing economic efficiency?

I'm a fervent supporter of competition and an equally fervent defender of the Polynesian Competition Authority (APC). Competition is absolutely essential to a well-functioning economy; it's what enables the healthy emulation needed for growth.

In a territory like Polynesia, entropy naturally leads to a lack of competition. In other words, if the public authorities do nothing, there will soon be no competition.

We often hear, for example, that given the size of local markets, there's "no room for two". This is often inaccurate, and if we look in detail we realise that there is often room for several players.

It is therefore essential that competition be regulated, and essential that it be regulated by an independent administrative authority, which can act in the same way in all sectors. The role of the APC is therefore very important.

I do, however, have some regrets, as the Assemblée has in the past somewhat clipped the wings of the APC, taking away two important tools: the ban on exclusive import agreements and the structural injunction. I note that the French and New Caledonian authorities have these tools at their disposal. I think it's important to reinstate them in Polynesia.

POSTFACE

"Informal contacts are numerous and help to clarify texts and case law"

Gina Cass-Gottlieb

Chair of the Australian Competition and Consumer Commission

As Chair of the Australian Competition and Consumer Commission (ACCC), it is my great honour to be invited to celebrate the 10th anniversary of the Polynesian competition regime and the achievements of one of our valued partners in the Pacific region, the Polynesian Competition Authority (APC).

The APC is among the pioneers of competition law and policy in the Pacific and has been a great champion of the key role competition plays in supporting and unlocking the great potential of Polynesian markets. Since being established in 2015, the APC has made great advancements in its enforcement and monitoring activities. During this time, it has completed investigations across nine sectors, considered 27 merger applications, and continued to grow its portfolio of work. I am also pleased to hear the news that, as a testament to the APC's emergent regulatory expertise, the authority has been entrusted with a new energy regulation remit.

The APC has also set a regional example in its competition education and compliance activities. Through workshops, community engagement, and annual 'Tahiti Competition Days', the APC has tirelessly worked to promote greater awareness of competition law. The Tahiti Competition Days are an important event in the regional competition law calendar and provide a key forum for businesses, academics, and regulators to come together and discuss competition challenges and opportunities in the Pacific region and beyond.

I would like to especially recognise Johanne Peyre's contribution to strengthening competition in our region through her role as Chair of the APC since July 2021. Under Johanne's leadership, the APC has become a regional leader in competition advocacy and a link between academics and competition authorities in the Pacific. In particular, Johanne has elevated awareness of the tailored solutions required for small island economies to effectively implement a competition regime.

At the regional level, last year saw the formation of the Pacific Island Network of Competition Consumer and Economic Regulators (PINCCER), a regional initiative established for the purpose of sharing information, investigative techniques, and authority best practice amongst Pacific regulators. I would like to acknowledge the APC's role in developing this network and its leadership in driving greater competition awareness and education amongst members.

PINCCER has strengthened relationships between regulatory authorities in the Pacific region and will support a path towards regionally coherent regulatory frameworks and robust competition enforcement. Although PINCCER is relatively new, its impact is already seen in the growing enthusiasm and commitment of its members to building a culture of competition in their own economies and across the Pacific region. The ACCC is honoured to be a part of this network.

A key feature of PINCCER is that its members represent diverse economies and different stages of their competition journey. This means that each member has unique individual contributions and perspectives to share and will always have something to learn from its counterparts. As a more established agency in the region, the ACCC has greatly appreciated this opportunity to hear about regional competition issues and connect with its Pacific peers.

Another important feature is that PINCCER provides a collective forum through which members can have an amplified voice and greater representation across larger international fora. Empowering the voices of Pacific authorities, both young and more established, in international forums and networks is also key to strengthening regional representation and increasing global awareness of the challenges faced by smaller economies.

At the global level, the APC has contributed to the International Competition Network (ICN) and Organisation for Economic Co-operation and Development (OECD) forums. These organisations enable the dissemination of best practices and effective international cooperation and are critical in facilitating cross-border cooperation between competition authorities amidst the emergence of global challenges demanding global solutions.

While younger authorities have historically had less of a presence in international forums, both the ICN and OECD have in recent years demonstrated their commitment to amplifying the voices of smaller and younger competition agencies. The ICN's Bridging Project, for example, is targeted at increasing the presence and participation of younger members, broadening the views of the ICN and ensuring that the network meets the needs of all members.

Providing opportunities and space for younger authorities, including those from the Pacific region, to be actively involved in international forums will improve the understanding by global authorities of challenges facing smaller economies, facilitate the effective transfer of knowledge and better cooperation, and lift the global standard of competition awareness and enforcement.

The ACCC is grateful for opportunities to partner with our Pacific neighbours for the purpose of strengthening competition laws and expertise across the region. The growing experience of Pacific nations can also be shared with other smaller economies around the world. I encourage other agencies to work with their young, regional counterparts where there is the opportunity to do so. The benefits of learning from each other cannot be overstated.

The 10th anniversary of the competition regime in French Polynesia serves as a well-timed opportunity for me to share in the celebrations, as Australia is also marking a milestone in the history of our competition law. This year marks the 50th anniversary of Australia's

Trade Practices Act, which, groundbreaking at the time, laid the foundation for the Competition and Consumer Act in Australia that is enforced by the ACCC today. Not only do Australia and French Polynesia share in celebrating the anniversaries of competition law in our respective countries, but we also share in celebrating the numerous advancements made towards implementing effective competition regimes across the Pacific. I am eager to celebrate the establishment and milestones of other competition authorities in our region in the years to come.

The ACCC takes great pride in its relationship with the APC and has cherished being part of the APC's journey over the past decade. We look forward to continuing to learn from each other and working together, alongside our other Pacific partners, to find effective solutions to shared regional challenges and build a regional culture of vibrant competition.

TABLE OF CONTENTS

PART II
A DECADE OF DECISIONS AND OPINIONS FROM THE POLYNESIAN COMPETITION AUTHORITY – A REVIEW

PART III
CONTRIBUTION TO THE REGULATION
OF KEY ECONOMIC SECTORS

PART V
ISSUES, CHALLENGES, AND FUTURE OF COMPETITION IN FRENCH POLYNESIA

Concurrences

Competition Laws Review

Concurrences Review

Concurrences is a print and online quarterly peer reviewed journal dedicated to EU and national competitions laws. It has been launched in 2004 as the flagship of the Institute of Competition Law in order to provide a forum for academics, practitioners and enforcers. Concurrences' influence and expertise has garnered contributions or interviews with such figures as Christine Lagarde, Bill Kovacic, Emmanuel Macron, Antonin Scalia and Magrethe Vestager.

Contents

More than 15,000 articles, print and/or online. Quarterly issues provide current coverage with contributions from the EU or national or foreign countries thanks to more than 2,500 authors in Europe and abroad.

Format

In order to balance academic contributions with opinions or legal practice notes, Concurrences provides its insight and analysis in a number of formats:

- Forewords: Opinions by leading academics or enforcers
- Interviews: Interviews of antitrust experts
- On-Topics: 4 to 6 short papers on hot issues
- Law & Economics: Short papers written by economists for a legal audience
- Articles: Long academic papers
- Case Summaries: Case commentary on EU and French case law
- Legal Practice: Short papers for in-house counsels
- International: Medium size papers on international policies
- Books Review: Summaries of recent antitrust books
- Articles Review: Summaries of leading articles published in 45 antitrust journals

Boards

The Scientific Committee is headed by Laurence Idot, Professor at Panthéon Assas University. The International Committee is headed by Frederic Jenny, OECD Competition Comitteee Chairman. Boards members include Douglas Ginsburg, Benoît Cœuré, Howard Shelanski, Richard Whish, Wouter Wils, Joshua Wright, etc.

Online version

Concurrences website provides all articles published since its inception, in addition to selected articles published online only in the electronic supplement.

Write for Concurrences

Concurrences welcome spontaneous contributions. Except in rare circumstances, the journal accepts only unpublished articles, whatever the form and nature of the contribution. The Editorial Board checks the form of the proposals, and then submits these to the Scientific Committee. Selection of the papers is conditional to a peer review by at least two members of the Committee. Within a month, the Committee assesses whether the draft article can be published and notifies the author.

e-Competitions

Antitrust Case Laws e-Bulletin

e-Competitions Bulletin

Case law database

e-Competitions is the only online resource that provides consistent coverage of antitrust cases from 85 jurisdictions, organized into a searchable database structure. e-Competitions concentrates on cases summaries taking into account that in the context of a continuing growing number of sources there is a need for factual information, i.e., case law.

- 26,000 case summaries
- 4,000 authors
- 85 countries covered
- 30,000 subscribers

Sophisticated editorial and IT enrichment

e-Competitions is structured as a database. The editors make a sophisticated technical and legal work on all articles by tagging these with key words, drafting abstracts and writing html code to increase Google ranking. There is a team of antitrust lawyers – PhD and judges clerks – and a team of IT experts. e-Competitions makes comparative law possible. Thanks to this expert editorial work, it is possible to search and compare cases by jurisdiction, legal topics or business sectors.

Prestigious Boards

e-Competitions draws upon highly distinguished editors, all leading experts in national or international antitrust. Advisory Board Members include: Sir Christopher Bellamy, Ioanis Lianos (UCL), Eleanor Fox (NYU), Frédéric Jenny (OECD), Jacqueline Riffault-Silk (Cour de cassation), Wouter Wils (King's College London), etc.

Leading Partners

- Association of European Competition Law Judges: The AECLJ is a forum for judges of national Courts specializing in antitrust case law. Members timely feed e-Competitions with just released cases.
- Academics partners: Antitrust research centres from leading universities write regularly in e-Competitions: University College London, King's College London, Queen Mary University, etc.
- Law firms: Global law firms and antitrust niche firms write detailed cases summaries specifically for e-Competitions: Allen & Overy, Baker McKenzie, Cleary Gottlieb Steen & Hamilton, Jones Day, Norton Rose Fulbright, Skadden, White & Case, etc.

www.ingramcontent.com/pod-product-compliance
Lightning Source LLC
Chambersburg PA
CBHW071413230926
51846CB00001B/75
9781939007582